TRAVELER'S WESTERN CANADA COMPANION

by Laura Purdom and Donald Carroll

Photographed by
Robert Holmes, Nik Wheeler, and David Henry

Kümmerly+Frey

Contents

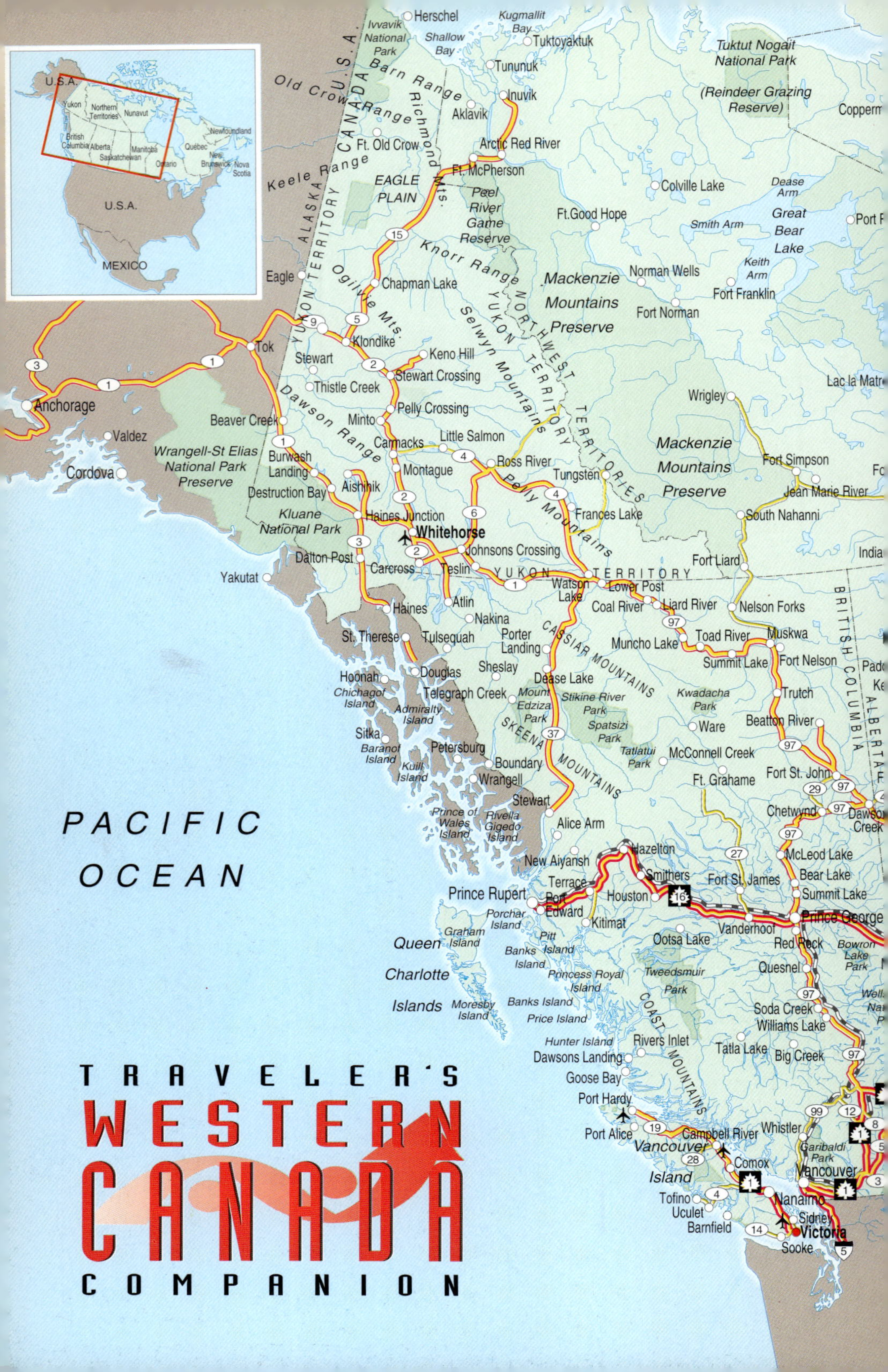

TRAVELER'S
WESTERN CANADA
COMPANION
PACIFIC OCEAN
U.S.A.
Yukon
Northern Territories
Nunavut
British Columbia
Alberta
Saskatchewan
Manitoba
Ontario
Quebec
Newfoundland
New Brunswick
Nova Scotia
U.S.A.
MEXICO
Herschel
Ivvavik National Park
Shallow Bay
Kugmallit Bay
Tuktoyaktuk
Tununuk
Tuktut Nogait National Park
(Reindeer Grazing Reserve)
Inuvik
Aklavik
Barn Range
Old Crow Range
Richmond Mts.
Ft. Old Crow
Arctic Red River
Ft. McPherson
Keele Range
EAGLE PLAIN
Peel River Game Reserve
Colville Lake
Dease Arm
Great Bear Lake
Smith Arm
Keith Arm
Ft.Good Hope
Knorr Range
Norman Wells
Fort Franklin
Fort Norman
Mackenzie Mountains Preserve
Chapman Lake
Ogilvie Mts.
Selwyn Mountains
YUKON TERRITORY
NORTHWEST TERRITORIES
ALASKA
CANADA
Eagle
Tok
Klondike
Keno Hill
Stewart
Stewart Crossing
Thistle Creek
Anchorage
Pelly Crossing
Dawson Range
Beaver Creek
Minto
Wrigley
Lac la Matre
Valdez
Little Salmon
Carmacks
Wrangell-St Elias National Park Preserve
Burwash Landing
Ross River
Fort Simpson
Jean Marie River
Cordova
Montague
Tungsten
Aishihik
Destruction Bay
Pelly Mountains
Frances Lake
South Nahanni
Kluane National Park
Haines Junction
Whitehorse
Johnsons Crossing
Dalton Post
Carcross
Teslin
Fort Liard
Yakutat
Watson Lake
Lower Post
Coal River
Liard River
Nelson Forks
Haines
Atlin
Nakina
St. Therese
Tulsequah
Porter Landing
Muncho Lake
Toad River
Muskwa
Summit Lake
Fort Nelson
CASSIAR MOUNTAINS
Hoonah
Douglas
Sheslay
Dease Lake
Chichagof Island
Admiralty Island
Telegraph Creek
Mount Edziza Park
Stikine River Park
Kwadacha Park
Trutch
Ware
Beatton River
Spatsizi Park
Sitka
Baranof Island
Petersburg
SKEENA MOUNTAINS
Tatlatui Park
McConnell Creek
Kuiu Island
Boundary
Wrangell
Ft. Grahame
Fort St. John
Stewart
Prince of Wales Island
Revilla Gigedo Island
Alice Arm
Chetwynd
Dawson Creek
Hazelton
New Aiyansh
McLeod Lake
Smithers
Bear Lake
Terrace
Fort St. James
Summit Lake
Prince Rupert
Port Edward
Houston
Prince George
Porchar Island
Kitimat
Vanderhoof
Graham Island
Red Rock
Queen Charlotte Islands
Pitt Island
Ootsa Lake
Bowron Lake Park
Banks Island
Quesnel
Tweedsmuir Park
Princess Royal Island
COAST MOUNTAINS
Moresby Island
Banks Island
Soda Creek
Price Island
Williams Lake
Hunter Island
Rivers Inlet
Tatla Lake
Big Creek
Dawsons Landing
Goose Bay
Port Hardy
Port Alice
Campbell River
Whistler
Garibaldi Park
Vancouver Island
Comox
Vancouver
Tofino
Ucluelet
Nanaimo
Barnfield
Sidney
Victoria
Sooke

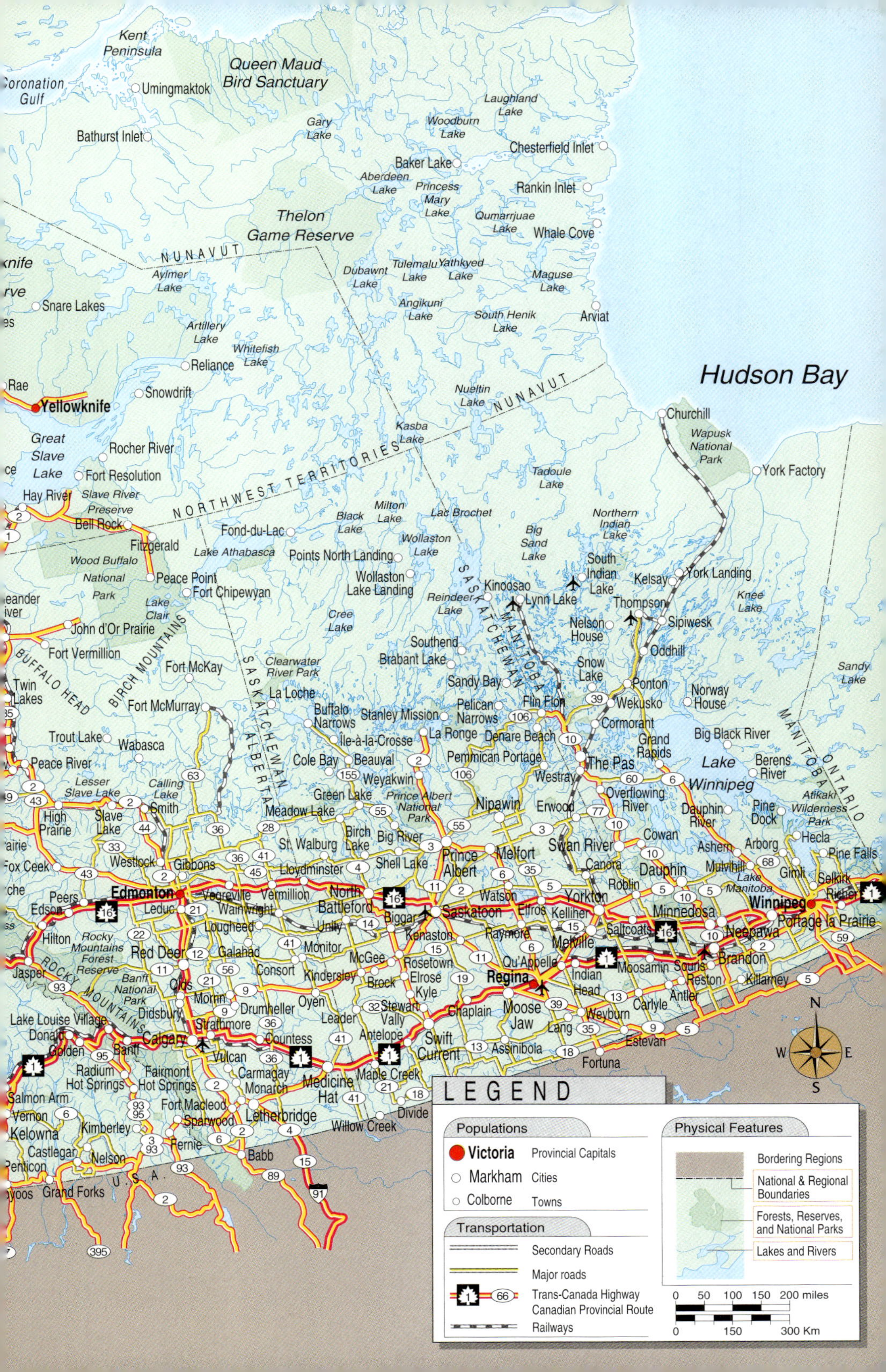

Kent Peninsula
Queen Maud Bird Sanctuary
Coronation Gulf
Umingmaktok
Bathurst Inlet
Gary Lake
Laughland Lake
Woodburn Lake
Chesterfield Inlet
Baker Lake
Aberdeen Lake
Princess Mary Lake
Rankin Inlet
Thelon Game Reserve
Qumarrjuae Lake
Whale Cove
NUNAVUT
Aylmer Lake
Dubawnt Lake
Tulemalu Lake
Yathkyed Lake
Maguse Lake
Snare Lakes
Angikuni Lake
South Henik Lake
Arviat
Artillery Lake
Whitefish Lake
Reliance
Hudson Bay
Rae
Yellowknife
Snowdrift
Nueltin Lake
Churchill
Great Slave Lake
Rocher River
Kasba Lake
Wapusk National Park
Fort Resolution
NORTHWEST TERRITORIES
York Factory
Hay River
Slave River Preserve
Tadoule Lake
Bell Rock
Milton Lake
Black Lake
Lac Brochet
Northern Indian Lake
Fitzgerald
Fond-du-Lac
Lake Athabasca
Points North Landing
Wollaston Lake
Big Sand Lake
Wood Buffalo National Park
Peace Point
Fort Chipewyan
Wollaston Lake Landing
South Indian Lake
Kelsay
York Landing
Lake Claire
Reindeer Lake
Kinoosao
Lynn Lake
Thompson
Knee Lake
John d'Or Prairie
Cree Lake
Nelson House
Sipiwesk
Fort Vermillion
BIRCH MOUNTAINS
Southend
Oddhill
BUFFALO HEAD
Twin Lakes
Fort McKay
Clearwater River Park
Brabant Lake
Snow Lake
Sandy Lake
SASKATCHEWAN
MANITOBA
Sandy Bay
Ponton
Fort McMurray
La Loche
Buffalo Narrows
Stanley Mission
Pelican Narrows
Flin Flon
Wekusko
Norway House
Cormorant
Trout Lake
Wabasca
Île-à-la-Crosse
La Ronge
Denare Beach
Grand Rapids
Big Black River
ALBERTA
Cole Bay
Beauval
Pemmican Portage
The Pas
Lake Winnipeg
Berens River
ONTARIO
Peace River
Weyakwin
Westray
Lesser Slave Lake
Calling Lake
Green Lake
Prince Albert National Park
Nipawin
Overflowing River
Atikaki Wilderness Park
High Prairie
Slave Lake
Smith
Meadow Lake
Erwood
Dauphin River
Pine Dock
Birch Lake
Big River
Swan River
Cowan
Hecla
Ashern
Arborg
Pine Falls
St. Walburg
Prince Albert
Melfort
Canora
Fox Creek
Westlock
Gibbons
Lloydminster
Shell Lake
Dauphin
Mulvihill
Gimli
Selkirk
Lake Manitoba
Roblin
Peers
Edmonton
Vegreville
Vermillion
North Battleford
Watson
Yorkton
Winnipeg
Richer
Edson
Leduc
Wainwright
Biggar
Saskatoon
Elfros
Kelliher
Minnedosa
Unity
Neepawa
Portage la Prairie
Hilton
Rocky Mountains Forest Reserve
Lougheed
Kenaston
Raymore
Saltcoats
Red Deer
Galahad
Monitor
McGee
Melville
Brandon
ROCKY MOUNTAINS
Jasper
Banff National Park
Consort
Rosetown
Qu'Appelle
Moosamin
Souris
Olds
Kindersley
Elrose
Regina
Indian Head
Reston
Killarney
Morrin
Brock
Kyle
Didsbury
Drumheller
Oyen
Stewart Vally
Chaplain
Moose Jaw
Weyburn
Carlyle
Antler
Lake Louise Village
Strathmore
Leader
Donald
Calgary
Countess
Antelope
Lang
Golden
Banff
Vulcan
Swift Current
Assiniboia
Estevan
Radium Hot Springs
Fairmont Hot Springs
Carmagay
Monarch
Medicine Hat
Maple Creek
Fortuna
Salmon Arm
Fort Macleod
Lethbridge
Divide
Vernon
Sparwood
Willow Creek
Kelowna
Kimberley
Castlegar
Fernie
Nelson
Babb
Penticton
U. S. A.
Osoyoos
Grand Forks
N
E
S
W
LEGEND
Populations
Victoria Provincial Capitals
Markham Cities
Colborne Towns
Physical Features
Bordering Regions
National & Regional Boundaries
Forests, Reserves, and National Parks
Lakes and Rivers
Transportation
Secondary Roads
Major roads
Trans-Canada Highway
Canadian Provincial Route
Railways
0 50 100 150 200 miles
0 150 300 Km

TOP SPOTS

Ride the Legendary Rails

UNTIL THE COMPLETION OF THE TRANS-CANADA HIGHWAY IN THE 1960S, IT WAS THE RAILWAYS THAT STITCHED CANADA TOGETHER AS A NATION. Over the years, many miles of track have closed, yet some historic and wildly scenic routes still remain, reminders of a romantic era in Canadian history.

"We're going to be highballing for the next few miles, folks, so hang on to your champagne glasses!" Thus begins a classic Canadian journey: the two-day train ride (daytime only, you overnight in Kamloops so as not to miss any of the splendor) through the Rockies from Calgary to Vancouver aboard the *Rocky Mountaineer*.

After a toast to the journey ahead, you settle into plush digs — a spacious two-level coach with a glass-domed roof allowing a 360° view of the thrilling rush of scenery. Downstairs is the dining room where — a brochure informs you — you'll enjoy West Coast cuisine prepared by the onboard chef. But lunch isn't for a few hours, and just now you have some sightseeing to do.

Right out of Banff you are in the midst of jaw-dropping mountain scenery. From this point on, every mention of a photo opportunity by the train crew is like a call to battle: cameras and binoculars bristle on one or the other side of the car — training their sights on blue-streaked glaciers and mile-high mountains, aerial bridges slung over thundering rivers with names like Jaws of Death and Suicide Rapids, and silent arcades of 1,000-year-old cedars. Over the course of the trip, wildlife sightings send passengers into yet higher ecstasies: a beaver paddling across a pond, Canada geese in V-formation, a black bear curious about the hulking giant that's passing through its berry patch, osprey fledglings in their eyrie. Across the Continental Divide and down into the Fraser Valley and onward to the Pacific shore, the *Rocky Mountaineer* is the journey of a lifetime.

Once you've crossed the Continental Divide by rail, the next adventure lies further north, where the White Pass & Yukon Railway (WP&YR crosses the 60th parallel, that latitudinal marker that for Canadians designates the transition from "north" to "true north."

White Pass. Anyone familiar with the history of the Klondike will know that this was the treacherous route to the gold fields that thousands attempted to cross on foot in the mad rush of 1898–1899. One of the most famous images of that era is that of an endless stream of humanity toiling up a snow-covered incline — the trail to White Pass.

So great was the lust for gold at the turn of the century that a group of entrepreneurs

The *Rocky Mountaineer* passing through Glacier National Park OPPOSITE on its way from Alberta to the Pacific coast; a bridal veil cascade ABOVE captures the attention of passengers.

conceived a plan to build a railroad over the pass. Most people said it couldn't be done, but with English capital, Canadian contractors, and American engineers, the "Stampede Rail" was completed in 1900 under extreme weather conditions.

Now the WP&YR is the last of the Canadian narrow-gage passenger service railways. All aboard! Following along a glacially fed river through the Tongass National Forest from Skagway, Alaska, to Fraser, British Columbia, you gain 900 m (3,000 ft) in elevation. Along the 32-km (20-mile) route you cross through Glacier Station, Slipping Rock, Inspiration Point, and Deadhorse Gulch, names which give an idea of both the magnificence and misery of the route. The tiny train wraps itself around each bend, by waterfalls which churn under half-melted snow bridges — so close that you could touch them. All too soon, the ride is over. At Fraser, you can transfer to a motor coach for the rest of the 176-km (110-mile) journey to the Yukon, or return the way you came — dreaming, perhaps, of yet another legendary rail journey somewhere in Canada's vast landscape.

The *Rocky Mountaineer* runs from early May to mid-October. For information and reservations, contact your travel agent or Rocky Mountaineer Railtours ☎ (604) 606-7245 TOLL-FREE (800) 665-7245 FAX (604) 606-7250, 1150 Station Street, First Floor, Vancouver, British Columbia V6A 2X7.

The White Pass & Yukon Railway runs four to six trips per day, from mid-May until late September. For information, contact the White Pass & Yukon Railway ☎ (907) 983-2217 TOLL-FREE (800) 343-7373 FAX (907) 983-2734, PO Box 435, Skagway, Alaska 99840 USA.

Walk with the Dinosaurs

WHEN YOU HEAR THE OMINOUS "BOOM... BOOM... BOOM," YOU'VE ENTERED THE ROYAL TYRRELL MUSEUM'S EXTREME THEROPOD EXHIBIT, which relates the gory tale of the *velociraptor* and other meat-eating dinosaurs that once roamed Alberta's badlands. The *Jurassic Park* connection is exploited to the fullest at this world-class paleontological museum; it's just one of the many enticements attracting 350,000 visitors here each year.

Situated in Alberta's Midland Provincial Park, 140 km (90 miles) northeast of Calgary, the Royal Tyrrell Museum collects, conserves, and exhibits paleontological history through to the appearance of man. That means dino bones, and lots of them. On view are 35 complete dinosaur skeletons — including the dramatic *Albertosaurus*, a fully-articulated skeleton in its death pose — along with some very impressive bits and pieces (among them, the rare "Black Beauty" *Tyrannosaurus rex* skull and a T-rex leg bone as thick as a tree trunk). Many of these specimens were found right in the extraordinary landscape of the Red Deer

Valley, where erosive conditions — nature's ongoing archeological dig — expose more petrified wood, fossils, and dinosaur bones with every gully-washing storm.

But, as museum staff like to point out: "It's not just bones!" Visitors with an aesthetic eye linger at display cases sparkling with million-year-old seed ferns in endless patterns and shades. There are fragile crystallized leaves imprisoned in stone; zebra-patterned blocks of Jurassic Period limestone; and rare multicolored ammolite gemstones, unique to the province.

Kids, needless to say, have a blast here. At the museum entrance youngsters crawl over the life-size dinosaur models, hanging from giant teeth and sliding down sloping backs. Inside they find plenty of interactive computers and touchable displays. A blacklight puppet show featuring the PaleoPlayers presents the story of the "Weird Wonders": the strange marine animals of the Burgess Shale, and the first multicellular animals in the fossil record. The Weird Wonders are also the subject of the museum's newest permanent exhibit, a three-dimensional Burgess Shale diorama that explores these extraordinary creatures and their underwater environment before they were buried 515 million years ago (see YOHO NATIONAL PARK, page 145, for information on hiking trips to the Burgess Shale fossil beds in British Columbia, or contact the Tyrrell Museum).

To would-be paleontologists, the Tyrrell offers not only a window through which to observe research in action, but a chance to get their hands dirty. At the museum's preparation-lab viewing area, visitors can watch technicians meticulously releasing fossilized remains from massive chunks of stone. Surrounding the museum, Midland Provincial Park's trails give explorers a chance to investigate the badlands on one- and two-hour loops. They can even pitch in and excavate alongside trained technicians with the museum's Day Digs program. At nearby Dinosaur Provincial Park, the Tyrrell Museum operates an important field station where volunteers can sign up for a more intensive field experience, working for stints of a week or longer in the park's fossil-rich fields.

In 1979, Dinosaur Provincial Park ☎ (403) 378-4342 FAX (403) 378-4247 WEB SITE discoveryweb.com/aep/parks/dinosaur, PO Box 60, Patricia, Alberta T0J 2K0, was designated a UNESCO World Heritage Site in recognition of its rich fossil deposits, which represent nearly 300 species of plants and animals. It is located a half-hour northeast of Brooks, Alberta.

OPPOSITE: Passengers peruse the British Columbia scenery from the *Rocky Mountainer's* "dome car." ABOVE: At Alberta's Royal Tyrrell Museum, *Tyrannosaurus rex* towers over a visitor.

The Royal Tyrrell Museum ☎ (403) 823-7707 FAX (403) 823-7131 E-MAIL rtmp@dns.magtech.ab.ca WEB SITE www.tyrrellmuseum.com, PO Box 7500, Drumheller, Alberta T0J 0Y0, is open from 9 AM to 9 PM daily from the end of May through Labor Day weekend; 10 AM to 5 PM, Tuesday to Sunday in winter. An admission fee is charged.

Paddle the Pacific Rim

HUGGING THE FJORD-PITTED COASTLINE OF VANCOUVER ISLAND IN SOUTHWEST BRITISH COLUMBIA, PACIFIC RIM NATIONAL PARK encompasses one of the most extensive temperate rain forests in the world. Kayakers paddle here in the calm waters surrounding the Broken Islands, alighting on tiny islets framed with white sand beaches. Day hikers out of Tofino roam the rain forest under a canopy of red cedars and through a damp profusion of sword fern. Beachcombers emerge from the muted colors of the forest to the sparkling tidal pools of the coast where green sea anemones feed and fat orange starfish cling to the rocks. Here, zealous backpackers follow the challenging West Coast Trail carrying all of their supplies for the six- to nine-day trip from Port Renfrew to Bamfield. This infamous trail covers the southern third of the park weaving through 77 km (48 miles) of woods and waterfalls, scaling slippery slopes, and tracing the shoreline that has been the death of many a ship. Killer and gray whales, sea otters and black bears are commonly seen along the route.

Pacific Rim National Park is also the setting for a somewhat more genteel adventure experience. In the midst of the rain forest, a small lodge nestles in a notch carved out of the granite hillside along the emerald waters of Barkley Sound. Eagle Nook Ocean Wilderness Resort offers a taste of the rich variety of flora and fauna to be found in the Pacific Rim National Park, but here guests rough it in style, enjoying a true wilderness experience — hiking and heli-hiking, kayaking, salmon fishing, whale-, seal- and bird-watching — and returning at the end of the day to the comforts of a warm hearth, a gourmet meal, a moonlit dip in the hot tub, and a soft bed.

One constant to a trip to the park is the weather, whether you're trekking or taking it easy. Some days the sky seems to hang within yards of the water. The air is liquid. "Classic west coast weather," you'll be told by Vancouver Islanders, who seem to thrive on the misty atmosphere as much as the cedars and ferns do. But rain or shine, rough or relaxed, Pacific Rim National Park is splendid.

No roads lead to Eagle Nook Wilderness Lodge. From Port Alberni, it's an hour's boat ride to the lodge. Float plane transportation can also be arranged. For information and

Pacific Rim National Park — OPPOSITE: Starfish and sea anemone. ABOVE: Kayaking.

reservations, contact Eagle Nook Ocean Wilderness Resort ☎ (250) 723-1000 TOLL-FREE (800) 760-2777 FAX (250) 723-9842 E-MAIL eaglenk@cedar.alberni.net, PO Box 575, Port Alberni, British Columbia V9Y 7M9.

Only experienced hikers should attempt to hike the West Coast Trail, and never alone. There is a strict quota system regulating the number of people who hike the trail. Advance reservations are strongly recommended (see PACIFIC RIM NATIONAL PARK, page 100).

Cruise the Inside Passage

WITH A DEEP GROAN AND A WHISTLE, THE FERRY SHIP, MV MATANUSKA *SWINGS ROUND ITS BOW AND SAILS OUT OF PRINCE RUPERT,* on British Columbia's northern coast. We will be aboard for three days, making our way along the Inside Passage, Canada's historic inland waterway.

We're following in the wake of hundreds of thousands of prospectors who blazed this route in 1898, when gold was discovered in the Klondike region of the Yukon Territory. One hundred years later, adventurers are still booking passage on Canada's inland waterway, in search of other sorts of riches — for this is one of North America's most scenic journeys, taking voyagers through and beyond the Pacific rain forest and into the glacier-locked Coast Mountains of the north. Along the way, the scenery is astounding, and opportunities for spotting wildlife, especially marine mammals, are unparalleled.

The voyage takes us along British Columbia's northern coast and the Southeast Alaska panhandle — which shares British Columbia's rainforest flora, composed of Sitka spruce, western hemlock, and the tall cedars. As we cruise further north, the landscape changes dramatically: Alaska — we're told by the onboard Forest Service interpreter — has glaciers the size of Rhode Island. She ticks off the wildlife we have a chance of seeing during the two-day passage through this icy wilderness: brown bears (grizzlies), black bears, bald eagles, orcas (killer whales), humpback whales, Steller's sea lions, and Pacific white-sided dolphins.

The 22-m (74-ft) long MV *Matanuska* looks like a hospital in *Mayberry RFD*. Snug, clean, solid. There's a cafeteria, a cocktail lounge, and an observation lounge. The top deck has a recliner lounge and the solarium where budget travelers can camp out for the duration of the trip. We have sprung for an outside cabin — with its two portals that blink out into the Pacific day. Along the way, in addition to a stopover in Prince Rupert, we dock briefly in the Alaskan ports of Ketchikan, Wrangell, Petersburg, Juneau, and Haines. It's possible to ferry hop along the coast of British Columbia and Southeast Alaska, debarking at these picturesque towns, many of which can only be reached by boat.

The second and final evening finds many of the passengers enjoying the waning day on the ship's port side. It's the orca watch. A couple of hours pass pleasantly enough, but tension is building: Where are those whales? A few false alarms set us to giggling: a log floats by… "Hey, look… oh, sorry." Then a resounding, "There they are!" comes from an upper deck, and we all rush to the rail. It's a large school of Pacific white-sided dolphins. Magnificent! But we still want whales. Finally, at dusk, they appear — a pod of five orcas, with their unmistakable tall black fins, curve majestically through the water. Seeing the orcas out on the open sea, it's not difficult to understand why the Pacific West Coast natives so revered these creatures, calling them sea wolves, incorporating them into their art, and endowing them with supernatural powers.

The journey ends at Skagway, Alaska, the very place where thousands of gold seekers erected a muddy tent-city 100 years ago in preparation for their trek over the White and Chilkoot passes to the Yukon.

Schedules and fare information and reservations are available from BC Ferries ☎ (604) 669-1211 TOLL-FREE IN BRITISH COLUMBIA (800) 223-3779 FAX (250) 381-2583, 1112 Fort Street, Victoria, British Columbia V8V 4V2, for trips between Vancouver, Vancouver Island, Port Hardy, and Prince Rupert, British Columbia; and from the Alaska Marine Highway System ☎ (907) 627-1744 or (907) 627-1745 TOLL-FREE (800) 642-0066, PO Box 25535, Juneau, Alaska 99802-5535 USA, for ports of call between Bellingham, Washington, and Skagway, Alaska. While the BC Ferries reservation system is slick and efficient, the Alaska Marine Highway is notoriously unresponsive. For better service, contact Alaska Northwest Travel Service ☎ (206) 787-9499 FAX (206) 745-4946, 3303 148th Street SW, Suite 2, Lynnwood, Washington 98037 USA. They can make bookings for you on both systems.

Note: If you're taking the Alaska Marine Highway out of a Canadian port of call, don't forget to bring along United States dollars.

The Inside Passage — ABOVE: The village of Petersburg in the Alaska panhandle. BELOW: Snowcapped mountains from the deck of the ferry ship MV *Matanuska*.

Listen to Ancient Voices

IT'S AN HOUR'S BOAT RIDE OUT OF DAWSON UP THE YUKON RIVER —A SHORT TRIP, BUT A LONG JOURNEY; taking visitors back many years as they sail into the Ancient Voices Wilderness Camp. Throughout the year, Dawson City visitors who want a change from the gold-rush hullabaloo, gladly embark on this quiet river journey where they can visit the descendants of the region's original inhabitants and learn about life in this valley before the gold seekers came and changed their lives forever.

This place in the woods may have originally been a Hän native hunting bivouac. Towards the turn of the century it became a logging camp, providing fuel for the riverboats that steamed up and down the Yukon at the height of the gold rush era. Now Marge and Peter Kormendy along with their family and their friends and colleagues are fulfilling a lifelong dream to reclaim and preserve their native heritage. They're part of an immensely exciting movement in the Yukon and throughout Canada of First Nations people regaining their land and their culture after a century of marginalization.

On the boat ride to the camp, Marge explains how she and Peter chose the camp's name. "We call this place Ancient Voices because it's a place of spirits. We're here because we want to keep alive our past. The voices are calling to tell us to come back to the past, because it is simple and true. The land is alive with our ancestors' voices."

Though it is a sacred place, Ancient Voices welcomes everyone. Some people come in winter to see *naoka*, the Northern Lights; some come for the summer women's retreat, knife-making workshops, wilderness survival courses, or leather- and bead-craft seminars. Others just want to be here amongst the voices — to sleep in rustic cabins, or learn the skills of building a lean-to out of spruce boughs, to bask in the *makivik*, the traditional steam-house, and to share a meal at the outdoor fire pit. While some visitors come for week-long stays, many come just for a few hours to see demonstrations of the traditional crafts being practiced: the fish wheel, moose-hide curing, storytelling, drumming and singing. After the demonstrations a picnic of traditional foods is served: *bannock*, a delicious fried biscuit, is eaten with highbush cranberry jam and dried caribou. A barbecue of moose steaks and salmon follows.

First Nations tourism is growing rapidly. These native-owned-and-run enterprises range from historical villages to tour companies to camps to lodges. What they offer in common is a chance to meet and talk to some of Canada's First Nations peoples and to learn about the culture, first hand, often in a participatory manner. These are not living history museums with costumed interpreters, but real encounters with a living culture — and one we have much to learn from.

The Yukon First Nations are among the country's most active and organized. The Yukon First Nations Tourism Association ((867) 667-7698 FAX (867) 667-7527, PO Box 4518, Whitehorse, Yukon Y1A 2R8, can assist you with a list of contacts in the territory. For information about Ancient Voices Wilderness Camp, contact Marge Kormendy ((867) 993-5605 FAX (867) 993-6532 E-MAIL avwcamp@yukon.net, PO Box 679, Dawson, Yukon Y0B 1G0. Day visits operate through the summer; workshops and conferences are offered throughout the year; package trips and customized vacations are also available year-round.

British Columbia is also an excellent place to encounter First Nations cultures. In the Vancouver area there is the Hiwus Feasthouse ((604) 980-9311 on Grouse Mountain, with a program of Coast Salish dancing and dining. Talapus Tours ((604) 734-1716 is a First-Nations-owned sightseeing company that takes visitors around the Vancouver to aboriginal sites and concludes with traditional dancing, *bannock*, and barbecue. On Vancouver Island, there are a number of cultural centers, including the U'Mista Cultural Centre at Alert Bay, the Cowichan Native Village, in Duncan, and the Kwagiulth Museum and Cultural Centre on Quadra Island. At Cape Mudge, you can stay at the Tsa-Kwa-Luten Lodge and dine in a longhouse on traditional native cuisine. Further north in British Columbia, Prince Rupert is steeped in Tsimshian history and culture (30% of the population is aboriginal) and there is much to see and do in and near the city. From here, you can sail to the Queen Charlotte Islands, ancestral home of the Haida, or head east to the Hazelton area to visit the 'Ksan Historical Village, a restored Gitksan native village.

The Nunavut Tourism Association ((867) 979-6551 TOLL-FREE IN CANADA (800) 491-7910, PO Box 1450, Iqaluit, Nunavut X0A 0H0, is the source of information for all things Inuit.

Finally, annual events and festivals are a good way to encounter First Nations culture. See FESTIVE FLINGS, page 35, and check with the tourism office or native tourism association of the region you are planning on visiting.

Ancient Voices Wilderness Camp, Dawson City, Yukon — ABOVE : After a barbecue of salmon and moose steaks, Nova Scotian visitors "jam" BELOW with native Canadians.

YOUR CHOICE

The Great Outdoors

Extending from the densely populated 49th parallel into the empty reaches of the north, Canada — the world's second largest country — encompasses not only a stunning breadth of wilderness, but also a mind-boggling variety of terrains. Within its embrace is an endless range of contrast: the treeless tundra of far north and the sea-battered fjords of Newfoundland; the lake-dotted interior of the Canadian Shield and the pocket deserts of British Columbia; the boundless wheat fields of the western prairie lands and the picket fences and potato patches of tiny Prince Edward Island.

Established throughout western Canada's distinct regions are some of the continent's grandest national parks. While these parks serve to protect the natural habitat, most are accessible to travelers, and most offer an array of facilities and activities. Boating, biking, skiing, dog mushing… take your pick. But a stout pair of hiking boots is all that is required to experience many of western Canada's wide-open spaces.

HIKING IN WESTERN CANADA'S NATIONAL PARKS

The five Rocky Mountain parks — Banff, Jasper, Kootenay, Yoho, and Waterton Lakes — straddle the provinces of Alberta and British Columbia. Banff alone has more than 1,500 km (900 miles) of marked trails. Jasper, larger than Banff, Yoho, and Kootenay combined, is the third-most visited park in Canada (after Banff and Kootenay), with some 800 lakes and mountain trails to satisfy every type of hiker. In both Banff and Jasper many trailheads are close to the townsites themselves, though for a true wilderness experience you'll want to climb to higher pastures. Yoho and Kootenay draw mountaineers and rock climbers from around the world, but also have trails for all levels of ability and interest.

Coastal British Columbia is the home of one of the world's most fabled long-distance treks, the West Coast Trail in **Pacific Rim National Park**. Originally used as a lifesaving route for shipwrecked sailors along Vancouver Island's sparsely populated coastline, it is a challenging 77-km (46-mile) trek that can take five to nine days to complete, and is only for experienced hikers.

Another long-distance hike with a fascinating history is the **Chilkoot Trail**. This grueling four- to five-day hike between Dyea, Alaska, and Lake Bennett, British Columbia,

Springtime in the Canadian Rockies, Alberta — OPPOSITE: A glacial lake mirrors its towering neighbor. ABOVE: A ground squirrel peers out from the rocks surrounding Lake Louise.

was the poor man's route to the Klondike gold fields in 1898. From Lake Bennet it's just a short hop to some of the best true-wilderness hiking in Canada, in the Yukon Territory's **Kluane National Park**. Canada's highest peak, Mount Logan (6,050 m or 19,844 ft) looms over vast ice fields in Kluane's back ranges, drawing alpinists from around the world. The park's front ranges are accessible to all, offering spectacular scenery and opportunities for spotting wildlife.

Some of Canada's parks are remote indeed, but well worth the effort and expense to reach. Bisected by the Arctic Circle, on Baffin Island in Nunavut, **Auyuittuq National Park Reserve** is an international draw for climbers and hikers; who follow traditional Inuit routes marked by *inukshuks*, rock cairns resembling human figures.

Most people don't think of Saskatchewan as a hiker's paradise, but **Prince Albert National Park**, where the prairie meets the forested northern region of the province, offers backpackers a 400,000-hectare (million-acre) playground. There are hiking trails for all abilities, ranging from short walks to lengthy backpacking treks. Another jewel of central Canada, **Riding Mountain National Park** has 30 hiking trails traversing Manitoba's highlands — where bison, elk, and deer roam.

In addition to local tourist information centers, park centers are often equipped with adequate trail maps. If you are venturing into the backcountry, you'll need a topographical map, available from the **Canada Map Office** ☎ (613) 952-7000 FAX (613) 957-8861 TOLL-FREE (800) 465-MAPS FAX (800) 661-MAPS, 130 Bentley Avenue, Nepean, Ontario K1A 0E9.

WILDLIFE

Canada's tundra, mountains, forests, and prairies support a profusion of wildlife. On Vancouver Island, **tidal pools** fascinate hikers who can gaze through clear waters at golden starfish and green sea anemone, while kayakers paddling the Broken Island Group drift through sparkling schools of sardines. Coastal British Columbia teems with **marine mammals;** from the majestic humpbacks to graceful orcas (killer whales), Steller's sea lions, and Pacific white-sided dolphins. In the northern interior of British Columbia, the rare white **kermode bear** is sometimes spotted around Terrace. The Tsimshian natives called these white bears "ghosts," and they figure prominently in their folklore. The kermode is cousin to the **black bear**, which roams Canada's boreal forest and can sometimes be seen foraging for berries along highways.

Grizzly bears (called brown bears in Canada) are found in greater numbers in the Yukon Territory's Kluane National Park than anywhere else in Canada. **Caribou**, **elk**, **timber wolves**, and **thin horn sheep** are abundant in the Kluane Range, which also has the world's largest population of **Dall sheep**.

In April, Yukon bird watchers flock to M'Clintock Bay for the annual migration of the **trumpeter swan**, and in the Northwest Territories some 300,000 **snow geese** migrate annually to the Mackenzie Delta, and other areas of the Arctic mainland and islands. In Wood Buffalo National Park, North America's largest herd of **bison**, commonly called buffalo, roam.

Visitors to Alberta are delighted at the sight of **elk** grazing the medians and yards in Banff and Jasper townsites. Outside the towns, a drive through the parks in summer virtually guarantees sightings of **bighorn sheep**; **black bears** are also often seen.

Saskatchewan is an important migratory stop for the endangered **whooping crane**, and in late August, Last Mountain Lake, northwest of Regina, is the place to watch cranes and **pelicans**. Churchill, Manitoba is the **polar bear** capital of the world; polar bears are also abundant along the Arctic coast as well as at Herschel Island in the Yukon.

OPPOSITE: The glacially-fed Lake Annette in Jasper National Park, Alberta. ABOVE: A bald eagle perched like a totem on Queen Charlotte Island, British Columbia.

Sporting Spree

Whatever your sporting passion, be it curling or croquet, watching a beer-soaked hockey match, or skiing solo down a pristine mountainside, Canada is likely to offer a time and a place for it.

CANOEING, KAYAKING, AND RAFTING

Canada is the world's most watery land, with lakes and rivers that contain half of the world's supply of fresh water, and with more than 240,000 km (151,000 miles) of coastline. With so much H_2O, it's no surprise that Canada's shores and inland waterways are an irresistible draw for paddlers from all over the world.

British Columbia is well-known for its water routes. In the Okanagan region, rafts bob and weave through the whitewater rapids of **Fraser Canyon**. The 120-km (72-mile) trip on the Cariboo River to **Bowron Lakes Provincial Park** is a classic. Sea-kayaking is splendid along the Vancouver Island shoreline, especially around the **Broken Islands** and in the **Gwaii Haanas (South Moresby National Park Marine Reserve,** part of the Queen Charlotte Islands), where most people hire a guide to help them navigate the archipelago's 180 islands.

In the Northwest Territories, the Mackenzie system presents a variety of challenging voyages, including a 300-km (180-mile) stretch of the **South Nahanni River** near Fort Simpson where the Nahanni National Park, a UNESCO World Heritage Site, has its headquarters. The Yukon river system has it all, from the gentle currents of the **Takhini** to the Class III rapids and spectacular river-level glaciers of the **Tatshenshini** and **Alsek** rivers.

SKIING

In this land of legendary winters, where snow covers hill and vale for five months (or more!) of the year, skiing — Canadians have discovered — is a good way to stay warm. Fine skiing can be had in just about every province and territory, even in Manitoba and Saskatchewan. But it is in British Columbia and the Rockies that you find ski slopes of a variety and grandeur unsurpassed anywhere on the globe.

The world-famous ski resort of **Whistler/ Blackcomb** is two hours north of Vancouver along the spectacular Sea-to-Sky Highway. Whistler Mountain has a rise of 1,530 m (5,020 ft) and Blackcomb Mountain has the greatest vertical rise in North America at 1,609 m (5,280 ft). Both are well served by high-speed lift systems, and between them they have 2,800 hectares (7,000 acres) of skiing, a good one and half kilometers (one mile) of it vertical, a third of it above tree-line. The area has some particularly beautiful cross-country skiing, with about 190 marked trails, and heli-skiing for intermediate or advanced skiers with Mountain Heli-Sports TOLL-FREE (888) HELISKI, or Tyax Heli-Skiing ☎ (604) 932-7007.

In the Canadian Rockies' Banff National Park, three world-class ski resorts are within easy reach of Banff townsite and Lake Louise: **Mount Norquay**, **Sunshine Village**, and the **Lake Louise Ski Area**. These three resorts combined offer 2,400 hectares (6,000 acres) of ski terrain with everything from groomed runs to pure powder. Over in Jasper National Park, **Marmot Basin** lays on another 400 hectares (1,000 acres) of snow.

Perhaps the best part of the Canada ski report is that skiing doesn't have to be an expensive undertaking. Many resorts, hotels and bed and breakfast inns offer affordable packages. In British Columbia and Alberta, some hostels offer ski packages. Hostelling International Southern Alberta ☎ (403) 283-5551 FAX (403) 283-6503 E-MAIL SAB@HostellingIntl.ca, Suite 203, 1414 Kensington Road NW, Calgary, Alberta T2N 3P9, will send you a brochure with the details.

SPECTATOR SPORTS

Though many North American professional spectator sports are dominated by United States leagues, on the ice rink Canada reigns supreme. There are three western Canada teams in the **National Hockey League** (NHL), whose season lasts from October to May: The Vancouver Canucks play at General Motors Place; the Edmonton Coliseum is home to the Edmonton Oilers, four-time winners of the Stanley Cup; while one-time Stanley Cup winners, the Calgary Flames, play at home in the splendid Canadian Airlines Saddledome in Stampede Park. For an **NHL season schedule**, contact the National Hockey League ☎ (514) 288-9220, 960 Sun Life Building, 1155 Metcalfe, Montréal, Québec H3B 2W2.

The Open Road

In the great tradition of ignoramuses who often say prescient things by accident, Al Capone once said, "I don't even know what street Canada is on." Everyone laughed, but old Scarface had put his chubby finger on one of Canada's most pressing needs: transportation. Nor could he have known that after his death Canada would come to live on one principal street, the **Trans-Canada Highway (TCH)**.

Completed in 1962, the TCH is only two lanes for much of its 6,978-km (4,361-mile) length from Victoria, British Columbia, to St. John's, Newfoundland. With more than 90% of all Canadians living within 80 km (50 miles) of this road, it truly is the country's main street. What's more, most of the major tourist attractions are within easy reach of the Trans-Canada Highway.

Adventurous vacationers and those with more time to spend will want to get off this well-beaten track to experience the country's more remote regions, including its incomparably beautiful national parks in the central and northern regions of the provinces. In Winnipeg, Manitoba — at about the halfway point of the TCH — cross-continental drivers can opt to veer northwest onto the **Yellowhead Highway**, the "other trans-Canada highway." Named after the blonde guide known as Tête Jaune (Yellow Head) who showed early fur traders a pass through the mountains, this road follows a First Nations trading route running 3,185 km (1,911 miles) from the prairies over the Rockies through Jasper National Park to the Pacific coast of British Columbia.

From Edmonton, Alberta, the Yellowhead Highway runs northwest to link up with "Mile 0" of the **Alaska Highway** at Dawson Creek, British Columbia. Running 1,500 km (900 miles) through often spectacular scenery,

OPPOSITE: Preparing a kayak at Eagle Nook Wilderness Lodge, Vancouver Island, British Columbia. ABOVE: Cyclists cruise the seawall in Stanley Park, Vancouver, British Columbia.

this historic route has beckoned four-wheeled adventurers since the United States government flung it hastily across the northern reaches of Canada during the early stages of World War II, when fears of a Japanese invasion via Alaska ran high. The Alaska Highway is no longer the rough-and-tumble affair that it was a decade or more ago. These days vehicles of every description, but particularly recreational vehicles, zip along the highway at a rate of one per minute. One of the most beautiful stretches of this road runs along Kluane National Park in southwest Yukon, where blue-green glacier-fed lakes and alpine scenery flank the road.

The Alaska Highway is just the tip of the iceberg when it comes to Yukon road adventures. From south of Dawson City, the **Dempster Highway** leads intrepid travelers into the wilder side of the north on an 18-hour drive that ends in Inuvik, Northwest Territories. Opened in 1979, the Dempster was Canada's first all-weather road to cross the Arctic Circle. It's a gravel surface all the way, but is well maintained. Autumn travelers are often rewarded with the sight of huge herds of caribou.

ABOVE: Train tracks head west out of Banff, Alberta, bound for the Pacific Coast. OPPOSITE TOP: Basset hound and a Ford Edsel, Jasper National Park. BOTTOM: A truck is covered with dust after the drive up the Dempster Highway to Inuvik, Northwest Territories.

If you're not bent on making one of Canada's many epic-length road trips, plenty of scenic loops and Sunday drives remain to be enjoyed. You will find many of them described in the regional chapters.

Backpacking

Perhaps it is the length and harshness of northern winters, but when summer rolls around, Canadians just can't stay indoors. **Vancouver**, in particular, is perfect for visitors on shoestring budgets — who can savor the city's vibrant street-life and many summer outdoor festivals without spending a thin Canadian dime. Alberta's and British Columbia's **Rocky Mountain parks** are obvious destinations, with 11 Hostelling International sites, inexpensive hikers' shuttle buses, and endless trails that are free for the taking. **Interior British Columbia** draws backpacking travelers with its miles of empty roads and spectacular waterways — perfect for long-distance biking and paddling. And the **Yukon Territory** has similar attractions as well as offering the far north's only youth hostel; at Dawson City, in the land of the midnight sun.

In short, penny-pinching travelers find much to like in Canada.

ACCOMMODATION

Canada's **hostels** are usually the least expensive places to lay your head down — especially for solo travelers — costing from $9 to $23 per night, per person. They have the added advantage of providing good company, a refreshing change from the isolation of hotels. Many of them provide cooking facilities for self-catering, offering additional savings on food cost.

Those who plan to do a fair amount of hostelling will benefit by becoming a member of Hostelling International ☎ (613) 237-7884 FAX (613) 237-7868 E-MAIL info@hostellingintl.ca WEB SITE www.hostellingintl.ca, 400-205 Catherine Street, Ottawa, Ontario K2P 1C3. A membership not only reduces your nightly fees, but also gets you discounts at local businesses. Write to obtain their *Official Guide to Hostels in Canada and the United States of America*.

YMCA and **YWCA** residences can be found in many Canadian cities. They are often quite comfortable with extras such as inexpensive cafeterias, fitness facilities, and swimming pools. Though some residences offer dormitory accommodation for as little as $15, others can cost as much as a budget hotel.

Coca-Cola
EDSEL

CHEVROLET

YMCA Canada ☏ (416) 967-9622 FAX (416) 967-9618, 42 Charles Street East, Sixth Floor, Toronto, Ontario M4Y 1T4, will send you the *YMCA-YWCA Residence Directory*, a complete list of all YMCA-YWCA residences in the country.

Some **university campuses** open their dormitories to travelers from May to August. Anyone can use the facilities, though preference is often given to students. Rates for single and double rooms start at $30 to $40. Most universities have an office that handles reservations, and it's a good idea to book well in advance. You'll find university accommodation contact numbers listed under WHERE TO STAY in the regional chapters.

GETTING AROUND

Have we mentioned that Canada is big? The largest part of your traveling budget will undoubtedly be transportation: gasoline is expensive in comparison to United States prices (but much cheaper than in Europe), and trains are outrageously expensive. **Greyhound Canada** TOLL-FREE (800) 661-8747 and the other bus lines ply just about every route in the country and are almost always cheaper than rail riding and driving, unless you are traveling in a group of three or more. Greyhound offers passes in seven-, 15-, 30- and 60-day limits, as well as discounts that allow a second person to ride for half price and children (under 16) to ride free with an adult (on certain routes). See GETTING AROUND, page 240, in TRAVELERS' TIPS.

Another way to reduce travel costs is with an **automobile drive-away**, whereby you deliver an automobile to a given destination. The demand for drive-aways is not as great in Canada as in the United States, but you might try Auto Driveaway TOLL-FREE (800) 346-2277, 310 South Michigan Avenue, Chicago, Illinois 60604-4298 USA, which has locations in Calgary ☏ (403) 289-7854, 232G, 3630 Brentwood Road NW, Calgary, AB T2L 1K8; Vancouver ☏ (604) 985-0936, 1080A Marine Drive, Vancouver, British Columbia B7P 1S5; and Winnipeg ☏ (204) 663-2966, 1579 Dugald Road, Manitoba R2J 0H3.

Living It Up

While some vacationers come to western Canada to test themselves against the great outdoors, others come to soak up the scenery at the region's luxury hotels and resorts. And, short of palm-shaded tropical beaches, western Canada has just about everything the sybaritic swinger could want.

EXCEPTIONAL HOTELS

THE CANADIAN ROCKIES

No roll call of Canada's top hotels would be complete without mention of the historic **Banff Springs Hotel**, opened in 1888 by the Canadian Pacific Railway Company. Its architecture, inspired by the baronial castles of Scotland, is now a revered Rocky

Mountain landmark, with 770 river- or mountain-view rooms and the European-style beauty and health spa, Solace. The equally luxurious **Rimrock Resort Hotel**, near Banff's hot springs, immerses its guests in modern opulence. Smaller than its venerable neighbor, yet equally refined, the Rimrock is our pick for the best place to stay in Banff — a more restful retreat than its popular neighbor. Nearly all rooms have views of the lovely Bow Valley.

But why stay in busy Banff when there is the laid-back Lake Louise, where our favorite Rocky Mountain retreat is nestled? The **Post Hotel**, owned by Swiss brothers André and George Schwarz, adds a European twist to mountain lodge accommodation, with its spacious and airy suites decorated in hunter green hues and Canadian pine. Some suites have cozy lofts and all have fireplaces with river-stone hearths. This Relais & Châteaux property is situated along the Pipestone River and ski lifts are just five minutes away by the hotel's complimentary shuttle service. Miles of cross-country trails start at the hotel's front door.

Further north, **Jasper Park Lodge** is another distinctive Canadian Pacific property, noted not only for its excellent and varied accommodation, but also for its plethora of recreational offerings: year-round swimming in a heated pool, tennis, golf, horseback riding, boating, cycling, ice skating, in-line skating, sleigh rides, and more.

VANCOUVER AND ISLAND

When we're in Vancouver and in the mood for pampering, we stay at the **Wedgewood Hotel**. This intimate 97-room hotel has everything the large luxury chain hotels have, as well as what they lack: a personal touch. Owner and general manager Eleni Skalbania decorated this gorgeous property, using her own antiques and works of art to embellish the lobby and halls. Her elegant taste and characteristic warmth are evident everywhere in this charming hotel. The suites are spacious and include fireplaces and balconies that look out over leafy Robson Square.

It is virtually impossible to think of Victoria without the image of the **Empress Hotel** springing instantly to mind. This ivy-clad dowager, a Canadian Pacific property, dominates the Inner Harbour and remains a bastion of Englishness and old-style glamour. Popular with honeymooners are the secluded rooms in the attic, which have four-poster beds, as well as window seats for enjoying the beautiful views of the harbor.

EXCEPTIONAL RESTAURANTS

THE CANADIAN ROCKIES

The latest entry in Banff's gourmet scene is the **Dining Room at Buffalo Mountain Lodge**, where main courses center on expertly prepared caribou, rack of Alberta lamb, and sea bass. Not to be missed is the **Post Hotel** in Lake Louise Village, which offers warm hospitality in their renowned dining room. Start with one of the delightful soups, such as squash with caramelized apples, and move on to a main course of grilled salmon on a bed of mashed potatoes mixed with heavenly chunks of boiled lobster. Ask for a window seat and enjoy a view of the Victoria Glacier as you dine. Breakfast is a treat here also: there's a generous cold buffet or you can tuck into eggs benedict with Pacific smoked salmon from the à la carte menu.

VANCOUVER AND ISLAND

Some say the best restaurant in Vancouver is **Diva at the Met** where the open kitchen serves "art you can eat." Others swear it's the **Chartwell** at the Four Seasons Hotel, with its inspired international cuisine. But never fear, this is one toss up you can't lose. Vancouver also has some excellent French *haute cuisine* with the upscale bistro **Le Crocodile** and the Pacific-Rim-influenced **Lumiere** leading the way in this category. Piloted by a Cordon Bleu Award-winning chef, **Floata** is the largest Chinese restaurant in Canada. Dinners are lavish, featuring such delicacies as shark fin and bird's-nest soups.

On Vancouver Island, the internationally acclaimed **Sooke Harbour House**, west of Victoria, has wonderfully inventive Pacific

OPPOSITE: The Post Hotel in Lake Louise Village is noted for its excellent cuisine. ABOVE: The lobby of the Château Lake Louise in Alberta.

Northwest cuisine; the couple who run the restaurant grow their own vegetables and herbs, and use only locally caught seafood and the meat of animals raised on nearby farms.

Family Fun

The bad news is: there is no Disneyland Canada. Or is this the good news? Whatever your opinion, this fact points to an essential, if subtle, difference between Canada and the United States when it comes to family vacations. The United States may have bigger thrill rides, glitzier cartoon characters, better-known superstars, but Canada has a small-town warmth and friendliness that we believe makes it just right for kids. It's safer, too. Canada, claims one of our American friends, reminds him of the United States of the 1950s. So, put Beaver and Wally in the car…

Skiing, as you might expect, is very big in western Canada. Families love British Columbia's Whistler and Blackcomb ski resorts, a short drive north of Vancouver. Both resorts have ski schools and daily supervised children's programs. Active teenagers will appreciate this resort's snowboarding facilities. If your tastes run to adventure, your Canadian winter break might include **dog sledding** and **snowmobiling** in the Yukon, a **canyon ice walk** in Jasper, or **backcountry skiing** and **winter camping** in one of the country's national parks.

When the snow melts, Canada's vacation offerings multiply. Teenagers are thrilled by **rafting** trips in British Columbia's Fraser Valley. Whether you join a tour or go it on your own, possibilities for **hiking** and **backpacking** are virtually endless and can be easily combined with **off-road biking** and **paddling** in Canada's lakes, rivers, and along its seashores. **Ranch vacations** and **farm stays** in southern Alberta, the Okanagan Valley (British Columbia), and the Qu'Appelle Valley (Saskatchewan) give everyone in the family a chance to share in the day-to-day operations of working ranches and farms: guests help with chores, ride horses, and round up cattle, along with a variety of leisure activities (see SPECIAL INTERESTS, below).

Children (and adults) are always delighted with animal encounters. There are zoos in most of the major western Canadian cities, but one of the country's great assets is its abundant wildlife. Each of western Canada's provinces and territories has its characteristic populations (see THE GREAT OUTDOORS, above), and an entire family vacation can easily be planned around wildlife watching.

Cultural Kicks

Canada is a mosaic of cultures, an assembly of immigrant groups and native peoples, many of whom have maintained their uniqueness rather than merging into a national Canadian identity. This makes Canada in many ways a more exciting cultural destination than its southern neighbor, where ethnic origins have been obscured by the "melting pot."

Vancouver is the place to stroll in the tranquil Dr. Sun Yat-Sen Classical Garden, browse a Japanese grocery stores, or watch a Punjabi parade. You can cultivate your

OPPOSITE: A boy checks out the orthodontics at the Royal Tyrrell Museum, Alberta. ABOVE: Another toothy creature clutches its catch of halibut at the 'Ksan Historical Village, British Columbia.

cowboy image in Calgary with its world-class rodeos, country-and-western music and Wild West bars. In Manitoba, Winnipeg's historical district of St. Boniface, with the largest French-speaking community in western Canada, will have you conjugating your verbs.

Canada's **First Nations** peoples are as culturally varied as the country's immigrant groups. In this spectrum of native bands, it is the Inuit and the Pacific Northwest Coast natives whose art first garnered international attention. The **Inuit** are known for their carvings on soapstone, ivory, antler, and whalebone, as well as for their printmaking. With the rising popularity of Inuit art, there are frequent temporary shows in galleries and museums throughout Canada. The **Pacific Northwest Coast tribes** developed a complex culture and a distinctive artistic style which can be seen today in the works of Haida, Tsimshian, West Coast (Nootka), Kwagiutl, Coast Salish, and 'Ksan artists. Animals such as the killer whale, the wolf, and the raven feature in prints, sculptures and ceremonial objects such as Chilkat blankets, totem poles, and masks. Like the Inuit, the Pacific Northwest Coast native artists are rising stars in the Canadian arts constellation, and every major city shows these magnificent works in a variety of venues.

European-Canadian painters began to distinguish their art from its continental influences at the beginning of the twentieth century, when the Group of Seven emerged as an artistic force, creating a uniquely Canadian school of landscape painting. Today, painters and sculptors are exhibiting their work in galleries and museums throughout Canada and the world. Western Canada's most prestigious art museum is the **Vancouver Art Gallery**.

The **Royal Winnipeg Ballet** perform on the international circuit. There are **opera** companies in most major cities; almost every city has an orchestra, as well as smaller ensembles. Vancouver, and Winnipeg have **symphony orchestras** of international status.

First Nations individuals and groups are also active in the performing arts. One of the best ways to see and learn about native art and artists is to go to the **Great Northern Arts Festival** that takes place in Inuvik, Northwest Territories, each July. Native drumming and dancing, exhibitions, sales of arts and crafts, and participatory workshops are part of this growing festival.

Canadian **pop musicians** such as Bryan Adams, Céline Dion, Leonard Cohen, Roch Voisine, and Daniel Lavoie are known the world over.

Shop till You Drop

The rule to remember is: look for local specialties. In **Prairie Provinces**, especially in Alberta, you will find every sort of cowboy attire you could possibly want. In **British Columbia** look for the elaborately carved handicrafts of the West Coast natives, including Cowichan sweaters from Vancouver Island and Haida carvings from the Queen Charlotte Islands. Also keep in mind that one of the specialties of this region is salmon, which you can buy smoked and gift-packed. In the **Yukon** gold-nugget jewelry is still in style. Fossilized mastodon ivory, most often seen beautifully carved, polished, and set in earrings, is unique to the region. In the **Northwest Territories**, seek out Dene specialties: snowshoes, baskets, and drums as well as traditional clothing such as parkas, mitts and moccasins. Also in the north, Fort Liard is noted for its birch-bark baskets, and Fort Simpson for the now-rare art of moose-hair tufting.

There are two caveats to bear in mind when shopping for native Canadian arts and crafts. Although these items, when genuine, are among the loveliest things to buy in Canada, they are often swamped by cheap imitations. Be suspicious of any handcrafted

OPPOSITE: The Dr. Sun Yat-Sen Classical Garden, Vancouver. ABOVE: West Coast native art on sale in Vancouver.

SnoCoach Tours
BREWSTER

article that strikes you as a bargain. To be certain that you are getting the real thing, buy from the artist or from a crafts guild or cooperative, or from a museum shop.

Short Breaks

Few visitors attempt to take in western Canada as a whole. Nor is there a single entry-point at which all international flights arrive. Rather, two metropolitan areas — Calgary, and Vancouver — serve as **primary transportation hubs**. Each of these cities has its unique attractions, and each has the distinct advantage of being within easy striking distance of the great outdoors, making them excellent choices for short vacations. Both Calgary and Vancouver are also within an hour's drive of the United States border — over which vast numbers of Americans flock to Canada each year.

CALGARY

Calgary is the jumping off point for trips into Alberta's **badlands**, where paleontology buffs can get their fill of *Tyrannosaurus-rex* bones and trilobite fossils. There's much to explore here, including Dinosaur Provincial Park, Royal Tyrrell Museum, and Midland Provincial Park. The **Rocky Mountains** are easily accessible from Calgary. Shuttles run direct from the Calgary International Airport to Banff townsite in under an hour. From here the field is wide open for all sorts of vacation pleasures, from spring and winter skiing to art and culture at the Banff Arts Festival in June. Five days allows you enough time to do some hiking and take in a few of the area's museums. Note that if your destination is Jasper rather than Banff, you should consider flying into Edmonton International Airport.

VANCOUVER

You could easily spend five days in Vancouver city limits without fear of repetition. For those who wish to venture further afield, great side-trips abound. **Whistler**, North America's premier ski resort, is a two-hour drive away. If it's cloudy in Vancouver, take the ferry (a 40-minute trip) or charter a float plane to the laid-back **Sunshine Coast** where seashore swimming, hiking in Canada's oldest forest, visiting charming villages, and bird watching are among the attractions. Although most British Columbia **wineries** are too far away from Vancouver to include in a day-trip, Domaine de Chaberton ☎ (250) 530-1736 is just an hour's drive east in the rural Fraser Valley. The winery offers tours and tasting, and also has a wine shop where you can pick up a bottle of their award-winning Chardonnay.

It would be a pity to visit Vancouver without a trip to British Columbia's provincial capital, **Victoria**. Thanks to the new "superferries" which sail out of Tsawwassen-Schwartz Bay, it's now possible to see Victoria on a day-trip from Vancouver (see HOW TO GET THERE, page 96, under VICTORIA). Allow time to explore the city's Inner Harbour, the Royal British Columbia Museum, Bastion Square and Chinatown. The fabulous Butchart Gardens is a half-hour drive away.

Festive Flings

Western Canada's rich cultural heritage, its grape harvest, and its glorious winter provide ample reason to celebrate throughout the year.

WINTER

In **Alberta**, Jasper-in-January ☎ (403) 852-3858 means nine days of alpine skiing, "canyon crawling," parades, and live entertainment. The Calgary Winter Festival (February) ☎ (403) 543-5480 emphasizes the city's Olympic spirit with bobsledding and ski-jumping events.

OPPOSITE TOP: The "Snocoach" shuttles passengers to the Athabasca Glacier, Alberta. BOTTOM: A cruise ship is docked at Canada Place, Vancouver. ABOVE: Alberta's badlands are an open book on the region's geological history.

Manitoba remembers the region's early French fur trading history in Winnipeg during the Festival du Voyageur (February) ☎ (204) 237-7692.

Way up north in the **Yukon Territory** when cabin fever reaches its height, the Yukon Sourdough Rendezvous (February) ☎ (867) 668-4711 in Whitehorse is the cure. Featured events include the crowning of the Rendezvous Queen as well as feats of strength such as the Tug-a-Truck Contest. The Yukon Quest International Sled Dog Race (February) ☎ (867) 668-4711 is called the toughest in the world. Mushers and their dog teams travel more than 1,600 km (1,000 miles) through frozen wilderness between Whitehorse and Fairbanks (the starting point alternates from year to year between the two cities) where revelers cheer them on.

SPRING

British Columbia welcomes spring with the Okanagan Wine Festival (April to May) ☎ (250) 861-6654 which takes place in the Okanagan Valley and features wine tasting, tours and gastronomic and sporting events.

In the **Northwest Territories** the Caribou Carnival (late March) ☎ (867) 873-4262 in Yellowknife is a three-day event celebrating traditional northern First Nations games, music, dancing and crafts.

SUMMER

Edmonton, **Alberta**, swings into summer with Jazz City International (June) ☎ (403) 432-7166, 10 days of concerts and free outdoor events. The Banff Arts Festival (June to August) ☎ (403) 762-6300 opens its season and continues through the summer with an internationally acclaimed lineup of performances and visual arts exhibitions. Calgary hosts the "greatest outdoor show on earth," the Calgary Exhibition and Stampede (July) ☎ (403) 261-0101, the highlight of which is the chuck wagon race and rodeo, while Edmonton's Klondike Days (July) ☎ (403) 479-3500 relive the gold rush with a week of festivities. Edmonton wraps up the summer with its Fringe Theatre Event (August) ☎ (403) 448-9000, one of the major festivals for alternative theater in North America.

Vancouver, **British Columbia**, hosts the World Championship Dragon Boat Festival (June) ☎ (604) 688-2382, which features Asian cuisine and the colorful ritual of the dragon boats.

In **Manitoba**, the Winnipeg Folk Festival (July) ☎ (204) 231-0096 features 200 gospel, bluegrass and other folk music concerts, and a crafts exhibition. The National Ukrainian Festival (July to August) ☎ (204) 638-5645 in Dauphin presents costumed interpreters, fiddling contests, dancing and workshops. Winnipeg celebrates its rich ethnic heritage with the colorful Folklorama (August) ☎ (204) 982-6210 where there are parades, traditional dancing, music, crafts, and wonderful opportunities to sample world cuisines.

The **Northwest Territories'** premier cultural event is the Great Northern Arts Festival (July) ☎ (867) 979-3536, when visitors and northerners gather in Inuvik to participate in a variety of visual arts events including exhibitions, workshops, live performances and crafts demonstrations.

Regina, **Saskatchewan**, presents the Mosaic Festival of Cultures (June) ☎ (304) 757-5990, celebrating the province's ethnic heritage. Regina returns to the days of the Wild West for a week of celebration known as the Buffalo Days Exhibition (end of July) ☎ (306) 781-9200. Citizens dress themselves and the town up in pioneer style to enjoy entertainment, livestock exhibitions, music, and parades. The Saskatoon Exhibition (July) ☎ (306) 931-7149 is a week of agriculturally based events also featuring livestock shows, tractor pulls, music, parades, and dances; while the Shakespeare on the Saskatchewan Festival (July to August) ☎ (306) 653-2300 brings the Bard to the bottomland.

The **Yukon** International Festival of Storytelling (June) ☎ (867) 633-7550, Whitehorse, draws storytellers from throughout the world to the North for four days of yarn-spinning. Everyone looks forward to the Dawson City Music Festival (July) ☎ (867) 993-5584, when Dawsonites break forth with five days of country and western and folk concerts, dances, and workshops.

AUTUMN

British Columbia bids adieu to summer with the Whistler Jazz & Blues Weekend (September) ☎ (604) 932-2394. The Vancouver International Film Festival (autumn) ☎ (604) 685-0260 presents 300 films from 50 countries. And the Okanagan Fall Wine Festival (October) ☎ (250) 861-6654 throws a 10-day celebration of wine and food.

See page 244 in TRAVELERS' TIPS for a listing of national holidays.

Galloping Gourmets

It must be said that western Canada has no Mobil-star-spangled restaurants. But that is not to say that you can't eat wonderfully well in every part of the region. The key is to concentrate on the local specialties.

Thus, in British Columbia, you will want to go for the Pacific salmon, shrimp, and king crab. For a change from all the wonderful seafood, you should try the lamb from Saltspring Island, British Columbia, or the moose steaks from the Yukon. Throughout the far north, fish, such as Arctic char, and game are particular specialties. You'll find such delicacies as caribou or musk-ox jerky, and scallops and giant shrimp fresh from the frozen Arctic waters.

In Alberta, steak is the thing. Even if you are not normally a beef eater, you will be won over by Alberta's beef. Only in Argentina have I ever tasted steaks to compare with the ones you can get here. In fact, across all the Prairie Provinces the beef is exceptional — as is the freshwater fish from the thousands of lakes and rivers carved into the prairies. In Saskatchewan and Manitoba, I would urge you to order wildfowl — especially the partridge and wild duck — and even the prosaic farm birds, which are tastier here than almost anywhere else because they eat better here. In these provinces, too, you will come across a sort of Borscht Belt, where the large Ukrainian population has left its mark on the menus in the form of spicy sausages, dumplings, and a variety of cabbage dishes.

On the other hand, if you are just looking for a pit stop where you can refuel quickly, you will find coffee shops, diners, and fast-food places just about everywhere you go.

As in the United States, Canadian restaurants tend to be informal and welcoming. They also tend to serve meals at earlier hours than Europeans are used to, so if you are counting on having a late dinner you would be wise to check on kitchen closing times first.

DRINKING

The first time I visited western Canada I asked a shopkeeper where I might find the nearest liquor store. This simple question caused utter consternation, followed by endless consultations, followed by — blank. The

Queen Charlotte Islands — OPPOSITE: A carving adorns the house of Haida artisan Alfie Collins. ABOVE: Traditional Haida foods.

reason was, it turned out, that spirits may only be purchased from specially licensed liquor stores. To buy liquor by the bottle, you have to go to one of these official stores — of which there are maddeningly few, which are maddeningly out of the way, and maddeningly closed at night and on Sundays and holidays — and there, but only there, are you allowed to conduct your thirsty transaction. Why this should be the case I cannot say. What I can say is that it interferes with one's budgeting more than with one's drinking, because even the happiest of Happy Hours is not as economical as a couple of self-catered cocktails, and a Rémy in your room is better value than any postprandial drink in a restaurant.

Even the most convivial imbibing is complicated by local laws, which come in various shades of blue. In some places you can get a drink if you're 18, in other places you have to be 19. In some places the bars close at midnight, in other places they stay open as late as 4 AM. In most places, on Sundays you can only order a drink at a restaurant or a hotel dining room, and then only if you order a meal. In a few places you can't buy a drink — period — whatever day it is.

Equally strange, Canadians are not great whiskey drinkers, even though they make some excellent whiskies. But they are great beer drinkers, although until recently the beer they make has been at best mediocre, at worst comparable to what passes for beer south of the border. Happily, Canadian beer has improved immeasurably with the growth of microbreweries, and now good local brews are available as far north as Whitehorse.

Though it is true that Canadian wines don't have an international reputation, there are also some happy exceptions here.

In British Columbia "ice wine" is enjoyed for dessert. It's made from grapes that are left on the vine until frozen: Quail's Gate is one of the best. Cedar Creek Wineries have an excellent Chardonnay as well as a widely respected Merlot. We enjoyed Mission Hill wines on our last visit.

Special Interests

LEARNING VACATIONS

From rustling cattle in the Alberta badlands to practicing your "Eskimo roll" in a Yukon kayaking class, western Canada is a veritable universe of learning opportunities.

Pacific Crest Outward Bound School ☎ (604) 737-3093 TOLL-FREE (800) 547-3312 FAX (604) 737-3109, 411-1367 West Broadway, Vancouver, British Columbia V6H 4A9, offers challenging

eight- to 22-day courses in **mountaineering** along British Columbia's interior Coast Range. Ice, snow and rock climbing, off-trail hiking, backcountry navigation, first aid, and minimum impact camping are all part of the curriculum. Voyageur Outward Bound School ☎ (612) 338-0565 TOLL-FREE (800) 328-2943 E-MAIL vobs@vobs.com, Mill Place, Suite 120, 111 Third Avenue South, Minneapolis, Minnesota 55104 USA, teaches the ins and outs of **canoeing** in Manitoba's Atikaki Provincial Wilderness Park, and **cross-country skiing** and **dog sledding** on Baffin Island, Nunavut, where would-be mushers learn to handle a team of huskies.

Ecological study tours are the specialty of Earthwatch ☎ (617) 926-8200 TOLL-FREE (800) 776-0188 E-MAIL info@earthwatch.org, 680 Mount Auburn Street, PO Box 9104, Watertown, Massachusetts 02471 USA, whose volunteers get a chance to contribute to ongoing studies by assisting researchers in the field. Call for a schedule of their current research projects. Elderhostel ☎ (613) 530-2222 TOLL-FREE (877) 426-8056, 4 Cataraqui Street, Kingston, Ontario K7K 1Z7, offers learning vacations for the 55-and-older set. Their "Take a Closer Look at Canada" series encompasses a variety of week-long tours that explore the **culture and history** of the country from Saskatchewan's Mounties to tours of the Arctic where you can learn about Inuktitut history and modern Arctic life. Elders of these First Nations communities often take part in providing the experience. Costs are very reasonable.

OPPOSITE: A canoe is waiting for you high in the Yukon's Kluane Range at St. Elias Lake. ABOVE: Coal Harbour Yacht Club, Vancouver.

FARM AND RANCH VACATIONS

Everybody say, "Yeehaw!" for Canada's guest farms and ranches. These vacation spots range from working cattle ranches, where guests can try their hand at cattle drives or branding, to remote lodges in pristine backcountry, and to luxury resorts complete with room service.

Alberta Outfitters Association TOLL-FREE/FAX (800) 742-5548, PO Box 277, Caroline, Alberta T0M 0M0, represents independent ranch and farm families located throughout the southern and central province. You can contact the **British Columbia Guest Ranchers' Association** ✆ (250) 374-6836 FAX (250) 374-6640, c/o BCFROA, PO Box 3301, Kamloops,

BC V2C 6B9, for a list of the provinces 14 guest ranches. There are a few places around Regina, Saskatchewan, that offer farm accommodation, mainly in the Qu'Appelle Valley. For details, contact the **Saskatchewan Country Vacation Association** ✆ (306) 931-3353, Rural Route 5, PO Box 43, Saskatoon S7K 3J8, which lists farm vacations as well as bed and breakfast accommodations. Manitoba vacation farms can be found through the **Pembina Valley Travel Association** ✆ (204) 324-8641 TOLL-FREE (800) 877-1874 E-MAIL pvdcorp@mts.net, PO Box 1180, Altona, Manitoba R0G 0B0.

WINE TASTING AND TOURS

The Okanagan Similkameen Valley is British Columbia's wine country, and wine-touring opportunities abound here. Contact the **Okanagan Similkameen Tourism Association** ✆ (250) 860-5999 FAX (250) 861-7493, 1332 Water Street, Kelowna, British Columbia V1Y 9P4. Motorists can follow the well-marked wine route through hill and valley, tasting the fruits of the season as they go (be sure to appoint a designated driver). Among the wineries to contact for details are: **Sumac Ridge Estate Winery** ✆ (250) 494-0451 FAX (250) 494-3456, 17403 Highway 97, Summerland, British Columbia V0H 1Z0; **Kelowna's Calona Vineyards** ✆ (250) 762-9144 or (250) 762-3332, 1125 Richter Street, Kelowna, British Columbia V1Y 2K6; **Mission Hill Winery** ✆ (250) 768-7611 or (250)

768-5125, 1730 Mission Hill Road, Westbank, British Columbia V4T 2E4; and **Quail's Gate Estate Winery** ☎ (250) 769-4451, 3303 Boucherie Street, Kelowna, British Columbia V1Z 2H3.

Taking a Tour

Ready for adventure? Whether your idea of a thrill is dog mushing through the Arctic or riding a luxury motor coach through British Columbia's wine country, western Canada has a tour for you. Aside from being lots of fun, a good tour takes the hassle out of trip planning, provides instant camaraderie, and puts a knowledgeable guide at your side.

ADVENTURE

Ecosummer Expeditions ☎ (604) 214-7484 TOLL-FREE (800) 465-8884 FAX (604) 214-7485 E-MAIL trips@ecosummer.com, 5640 Hollybridge, Richmond, British Columbia V7C 4N3, has one- to two-week kayaking trips through the misty archipelago of the Queen Charlotte Islands and rafting trips on the Tatshenshini and Alsek rivers of the Yukon and northern British Columbia.

Butterfield & Robinson's ☎ (416) 864-1354 TOLL-FREE (800) 678-1147 FAX (416) 864-0541, 70 Bond Street, Suite 300, Toronto, Ontario M5B 1X3, offers backcountry walks in British Columbia, Gulf Islands biking and walking trips, and a hikes in the Rockies.

Backroads ☎ (510) 527-1555 TOLL-FREE (800) 46A-2848 FAX (510) 527-1444, 801 Cedar Street, Berkeley, California 94710 USA, specializes in active adventures in an irresistible framework of luxury lodging and gourmet dining. Trips include walking tours of Banff and Yoho national parks. There are also multi-sport trips in the Rockies that can include hiking, mountain biking and rafting, heli-hiking, cross-country skiing, and snowshoeing.

Wells Gray Provincial Park, in British Columbia's Cariboo Mountains, is the destination for **GAP Adventures** ☎ (416) 922-8899 TOLL-FREE (800) 465-5600 FAX (416) 922-0822 E-MAIL adventure@gap.ca, 266 Dupont Street, Toronto, Ontario M5R 1V7, which offers five- to nine-day hut-to-hut hiking trips. GAP also has week-long and three-day trips to Churchill, Manitoba, the "Polar Bear Capital of the World." On Vancouver Island, GAP has trips that take in killer-whale watching, grizzly bear tracking, and sea kayaking. GAP Adventures feature grassroots-style traveling, basic accommodation in simple hotels and hostels, or camping.

In the Yukon Territory, **Walden Guiding and Outfitting** ☎ (867) 667-7040 TOLL-FREE (877) WALDENS (9259) E-MAIL Bwalden@hypertech.yk.ca, PO Box 4845, Whitehorse,

OPPOSITE TOP: Life in the tidal pools fascinates a golden retriever. A beluga whale BELOW at the Vancouver Aquarium. ABOVE: Downtown Calgary gleams from the Calgary Tower.

Yukon Y1A 4N6, offers dog-mushing adventures in winter and in summer canoeing on the Big Salmon River. **Arctic Vision** ☎ (867) 668-2411 FAX (867) 668-2642 E-MAIL arctic@yknet.yk.ca, PO Box 31210(v), Whitehorse, Yukon Y1A 5P7, specializes in tours to the Western Arctic, including day tours from Inuvik to Tuktoyaktuk where you can dip your toes in the Arctic Ocean, and flights to the remote Herschel Island. **Cloudberry Adventures Yukon** ☎/FAX (867) 668-7711 E-MAIL cloud@cloudberry.ca, PO Box 6113, Department C, Whitehorse, Yukon Y1A 5L7, journeys to "Little Switzerland," Atlin, British Columbia, and the remote Coal River Springs Territorial Park with combined hiking, paddling and wildlife watching activities.

You can canoe on the Nahanni River, in the Northwest Territories, with **Black Feather Wilderness Adventures** ☎ (705) 746-1372 TOLL-FREE (800) 574-8375, Rural Route 3, Parry Sound, Ontario P2A 2X1. Trips combine paddling with a four- to five-day alpine hike in the Cirque of the Unclimbables, as well as rugged 16-day kayaking and hiking trips on Ellesmere Island — the top of the world.

There are a number of excellent First Nations-owned and run tour companies. One of the longer-established of them is the **Arctic Tour Company** ☎ (867) 977-2230 FAX (867) 977-2276 E-MAIL atc@dauroranet.nt.ca, PO Box 325, Tuktoyaktuk, Northwest Territories X0E 1C0, which offers various winter and summer tours, including dog team and snowmobile excursions, wildlife viewing and bird watching, Northern Lights viewing, camping, hiking, and community tours, and native cultural and traditional tours.

GUIDED COACH AND CRUISE TOURS

Globus Tours ☎ (303) 797-2800 TOLL-FREE (800) 851-0728 extension 7518, 5301 South Federal Circle, Littleton, Colorado 80123 USA, is a Swiss-owned company offering deluxe coach tours. Their sister company, **Cosmos** (contact Globus offers bargain-priced motor coach tours with accommodation in modest hotels. **Maupintour** ☎ (913) 843-1211 TOLL-FREE (800) 255-4266 FAX (913) 843-8351, 1515 St. Andrews Drive, Lawrence, Kansas 66047 USA, and **Tauck Tours** ☎ (203) 226-6911 TOLL-FREE (800) 468-2825 FAX (203) 221-6828, PO Box 5027, Westport, Connecticut 06881 USA, are two more well-established luxury coach tour operators with many Canadian destinations.

In the northwest the trend is two- to three-week combination tours that include a cruise along the Inside Passage and a motor coach ramble over the White Pass into the Yukon.

Brendan Tours ☎ (818) 785-9696 TOLL-FREE (800) 421-8446 FAX (818) 902-9876, 15137 Califa Street, Van Nuys, California 91411 USA, makes an interesting two-week combination cruise and motor coach tour that takes you from Vancouver to Anchorage. On the way you spend three nights aboard the MS *Westerdam*, take a scenic ride on the White Pass & Yukon Railway, and enjoy a riverboat cruise out of Dawson City.

The city-sized ships of **Holland America** ply the North Pacific coastline; contact Travelon Vacations ☎ (630) 271-6004 TOLL-FREE (800) 392-2277 (no mailing address available) for information. There is an abundance of cruises that sail the glacier-bound west coast of British Columbia, typically making their way to Anchorage, Alaska. The cruise season is late May through early September (see CRUISE THE INSIDE PASSAGE, page 16, in TOP SPOTS).

The Canadian Rockies — OPPOSITE: Along Alberta's Icefields Parkway, Athabasca Falls roars through a canyon created by eons of erosion. ABOVE: Atop Athabasca Glacier.

NOBLE RANGER

Welcome to Western Canada

IF YOU LIKE THE IDEA OF A GIGANTIC COUNTRY THAT can be enjoyed without a gigantic wallet, a New World nation that has taken care not to squander its Old World inheritance, a place where the dazzle of the landscape is matched by the kaleidoscopic mix of peoples who inhabit it, then you will like Canada — a lot.

And there is a lot of it to like. Covering almost 10 million sq km (3.9 million sq miles), it is the second largest country in the world (after Russia). Unlike Russia, however, or its next-door neighbor to the south, Canada has only 30.3 million inhabitants — slightly more than California. While the land extends northward well into the Arctic Circle, the vast majority of the population is concentrated in a narrow band along the long border with the United States.

From a strictly demographic point of view, the two most striking things about this population are that it is overwhelmingly urban — over 75% of Canadians live in cities or towns — and surprisingly heterogeneous. Unlike their American counterparts who have been historically quick to jettison their cultural baggage in the rush to become assimilated, immigrants to Canada have tended to cherish and safeguard their distinctive traditions, preserving the old in order to civilize the new. Thus it is not uncommon to see signs in Finnish by Lake Superior or to hear Ukrainian spoken on the Manitoban prairies. Likewise, members of various other nationalities and ethnic groups in Canada have created cheery enclaves without creating dreary ghettos.

It's a pity that President Kennedy appropriated the phrase "a nation of immigrants" to describe the United States, because it applies more accurately to Canada. Whereas the United States may have been founded by immigrants, and substantially populated by them for a century or more, Canada is still being shaped by immigration. At the beginning of the nineteenth century the country had a population of barely five million; since then two tidal waves of immigrants — the first before World War I and the second following World War II — have washed up on Canada's shores, helping to boost the population to its present level and helping to determine what kind of nation will enter the twenty-first century.

Unhappily, it is still uncertain whether or not this nation — whose greatest triumph has been the achievement of a multicultural, bilingual state — will unravel as the friction between the two predominant cultures, the British and the French, provokes Québec to tear itself away from the Confederation. But of this more later. Happily, Canada's other great achievement, which is to have shared a continent with America without becoming totally Americanized, looks like it will continue to be a distinguishing feature of the Canadian way of life.

It won't be easy. For one thing, most Canadians live close to the United States border, the longest unguarded national boundary in the world. This means, among other things, that most Canadians are within reach of American radio and television stations. This has been a major concern of Canadian intellectuals for the better part of the twentieth century. It first surfaced as a worry in the 1920s, when Canada was absorbed into the American radio system at a time when the United States was beginning to flex its imperial muscles. Then, after the end of World War II, when America was at the zenith of its power and influence, there came the new threat of cultural annexation by television.

So seriously was this threat viewed that no fewer than three royal commissions were set up between 1949 and 1961 to address "the problem of American culture in Canada," and specifically to seek ways of organizing "resistance to the absorption of Canada into the general cultural pattern of the United States." There was little the commissioners could do, however, apart from encouraging the Canadian Broadcasting Corporation (CBC) in its policy of featuring homegrown material. Even this rearguard action, faithfully pursued by the CBC since its creation in 1936, has never received wholehearted government support. Today that support is decidedly half-hearted: during the 1990s, 11 CBC television stations had to close down because of cuts in government funding. Meanwhile, the most recent surveys show that 80% of total television viewing in the big metropolitan areas near the border is of American programs; even in Edmonton, which receives only Canadian stations, the figure is 66%.

Nor is the cross-border invasion limited to the airwaves. American films occupy most of the cinema screens, while American magazines dominate the newsagents' shelves. Even Canadian sports have not escaped American colonization. All of the top teams in the one sport about which Canadians are passionate — ice hockey — play in America's National Hockey League. Having been (quite rightly) converted to the glories of baseball, Canadians see their two baseball teams — the Toronto Blue Jays and the Montréal Expos — competing in the American major leagues. Not even their individual sporting heroes seem able to resist the Americans: within the last decade, Wayne Gretzky, "The Great One" — ice hockey's

OPPOSITE TOP: A farm off Highway 1 in southern British Columbia. The Fraser Valley is western Canada's "bread basket." BOTTOM: A mountain lake on the remote Queen Charlotte Island in northern British Columbia.

all-time superstar — abandoned Edmonton for Los Angeles, and Ben Johnson, Canada's greatest-ever sprinter, was stripped of his Olympic gold medal after failing a drug test, and then had to watch while the medal was awarded to his archrival, the American Carl Lewis. Perhaps the only sport in which Canadians have managed to remain somewhat aloof is American football, but that is only because they enthusiastically embraced the game, made a few minor adjustments here and there, and then renamed it Canadian football. I have watched it (with more enthusiasm, it must be said, than most Canadians) and I have to say that one needs to be a real aficionado, or perhaps a theologian, to explain how it differs from the original.

Canadian football is symbolic of Canadian society insofar as it presents the outsider with difficulties in distinguishing it from its more familiar American counterpart. This, not surprisingly, fills Canadians with an overwhelming sense of frustration. So much so, in fact, that when I told a prominent Canadian businessman over lunch (truthfully) that I had never met a Canadian I didn't like, he reacted with exasperation bordering on disgust. "That's precisely our problem," he said. "Nobody dislikes us, because nobody knows us. To the rest of the world we're just nicer, quieter Americans." Although I felt constrained to insist that this was not a bad thing to be, I could see his point: it must be maddening to be treated forever like the Canadian dollar is treated, as a slightly discounted version of the real thing.

Equally maddening, if not more so, is the fact that most Americans regard Canadians as nicer, quieter versions of themselves. No wonder, then, that Canadians are forever worrying about their national identity being obliterated by the long shadows cast by the colossus to the south. As former prime minister Pierre Trudeau, in a celebrated quip, told Americans on a visit to Washington in 1969: "Living next to you is in some ways like sleeping with an elephant. No matter how friendly and even-tempered the beast, one is affected by every twitch and grunt."

John Bierman, the distinguished English biographer and author of *Dark Safari* who now lives in Toronto, puts it this way: "If you could perforate along the 49th parallel, tear along the dotted line and push Canada out into the Pacific or Atlantic, I'm sure they'd be a totally different people. But the identity crisis is perpetual."

To deal with this "crisis" many Canadians have chosen to reach back, sometimes way back, into their colonial past for a suitable identity. Thus there are parts of the country where stylized versions of the British and French ways of life have been lovingly, not to say fanatically, preserved. This understandably leads outsiders to the frequent conclusion that Canadians have a neurotic preoccupation with being seen as Not-Americans. Indeed in some cases they have. But in my travels around the country I have found that for all the agonizing over their soft-focus national profile, the great majority of Canadians sensibly realize that they quite probably live in the best of all possible worlds.

After all, their country is situated in a neighborhood where there is only one neighbor — and that one is so friendly that neither of them has ever bothered to put up a fence. They have the luxury of living in cities that are not only handsome and comfortable but come equipped with the world's largest backyard, in the form of wilderness areas of awe-inspiring beauty.

Their society has the civilizing patina of history while enjoying all the benefits of modern technology. In short, as a member of the Commonwealth of Nations with a large Francophone population, Canada is in the privileged position of being able to boast of a British monarch but American telephones, French cooking but American plumbing.

In this book we explore western Canada. Since the great preponderance of major tourist attractions in western Canada are within easy reach of the Trans-Canada Highway, we journey along the nation's "main street" as far west as Victoria, British Columbia, on the Pacific coast, and as far east as Winnipeg, Manitoba, the cultural capital in the heart of the prairie. En route, we make those classic detours that are necessary in order to experience the incomparable beauty of the great Rocky Mountain national parks and the wild grandeur of the Yukon Territory in the Far North. (For would-be visitors to Canada's Arctic north, there are a number of specialist publications available. See RECOMMENDED READING, page 247.) Travel along with us, then, and discover the places and people that have made western Canada one of the best-loved travel destinations in the world.

As the country's Chinatowns attest, Canadians have managed to create cheery enclaves without creating dreary ghettos.

Canada and Its People

HISTORICAL BACKGROUND

Just when people first came to Canada is a matter of considerable debate among the experts — some say it could have been up to 40,000 years ago, while others insist that it was no more than 11,000 years ago — but there is no argument over who they were or where they came from. They were nomadic tribes from Asia, principally Siberia and Mongolia, who came into North America across a land bridge that crossed the Bering Strait during successive ice ages. This migration, often imagined as a mass exodus like Moses crossing the Red Sea, in fact happened gradually as bands of hunters traveled east in search of game. And the land bridge from Asia, now referred to as Beringia, was actually hundreds of miles wide, more like a small continent.

Over thousands of years, these bands and their descendants fanned out across North America, establishing different Amerindian societies and civilizations which in some cases became highly developed as early as the eighth millennium BC.

THE FIRST EUROPEANS

There is evidence, although inconclusive, to suggest that the first European to set foot in North America was a sixth-century Irish monk who, according to legend, landed briefly on the coast of Newfoundland. But Vikings sailing from Greenland around AD 1000 made the earliest verified landing. Arriving at the northwestern tip of Newfoundland, which they named Vinland ("land of grapevines"), they established a settlement at the site of present-day L'Anse aux Meadows. Unfortunately, the archaeological remains don't tell us how long the settlement survived or what finished it off, but it is generally assumed that a combination of the harsh winters and clashes with the region's natives drove the settlers away before they had a chance to establish a viable colony.

The next proven landing in Canada was not for another five centuries, when in 1497 the Venetian John Cabot (*né* Giovanni Caboto) arrived in Newfoundland, and then Nova Scotia, to claim these new-found lands for England and Henry VII. (For all practical — i.e., fishing — purposes the nearby sea had already been claimed by the Portuguese, Basque, and Breton fishermen who in the previous century had discovered the Grand Banks fishing grounds off the coast of Newfoundland to be among the richest in the world.) The next claimant to what was already shaping up as another stage for the worldwide Anglo-French rivalry was the Breton Jacques Cartier, who in 1534 sailed into the Gulf of St. Lawrence, landing at Prince Edward Island (which he named Île St-Jean) and the Gaspé Peninsula before sailing down the St. Lawrence as far as a native village in the shadow of an impressive hill, which he named *Mont Réal* (royal mountain). He claimed the entire area for France, referring to it by the Algonquin word for "settlement": Kannata.

NEW FRANCE

Since Cartier didn't return to France laden with the hoped-for gold and gems, French interest in Canada quickly waned, only to be revived at the start of the seventeenth century by, of all things, the demands of *haute couture*. In a word, furs. Thus in 1605 the French explorer Samuel de Champlain established the first permanent European settlement in Canada at Port Royal, Nova Scotia, on the Bay of Fundy, in hopes of trading with the natives for their beaver pelts. Three years later Champlain founded another settlement on a plateau overlooking the St. Lawrence River at the bend where the river suddenly narrows. He named the village Québec, and as the center of the fur trade it rapidly grew into the most important city in New France.

Following in the footsteps of the explorers and the fur traders, the Jesuits swiftly began the spiritual and intellectual colonization of the region. Their more contemplative lay counterparts, the Société de Notre-Dame, moved in on Cartier's "royal mountain" and founded the settlement of Montréal in 1642. Before long it had supplanted Québec as the center of the fur trade in New France.

The two decades spanning the middle of the seventeenth century were difficult ones for the French settlers, as they became inexorably drawn into the bitter tribal conflicts between the Hurons, their principal trading partners, and the warlike Iroquois. But the real threat to their colonial supremacy came, as always, from the British. Although the British had watched uneasily as New France expanded, their primary concerns had remained the settling and securing of their American colonies and the exploitation of the fertile fishing grounds off the Canadian coast. Canada itself was of interest only insofar as somewhere within its precincts there had to be the long-sought Northwest Passage to the Orient. Gradually, however, it began to dawn that Canada, or New France, was part of a continent that was itself a treasure trove of riches — and Britain had the key to the back door.

In 1610 the English navigator Henry Hudson sailed into the giant bay that now bears his name. Sixty years later Hudson Bay in turn gave its name to a commercial enterprise, the Hudson's Bay Company, which was to leave an indelible mark on the history of Canada. Formed by British fur merchants to provide an alternative to Québec as an outlet for the fur trade, it was granted by Charles II right to all the lands drained by rivers flowing into Hudson Bay. Thus backed by a solicitous sovereign and a powerful navy, it was to become the largest fur trading company in North America, and today is still a force to be reckoned with in Canadian retailing.

Although British military activity in Canada was minimal during the War of the Spanish Succession (1701–1713), under the Treaty of Utrecht France was forced to relinquish all claims to

OPPOSITE: A bridal party of Kwakiutl Indians, photographed by Edward Curtis in 1914, arrives at the groom's village. ABOVE: Yukon native women and their children.

Hudson Bay and Newfoundland, and to give up Acadia, which the British promptly renamed Nova Scotia ("New Scotland"). There was a period of relative peace and tranquillity for the next 40 years, broken only in 1744 by the British seizure of the French fortress of Louisbourg on Cape Breton Island. It was handed back four years later under the Peace of Aix-la-Chapelle.

The Seven Years' War, known in America as the French and Indian War, was to be the decisive turning point in Canadian history. The war began well for the French and their native allies, as in battle after battle the British forces showed themselves to be tactically unprepared for what amounted to quasi-guerrilla warfare. But the tide began to turn in 1758 with the arrival of British land and naval reinforcements. A successful siege of the fortress at Louisbourg led to its recapture, giving the British control of the entrance to the Gulf of St. Lawrence, while at the Lake Ontario end of the St. Lawrence River the British took the vital Fort Frontenac. Then, in the summer of 1759, an assault force under the command of 32-year-old General James Wolfe, the youngest general in the British army, sailed from the Atlantic down the St. Lawrence to Québec. All summer long Wolfe's artillery pounded the city, reducing it to rubble but without budging the French forces under the Marquis de Montcalm in their citadel atop the steep cliffs above the town. Then, on the night of September 12, Wolfe tried a daring maneuver. He led a force of 5,000 infantrymen in boats to a point behind the city, where they silently scaled the cliffs and assembled on the Plains of Abraham. The next morning, the startled French forces, flushed out of their fortified redoubt, were slaughtered. Québec had fallen. Both Wolfe and Montcalm were killed. The battle had lasted 15 minutes.

Although it was one of the shortest battles on record, its consequences ultimately reverberated around the world. The fall of Québec effectively marked the fall of New France, and when the French handed over all of Canada under the terms of the Treaty of Paris in 1763, the British were left as undisputed masters of the entire North American continent. Some historians argue, however, that it was a Pyrrhic victory in that the British were also left overconfident and overstretched, not to mention out-of-pocket, while the many American colonists who fought on the British side, including one George Washington, had gained wartime experience as well as insights into British military strategy that would prove invaluable a few years later when the Americans launched their War of Independence.

BRITISH CANADA

The conquest of Canada brought another problem for Britain: what to do about the predominantly French population in the new territory over which they now ruled. In the end, they did the decent thing — and paid dearly for it. By passing the Québec Act of 1774, the British gave the French Canadians the right to continue using their own language, the secure ownership of their property, the primacy of French civil law, and the freedom to practice the Roman Catholic religion (including the Church's right to collect tithes). This did not go down at all well with the overwhelmingly Protestant population in the 13 American colonies, who were already incensed over what they considered unjust taxes imposed by Britain to help pay for the war against France. When the boundaries of the province of Québec were extended to protect the French Canadian fur traders operating in the Ohio and Mississippi River valleys, the American colonists decided that they had had enough.

The colonial rebellion became the American Revolution late in 1775 with attacks on Montréal and Québec City which, had they been successful, would almost certainly have heralded a fairly swift victory for the Americans. In fact, the attack on Montréal was successful, but so brutish was the behavior of the "liberators" that most French Canadians decided they would prefer not to be thus liberated and went on to fight fiercely alongside the British, thus denying the Americans an early knockout.

By the time the war ended in 1783, Canadians had a new neighbor, the United States of America, and also a lot of new Canadians, for about 50,000 Americans who remained loyal to the British Crown had fled northwards. Most of them settled in Nova Scotia and what is now New Brunswick, although about 7,000 made their way to present-day Ontario. More still arrived at the end of the war claiming to be Loyalists, but their devotion to George III might possibly have been influenced by the offer of free land to Loyalist immigrants. In any case, as a result of the American Revolution, Canada received a large transfusion of English-speaking immigrants, many of whom were well-educated and had occupied positions of responsibility and influence under the old colonial regime. Thus did the balance of power in Canada begin to shift away from the French Canadians.

In the years following the war Canada became transformed both politically and territorially. In 1791 the province of Québec was divided into Upper Canada (mainly English-speaking: now Ontario) and Lower Canada (mainly French-speaking: now Québec), each with its own Lieutenant Governor and parliament. Meanwhile, the vast and hitherto neglected lands to the west were gradually being opened up in the wake of the pioneering explorations of Alexander Mackenzie, who in 1793 became the first white man to cross Canada all the way to the Pacific coast, and Simon Fraser and David Thompson, who were the first to map the great mountains and rivers from the Rockies to the Pacific.

The War of 1812 was the last neighborhood brawl before the United States and Canada settled down to live together more or less happily ever after. The war had a number of causes: border disputes, British interference with American shipping, fierce rivalry in the lucrative fur trade, American claims that the British were behind native raids on American border settlements, British claims that Americans were trying to export republicanism to Canada, and so forth. Whatever the justice of any of these claims, they added up to war. Although both sides suffered some telling blows — the Americans captured Toronto (or York, as it was then called) and burned it to the ground, whereupon the British retaliated by capturing Washington and burning the White House — neither side really seemed to have much appetite for the fight. The Americans wanted to get on with nation-building and the British wanted to get on with countering the Napoleonic threat at home,

while the Canadians wanted to be left in peace. In 1814 they got together and declared the war over.

Not surprisingly, considering the enormous size of the two countries, the border issue was not resolved immediately. The first major step was taken in 1818 when they agreed on the 49th parallel as their mutual border from the Great Lakes to the Rockies, but it was not until 1842, after much haggling and a little skirmishing, that the Canadian border with the New England states was established. The last link, the border with the Oregon Territory west of the Rockies, was established along the 49th parallel in 1846.

As increased immigration swelled the population, French Canadians became convinced that the British were deliberately trying to dilute their

OPPOSITE: Expo '86 in Vancouver.
ABOVE: A rugged face in Inuvik bears the traces of the north's harsh climate.

power by swamping them with English-speaking newcomers. As a result, in 1837 French Canadians under the leadership of Louis-Joseph Papineau demanded autonomy for Lower Canada (Québec) so that they could establish an independent republic. When the British refused, a violent rebellion broke out which was not finally defeated until 1838. It was the first time that the call for an independent Québec had been heard. It would not be the last.

Nor were the French Canadians the only ones growing impatient with British rule around this time. In Upper Canada (Ontario) a rough and ready coalition of economic have-nots led by newspaper editor William Lyon Mackenzie rose up against the oligarchic Tory establishment and demanded that the government be remodeled along American lines. When these demands, predictably, were not met, Mackenzie too resorted to armed rebellion with even less success than Papineau, whom he soon joined in exile in the United States.

Although both insurrections had been easily put down, they succeeded in lighting an anti-colonialist fuse that would prove unquenchable.

Nevertheless, Canada at mid-century was a picture of expansion and growth. New waves of immigrants boosted the population of the Maritime Provinces, which were beginning to prosper as a result of their flourishing lumber, fishing, and shipbuilding industries. The population explosion also led to the creation of settlements further westward, in addition to providing the labor needed to build the canals, roads, and railways that made the westward expansion possible. In less than 20 years, over 3,000 km or 2,000 miles of railroad tracks were laid. All that was needed for Canada to become a truly coast-to-coast country was for some sort of tug to be exerted from the other side of the Rockies. That tug, when it came, turned out to be a powerful yank: in 1858 gold was discovered in the Fraser River valley.

The gold rush that followed was so frenetic, and so dominated by Americans rushing northwards to stake their claims, that Britain quickly proclaimed a new Crown colony, British Columbia, to control the stampede into the territory.

British colonies now straddled the continent from the Atlantic to the Pacific.

THE DOMINION OF CANADA

With the old Anglo-French tensions still causing problems, and with the turmoil to the south caused by the American Civil War, not to mention the ordinary growing pains brought on by rapid population growth and territorial expansion, it was widely felt that the colonies should come together and forge a stronger union among themselves. So in 1864, delegates from the various colonies convened in Charlottetown, Prince Edward Island,

to begin laying the groundwork for a new confederation. Three years later, the British North America Act of 1867 created the Dominion of Canada, in which the colonies of Nova Scotia, New Brunswick, and Québec became provinces in a confederated union with self-rule under a parliamentary system of government. Manitoba joined the Confederation in 1870, British Columbia in 1871, and Prince Edward Island in 1873. The Yukon, formerly a district of the Northwest Territories, was made a separate territory in 1898 at the height of the Klondike gold rush. Alberta and Saskatchewan, also carved out of the old Northwest Territories, joined in 1905; Newfoundland, typically, held out until 1949, when it finally became Canada's tenth province.

As important as this political union was to Canada's development, it was more symbolic than real so long as there was no corresponding physical link between the provinces. In fact, three of the

provinces — Nova Scotia, Prince Edward Island, and British Columbia — only agreed to join the Confederation on condition that a transcontinental railway was built to tie the new nation together. Work on this mammoth project began in 1881 and, incredibly, was completed in only four years. In 1885, at Rogers Pass in the Selkirk Mountains, the last spike was driven: the Canadian Pacific Railway was in business.

As was to be expected, however, this mighty triumph of engineering was not achieved without casualties. The coming of the Iron Horse meant the virtual disappearance of the buffalo, the driving of natives from their ancestral homelands, and the deaths of hundreds of (mostly Chinese) laborers on the railroad itself. It also precipitated a bloody uprising in 1885 on the part of the Métis, who were the descendants of French trappers and Cree women, aided and abetted by several tribes of Plains natives, all of whom felt threatened by the armies of new settlers swarming over their land. Already driven out of Manitoba as far west as the southern banks of the Saskatchewan River, the Métis and their native allies, under the leadership of Louis Riel, overwhelmed the Mounted Police post at Duck Lake, attacked the town of Battleford, and captured and burned Fort Pitt. But their successes were short-lived. Before long they were subdued by the superior firepower of the Canadian forces, and Riel was hanged. His execution became another source of resentment among French Canadians, who felt that he would not have been treated so harshly had he not been a Roman Catholic of French ancestry.

With the country now linked literally and politically from sea to sea, the final years of the nineteenth century saw Canada blossom dramatically as a nation. As thousands upon thousands

The entrance to Ottawa's Confederation Building.

of new immigrants arrived, new lands were settled and cultivated, hydroelectric projects were initiated, new manufacturing industries were started up alongside the already-thriving industries of lumbering, fishing, mining, pulp and paper. Above all, agriculture boomed as the Prairie Provinces became one of the great grain-producing areas of the world. And, for icing on the national cake, in 1896 gold was discovered in the Klondike, setting off one of the biggest gold rushes in history as 100,000 (mostly American) fortune-seekers poured into the Yukon. These were heady times.

Thus Canada entered the twentieth century in a buoyant mood. It was also blessed from 1896 to 1911 with one of its greatest prime ministers,

Sir Wilfrid Laurier, a French Canadian and Roman Catholic who set himself the Herculean task of ending the antagonism and suspicion between Canada's English and French communities. But World War I came along and deepened the rift: French Canadians violently objected to military conscription, which was introduced in 1917 after the Canadian volunteer forces fighting alongside the British in the trenches had suffered such appalling losses that there were no volunteers left to fight. The French Canadian point of view — that the war had nothing to do with them, and therefore they shouldn't be drafted to fight in it — left much residual bitterness on both sides after the war was over.

A happier legacy of the war was an economy enriched by a vastly increased manufacturing capacity, streamlined industrial development, expanded mining activity, and burgeoning exports of wheat. Along with Canada's postwar prosperity came growing independence from Britain, acknowledged by the British at the Imperial Conference of 1926 when Canada was granted the right to conduct its own international affairs without reference to London, and sealed by the Statute of Westminster in 1931, which made Canada an independent nation.

Then came the Depression, which was even worse in Canada than in the United States. Suddenly the Promised Land was a ravaged land, as drought erased the wheat fields and unemployment stalked the cities. The misery of the "Dirty Thirties," as the Canadians called the decade, lasted until September 1939 when Hitler marched into Poland. Canada, following Britain's lead, immediately declared war on Germany, whereupon the economy coughed, spluttered, then roared back to life.

Also revived, sadly, was the bitter Anglo-French debate over military conscription, which once again split the country. Again, Canada suffered battlefield losses out of all proportion to its population. On the other side of the ledger, the Canadian economy prospered out of all proportion to its prewar capacity as almost 10% of the population were engaged in war-related industries. Thanks to the war, Canada became one of the world's major industrial nations as well as an important military power, a cofounder of the United Nations, and a member of NATO.

Peace was as good to Canada as the war had been. A huge oil field was discovered near Edmonton, Alberta, in 1947. Giant uranium deposits were discovered in Ontario and Saskatchewan, and its extraordinary mineral riches made Canada the world's leading producer of nickel, zinc, lead, copper, gold, and silver. Its inexhaustible water resources made countless hydroelectric projects possible, including the world's biggest, its forests made it the world's foremost exporter of newsprint, and its oceans made it the world's foremost exporter of fish. As if that weren't enough, Canada was fortunate in having the world's best customer for raw materials right on its doorstep.

Another milestone in Canada's rise among the world's top industrial nations was the opening in 1959 of the St. Lawrence Seaway, a joint United States–Canadian project that made possible shipping from the Great Lakes to the Atlantic. Three years later the Trans-Canada Highway was completed, a concrete link spanning all 10 provinces.

In 1967 Canada celebrated its hundredth birthday by throwing itself a big party in the form of a World's Fair — Expo '67 — in Montréal. Canadians had much to celebrate: a vigorous and rapidly expanding economy; one of the highest standards of living in the world; advanced social welfare programs providing health care and other benefits for all citizens; virtually unlimited natural resources; and a history of international conduct such that Canada had managed to join the front rank of the world's nations without making any enemies. What better reasons to have a party?

CANADA TODAY

Alas, there was a ghost at the birthday party. The old specter of separatism which had haunted the federation during the entire century of its existence was suddenly summoned up in a speech by visiting French President de Gaulle. Speaking to a large throng outside the Montréal City Hall, he declared, *"Vive le Québec libre!"* With their clamoring having thus been endorsed by the President of France,

Québec's separatists found new heart for the struggle to wrench the province away from the rest of the nation. With the ultimate goal of full independence, the Parti Québécois (PQ) was formed and won 23% of the vote in the 1970 provincial elections. They set about developing the province's economy, instituting educational reforms, and making Québec monolingual, all the while pressing for a referendum and secession from the Canadian federation. But, in 1980, when the referendum came, 60% of the province voted "non" to secession. Yet the issue blazed back into prominence a decade later: In 1992 and again in 1995, referenda for sovereignty were held in Québec. In both cases, the electorate rejected the idea. But the 1995 vote was nearly a dead heat. Now, at the end of the twentieth century, the PQ has once again been reelected, and another "neverendum" — as Canadians have named them — may be imminent.

The future of the federation is still Canada's most troublesome political issue. But it's not the only one. In 1989, the free trade agreement with the United States (NAFTA) was pushed through parliament by Prime Minister Brian Mulroney; causing the loss of thousands of jobs, and exposing Canada's industries to American competition. The collapse of the North Atlantic cod fishery has brought hard times to Newfoundland and Nova Scotia, where unemployment now runs very high. How far the current Liberal administration will succeed in patching up the economy and easing the straining bonds of the federation remains to be seen.

One thing, however, is clear: After centuries of exploitation and marginalization, Canada's native peoples are beginning a new and happier era. Having gained political strength throughout the late 1960s and early 1970s, the First Nations of the north launched a series of land claims against the Canadian government in the late 1970s, demanding financial compensation, funding for social programs, hunting rights and a greater role in wildlife management and environmental protection. The success of these land claims has lead to a native cultural revival and, finally, to redrawing the very map of Canada. On April 1, 1999, Canada, formerly comprised of 10 provinces and two territories — gained a new territory, when the present Northwest Territories were divided in two. The eastern part of the existing territories is now known as Nunavut, "Our Land" in the Inuit language. The western lands will remain the Northwest Territories until a name is chosen.

Both in the north and throughout the rest of the country, native Canadians (excluding the Inuit) number around 282,000 and are members of 574 separate communities, called "bands." Ethnically, many of Canada's native peoples have the same heritage as certain United States tribes: Cree, Sioux and Blackfoot, for example, are found in both countries. In Canada native people belong to 10 linguistic groups, each of which has many local dialects.

Since 1973, when the Canadian government accepted a proposal by the National Indian Brotherhood, increasing numbers of bands have begun to manage their own schools. These schools have introduced new curricula, which often include the history of native Canadians and native-language courses.

GEOGRAPHY AND CLIMATE

William Lyon Mackenzie King, Canada's longest-serving prime minister (1921–1930, 1935–1948), observed at the beginning of his third term of office

OPPOSITE: Canada — a land called Winter.
ABOVE: Formed by eons of erosion, a hoo doo towers over the sweltering Alberta badlands.

in 1936: "If some countries have too much history, we have too much geography."

It's hard to argue with that. Western Canada alone spreads over 6.7 million sq km (2.6 million sq miles), stretching from the eastern edge of Manitoba to the Alaskan border in the west, and from the United States border in the south to Cape Columbia on Ellesmere Island in the north (which is only 800 km or 500 miles from the North Pole).

Within this vastness one finds stunning topographical extremes. Almost half the entire country, for example, is forested — one single forest zone of conifers extends for 6,000 km (3,730 miles) in a wide sweep from the eastern seaboard to the far north — while similarly enormous tracts of land are empty, treeless prairies. There are millions of acres of flood plains and marshy lowlands, and there are the majestic Rocky Mountains, though Canada's highest mountain, at 6,050 m (19,844 ft), Mount Logan, is not in the Rockies but in the St. Elias Mountains of southwestern Yukon.

And then there is the water. Canada is awash in lakes and rivers; they account for over seven percent of the country's total area. Three of the 20 longest rivers in the world are to be found in Canada. In all, the country has a staggering 25% of the world's fresh water resources.

Geologically, western Canada can be divided into three distinct regions, not counting the archipelago of islands inside the Arctic Circle. The Prairies spread across the provinces of Manitoba, Saskatchewan, and Alberta, and on up into the Northwest Territories. The rich soil in the southern reaches, where the prairies join the Great Plains of the United States, yields great golden seas of wheat which gradually dry up in Alberta, giving way to huge cattle ranches.

The Western Cordillera is bounded on the east by the Rocky Mountains and on the west by the Coast Mountains. In between is the spectacular diversity of British Columbia, a province of soaring mountain peaks, alpine lakes and meadows, large boreal forests, intricate networks of rivers, deep blue lakes, hot springs and long green valleys.

The third region, the Canadian Shield, encompasses everything else: the immense, horseshoe-shaped land mass that surrounds Hudson Bay, and stretches from the east coast over to the Prairies, and up to the Arctic. Covering some 4.7 million sq km (1.8 million sq miles), about half the entire area of Canada, this rough-hewn, rock-strewn, lake-pitted wilderness is one of the oldest sections of the earth's crust.

The flora and fauna naturally vary from region to region. There are, however, some animals that can be found just about everywhere: squirrels and chipmunks, rabbits and hares, porcupines and skunks. Equally widespread throughout the country's forests and woodlands are deer, moose, black bears, beavers, wild geese, and ducks.

In the prairies, one animal in particular is conspicuous by its absence: the plains buffalo (also called bison). The few who have survived are now in the national parks, while their place has been taken by great herds of cattle. Denizens of the semi-arid grasslands of the southern prairies include kangaroo rats, hares, pronghorn antelopes, and the ranchers' nemesis, coyotes.

In the mountain ranges of the Western Cordillera one can find, if one tries hard enough, brown bears, elk, mountain goats, bighorn sheep, and the bosses of the upper slopes, grizzly bears. In the lakes and rivers there is some of the best trout and salmon fishing to be found anywhere in the world.

In the great expanse of forests across northern Canada are the largest concentrations of fur-bearing animals: mink, ermine, marten, muskrat, beaver, river otter, weasel, lynx, bobcat, wolves, and wolverines. Further north, in the tundra, are arctic foxes, lemmings, musk oxen, and caribou, as well as snow geese and trumpeter swans. Still further north, where the frigid waters are full of whales, seals, and walrus, the mighty polar bear patrols the ice packs of the Arctic.

Because words like "frigid" and "polar" and "ice" and "Arctic" — and even the subtly prejudicial "north" — are all words that we readily associate with Canada, most foreigners think that Canada's climate can probably be summed up in one word: cold. This is a mistake. True, Canada occupies the northern — and therefore colder — part of the continent, but this ignores the fact that Victoria, British Columbia is on the same latitude as Paris. True, the dominant images of western Canada are the snow-capped peaks of the Rockies, but this obscures the fact that those same Rockies form a protective wall that guarantees Vancouver milder winters than, say, Dallas.

Having said that, one has to admit that for much of the year Canada is a theme park called Winter. Harold Town, one of Canada's leading artists, once said: "We are a nation of thermometers monitoring cold fronts. We jig to the crunch of snow." Indeed, over a third of the annual precipitation in Canada falls as snow, compared to a worldwide average of five percent. Winnipeg is the coldest city in the world with a population of more than half a million.

But there is a bright side to all this. It's just that: brightness. Canada may be refrigerated half the time, but it is sunlit most of the time. Which means that it is beautiful all the time, brilliantly white in winter, infinitely and variously green the rest of year. What's more, its meteorological diversity mirrors its geographical diversity, so that the visitor has the luxury of choosing not only the scenery and activities that most appeal, but also the precise climate in which to enjoy both.

In the following chapters, and in the WHEN TO GO section of TRAVELERS' TIPS, page236, we provide information about the sort of weather you can expect to find in different places at different times. For now, though, be assured that in western Canada there is truly a time and place for everything.

OPPOSITE: In Kluane National Park, a forest canopy of birch trees, Yukon Territory. ABOVE: The Canadian prairies in bloom.

British Columbia

BRITISH COLUMBIA IS THE COUNTRY'S THIRD LARGEST and most westerly province, and perhaps its most beautiful. It stretches from the Rockies to the Pacific and from the 49th to the 60th parallel. It is thus bordered by the United States' states of Washington, Idaho, and Montana at its southern edge, the Yukon and Northwest Territories to the north, Alaska at its northwest corner, and Alberta to the east beyond the Rockies. The rugged, snowcapped Coast Mountains rise above the deeply indented Pacific coastline, and beyond them the landscape is rippled by mountain ranges running northwest to southeast that give way to valleys and wide, rolling prairies carpeted with ancient forests and dotted with lakes.

British Columbia's climate is as varied as its landscape. The coast, warmed by the Pacific current and shadowed by the high Coast Mountains, has mild, wet winters and cool summers. The more exposed interior is generally drier, with more extreme temperatures, while northeastern winters are the coldest of all and have the heaviest snowfall.

The province covers an enormous area — 947,800 sq km (366,255 sq miles) — big enough to hold a handful of European countries. There are less than four million inhabitants in the entire province, the majority of whom live in the southwestern corner, and almost half the entire population can be found in Greater Vancouver. This leaves an awful lot of space. There are literally hundreds of parks covering millions of acres of wilderness, making ideal habitats for all kinds of wildlife and a heaven for outdoor enthusiasts. With so many people huddled in its bottom corner, and with the great barrier created by the Rockies, it is not surprising that British Columbia seems separated from the rest of the country. It has often been observed that its lifestyle and easygoing attitudes owe more to California than to Canada.

The First Nations tribes who once populated the West Coast enjoyed prosperity and had a highly developed culture, expressed in art forms that are still much in evidence. Stunning examples of woodcarving are carefully preserved, most strikingly in the form of totem poles. Many First Nations communities still exist in British Columbia and, like the bands of the far north, they are in the midst of an exciting cultural renaissance, resulting in the revival of their languages and traditional arts and crafts.

Europeans were slow to arrive here because of the enormous physical barriers presented by the terrain. It was 1774 when tentative Spanish exploration began, and 1778 when Captain James Cook landed on Vancouver Island, where he traded with natives for furs which he later sold to the Chinese at a large profit. News of this began to speed things up, and the inevitable skirmishes ended with the Spanish conceding control to the British. So in 1792 Captain George Vancouver was dispatched by the British to map the coast. In the meantime intrepid fur traders were exploring overland routes to the Pacific and establishing trading posts.

The Hudson's Bay Company established its headquarters on Vancouver Island. In 1849 the English colonized the island in the name of the Crown, and Victoria was declared its capital. The discovery of gold along the banks of the Fraser River brought a rush of prospectors, and to secure its hold on their territories the British Government made the mainland (then known as New Caledonia) a British colony and renamed it British Columbia in 1858. In the 1860s the construction of the Cariboo Highway opened up the area. Lumber mills and canneries began to spring up, and in 1866 the colonies of Vancouver Island and British Columbia joined together. When the United States acquired Alaska, a further attack of nerves prompted British Columbia to consider joining the Canadian confederation as a security measure against American invasion, but it was with caution and only upon the promise that a transcontinental railway would reach its coast that in 1871 British Columbia finally joined.

This promise was fulfilled by 1885, and industries based on the province's natural resources were able to develop. A further boost came with the opening of the Panama Canal, which made transportation easier and therefore cheaper. Today

ABOVE: Vancouver's Marine Building with its art deco façade. OPPOSITE: A fjord parts the mountains in the Queen Charlotte Islands.

the economy still rests largely on natural resources such as fishing, forestry, mining, energy, agriculture (particularly in the lower Fraser Valley and the irrigated Okanagan), and the tourism attracted by the area's extraordinary natural beauty. The logging industry is currently at the center of a battle between conservationists, First Nations activists and the British Columbia government, with the province's image of caring environmentalism being severely challenged by the rapid destruction of the rain forests and the pollution resulting from logging activities.

VANCOUVER

Magnificent in its setting, sophisticated and cosmopolitan in character, Vancouver must rate as one of the world's most livable and beautiful cities. The air is fresh, the atmosphere is vibrant and youthful, and being only a little over 100 years old, this youngster is suitably seated in the lap of nature. To the north it is shadowed by the Coast Mountains, to the west are the peaks of Vancouver Island, and wilderness surrounds the city. Water is all around: Burrard Inlet separates the city core from the residential North Shore area, while the Strait of Georgia lies to the west and the Fraser River to the south. Water of another kind also figures largely in the life of Vancouverites. The rain is a popular topic of conversation — which is hardly surprising, as the city averages 145 cm (57 inches) of it a year. However, protected by the bulk of Vancouver Island and warmed by the Japan Current, Vancouver has a gentle climate and, unlike so much of Canada, has very little snowfall. May to September are the warmest months with the least rainfall, although even in July and August there may be days when the mountains will be shrouded in mist. On the bonus side, the rain keeps the air fresh and the city green.

Vancouver is the third largest city in Canada as well as being British Columbia's business center, but with a metropolitan population of only 1.8 million, and being so close to nature, it can afford a small-town lifestyle. Here, where there is a noticeable tendency to stroll instead of rush, the residents positively rejoice in the delights of their parklike city. It is said that Vancouverites are considered by Eastern Canadians to be a little too hedonistic. With the endless recreational opportunities offered them by the sea and mountains, who can blame them? There are over 14 km (nine miles) of beaches within the city limits, a rain forest within walking distance of the business core, and ski slopes only 20 minutes away.

The sea plays a major role in the city's economy, for Vancouver has the largest port on the North American Pacific coast. It's from here that grain, timber, and minerals are exported, and especially valuable trade links with Japan have been forged.

Timber, fishing, and tourism are Vancouver's major industries, but increasingly the economy is becoming more dependent on international finance. With the high rate of foreign investment here and the latest wave of immigration from Hong Kong, in some quarters the city has been dubbed "Hongkouver."

BACKGROUND

When the Spanish explorer José María Narváez sailed up the Georgia Strait in 1791, the shores on which Vancouver now stands were densely carpeted with trees and inhabited by Salish natives who fished the waters. The following year Captain George Vancouver quite literally put the area on the map when he explored and charted Burrard Inlet on behalf of the British Navy. The next white man to explore the area was Simon Fraser who in 1808 reached the Pacific by means of an overland

route. This brought him to the mouth of the river now named after him, and in his wake fur trading posts were set up.

The site then seems largely to have been ignored until the 1860s when sawmills started to appear around Burrard Inlet. Alcohol was not allowed on company land, and so when a Yorkshireman named Jack Deighton turned up with a keg of whiskey, he answered the prayers of the thirsty workers. He persuaded the men to help him build a saloon, and that was when things began to happen. The year was 1867, and the rough-and-ready community that quickly sprang up around the bar was named Gastown after its loquacious saloonkeeper, who by then had become known as "Gassy Jack." The town kept on growing and in 1869 the provincial government officially renamed it Granville.

The next major development came in 1884 when William Van Horne, builder of the Canadian Pacific Railway (CPR), decided to make Granville the site of the West Coast terminus. He also suggested that the town be renamed; and in 1886 it became incorporated as the city of Vancouver. Within months the city was destroyed by fire but with speed and determination it was rebuilt by the time the first CPR passenger train chugged into town in 1887.

It was at this time that unpleasantness and disgrace shadowed Vancouver's history. Many Chinese had arrived to work on constructing the railroad, and a series of clashes between them and the white community spurred Vancouver authorities to deport them to Victoria. The incensed provincial government intervened to right this injustice and the Chinese community continued

The Vancouver skyline at dusk seen from Stanley Park. On the left-hand side of the photograph is the city's most recognizable landmark, Canada Place with its white sails.

to live in the area that developed into the city's Chinatown. The racism did not end there, however, and to the city's further shame until the late 1940s the Chinese were denied many of the rights granted to other citizens.

The twentieth century saw Vancouver's rapid growth: The port grew in importance as trade with the Far East developed, the fishing and timber industries thrived, the opening of the Panama Canal in 1914 facilitated export of grain to Europe, thus increasing the port's importance, and the demands created by World War II served to boost the mining and timber industries. After that, urban development hurtled onwards, making Vancouver the envy of many older cities.

Where once a wilderness of 1,000-year-old trees greeted the eyes of the first explorers, shiny highrise buildings glitter against the splendid background of the Coast Mountains. The city gently tends the little history it has: old buildings have been restored and First Nations art has been carefully preserved.

GENERAL INFORMATION

For information on Vancouver, contact or drop by the excellent **Visitor Information Centre** ((604) 683-2000 WEB SITE www.tourism-vancouver.org/, Plaza Level, 200 Burrard Street, Vancouver V6C 3L6. The main **North Vancouver Visitor Information Centre** ((604) 987-4488 is at 131 East Second Street. There is an information kiosk at Lonsdale Quay by the SeaBus Terminal, another at the airport, and several more dotted within and around the city. **Internet access** is available at the Electric Zoo ((604) 801-5788, located at 679 Denman Street at Georgia. It's open 24 hours a day.

Many of Vancouver's points of interest can be reached by public transportation. The Visitor Information Centre (above) provides schedules and maps. **BC Transit** ((604) 521-0400 bus stops are clearly marked and often list the route numbers serving the stop. The **SkyTrain** is an automated light rail that follows an elevated 29-km (17-mile) route with 20 stations, running from downtown east to the suburb of Surrey. The **Aquabus** ((604) 689-5858 runs to Granville Island from the Hornby Street dock, and the **SeaBus** ((250) 521-0400 takes passengers and their bicycles (but not cars) to the North Shore via a scenic 12-minute harbor crossing. It sails are every 15 minutes, departing from the SkyTrain Waterfront station downtown, and from the south foot of Lonsdale Avenue at Lonsdale Quay on the North Shore.

Gastown shops offer a wide variety of Canadian crafts such as this pottery proudly displayed by a neighborhood shopkeeper.

WHAT TO SEE AND DO

Downtown

One of the city's most distinctive landmarks is **Canada Place** ((604) 775-8687, which boldly projects into the harbor north of Burrard Street. With its unmistakable roof of white Teflon-coated "sails" that whiten in the sunlight, it has inevitably been referred to as "Vancouver's answer to the Sydney Opera House," and like the Opera House it quickly became an emblem of the city it graces. Originally built as the Canada Pavilion for 1986 World's Fair, the complex now comprises the World Trade Centre, the Vancouver Trade and Convention Centre, a luxury hotel, restaurants, shops, and a major cruise ship terminal. An outdoor promenade runs around the structure and offers excellent views of the harbor and mountains of the north shore.

Also of architectural note is the nearby **Canadian Pacific Railway Station** on Cordova Street. This splendidly restored structure was built in the 1880s as the Canadian Pacific Railway terminus, and now the SkyTrain elevated rail line to the eastern suburbs and the SeaBus ferry operate from here.

To fully appreciate the city's glorious setting you should take a trip up the nearby 40-story-tall **Harbour Centre** at 555 West Hastings Street. The views from the top will take your breath away, if you have any left to take after the journey up the outside of the building in the glass "Skylift" elevator. The circular observation deck is equipped with telescopes and information plaques, and an excellent special-effects film about the city is

shown. It is open May to September daily from 8:30 AM to 10:30 PM and October to April from 10 AM to 8 PM; an admission fee is charged.

Three blocks south of the Harbour Centre and then a couple east along Georgia Street lies **Robson Square**, which covers the area between Howe and Hornby streets. This complex, built in 1979, contains government buildings, a seven-story law court building with a vast sloping glass roof, restaurants, terraces, waterfalls, and, during the colder months, an ice-skating rink in the open-air plaza. The old courthouse building still stands across from the modern complex, and this dignified neoclassical building has been converted to house the **Vancouver Art Gallery (VAG)** ☎ (604) 662-4700, 750 Hornby Street. The building was designed in 1907 by British Columbia's foremost architect of the time, Francis Rattenbury, and it seems fitting that the interior of the building was redesigned by Arthur Erickson, the internationally renowned Vancouver architect who was responsible for the square's modern complex. The gallery holds temporary exhibitions of international and Canadian art and its permanent collection includes Canadian, European, and North American paintings. One of its main attractions is the large collection of works by the famous British Columbia artist Emily Carr, whose paintings capture the mystery of the rain forests and echo the native art of Canada's Pacific coast. During June to September the VAG is open Monday to Wednesday and Friday from 10 AM to 6 PM, Thursday from 10 AM to 9 PM (pay what you can 5 PM to 9 PM), Saturday from 10 AM to 5 PM, and Sunday from noon to 5 PM. From October to May the hours are reduced to Monday, Wednesday, Friday, and Saturday from 10 AM to 5 PM. An admission fee is charged.

You can soak up a bit of European atmosphere when you stroll along the section of Robson Street that runs between Howe and Broughton streets. Once a mainly German neighborhood, this stretch is known locally as **Robsonstrasse**, and here you can sample all varieties of European food in the restaurants, cafés, and delicatessens that line the street, or take a look at the high fashion shops.

Gastown

A few blocks east of the Harbour Centre between Richards and Columbia streets lies the neighborhood of Gastown, the birthplace of Vancouver and the oldest part of the city. In 1867 it was here that the Englishman John "Gassy Jack" Deighton built his saloon with the willing help of thirsty mill workers. The shantytown that sprung up around it grew to eventually become Vancouver, and although the 1886 fire destroyed the town, it was quickly rebuilt using more robust materials. By the 1960s these buildings had degenerated into slums, and so it came about that during the 1970s Gastown underwent the familiar rags-to-riches story of gentrification. The nineteenth-century buildings were restored, modern but matching additions were built, streets were cobbled, imitation nineteenth-century streetlights popped up, and the area filled with bistros, restaurants, galleries, and shops. This recipe proved successful yet again and Gastown is now a major tourist draw both by day and by night. The center of Gastown is Maple Tree Square, where the original Globe Saloon once lay and where a statue of Gassy Jack and his barrel of whiskey now stands in memory. At the corner of Cambie and Water streets there's an unusual object, which a plaque proudly proclaims to be the first **steam-powered clock** in the world. It pipes out its very own version of the Westminster chimes on the quarter-hour and truly lets off steam on the hour.

Gastown has the city's largest selection of cheap souvenirs, but also offers good shopping for quality Canadian crafts. **Frances Hill's** ☎ (604) 685-1828, 151 Water Street, is one of the best outlets carrying Canadian-made crafts, clothing and gifts. Water Street is also the place for Northwest Coast and Inuit arts and crafts, including Cowichan sweaters, moccasins and carved silver jewelry, which can be purchased at the government-licensed **Inuit Gallery of Vancouver** at No. 345 and **Images for a Canadian Heritage** at No. 164.

Chinatown

Just south of Gastown between Carrall Street and Gore Avenue, centered along Pender and Main streets, is **Chinatown**, home to Canada's third largest Chinese community. The neighborhood developed in the 1880s and some of the original buildings still stand. It's a bustling area filled with the noises and smells of Hong Kong, and it brims with restaurants, bakeries, herbalists, and shops selling all kinds of Chinese goods from ginseng, green tea and exotic fresh produce to embroidered linens and silk robes.

Behind the Chinese Cultural Centre on East Pender Street is the delightful **Dr. Sun Yat-Sen Classical Garden** ☎ (604) 689-7133 or (604) 662-3207, at 578 Carrall Street, which offers a peaceful sanctuary from the city. The only one of its kind outside China, it was designed in Ming Dynasty style by a team from the city of Suzhou, in honor of the revolutionary Sun Yat-Sen, who visited Vancouver while planning the overthrow of China's last dynasty. Everything in the garden was manufactured in China and brought over for the 1986 World's Fair, the 100th anniversary of the founding of Vancouver. (That same year was an important anniversary for the city of Suzhou — its 2,500th.) The garden is an exquisite composition of sculptural limestone rocks, plants, trees, bridges and water, and it's a good idea to join the guided tour which explains the principles behind the design. It's open daily year-round; an admission fee is charged. A small section of the garden is accessible free of charge.

While you're in the area, keep your eyes peeled so not to miss the **Sam Kee Building**, reputedly the world's narrowest building, which stands at the corner of Pender and Carrall streets, one block wide and a mere 1.3 m (six feet) deep.

Stanley Park

The city's pride and joy, Stanley Park is regarded by Vancouverites with great reverence. This 400-hectare (1,000-acre) urban park covers the whole of the western tip of the downtown peninsula that juts out into Burrard Inlet, and consists of some 280 hectares (700 acres) of lush rain forest. The rest is given over to gardens, sandy beaches, and public facilities.

Back in 1886 Ottawa granted this land to Vancouver, and in 1889 Canada's governor-general Lord Stanley dedicated it "to the use and enjoyment of people of all colors, creeds and customs for all time." It is laced with hiking trails and dotted with picnic sites. There are tennis courts, a biking, in-line skating and running track, a walking path, miniature golf courses, cricket pitches, restaurants and snack bars, and an open-air theater. At the Georgia Street entrance is the marshy lake known as the Lost Lagoon, a bird sanctuary where you'll see Canada geese, Trumpeter swans, great blue heron, and other wildfowl. The 10-km (six-mile) scenic **seawall** that encircles the park is popular with cyclists and strollers, and for the less energetic there's a **scenic drive** which starts from the Georgia Street entrance to the park, taking you around the peninsula in an counterclockwise direction. Stanley Park is within easy reach of downtown on foot or via No. 19 city bus along West Pender Street. There is a free shuttle bus around the park from mid-May to mid-September. Information is available from the Park Board ☏ (604) 257-8400.

At **Brockton Point** there are great views across Burrard Inlet of the north shore mountains, and nearby is a display of totem poles. At **Prospect Point**, the Lion's Gate Bridge forms the only land link between the downtown area and the north shore, and from here you get a good view of the ships passing through First Narrows to and from the port. At the southwest tip of the park peninsula, **Ferguson Point** looks over to Third Beach and the peaks of Vancouver Island.

Also in the park is the **Vancouver Aquarium** ☏ (604) 268-9900. This award-winning exhibition of marine life is the largest of its kind in North America: over 8,000 aquatic specimens are on display here. Star performances are given by the acrobatic orcas (killer whales), who can be watched through glass, with strong support from the playful beluga whales, Pacific white-sided dolphins, and sea otters. While you're here you can take a turn in the Amazonian jungle, recreated under cover with sloths, turtles, and bird life indigenous to that area. It's open July to September 4, daily from 9:30 AM to 8 PM; the rest of the year, daily from 10 AM to 5:30 PM. An admission fee is charged.

OPPOSITE: Vancouver's Chinatown not only has the largest Chinese Community in Canada, but many of its buildings were erected by the original settlers. ABOVE: The Dr. Sun-Yat Sen Classical Garden is an oasis of calm.

Outside Downtown

Over on the south side of False Creek is **Granville Island**, which is in fact a small peninsula connected to the downtown core by Granville Bridge. Once the center of Vancouver's shipbuilding industry, by the 1960s the area had degenerated into a grim spot full of dingy factories and warehouses. Renovation began in the 1970s and it is now a lively neighborhood of businesses, craft studios, industry, theaters, galleries, restaurants, markets, and shops. A huge warehouse underneath Granville Bridge has been converted to house the popular **Public Market**, where stalls sell seafood, produce, and foods of many countries. It's open daily in summer and Tuesday to Sunday in winter. On the west of the island you'll find the **Maritime Market** which sells just about everything needed for pleasure boating. The island is a fun place to have lunch and enjoy some views. There is also a collection of shops known as the **Kid's Only Market** with children's clothing and toys and lots of arts and crafts studios. To get there from the center peninsula you can take the passenger ferry that runs from Sunset Beach near the Aquatic Centre or take a bus from downtown.

Close by and to the west of Burrard Bridge in Vanier Park stands the **Vancouver Museum** ✆ (604) 736-4431, 1100 Chestnut Street. The museum has a gallery devoted to West Coast native culture, where some stunning examples of native art and artifacts are displayed. In a gallery that charts the area's history, exhibits include a replica of a Hudson's Bay Company trading post and reconstructed period interiors. It's open daily in summer from 10 AM to 5 PM; winter, Tuesday to Sunday from 10 AM to 5 PM. A general admission is charged with an extra charge for special exhibitions. Situated on the second floor of the museum is the **H.R. Macmillan Planetarium**, which has up to four astronomy shows daily, and laser shows set to rock music at night. It is open July to early September daily, from 11 AM to 4 PM; admission fee varies. Next to the museum is the **Gordon Southam Observatory**, where you gaze at the heavens with the aid of a Zeiss telescope. Hours are daily 7 PM to 11 PM; ring for opening times as they are subject to weather conditions. Admission is free.

Also in Vanier Park, the **Pacific Space Centre** ✆ (604) 738-7827, which underwent major renovation in 1997, has dozens of hands-on space-themed exhibits from laser shows to space artifacts. Computer games take you around the solar system, give you the chance to dock a space shuttle, touch a real moon rock, and then "morph" yourself into an alien. It's open daily in July and August; an admission fee is charged. Nearby, the **Vancouver Maritime Museum** ✆ (604) 257-8300, 1905 Ogden Avenue, north end of Cypress Street, looks at voyagers of an earlier era. Here exhibits trace the history of shipping in the region and the development of the port of Vancouver. The centerpiece is the *St. Roch*, a fully restored Royal Canadian Mounted Police ship that during World War II became the first vessel to navigate the Northwest Passage in both directions. Guided tours are given. It's open May to August, daily from 10 AM to 5 PM;

September to April, Tuesday to Sunday from 10 AM to 5 PM; an admission fee is charged. Outside you can see some of the museum's restored boats in **Heritage Harbour**.

Moving west, the **University of British Columbia** is magnificently sited on the headland of Point Grey, which is tipped with forest and overlooks the Georgia Strait and English Bay. Its **Museum of Anthropology (MOA)** ☎ (604) 822-3825, at 6393 NW Marine Drive, is a concrete and glass building worthy of its dramatic setting. Designed by Vancouver architect Arthur Erickson, the building's huge glass windows embrace the splendid views of cliffs, mountains, sea, and trees, giving context to one of the world's finest exhibits of Pacific Northwest Coast First Nations art. The MOA has a splendid collection of totem poles, some of which are displayed alongside other huge exhibits in the vast **Great Hall**. The museum does not limit itself to representing the Northwest Pacific area and there are works of art and artifacts from many other cultures. Some galleries are set aside for temporary exhibitions and some house the research collections where items are thoughtfully stored in glass filing drawers and clearly catalogued. On the museum grounds, totem poles and reconstructed Haida dwellings are set in the rain forest. The museum is open Tuesday from 11 AM to 9 PM; Wednesday to Sunday from 11 AM to 5 PM. An admission fee is charged, free all day on Tuesday.

Should you feel so inclined, from here you can follow the marked trails that lead down to **Wreck Beach**, a well-known and popular nudist beach. Or you can enjoy nature in a more cultivated form at the **Nitobe Memorial Garden** ☎ (604) 822-6038, 6565 NW Marine Drive, a serene Japanese garden with a ceremonial teahouse. It's open in summer, daily from 10 AM to 6 PM; in winter, weekdays from 10 AM to 3 PM; an admission fee is charged. At the southwest end of the campus there's the **UBC Botanical Garden** ☎ (604) 822-9666, at 16th Avenue and SW Marine Drive, where highlights include the **Asian Garden** and the **Physick Garden**, a sixteenth-century-style garden of medicinal plants. It's open daily 10 AM to 6 PM; an admission fee is charged.

In the eastern corner of False Creek, the silver geodesic dome that was built for the 1986 World's Fair is now home to **Science World** ☎ (604) 268-6363, 1455 Québec Street at Terminal Avenue, where visitors come to grips with science and have fun through imaginative hands-on displays. The SkyTrain runs to the nearby Main Street Station. It's open daily; an admission fee is charged.

Keen gardeners and those who enjoy floral displays will love **Queen Elizabeth Park** ☎ (604) 872-5513, at 33rd Avenue and Cambie Street. At a height of 150 m (492 ft) it's the city's highest point, where wonderful views and magnificent gardens make a delightful place to stroll. Inside its dome-shaped **Bloedel Conservatory** exotic plants grow and brightly colored tropical birds fly free. It is open April to September, weekdays from 9 AM to 8 PM, weekends from 10 AM to 9 PM; the rest of the year, daily from 10 AM to 5 PM; an admission fee is charged. A few blocks away there's yet another manifestation of Vancouver's love affair with nature at the **Van Dusen Botanical Gardens** ☎ (604) 261-0011, at 5251 Oak Street at 37th Avenue. In this 22-hectare (55-acre) garden there are geographical and botanical groupings of plants, a fragrance garden, a children's topiary garden where hedges are cut into animal shapes, and a maze. It's open July to August, daily from 10 AM

to 9 PM; October to April, daily from 10 AM to 4 PM; May, June and September, daily from 10 AM to 6 PM. An admission fee is charged, half price October to May.

The North Shore

On Vancouver's north shore the Coast Mountains rise steeply out of the sea, cut deeply by inlets and canyons. On the lower slopes are the smart residential suburbs of North and West Vancouver and beyond them, peaks and parks beckon hikers in the summer, skiers in the winter, and lovers of the great outdoors all the year round. To get there you can cross the spectacular **Lions Gate Bridge** that links the northern end of Stanley Park to Western Vancouver or the Second Narrows Bridge at

OPPOSITE: The seawall in Stanley Park, attracts cyclers, skaters, and a lone runner.
ABOVE: Downtown Vancouver.

Burnaby in East Vancouver. Alternatively, take the SeaBus. From there buses will take you to the viewing point of your choice.

Next to the SeaBus terminal is the **Lonsdale Quay Market** ☎ (604) 985-6261, a lively waterfront development of shops and eateries centered around a busy public market selling produce. There are lovely views across Burrard Inlet of the city and it is a good spot to pause and orient oneself before exploring the spectacular sights the north shore has to offer. The market is open daily from 9:30 AM to 6:30 PM, Fridays until 9 PM.

At the north end of Capilano Road, the **Skyride** ☎ (604) 984-0661, 6400 Nancy Green Way, awaits to lift you 1,100 m (3,700 ft) up **Grouse Mountain**. The ride takes about eight minutes, and on a clear day it's a chance to enjoy panoramic views that take in Washington's Olympic Peninsula. In the winter this is one of the most popular ski resorts, being the closest to the city, but in the summer it's known as Cypress Beach because it's a great place to laze around soaking up the brilliant sunshine. There's a restaurant and bistro up here, as well as the new Feasthouse, which offers a sunset program combining traditional First Nations song and dance with a dinner of native foods. For information on the restaurants call ☎ (604) 984-0661.

Near the foot of Grouse Mountain, the fantastically dramatic **Capilano Suspension Bridge** ☎ (604) 985-7474 offers thrills for those with a head for heights. Set in a wild and wonderful parkland, this plank-and-cable bridge is 137 m (450 ft) long and sways 70 m (230 ft) above the Capilano River as it rushes through a deep and narrow canyon surrounded by Douglas firs and Western Red cedars. It's a commercialized place and you are charged to cross the bridge; nevertheless it is a beautiful and awe-inspiring sight. It's at 3735 Capilano Road; if you're driving from downtown, pick up the Capilano Road from Lions Gate Bridge. The park is open daily year-round.

You can enjoy a similar but less commercialized experience at **Lynn Canyon Park and Ecology Centre** ☎ (604) 981-3103. This thickly-forested parkland has nature trails through the rain forest, an ecology center, and a suspension bridge that crosses Lynn Creek. Like the bridge at Capilano though only half as long, it crosses the creek at a height of 80 m (240 ft). There is no admission charge. If you're traveling by car, cross at Second Narrows Bridge, take Lynn Valley Road, and then head east along Peters Road.

A little further afield, the **Mount Seymour Provincial Park** overlooks the waters of Indian Arm, offering opportunities for hikers, horse riders, mountaineers, picnickers, view-seekers, and during the winter months skiers. Walking trails and a road climb eight kilometers (five miles) up the mountain to a lookout where there's a café, an information center, more walking paths, and views of eastern Vancouver. From here a chair lift takes visitors to the mountain top in July and August, while the more rugged follow the trail to the summit. To get there by car, take the Mount Seymour Parkway from Second Narrows Bridge, then turn off to the north on Mount Seymour Road.

A delightful way to see the impressive coastal scenery of **Howe Sound** is to take a trip aboard the refurbished ***Royal Hudson***, a stately old Canadian Pacific Railway steam locomotive that pulled trains across Canada in the 1940s and 1950s. With a shrill whistle, a hiss, and the squealing of wheels, the train pulls away from North Vancouver Station at 10:30 AM and begins its 66-km (41-mile) journey northwest to the small logging community of Squamish along a route that runs through forests, up mountains, by waterfalls, all at a leisurely 20 mph. The train arrives at Squamish at approximately 12:30 PM and passengers have one and a half hours to explore — enough time to get to **Shannon Falls** for some lunch. There's an attractive option of returning to Vancouver by sea aboard the **MV *Britannia***, a route that takes a little longer. The *Royal Hudson* runs Wednesdays through Sundays and holiday Mondays from early June to mid-September, and as it's a popular excursion you must book in advance. Contact BC Rail ☎ (604) 631-3500 or (604) 984-5246 TOLL-FREE IN BRITISH COLUMBIA (800) 339-8752 TOLL-FREE ELSEWHERE IN NORTH AMERICA (800) 663-8238 FAX (604) 984-5505. Train buffs who've come this far will be delighted with Canada's second-largest collection of railway equipment at the new **West Coast Railway Heritage Park** TOLL-FREE (800) 722-1233 in Squamish, with vintage rail cars filled with artifacts, photos and information about the history of railroading in British Columbia. It's open daily from 10 AM to 5 PM, May to October; an admission fee is charged.

Southeast of Vancouver

To the east of Vancouver lies the fertile **Fraser Valley**, an area of parklands shadowed by mountains all around, a popular weekend escape for Vancouverites. The Trans-Canada Highway follows the Fraser River along its south shore, while Highway 7 runs along the north side. **Fort Langley National Historic Park** ☎ (604) 513-4777, 56 km (35 miles) from Vancouver on the south side of the river makes an interesting stop. Once a trading post for the Hudson's Bay Company, the fort dates from 1827, and it was here in the Big House that British Columbia was officially proclaimed a crown colony. The fort with its wooden palisade has been restored and the buildings are open daily to the public.

SPORTS AND OUTDOOR ACTIVITIES

With so many excellent opportunities within easy reach of the city center, outdoor pursuits are very much part of the Vancouver lifestyle.

From late November through Easter, it's a paradise for **skiing**. Just 15 minutes from downtown, Grouse Mountain ☎ (604) 984-0661, 6400 Nancy Greene Way, offers runs that are suitable for those of all abilities. An aerial tramway takes skiers to the top; runs are lit at night. With your daily Skyride ticket (see WHAT TO SEE AND DO, above), you can also enjoy **snowshoeing**, **cross-country skiing**, **ice skating**, and **sleigh rides**. Neighboring Mount Seymour ☎ (604) 986-2261,

OPPOSITE: B.C. Place Stadium in Vancouver.
ABOVE: Sails charmingly interrupt Vancouver's shoreline and skyline.

1700 Mount Seymour Road, and Cypress Bowl ☎ (604) 922-0825 (end of Cypress Bowl Ski Area Road, Exit 8 off Highway 1 westbound) also have good skiing and nighttime illumination. For ski information and conditions in the Vancouver area call the Snowphone ☎ (604) 986-6262.

North of Squamish and 120 km (75 miles) northwest of Vancouver is the fashionable Whistler Resort. It is primarily famous for its skiing but also offers all manner of recreational activities that include **fishing, hiking, water sports, heli-hiking**, and simply sightseeing. The pseudo-European Whistler Village nestles between Blackcomb and Whistler Mountains, and caters to every need. For information contact Whistler Resort Association ☎ (604) 932-3928 TOLL-FREE (800) 944-7853, 4010 Whistler Way, Whistler V0N 1B4. All lodgings in Whistler can be book through this agency. You can get there by train from North Vancouver, by hourly bus with Maverick Coach Lines ☎ (604) 662-8051, Suite 210, 1150 Station Street, that operate from downtown Vancouver, or by car along Highway 99, the scenic Sea-to-Sky Highway.

Two more of Vancouver's popular pastimes are **cycling** and **in-line skating**, and there's no problem with rentals. The most convenient rental place is located next to the Westin Bayshore. It's open 9 AM to 6 PM. From the Bayshore you can roll your way along the seafront path which leads into Stanley Park and to the seawall promenade, where there are specially marked areas for skaters, bikers and joggers.

There are countless hiking trails of all kinds and lengths throughout the north shore parks. Close to the city center, Stanley Park has some scenic trails.

There's plenty of action to be had both in and on the water. If you fancy **sailing**, there are schools to teach you how to do it, and plenty of places where you can charter something, particularly around the Coal Harbour area and on Granville Island. **Windsurfing** tuition and equipment rentals are available at Kitsilano, Jericho, and English Bay beaches. Fraser Canyon is a good area for **canoeing** and **whitewater rafting**, while nearer downtown there's canoeing at False Creek. The Vancouver area has some excellent **scuba diving**, particularly in Howe Sound. Diver's World ☎ (604) 732-1344, at 1817 Fourth Avenue West, and The Diving Locker ☎ (604) 736-2681, 2745 Fourth Avenue West, rent out equipment, offer instruction, and organize scuba trips.

With 10 bathing beaches within the city limits **swimmers** are also spoiled for choice. The closest to downtown are the beaches in Stanley Park, all of which are good for swimming. Beaches are open from Victoria Day to Labor Day, guarded daily from 11:30 AM to 8:45 PM. Call the Vancouver Board of Parks and Recreation (swimming information) ☎ (604) 738-8535 for more information. At Sunset Beach there's the Aquatic Centre ☎ (604) 665-3424, 1050 Beach Avenue, which has indoor Olympic pools, a saltwater pool and a diving tank, and there's also the Kitsilano Pool ☎ (604) 731-0011, an outdoor saltwater pool at Kitsilano Beach.

The Vancouver area has exceptionally good freshwater and saltwater **fishing**, with a good choice of lakes, rivers, streams, bays, and a variety of fish, being particularly well known for its salmon. You'll need a license and you should check the regulations carefully. Tackle shops sell licenses and can provide you with a list of current regulations: Bonnie Lee Fishing Charters ☎ (604) 290-7447, 744 West King Edward Avenue; and Granville Island Boat Rentals ☎ (604) 682-6287, 1696 Duranleau Street, on Granville Island, are two reputable outfitters.

NIGHTLIFE AND THE ARTS

True to its pleasure-seeking reputation, Vancouver is geared to entertainment. **Gastown** has a vibrant nightlife that draws visitors and residents alike. **Granville Island** has a concentration of theaters and art centers, as well as trendy microbreweries, while **Yaletown** is fashionable historic district of pool halls, art galleries and cafés. To check the listings you can pick up a free copy of the weekly arts and entertainment paper the *Georgia Straight*, or check the *Vancouver Sun* entertainment section, which appears each Thursday. There's also an **Arts Hotline** ☎ (604) 684-2787 for the latest on performing and visual arts events in the city. Tickets for most cultural events are available, subject to handling charge, through **Ticketmaster** ☎ (604) 280-3311, which has lots of outlets around the city. Bear in mind that reduced-price tickets are often available as the time of performance approaches.

The cultural heart of Vancouver beats downtown at the new Ford Centre for the Performing Arts, together with the Vancouver Playhouse and the Queen Elizabeth Theatre. The **Ford Centre** ☎ (604) 280-2222, 777 Homer Street, presents world-class musicals, while the modern 3,000-seat **"Queen E"** ☎ (604) 280-4444, Hamilton at Georgia, is the place to see ballet, opera, Broadway musicals and celebrity performers. The **Vancouver Playhouse** ☎ (604) 872-6622, 160 First Street, is home to the city's main theatre company of the same name, presenting a mix of new drama and classic theater. Visiting dance companies also perform here.

The Arts Club Theatre ☎ (604) 687-5315, 1585 Johnston Street, Granville Island, stages major theatrical productions, while smaller ones are performed in the adjoining Arts Club Revue. **The Vancouver East Cultural Centre** ☎ (604) 254-9578, 1895 Venables Street, holds musical and theatrical events, and in Gastown the **Firehall Arts**

Centre, 280 East Cordova Street, the Touchstone theater company ☎ (604) 687-8736 offers innovative theatre.

There are Theater-sports twice nightly on Fridays and Saturdays at the **Back Alley Theatre** ☎ (604) 738-7013, 715 Thurlow Street, when two teams of actors compete for laughs by improvising plays on themes suggested by the audience. Front seats run the risk of audience participation.

Second only to Montréal as a major Canadian dance center, Vancouver's dance scene is as diverse as its cultural makeup, and ranges from traditional Japanese and Chinese dance to classical ballet. The **Vancouver East Cultural Centre** ☎ (604) 254-9578 is home to the innovative Kokoro Dance Company, and the **Firehall Arts Centre** ☎ (604) 689-0926 (for dance company information) presents an annual series as well at the Dancing on the Edge Festival each July. The **Ballet British Columbia** ☎ (604) 732-5003 can be seen at the Queen Elizabeth Theatre (see above) where world-class companies can also be seen. In **Robson Square Plaza**, free dance performances are held during the summer months.

Another cultural mainstay, the **Orpheum Theatre** ☎ (604) 684-9100, at 601 Smithe Street, is a splendidly restored 1920s building that is home to the widely acclaimed **Vancouver Symphony Orchestra** ☎ (604) 684-9100 and is the major venue for musical events. The **Vancouver Opera** ☎ (604) 682-2871 presents four productions each season at the Queen Elizabeth Theatre.

Vancouver likes its jazz, and there's quite a mixture of venues. **Hot Jazz** ☎ (604) 873-4131, at 2120 Main Street, features the Big Band sound. Good places for mainstream jazz are the **Alma Street Café** ☎ (604) 222-2244, 2505 Alma Street, and also at the **Glass Slipper** ☎ (604) 877-0066, 185 East 11th Avenue. Blues fans should check out the **Purple Onion** ☎ (604) 602-9442, at 15 Water Street, and the Arts Club Theatre (above) on Granville Island. The Coastal Jazz and Blues Society ☎ (604) 687-0706 has a **hotline** with listings and directions to regular venues.

The spot for serious rhythm and blues is the **Yale Hotel** ☎ (604) 681-YALE, at the north end of the Granville Bridge. **WISE Hall** ☎ (604) 254-5858, 1882 Adanac Street, is the major venue for Celtic and other folk music, and big rock concerts are often held at **GM Place** ☎ (604) 280-4444, Pacific Boulevard North at Abbott Street. The **Commodore Ballroom** ☎ (604) 681-7838, 870 Granville Street, is another major venue for rock and many other kinds of music.

On the dance club circuit, the classy-yet-cool **Richard's on Richards** ☎ (604) 687-6794, 1036 Richards Street, one of the longest-running venues in the city, features live rock music and dancing nightly, while the very hip **Babalu's** ☎ (604) 605-4343, 654 Nelson at Granville, has a versatile house band playing jazz, funk, soul, and rhythm and blues. Formerly called Graceland, **The Palladium Club** ☎ (604) 688-2648, 1250 Richards Street, presents a diverse lineup of live dance music nightly. The dark and shiny **Luvafair**, at 1275 Seymour,

A stunning sculpture greets visitors to the University of British Columbia's Museum of Anthropology.

is one of Vancouver's see-and-be-seen spots, and the **Town Pump**, 66 Water Street, has live rock bands, a good location in one of the city's oldest neighborhoods, and a casual atmosphere.

WHERE TO STAY

Expensive

One of the city's top hotels is the **Four Seasons** ☎ (604) 689-9333 TOLL-FREE (800) 286-6282 FAX (604) 689-3466, at 791 West Georgia Street, Vancouver V6C 2T4. Rising above the 200 fine shops of Pacific Centre Mall, this hotel embodies the excellent service, ultimate comfort and good taste which has become the trademark of this first-rate hotel chain. Rooms and suites are beautifully furnished, and there are indoor and outdoor swimming pools and tennis courts. There are several restaurants, including the first-rate Chartwell, and piano music plays in the delightful lounge.

The **Metropolitan Hotel Vancouver** ☎ (604) 687-1122 TOLL-FREE (800) 667-2300 FAX (604) 689-7044, 645 Howe Street, Vancouver V6C 2Y9, is another leading hotel. The 197 well-furnished rooms and suites are individually designed and have marble bathrooms. The hotel has a business center, one of the city's best restaurants, an indoor swimming pool, a sun deck, racquetball courts, and even a library. Everywhere the needs and comforts of its guests are anticipated, and service is always close at hand.

For old-fashioned grandeur look to the **Canadian Pacific Hotel Vancouver** ☎ (604) 684-3131 TOLL-FREE (800) 441-1414 FAX (604) 662-1929, 900 West Georgia Street, Vancouver V6C 2W6, one of the great railway hotels with over 500 accommodations. With a classical façade crowned with a steep green copper roof, this hotel is a Vancouver landmark, and within it the spacious public areas are furnished in grand style with chandeliers, antiques, an ocean of marble, and comfortable old-fashioned sofas and armchairs. The rooms are also spacious, but decorated in a much more low-key fashion, and business- and executive-class accommodation is offered. There's an indoor swimming pool, shops, cocktail lounges, a couple of good restaurants, and a popular nightspot. The service here is impeccable and the overall picture one of comfort and elegance.

Rising above the Royal Centre mall is the city's largest hotel, the **Hyatt Regency Vancouver** ☎ (604) 683-1234 TOLL-FREE (800) 233-1234 FAX (604) 689-3707, 655 Burrard Street, Vancouver V6C 2R7. There are 644 accommodations and several floors set aside for executive suites. Rooms are smartly decorated, some have balconies, and there are lots of nice touches. It has a good seafood restaurant, Fish & Co., pleasant lounges, a heated outdoor swimming pool, and access to racquetball and squash courts. The staff are knowledgeable and extremely helpful, and there's a bright and lively atmosphere.

Magnificently situated in the remarkable Canada Place waterfront complex is the **Pan Pacific Vancouver Hotel** ☎ (604) 662-8111 TOLL-FREE IN CANADA (800) 663-1515 TOLL-FREE IN THE UNITED STATES (800) 937-1515, 300-999 Canada Place, Vancouver V6C 3B5. This hotel really does have everything. It's a member of the Leading Hotels of the World group, and all rooms and suites are luxurious, although there is an ultra-deluxe class available. With the Trade and Convention Centre also in the complex, it comes as no surprise to find that the excellent restaurants offer Japanese, Italian, and Pacific Rim cuisine along with spectacular harbor views. It has a business center, and a soaring, glass-topped lobby complete with waterfall.

Sutton Place ☎ (604) 682-5511 TOLL-FREE (800) 961-7555 FAX (604) 682-5513, 845 Burrard Street, Vancouver V6Z 2K6, has a distinctly European accent. This is a relatively new hotel, furnished in classical French style with marble, antiques, and great elegance. The rooms, although on the small side, match the public areas for style and grace, and the service is superb and personal. The hotel has 397 units and an adjoining block provides suites for long-stay guests. There's an attractive café, piano bars, an indoor pool, and tennis courts. Also European in style the **Georgian Court Hotel** ☎ (604) 682-5555 TOLL-FREE (800) 663-1155 FAX (604) 682-8830, 773 Beatty Street, Vancouver V6B 2M4, is located opposite the BC Stadium and only a block away from the Queen Elizabeth Theatre. Antiques adorn the elegant lobby, the airy rooms are beautifully furnished, well-equipped, and many offer splendid views. There is an executive floor, and the first-rate William Tell restaurant.

Across from Robson Square the **Wedgewood Hotel** ☎ (604) 689-7777 TOLL-FREE (800) 663-0666 FAX (604) 688-3074 E-MAIL wedgwood@portal.ca, 845 Hornby Street, Vancouver V6Z 1V1, is a smaller, privately owned hotel with 93 accommodations. Rooms and suites are small but elegant with every amenity one could wish for. Some rooms have large balconies with views over Robson Square and fireplaces. Owner and general manager Eleni Skalbania's dedication to excellence is evident everywhere, and her personal touch makes this hotel a favorite of knowledgeable travelers. Executive facilities are available, and there's an excellent restaurant, The Bacchus, with its cozy fire-lit room romantically decorated in cherry wood and velvet. At high tea each afternoon guests choose from a street-side table by the French windows or a cozy fireside spot.

In the city's west end the **Westin Bayshore** ☎ (604) 682-3377 TOLL-FREE (800) 228-3000 FAX (604) 687-3102, 1601 West Georgia Street, Vancouver V6G 2V4, is beautifully positioned near the edge of Stanley Park and set in grounds overlooking Coal Harbour. Rooms have large windows and lovely views, and the hotel offers a wide range of services including a children's activity program, restaurants, and an outdoor pool. The *pièce de résistance* is the private marina which brings float planes, fishing trips and cruises to the doorstep. This is the only hotel in Vancouver that is accessible from land, sea, and air.

Moving a few blocks away from Coal Harbour, the highrise **Shangri-La Pacific Palisades Hotel** ☎ (604) 688-0461 TOLL-FREE (800) 663-1815 FAX (604) 688-4374, 1277 Robson Street, Vancouver V6E 1C4,

OPPOSITE: It's time for breakfast in bed in the penthouse suite at Vancouver's Wedgewood Hotel. ABOVE: The Pan Pacific Vancouver Hotel in the Canada Place waterfront complex.

is the pick of the hotels in the Robson Street area with its generous rooms with balconies overlooking Coal Harbour and Stanley Park. Its suites are particularly well-adapted for business travelers, but leisure travelers also enjoy the amenities, that include an indoor pool and bike rental.

In North Vancouver, the **Lonsdale Quay Hotel** ((604) 986-6111 TOLL-FREE (800) 836-6111 FAX (604) 986-8782, 123 Carrie Cates Court, North Vancouver V6M 3K7, is located next to the SeaBus Terminal on the top floors of the lively Lonsdale Quay Market. Its rooms and suites are attractively decorated, and there are some good views across Burrard Inlet. It has a restaurant, and a pub, and downtown is only 12 minutes away by SeaBus.

throughout in European style. It has a French restaurant and licensed lounge.

Just north of Lions Gate Bridge, you'll find the lovely **Park Royal Hotel** ((604) 926-5511 FAX (604) 926-6082, 540 Clyde Avenue, West Vancouver V7T 2J7, set in attractive grounds on the banks of the Capilano River, well-situated for beaches and mountains, and close to the Park Royal shopping center. The 30 accommodations are all attractive and airy, and there is a restaurant, an outdoor terrace for dining, and an English-style pub.

At the edge of Stanley Park on English Bay stands the much-loved **Sylvia Hotel** ((604) 681-9321, 1154 Gilford Street, Vancouver V6G 2P6. This delightful ivy-covered stone building has 115 rooms

and suites (including housekeeping suites) some of which are located in a modern extension. The decor throughout is attractive, each room is different, and there's a restaurant and bar which both have beautiful views of the bay. Its popularity means that it is necessary to book well in advance.

South of downtown, the **Granville Island Hotel** ((604) 683-7373 TOLL-FREE (800) 663-1840 FAX (604) 683-3061 E-MAIL GIHotel@netminder.com, 1253 Johnston Street, Vancouver V6H 3R9, is a lively waterfront place that tends to attract a sporty crowd who take advantage of the tennis courts and the various charters that operate from the marina. The building has the warehouse-like appearance characteristic of Granville Island, and most rooms have waterfront views. The building incorporates a nightclub, restaurant, and a popular pub.

Mid-range

The **Barclay Hotel** ((604) 688-8850 FAX (604) 688-2534, at 1348 Robson Street, Vancouver V6E 1C5, is within walking distance of Stanley Park and offers some of the best value around. It has 90 accommodations and is attractively decorated

For accommodation in the Gastown area, try the **Dominion Hotel** ((604) 681-6666 FAX (604) 681-5855, 210 Abbott Street, Vancouver V6B 2K8. This charming hotel is a late nineteenth-century brick building with antiques and relics of old Vancouver scattered throughout, and rooms that have been renovated. There is a restaurant, and breakfast is included in the room rate.

Inexpensive

The **Kingston Hotel Bed & Breakfast** ((604) 684-9024 TOLL-FREE (888) 713-3304 FAX (604) 684-9917, 757 Richards Street, Vancouver V6B 3A6, is a

European-style place where continental breakfast is included in the price. The rooms are small but clean; some have private bathrooms while others have hand basins. The hotel has a sauna and laundry facilities. Room rates range from inexpensive to moderate, and it is excellent value for money. East of downtown, the **Budget Inn-Patricia Hotel** ☎ (604) 255-4301 FAX (604) 254-7154, 403 East Hastings Street, Vancouver V6A 1P6, has 24 simply furnished rooms with private bathrooms.

There's a wide range of **bed and breakfast** accommodation in metropolitan Vancouver. Among the agencies are: the Old English Bed and Breakfast Registry ☎ (604) 986-5069 FAX (604) 986-8810, 1226 Silverwood Crescent, North Vancouver V7P 1J3; and Canada-West Accommodation B&B Registry ☎ (604) 929-1424 FAX (604) 929-6692 TOLL-FREE (800) 561-3223, PO Box 86607, North Vancouver V4L 4L2.

Vancouver has two large Hostelling International **hostels**: Vancouver Downtown ☎ (604) 684-4565 FAX (604) 684-4540 E-MAIL vandowntown@hihostels.bc.ca, at 1114 Burnaby Street, Vancouver V6E 1P1, with 240 beds; and Vancouver Jericho Beach ☎ (604) 224-3208 FAX (604) 224-4852 E-MAIL van-jericho@hihostels.bc.ca, 1515 Discovery Street, Vancouver V6R 4K5, where there are over 300 beds and good self-catering facilities.

University accommodation is available from May to August at the Simon Fraser University, 20 km (12 miles) east of downtown. For details contact SFU Accommodations ☎ (604) 291-4503 E-MAIL conference-accommodations@sfu.ca, Simon Fraser University, Room 212 McTaggart-Cowan Mall, Burnaby, Vancouver V5A 1S6. The University of British Columbia at Point Grey 16 km (10 miles) southwest of the center also offers year-round accommodation; information is available from the UBC Conference Centre ☎ (604) 822-1010 FAX (604) 822-1069 E-MAIL reservations@brock.housing.ubc.ca, 5961 Student Union Boulevard, Vancouver V6T 2C9.

WHERE TO EAT

Vancouver's large number of restaurants reflect the city's rich ethnic mix in the wide variety of food they offer. You'll also find Pacific Northwestern cuisine here, the region's own brand based on plentiful supplies of salmon and other seafood, game, herbs, and flowers. *City Food* is a free publication that comes out monthly and can be picked up at restaurants and bookstores. It's a good source of up-to-date information on the Vancouver area dining scene.

Expensive

Named Top Table by *Gourmet* magazine, **Diva at the Met** ☎ (604) 602-7788, Metropolitan Hotel, 645 Howe Street, is known for its open kitchen from whence emanates the restaurant's unique international cuisine. Seasonal ingredients are emphasized and flavors are bold. The terraced room offers atmospheres ranging from lively to

OPPOSITE: Salmon on ice at Granville Market. ABOVE: Produce for sale in Chinatown.

intimate. **Chartwell** ☎ (604) 844-6715, at the Four Seasons Hotel, 791 West Georgia Street, is named after the English country home of Winston Churchill, and the restaurant imitates that ambiance with its warm wooden paneling and a glowing fireplace. Amid these gracious and tasteful surroundings, diners enjoy a wide-ranging progressive menu with strong Pacific Rim influences. Those who count the calories will find the menu especially pleasing.

William Tell ☎ (604) 688-3504, at the Georgian Court Hotel, 765 Beatty Street, is another top Vancouver restaurant where a traditional interior and tables set with the finest china and crystal provide the setting for its haute cuisine. Swiss-French specialties appear alongside the classics, and local produce is mostly used. The wine list here is particularly good and the service superb.

Vancouver has some excellent French restaurants, and **Lumière** ☎ (604) 739-8185, 2551 West Broadway, is among the best. French cuisine with influences from the East and West are served amidst furnishings of polished chrome and wood. The wine list is global. **Étoile** ☎ (604) 681-4444, 1355 Hornby Street, also serves classical French cuisine adding its own contemporary spin. The *prix-fixe* menu changes every two weeks. A long-running favorite, **Le Gavroche** ☎ (604) 685-3924, at 1616 Alberni Street, is set in a lovely old house in the city's west end. This restaurant has a mouth-watering menu, a democratic wine list, and excellent service. It is an ideal choice for a special occasion.

For a Chinese experience, try **Floata** ☎ (604) 602-0368, 400-180 Keefer Street, located near the Dr. Sun Yat-Sen Park, in the third floor of a bright-red shopping plaza. It is the western flagship of a renowned Hong Kong restaurant, and despite its cavernous size, it's usually packed with diners enjoying dim sum served from steaming carts and lavish dinners of delicacies cooked up by its award-winning chef.

Moderate

South of the downtown peninsula, **Tojo's** ☎ (604) 872-8050, at 202-777 West Broadway, offers Japanese food in sleek, sophisticated surroundings with an outdoor terrace and mountain views. You can choose to dine in a traditional tatami room, at a conventional dining table, or at the small sushi bar. The menu features all kinds of Japanese specialties as well as the chef's own innovative dishes, and freshness is the hallmark. Prices here range from expensive to moderate.

The best place in Vancouver specializing in Pacific Northwest cuisine is the highly acclaimed **Raintree at the Landing** ☎ (604) 688-5570, 375 Water Street. The imaginative use of local seafood and organically grown produce results in some wonderful dishes, and an exceptionally good wine list together with stunning views over the water of Grouse Mountain make a memorable meal. Over in West Vancouver, **Salmon House on the Hill** ☎ (604) 926-3212, 2229 Folkstone Way, is another good place to sample Pacific Northwestern cuisine. Perched high above Vancouver, the restaurant commands wonderful views of Stanley Park and the city across the inlet. Seafood dominates the menu here, and it really is delicious.

At a beautiful location on Granville Island's waterfront, **Bridges** ☎ (604) 687-4400, 1696 Duranleau Street, has a good seafood restaurant, a bistro, and a large terrace where you can enjoy beautiful mountain views. Across the creek, **A Kettle of Fish** ☎ (604) 682-6661, 900 Pacific Street, serves deliciously fresh fish in a conservatory-style setting, and east of downtown, **The Cannery** ☎ (604) 254-9606, 2205 Commissioner Street, has an extensive seafood menu and great harbor views.

For excellent and moderately priced French food, few places better the bistroesque **Le Crocodile** ☎ (604) 669-4298, 100-909 Burrard Street, and in Stanley Park at Ferguson Point, the **Teahouse Restaurant** ☎ (604) 669-3281, serves fine continental fare in a delightful Victorian house overlooking the bay.

Over in Kitsilano, at **Bishop's** ☎ (604) 738-2025, 2183 West Fourth Avenue, exciting continental cuisine is presented with great style and served with enthusiasm. The restaurant is small and chic, and the atmosphere relaxed. Celebrated Italian chef Umberto Menghi has several restaurants in Vancouver, the most popular being **Il Giardino** ☎ (604) 669-2422, 1382 Hornby Street. Here Italian classics reign, with game featuring prominently on the menu. It's extremely popular and reservations are required for both lunch and dinner. For imaginative Italian country cooking, go to **Piccolo Mondo** ☎ (604) 688-1633, 850 Thurlow Street, where you'll find a seemingly endless menu and some very interesting dishes.

Some of the best Cantonese food can be found at the **Pink Pearl** ☎ (604) 253-4316, 1132 East Hastings Street, a large restaurant where the emphasis is on seafood. A favorite for Northern Chinese cuisine is **Kirin Mandarin Restaurant** ☎ (604) 682-8833, 102-1166 Alberni Street, where the menu is diverse, the surroundings sophisticated, and lobster and crab come fresh from the tanks. For a taste of Japan, try the **Kamei Sushi** ☎ (604) 732-0112, 1414 West Broadway.

Inexpensive

We never miss a chance to drop by **La Bodega Tapas Bar** ☎ (604) 684-8815, 1277 Howe Street, with its Spanish decor and intriguing specials

Coal Harbour divides Stanley Park from downtown's forest of highrise apartment buildings.

emphasizing creatively prepared meat dishes. If it's seafood you want, drop in on the **Only Other Fish and Oyster Café** ☎ (604) 682-3474, 1517 Anderson Street, or rather, join the queue, because although this well-known and well-loved café has absolutely no finesse and no alcohol, it does have the freshest seafood you'll find anywhere.

Chinatown has a wealth of restaurants. The cheerful and unpretentious **Gain Wah** ☎ (604) 684-1740, 218 Keefer Street, has authentic Cantonese fare including good *congee*, and you can enjoy Korean barbecue and sizzling hot pots in a casual atmosphere at **Arirang House** ☎ (604) 879-0990, 221 Cambie Street. Our favorite lunch spot is **Ezugiku Noodle Café** ☎ (604) 685-8606, 1329 Robson Street, where steaming noodles are served at the stainless steel counter. In addition to Japanese fare, Robson Street is noted for its European restaurants, and one of its old favorites is **Heidelberg House** ☎ (604) 682-1661, at 1256 Robson Street, a pleasant place in which to sample German specialties.

Pezzo ☎ (604) 669-9300, at the corner of Robson and Thurlow, has cheap and good pizza and pastas, local beer and a stereo featuring the mellow voice of Mario Lanza. If Californian-Mexican food appeals, go to **Topanaga** ☎ (604) 733-3713, 2904 West Fourth Avenue, a small café that serves hearty portions. For East Indian food, try the **Heaven and Earth India Curry House** ☎ (604) 732-5313, 1754 West Fourth Avenue, in the Kitsilano area.

How to Get There

Vancouver International Airport — Canada's second largest — is 15 km (nine miles) from downtown and about a 25- to 40-minute drive from town. The **Vancouver Airporter Service** ☎ (604) 946-8866 TOLL-FREE (800) 668-3141, runs shuttles from the airport at 15-minute intervals, which stop at major downtown hotels and the Greyhound Bus Terminal, and operate from 6 AM to midnight. Ask the ticket agent to advise you of the hotel stop closest to your destination. Taxi stands can be found in front of the terminals.

When leaving Vancouver by air there is a $10 to $20 "Airport Improvement Fee."

VIA Rail ☎ (604) 669-3050 TOLL-FREE IN CANADA (888) 842-7733 TOLL-FREE IN THE UNITED STATES (800) 561-3949 FAX (604) 640-3757 operates the *Canadian* three times a week from Toronto to Vancouver. Other points in the province connected to Vancouver by VIA Rail service include Kamloops, Prince Rupert, and Prince George. (Vancouver Island is accessed via bus ferry to Victoria or Nanaimo where there is train service up to Courtenay.) Trains depart from Pacific Central Station ☎ (604) 669-3050 TOLL-FREE (800) 665-8630, at 1150 Station Street. **Amtrak** TOLL-FREE (800) 872-7245 TOLL-FREE IN THE UNITED STATES (800) 835-8725 operates one train daily from Seattle to Vancouver's Pacific Central Station. **BC Rail** ☎ (604) 631-3500 TOLL-FREE (800) 663-8238 has daily service into North Vancouver from Squamish,

The First Narrows leads out from Vancouver into the Strait of Georgia.

Whistler, Lillooet, and points in between, as well as regular service to 100 Mile House, Williams Lake, Quesnel, and Prince George. Its station is at 1311 West First Street, North Vancouver. **Rocky Mountain Railtours** ☎ (604) 606-7200 TOLL-FREE (800) 665-7245 FAX (604) 606-7201, 1150 Station Street, Vancouver V6A 2X7 operates between Calgary, Banff and Jasper to Vancouver between May and October (see RIDE THE LEGENDARY RAILS, page 11, in TOP SPOTS).

BC Ferries ☎ (604) 669-1211 TOLL-FREE IN BRITISH COLUMBIA (800) 223-3779 FAX (250) 381-2583 run from the Tsawwassen Ferry Terminal, 30 km (19 miles) south of downtown Vancouver, to Victoria (Swartz Bay), Nanaimo on Vancouver Island, and to the Southern Gulf Islands. They also operate a ferry from Horseshoe Bay, west of Vancouver, to Nanaimo, Bowen Island, and the mainland's Sunshine Coast. Twenty-four-hour recorded schedule information ☎ (250) 386-3431 is also available.

Long-distance buses arrive at Pacific Central Station, Main Street at Terminal Avenue, including **Pacific Coach Lines** ☎ (604) 662-8074 (from Victoria), **Maverick Lines** ☎ (604) 662-8051 (from Squamish, Whistler, Pemberton, and Nanaimo), and **Greyhound** ☎ (604) 482-8747 (from most mainland cities).

Motorists coming from the east will want to take the Trans-Canada Highway, while those coming from Seattle, Washington will take Highway 5, which becomes Highway 99 at the British Columbia border. The drive from Seattle to Vancouver takes about three hours.

VANCOUVER ISLAND

Moored alongside the west coast of the British Columbia mainland and separated from it by the Georgia Strait, Vancouver Island stretches 450 km (280 miles) and covers an area of 32,000 sq km (12,000 sq miles). It is thus the largest island off North America's Pacific coast, and violates the 49th parallel, much to the annoyance of some. A chain of snow-tipped mountains runs north-south through the center of the island, splitting its personality between a rugged and sparsely populated west, with an exposed Pacific coastline cut by deep inlets, and a sheltered eastern shore of a much more tame character with white sandy beaches, gentle slopes, farmlands, and seaside towns.

The island is blessed with a gentle climate throughout the year, although the rainfall varies dramatically from place to place. The lowest rainfall and mildest temperatures are found at the southern end of the island, which is sheltered by the Olympic Mountains across the Juan de Fuca Strait. It is not surprising therefore that most of the island's population of 500,000 live in Victoria and the cozy seaside towns of the southeast, leaving the west side uninhabited for the most part, with a few small fishing communities dotted around.

The rain forests with their soaring red cedars and the lonely west coast shores seem a far cry from the neat lawns of Victoria and the snug towns of the southeast. It is this combination of ruggedly beautiful scenery, the sedate charm of Victoria, and people as gentle as the climate itself that makes

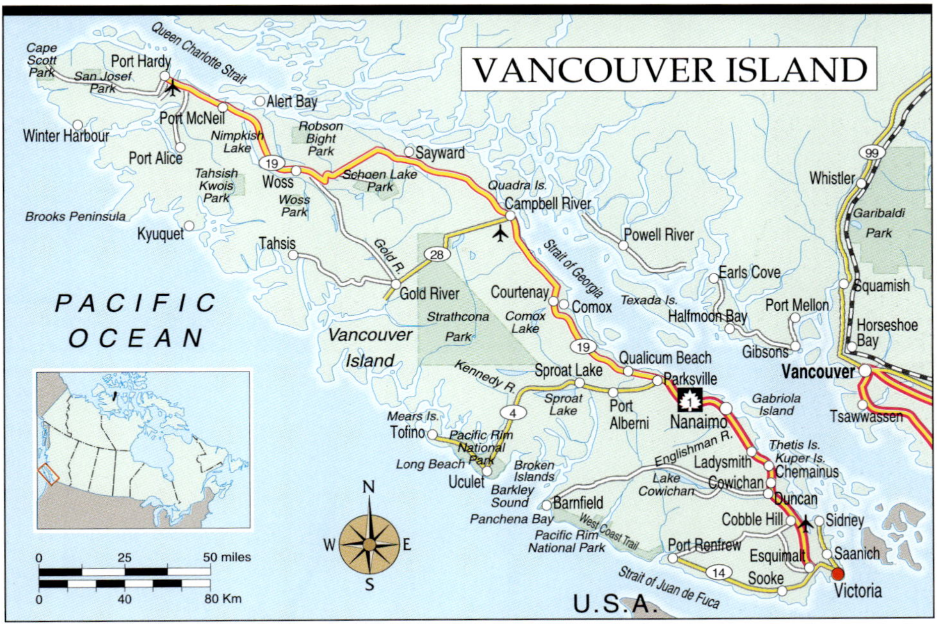

THE EMPRESS
Sightseeing Tours

Vancouver Island so appealing to vacationers. The culture is equally diverse, for the British Empire was not the only society to leave its mark. The Haida, Kwagiutl, Cowichan, and Sooke natives who lived in fishing villages here long before the arrival of the white man have scattered the island with their totem poles, their crafts and legends, while their fishing skills seem to have found their way into the blood of the inhabitants.

Together with fishing, mining and logging are the island's main industries, and they are mostly found to the east of the mountain range. Stubbled mountainsides stand testimony to the latter and an impassioned battle rages over the island's particularly active logging program.

BACKGROUND

In 1774 Juan Perez of Spain visited Vancouver Island, and when Captain Cook landed at Nootka Island on the west coast in 1778 he did a little trade with the natives. In 1792 Captain George Vancouver put the island on the map when he charted the waters of Johnstone Strait. These visits had little effect on the lives of the island's native tribes and it wasn't until 1843, when the Hudson's Bay Company took control and founded a trading post on the island's southeastern tip, that things started slowly to change.

In 1849 Vancouver Island was declared a crown colony, with the Hudson's Bay Company administering it from Fort Victoria. Apart from some company farms established by the subsidiary Puget Sound Agricultural Company, little happened by way of colonization and the main concern remained fur trading.

The discovery of gold in the Fraser River during the 1850s and 1860s brought prospectors to Victoria, British Columbia's only port and source of provisions. As a result, the area developed into a typical boomtown, but when the gold fields were exhausted Victoria continued as an administrative center. The island united with British Columbia in 1866, and in 1871 Victoria was declared the provincial capital. It was intended to be the western terminus of the Canadian Pacific Railway, but this did not come to pass and the railroad stopped at Vancouver. This meant that industrialization also stopped at Vancouver and Victoria was left free to build itself a reputation as a center of genteel society. The other gift that the Canadian Pacific Railway gave Victoria was the building of the beautiful Empress Hotel in 1908, boosting a tourist industry that has flourished ever since.

GENERAL INFORMATION

Victoria's **Visitor Information Centre** ☎ (250) 953-2033 FAX (250) 382-6539, 812 Wharf Street, Victoria V8W 1T3, is located on the waterfront across from the Empress Hotel. The office is open daily. For **hotel reservations** in Victoria call TOLL-FREE (800) 663-3883. For information on the rest of Vancouver Island, contact the **Tourism Association of Vancouver Island** ☎ (250) 382-3551 FAX (250) 382-3523, 302-45 Bastion Square, Victoria V8W 1J1. There are also information centers in towns throughout the island, including a major branch, the **Nanaimo Travel Infocentre** ☎ (250) 756-0106, at 2290 Bowen Road, Nanaimo.

VICTORIA

Victoria has overcome its rough and ready beginnings, and has developed into a graceful city

that is both conservative and relaxed. Baskets of flowers adorn the lampposts, nineteenth-century buildings have been carefully renovated, tidy lawns and flowerbeds are all around. Victoria has been transformed from a raucous gold rush town into a colonial fantasy of a British seaside resort.

Victoria is British Columbia's capital, and with a population of 313,000 it is the province's second largest city. It is situated around a beautiful natural harbor at the southeastern tip of the island, sheltered by the mountains of Washington State, which lies only 32 km (20 miles) away across the Juan de Fuca Strait to the south. It boasts Canada's mildest climate with only 68 cm (27 inches) of

OPPOSITE TOP: Dignified survivors from the last century: a horse and carriage and the Parliament Buildings in Victoria. BOTTOM: The Empress Hotel. ABOVE: A Morris dancer.

rainfall a year and plenty of sunshine. While the rest of Canada is struggling through snow, Victoria is busy taking its official bloom count.

The love of beautiful gardens is not the only feature that Victoria has inherited from its British connections. It is a place that revels in and capitalizes upon its image as a last bastion of the British Empire. Old British traditions are fiercely preserved. Wander through one of the city's parks and the chances are that you'll see some croquet, cricket, or English bowls being played. You can ride around the city on a double-decker bus, stock up on Wedgwood china, Waterford crystal and tweeds in the shops, or take refreshment in one of the many pubs or tearooms. Just to make sure you get the picture, somewhere around the Parliament Buildings you'll hear the whine of bagpipes.

Part of the reason for this "forever England" image is that the population is largely of British extraction, and the mild weather and low rainfall continues to make Victoria an attractive retirement home for the British. The main employers here are the government and tourism, and to keep the latter industry thriving the Britishness is carefully preserved and reinforced wherever possible, sometimes in ways that are rather garish, but it still keeps the visitors coming.

WHAT TO SEE AND DO

Downtown

Downtown Victoria is compactly laid-out within a small area, so walking is the easiest and most pleasant way of exploring it. The hub of the city is the **Inner Harbour** area, where Victoria's most majestic buildings overlook the lively little harbor which is constantly busy with the comings and goings of ferries, fishing boats, and yachts.

A large portion of the Inner Harbour is filled with the ivied grandeur of the **Empress Hotel** ☎ (250) 384-8111, a resplendent castle-like building that is the heart and very much the soul of Victoria. Designed by Francis Rattenbury and built by the Canadian Pacific Railway in 1908, the Empress became the place where Victorian polite society came to take tea. Today visitors flock here to experience an afternoon tea of cucumber sandwiches and scones with jam and clotted cream, served among silver teapots and cake stands in the desperately British ambiance of the Empress lobby. Tea at the Empress is very popular and should you wish to partake you should telephone to make a reservation. Behind the hotel stands the **Crystal Garden** ☎ (250) 381-1213, 731 Douglas Street, a large glass structure that was designed by Rattenbury and built in 1925. It once held an enormous saltwater pool, and its elegant ballroom was the scene of many social events. It is now an exotic conservatory with colorful tropical birds and monkeys among the greenery, overlooked by the ever-popular tearooms. It's open daily, year-round, and an admission fee is charged. You'll also find some of the best outlets for **native arts and crafts** along Douglas Street.

Across from the Empress, neatly clipped lawns and carefully arranged flowerbeds surround the stately **Parliament Buildings** ☎ (250) 387-3046, a

Gothic extravaganza of towers and domes that also overlooks the lovely harbor. Completed in 1897 and designed by the irrepressible Francis Rattenbury, these buildings remain the home of the provincial legislature. A statue of Queen Victoria dignifies the lawn to the front, statues of eminent Victorians stand on either side of the elaborate arched entrance, and the central copper-covered dome is crowned with a gilt statue of Captain George Vancouver. Free guided tours of the interior in a choice of languages operate daily during the summer months and on weekdays only during the winter. The buildings are also a remarkable sight at night, when they are outlined by thousands of little lights.

On the corner between the Empress and the Parliament Buildings stands the excellent **Royal British Columbia Museum** ☎ (250) 387-3014. This is one of Canada's very best museums and the skill and imagination of its displays have made it one of Victoria's top attractions. It is devoted to all aspects of British Columbia's natural and cultural history from prehistoric times through to the present day. The second floor covers the province's natural history, while beautifully constructed dioramas depict aspects of the region's natural environment such as the rain forest, seashore, mountains, and ocean. The section dealing with the province's cultural history has some of the most popular and fascinating displays where sight, sound, and smell combine to give vivid and memorable impressions of life in the past. There is, for example, a detailed recreation of an early twentieth-century street, complete with a cinema that runs old movies, a pioneer village, a sawmill, and a reconstructed section of Captain George Vancouver's ship, *The Discovery*. In the section that deals with First Nations history, realistic displays allow the visitor to glimpse life in a Pacific Coast native village, and the museum's extensive collection of First Nations art and artifacts includes a collection of totem poles. The museum is open daily September to June from 10 AM to 5:30 PM, July and August from 9:30 AM to 7 PM; an admission fee is charged.

To the rear of the museum is a small grassy plot known as **Thunderbird Park** which is forested with modern totem poles carved with the image of the legendary thunderbird. At the southern edge of this park stands **Helmcken House** ☎ (250) 361-0021, a heritage building dating from the 1850s that was originally the home of Fort Victoria's surgeon. Inside you can see period furnishings and a display of the doctor's medical equipment. It's open daily May to September with reduced winter hours; an admission fee is charged.

Victoria has its share of commercialized attractions, especially in the area around the Parliament Buildings. One of the better ones is the **Pacific Undersea Gardens** ☎ (250) 382-5717, 490 Belleville Street, where you descend to the bottom of the harbor to look, through glass, at the marine life and some frolicsome scuba divers. Next to it the **Royal London Wax Museum** ☎ (250) 388-4461 is

Victoria — OPPOSITE: Highland dancers step out. ABOVE: Rugby is another Old World activity that thrives here.

worth a look. The building was designed by Rattenbury and originally built in 1924 as the CPR Steamship Terminal. Inside you'll find 300 wax figures, including, of course, Queen Victoria. Both attractions are open daily, year-round; both charge an admission fee.

For a pleasant waterfront stroll continue westwards along Belleville Street past the ferry terminals and follow the coast to **Fisherman's Wharf**, a lively spot where fishing boats come and go and houseboats are moored. If you'd like to see Victoria from the water, boat trips leave from the Inner Harbour, in front of the Empress. Also along the waterfront, the brightly painted houses of **Waddington Alley** contain some interesting boutiques and art galleries.

The **Old Town** section of Victoria lies to the north of the Empress, along Wharf Street and the nearby streets and alleys. This is an area of narrow streets, squares, gaslights, cobbles, and buildings that date from the 1860s. The area has undergone extensive renovation and, as is so often the case, many of the old buildings now house chic cafés, restaurants, and shops. At **Centennial Square** you can see Victoria's original City Hall, and at nearby **Bastion Square**, site of the original Fort Victoria in 1843, the old criminal courthouse now houses the **Maritime Museum of British Columbia** ☎ (250) 385-4222. On display here are model ships, nautical paraphernalia, and a Native American dugout canoe that voyaged from Victoria to England a hundred years ago.

Government Street, particularly where it runs through the Old Town, has some of the city's most interesting stores. Here are shops that have remained unchanged for the last 70 or so years and they wouldn't seem out of place in London's Jermyn Street. You can buy plaids, tartans, Waterford crystal, Wedgwood china, have yourself measured for a suit that will be made for you in England, buy your cigars at an old-fashioned tobacconist, or treat someone to delicious handmade chocolates. Also along the street are outlets for Canadian arts and crafts, and you'll see hardwearing Cowichan sweaters on sale that are made of naturally waterproof undyed wool and decorated with traditional First Nations designs.

Just north of Centennial Square, on the corner of Fisgard Street and Government Street, an ornate red gateway known as the **Gate of Harmonious Interest** marks the entrance to Victoria's old and colorful **Chinatown**. Once a flourishing community, it came into being in the 1850s when many Chinese arrived to work on constructing the Canadian Pacific Railway. Over the years Chinatown has dwindled in size and now scarcely covers two blocks, but it is still the site of the narrowest street in Canada and has a few interesting buildings, along with shops selling souvenirs, crafts, and exotic groceries.

At the southeastern edge of downtown, behind the British Columbia Provincial Museum, **Beacon Hill Park** offers a delightful retreat and a lovely spot to picnic. This hilly parkland of gardens, trees, ponds, and views stretches southwards to the Juan de Fuca Strait. At its southwestern corner a plaque marks the terminus of the Trans-Canada Highway.

Outside Downtown

About one and a half kilometers (a third of a mile) east of downtown in the Rockland area, a nineteenth-century mansion houses the **Art Gallery of Greater Victoria** ☎ (250) 384-4101, 1040 Moss Street. It exhibits art from a variety of countries and periods, and has a particularly fine collection of Asian art that includes a Shinto shrine. The gallery is open daily; an admission fee is charged, free on Monday. Nearby stands the imposing **Craigdarroch Castle** ☎ (250) 592-5323, 1050 Joan Crescent, a turreted baronial-style mansion of palatial proportions. It was built in 1890 by Robert Dunsmuir, a wealthy Scottish coal tycoon, in order to persuade his wife to leave her home in Scotland. The interior is richly decorated with wood paneling, stained glass, and period furniture. It is open daily, and an admission fee is charged.

Moving west of downtown, **Craigflower Manor** ☎ (250) 387-4697, at Admirals and Craigflower roads, is one of Victoria's earliest buildings, dating from 1856. It was built on a farm for the Hudson's Bay Company subsidiary, Puget Sound Agricultural Company, in an early attempt to develop a settlement around the trading post. With original furnishings and household appliances, it makes for an interesting visit. Nearby stands the **Craigflower Schoolhouse**, which was built in 1855 and ended its days as a schoolhouse in 1911 to serve as a museum. It's open daily.

To the west of Victoria Harbour, the **English Village** ☎ (250) 388-4353, at 429 Lampson Street, is a collection of replicated old English buildings. The highlight is the accurately reconstructed **Anne Hathaway's Cottage** furnished with sixteenth- and seventeenth-century antiques. The **Olde England Inn** offers accommodation and a restaurant serving English-style meals. The village is open daily, and an admission fee is charged.

Excursions from Victoria

The outstanding **Butchart Gardens** ☎ (250) 652-5256, are located 21 km (13 miles) north of downtown Victoria on Brentwood Bay at 800 Bennevuto Avenue. Their history makes a classic ugly-duckling-to-swan story. Jenny Butchart was the wife of a wealthy cement manufacturer who, in the process of beautifying their large estate, decided to do something about the unsightly hole left by her husband's abandoned limestone quarry.

In 1904 she began the task of landscaping this eyesore by setting lawns, planting trees, creating beautiful arrangements of flowers, and by covering the sides of the pit with ivy. The success of this sunken garden inspired the Butcharts to continue their horticultural activities, and now their gardens cover an area of some 20 hectares (50 acres). There's a magnificent rose garden, which is best seen in July; a Japanese garden with lacquered bridges, summerhouses, and a waterfall; and a formal Italian garden with topiary hedges, a lily pond, and statuary. In the summer you can enjoy music in these delightful surroundings on the Concert Lawn and take a nighttime tour of the illuminated gardens.

These are pleasure gardens so you won't find botanical labels among the flowerbeds, but the Horticultural Centre can answer any questions you may have.

Even in their winter greenery the gardens are worth the trip, and flowers will still be blooming in the greenhouses. You can have lunch or dinner in the Blue Poppy or the Dining Room restaurants making the leisurely visit that the gardens deserve. To get there from downtown Victoria, either take Highway 17 to the Keating Cross Road turnoff, from where you continue your journey in a westerly direction, or take the 17A direct. It's open daily at 9 AM; an admission fee is charged with discounts in the winter months.

To take a look at the coastal scenery northwest of Victoria, travel north out of the city on the Trans-Canada Highway, and after 16 km (10 miles) you'll hit **Malahat Drive**. The road skirts along Finlayson Arm and then climbs Malahat Ridge where you have views across Saanich Inlet of the Gulf Islands, the mainland, and the distant peak of Mount Baker in Washington State.

If you'd like to explore some of the beaches and forests of the southwest corner of Vancouver Island, then pack your picnic hamper, maybe your tent as well, and head out of Victoria picking up Highway 14 bound for **Sooke**, some 42 km (26 miles) west of Victoria. In this logging town you'll find the Sooke Regional Museum and Travel Infocentre ☎ (250) 642-6351, at 2070 Phillips Road, with its displays of local native craft (open daily in summer, closed Mondays in winter; admission is free). You can also pick up supplies for the rest of your journey in town. North of Sooke along Highway 14 you'll probably stop and follow a forest trail to one of the lovely beaches that line the coast here. The highway ends at the one-horse settlement of Port Renfrew, where you can observe some marine life in the tidal pools at **Botanical Beach** when the tide is low. The rugged West Coast Trail — a serious hiking undertaking — runs from here to Bamfield and forms a section of the famous Pacific Rim National Park. From here you can either retrace your steps along Highway 14 back to Victoria or you can take the logging road to Lake Cowichan where you have a choice of two roads, both of which connect with the Trans-Canada Highway at Duncan.

The beautiful Butchart Gardens on Tod Inlet outside Victoria.

Northeast of Victoria in the Strait of Georgia lie the lovely and temperate **Southern Gulf Islands**. Artists, retirees, and others drawn by the peace or the prospect of an alternative lifestyle inhabit some of the islands, which offer the visitor quiet beaches, beautiful vistas, accommodation, fishing, diving, and a host of other outdoor opportunities. From Swartz Bay, BC Ferries ☎ (250) 386-3431 or (604) 669-1211, runs at regular intervals to Salt Spring Island, and operates another service to Pender, Mayne, Galiano, and Saturna Islands. Reserve ahead, and in the summer arrive well in advance of the departure time. For **bed and breakfast** accommodation, contact the Accommodations Group

of Salt Spring Island ☎ (250) 537-5252 FAX (250) 537-4276 E-MAIL chamber@saltspring.com, Chamber of Commerce, Tourist Information Centre, 121 Lower Ganges Road, Salt Spring Island V8K 2T1.

SPORTS AND OUTDOOR ACTIVITIES

There are plenty of places offering **boating** or **sailing** charters, with or without crew. If you'd like to learn how to do it, there are a few schools around the Oak Bay Marina ☎ (250) 598-3369. There are plenty of opportunities for **canoeing** in the area and sports outfitters can often supply information on package trips. There's **freshwater fishing** at Elk and Beaver lakes, which are only about a 15-minute drive north of Victoria, and there are several other lakes and streams a little further out. The waters that surround Victoria are renowned for salmon and offer some excellent **deep-sea fishing**, and many companies in town offer charter trips. Fishing licenses are required, and regulations are complicated and constantly in flux; call ☎ (604) 666-5835 for fish licensing information. Licenses are available province-wide from marinas, sporting goods stores, charter boat operators, and department stores.

The waters, particularly in the Georgia Strait, are excellent for **diving**, and are inhabited by a wide variety of marine life. Thetis Lake Park is a very pleasant spot for **swimming**. It is only a short drive northwest of downtown, and has a popular beach as well as more secluded spots. You'll also find some beautiful beaches on the southwest coast along the stretch of Highway 14 between Sooke and Port Renfrew. There are several recreation centers in the Victoria area with pools. One of the best is the Crystal Pool Recreation Centre ☎ (250) 380-7946, at 2275 Quadra Street.

Windsurfing is quite a popular pursuit in these parts, and there are plenty of places that give lessons. Some popular spots are Cadboro Bay, east of downtown near the university, and Elk Lake, which is about a 15-minute drive north of Victoria.

There are good **hiking** trails around some of the parklands northwest of Victoria, and lots more along the southwest coast between Sooke and Port Renfrew. At Port Renfrew, about 107 km (66 miles) from Victoria, there's the very challenging West Coast Trail to Bamfield (see PACIFIC RIM NATIONAL PARK, page 100).

NIGHTLIFE AND THE ARTS

Several free magazines are available that carry entertainment listings for the area. The Arts Council of Greater Victoria publishes *Arts Victoria*, and there's the *Monday Magazine* that, despite its title, comes out on Thursday.

The **Royal Theatre**, 805 Broughton Street, and the **McPherson Playhouse**, 3 Centennial Square, are both renovated older theaters that stage plays and concerts. Information on both can be obtained at ☎ (250) 386-6121. The **University Centre Auditorium** ☎ (250) 721-8480 at Finnerty Road also stages plays and dance events, and the intimate **Belfry Theatre** ☎ (250) 385-6815, 1291 Gladstone Street, tends towards contemporary drama.

The **Pacific Victoria Opera** stages three productions a year at the McPherson Playhouse, while the **Victoria Symphony** performs year-round, mainly at the Royal Theatre but can also can be heard at the University Centre Auditorium.

Victoria holds its own annual **Jazz Festival International** in late June. You can obtain information from the **Victorian Jazz Society** ☎ (250) 388-4423. There's also the **Jazz Hotline** ☎ (250) 658-5255 to contact for club and restaurant shows throughout the year. Downtown, **Hermann's Dixieland Inn** ☎ (250) 388-9166, 753 View Street, has lots of atmosphere, hearty food, and the kind of jazz you'd expect from its name.

For jazz as well as live rock and blues, there's **Harpo's** ☎ (250) 385-5333, at 15 Bastion Square, where top names often play.

Priding itself on its Englishness, Victoria has several pubs that serve British-style beer. **Spinnaker's Brew Pub** ☎ (250) 386-2739, at 308 Catherine Street overlooks the harbor to the west of downtown, and is a pleasant place where you can sample some good ale brewed on the premises, take a brewery tour or just relax with a dart game. There is live music some nights.

WHERE TO STAY

Expensive

The château-like **Empress Hotel** ☎ (250) 384-8111 FAX (250) 381-4334 TOLL-FREE (800) 441-1414, 721 Government Street, Victoria V8W 1W5, underwent major renovation in 1989 and has emerged triumphantly with upgraded facilities and sympathetic redecoration. It is the island's largest hotel with 475 rooms and suites, all beautifully decorated with traditional prints and fresh flowers. Formal dining is in the lovely Empress Room. There is a modern bistro, and the famous afternoon tea is served in the 1920s elegance of the Palm Court or the Tea Lobby. There is an indoor pool, and shops complete the amenities.

Close to Beacon Hill Park, the **Beaconsfield Inn** ☎ (250) 384-4044, 998 Humboldt Street, Victoria V8V 2Z8, is a restored early twentieth-century mansion beautifully decorated with wood paneling, stained glass, and furnished with antiques. This Old World elegance extends to the

OPPOSITE: The Victoria Eaton Centre. ABOVE: Afternoon tea in the Empress Hotel.

10 unique and lovely rooms, some of which have special features such as canopied beds or wood-burning fireplaces, and there are also a few "celebration suites" for honeymooners and lovers of luxury. The old-fashioned atmosphere is preserved by the absence of telephones or televisions in the rooms. The hotel has a lovely library where guests can attend a hospitality hour each afternoon, and breakfast — included in the room rate — is served in the attractive conservatory. Its sister hotel is the nearby **Abigail's Hotel** ((250) 388-5363, 906 McClure Street, Victoria V8V 3E7, which is a heritage Tudor-style mansion in much the same mold. It has 16 accommodations with similar features to the Beaconsfield, and again the library serves as a delightful social center. A gourmet breakfast is included in the room rates, which vary between expensive and mid-range.

In complete contrast is the modern highrise **Executive House Hotel** ((250) 388-5111 TOLL-FREE (800) 663-7001 FAX (250) 385-1323, 777 Douglas Street, Victoria V8W 2B5. It is one block away from the Inner Harbour and has 179 large accommodations, including suites with self-catering facilities. There's a restaurant, a popular pub, and an oyster bar. Rates range from expensive to mid-range. The **Clarion Hotel Grand Pacific** ((250) 386-0450 TOLL-FREE (800) 458-6262 FAX (250) 386-8779, at 450 Québec Street, Victoria V8V 1W5, is another modern hotel that overlooks the Inner Harbour. Rooms and suites are attractive, well-equipped, and each has a balcony and bathroom. The hotel has a pleasant dining room.

The **Laurel Point Inn** ((250) 386-8721 TOLL-FREE (800) 663-7667 FAX (250) 386-9547, at 680 Montréal Street, Victoria V8V 1Z8, stands on a headland overlooking the Inner Harbour and is surrounded by gardens. The coolly elegant rooms all have balconies with harbor views, and there is an indoor swimming pool, a tennis court, and a bistro.

The **Victoria Regent Hotel** ((250) 386-2211 TOLL-FREE (800) 663-7472 FAX (250) 386-2622, 1234 Wharf Street, Victoria V8W 3H9, stands at the water's edge and has excellent harbor views. There are 40 well-appointed accommodations, mostly one- and two-bedroom suites, some with fireplaces and all with kitchens. There's a waterside restaurant and marina facilities.

Close to the Parliament Buildings, the **Château Victoria Hotel** ((250) 382-4221 TOLL-FREE (800) 663-5891 FAX (250) 380-1950, 740 Burdett Avenue, Victoria V8W 1B2, is a highrise building with 178 accommodations each with a balcony. The hotel offers a good range of services; rooms and suites are available, some with a kitchen.

If you're considering a trip to the South Gulf island of Saltspring, you should make sure to stay at **Hastings House** ((250) 537-2362 E-MAIL hasthouse @saltspring.com, PO Box 1110, Ganges V0S 1E0. If you weren't considering it, it's worth the trip just for the delight of staying at this inn. It belongs to the prestigious Relais & Châteaux chain and has 12 lovely rooms and suites well stocked with life's little luxuries. The half-timbered house resembles an old English country manor set in lovely grounds with views of Ganges Harbour, and first-class gourmet food is served in the graceful dining room. Guests can enjoy fishing, sailing and hiking nearby. The price includes full English breakfast. Book well in advance.

Some five kilometers (three miles) east of downtown there's the delightful Tudor-style **Oak Bay Beach Hotel** ((250) 598-4556, at 1175 Beach Drive, Victoria V8S 2N2. This seaside hotel has antiques in the lovely lobby and rooms which all differ in size and design. The hotel operates dinner cruises, whale watching tours, and fishing charters from the nearby marina, and it has an English-style pub and a seaside dining room.

Just outside Victoria (about 40 km or 24 miles from Victoria International Airport), **The Aerie** ((250) 743-7115 FAX (250) 743-4766 PO Box 108, Malahat V0R 2L0, is a lovely Relais & Château property, with a superb location offering breathtaking views across the fjords and Olympic Mountains. Sumptuous Mediterranean-style villas, including 10 rooms and 10 suites, are surrounded by acres of parkland. Activities abound with tennis courts, fishing, sailing, and hiking on site. When the day is done the spa, sauna, and whirlpool soothe the body from the day's exertions.

If you're planning an excursion to the southwest coast of the island, you might consider staying at the **Sooke Harbour House** ((250) 642-3421 FAX (250) 642-6988, 1528 Whiffen Spit Road, Rural Route 4, Sooke V0S 1N0, about 37 km (23 miles) from Victoria. Primarily an internationally famous gourmet restaurant, this large white house perched high above a bay also has 23 wonderful guestrooms. Rooms are lovingly decorated with original artworks and antiques, each with a name that underlines the theme reflected in the decor. All rooms have fireplaces, and some have four-poster beds, double Jacuzzis, balconies, or sun decks. Rates include breakfast and lunch, and special honeymoon packages are available.

Mid-range

Close to Parliament Buildings you can enjoy some old-fashioned comfort in an intimate atmosphere at the **Holland House Inn** ((250) 384-6644, 595 Michigan Street, Victoria V8V 1S7. This is a 1930s house, casually elegant with contemporary art adorning its public areas. There are 10 cheerful, antique-furnished rooms with balconies, some of which have four-poster beds and fireplaces. It's worth staying here for the gourmet breakfast alone. Rates include breakfast and vary from expensive to mid-range. Also close to Parliament, the **James Bay Inn** ✆ (250) 384-7151 TOLL-FREE (800) 836-2649 FAX (250) 385-2311, 270 Government Street, Victoria V8V 2L2, is a large old house with character that offers good value and is thus very popular. The 48 rooms vary in amenities and size — some have private baths and some have kitchenettes.

For some fantasy accommodation try the **Olde England Inn** ✆ (250) 388-4353 FAX (250) 382-8311, 429 Lampson Street, Victoria V9A 5Y9. It is part of a group of reconstructed sixteenth-century English buildings that include replicas of Shakespeare's birthplace and Anne Hathaway's

cottage and the like, and are just a short drive west of downtown in the Esquimalt district. Genuine antiques, including some canopy beds, furnish the rooms. The bathrooms are not, thankfully, sixteenth-century replicas. Prices vary widely from low mid-range to expensive.

The **Strathcona Hotel** ✆ (250) 383-7137 TOLL-FREE (800) 663-7476 FAX (250) 383-6893, at 919 Douglas Street, Victoria V8W 2C2, is an old building that also houses a pub, a restaurant, and several nightspots. The rooms are modern with private bathrooms and lots of features that make it very good value. The **Hotel Douglas** ✆ (250) 383-4157 TOLL-FREE (800) 332-9981 FAX (250) 383-2279, at 1450 Douglas Street, Victoria V8W 2G1, is also an older building with nice, modern rooms, some of which have private baths. There's a 24-hour café, a bar and laundry facilities. Room rates vary from the top of the inexpensive range to mid-range.

Inexpensive

Conveniently situated, the **Cherry Bank Hotel** ✆ (250) 385-5380 TOLL-FREE (800) 998-6688, 825 Burdett Avenue, Victoria V8W 1B3, is a late nineteenth-century building with new extensions. The rooms are simply furnished and have no phones or television, but they are clean and adequate. There's a restaurant and bar, and you can join other guests in the Trivial Pursuit lounge. A full English breakfast is included in the price.

Victoria has an abundance of **bed and breakfast** accommodations ranging from the basic to the luxurious (see WHERE TO STAY, page 78, under VANCOUVER).

Hostelling International-Victoria (HI) ✆ (250) 385-4511 FAX (250) 385-3232 E-MAIL victoria@hihostels.bc.ca, downtown at 516 Yates Street, Victoria V8W 1K8, is a large, modern place with single-sex dormitories and good kitchen facilities.

The University of Victoria six kilometers (four miles) east of downtown offers **campus accommodation**. For details contact the University of Victoria Housing and Conference Services ✆ (250) 721-8395, PO Box 1700, Victoria V8W 2Y2.

WHERE TO EAT

Expensive

Sooke Harbour House ✆ (250) 642-3421, 42 km (26 miles) west of Victoria at 1528 Whiffen Spit Road, Rural Route 4, is one of Canada's best restaurants and offers some truly memorable dining. This is a large white house perched on a bluff overlooking a bay, with a spectacular view of the Juan de Fuca Strait and the Olympic Mountains beyond. The menu changes according to what is available that day, but you can expect to find flowers liberally used in delightful salads and as garnish, the freshest of fish, and free-range chicken. The presentation is pure artistry, the service knowledgeable, and the atmosphere informal.

Dinner is a far more formal affair at the distinguished **Empress Room** ✆ (250) 384-8111, in the Empress Hotel, 721 Government Street. Wooden ceilings, pillars, and chandeliers create a setting that is splendidly traditional while the menu features Pacific Northwest cuisine and holds some pleasant surprises. Gentle piano or harp music enhances one's enjoyment of the excellent food.

Moderate to Inexpensive

Pagliacci's ✆ (250) 386-1662, at 1011 Broad Street, serves dependable Italian food. There's usually a line outside and it is cramped inside, but everyone is fortunately very friendly, and putting your elbow in somebody else's pasta can prove to be a great icebreaker. There's a slightly Bohemian air about the **Herald Street Caffe** ✆ (250) 381-1441,

An outdoor café in Victoria.

546 Herald Street, where you can inspect the work of local artists on display and enjoy some extremely good Italian and Californian food.

For Indian food try the **Taj Mahal** ☎ (250) 383-4662, 679 Herald Street, where vegetarians will find themselves well-catered for. Along Fisgard Street in Chinatown, a goodly number of restaurants serve Sichuan, Hunan, and Cantonese food; for authentic Japanese food try the **Japanese Village Steak & Seafood House** ☎ (250) 385-1615, at 734 Broughton Street. For an altogether English experience go to **Old Vic Fish 'n' Chips** ☎ (250) 388-4536, at 1316 Broad Street, or on a rather more dignified note, take afternoon tea at the **James Bay Tearoom** ☎ (250) 382-8282, 332 Menzies Street.

How to Get There

Victoria International Airport is about 26 km (16 miles) north of downtown. There is an **airport bus service**, operated by PBM Transport ☎ (250) 475-2010, that runs frequently. The trip to downtown takes around half an hour. Victoria is served by 50 flights each day that make the short trip from Vancouver International Airport and Seattle-Tacoma Airport, in addition to numerous direct flights from other major cities. Regular float plane and helicopter service to downtown Victoria is available from Vancouver and Seattle.

The *Princess Marguerite III* (which also carries cars) cruises daily between Seattle and Victoria's Inner Harbour from mid-May to mid-September. The journey takes approximately four and a half hours. Contact **Clipper Navigation** ☎ (250) 480-5555 TOLL-FREE IN THE UNITED STATES (800) 888-2535, for details and reservations. The *Victoria Clipper* is a jet-propelled catamaran, also operated by Clipper Navigation, that crosses between Victoria and Seattle in a mere two and a half hours, year-round. **BC Ferries** ☎ (604) 277-0277 (24-hour recorded information) or (604) 669-1211 (reservations) TOLL-FREE IN BRITISH COLUMBIA (800) 663-7600 operate between Vancouver and Vancouver Island. From Tsawwassen, which is south of Vancouver on the mainland, ferries sail to Victoria and Nanaimo on Vancouver Island and to the Southern Gulf Islands. BC Ferries also operate between Horseshoe Bay (30 minutes north of Vancouver) and Nanaimo.

Black Ball Transport ☎ (250) 386-2202 or ☎ (206) 457-4491 in Port Angeles runs a ferry between Victoria's Inner Harbour and Port Angeles on Washington's Olympic Peninsula; it takes an hour and 35 minutes. **Washington State Ferries** ☎ (250) 381-1551 or ☎ IN THE US (206) 464-6400, operate daily, year-round between Sidney, just north of Victoria, and Anacortes, Washington with ports of call in the San Juan Islands. The approximate crossing time is three hours.

The **Pacific Coach Line** ☎ (250) 385-4411 operates frequent service from Vancouver to Victoria via the Tsawwassen-Swartz Bay ferry crossing, with a journey time of three and a half hours. **Island Coach Lines** ☎ (250) 385-4411 connects with other Vancouver Island towns. **Maverick Coach Lines** ☎ (250) 662-8051 operates between Nanaimo and Vancouver also via the BC Ferries.

The **Esquimalt & Nanaimo Rail Liner** (VIA Rail) ☎ (250) 383-4324 TOLL-FREE (888) 842-7733 runs to Duncan, Nanaimo, Qualicum Beach, Courtenay and points in between. The station is near downtown Victoria at 450 Pandora Avenue.

ELSEWHERE ON THE ISLAND

Duncan and Vicinity

The rural town of Duncan, 60 km (38 miles) north of Victoria on the Trans-Canada Highway, is the gateway and supply center to the **Cowichan Valley**. The valley is still home to many Cowichan, and native craftsmen have collaborated with the town to produce the 80 or so totem poles clustered along the roadside. This is a good place to buy one of the famous Cowichan sweaters, as well as other native arts and crafts. Duncan's premiere attraction is the **Cowichan Native Village** ☎ (250) 746-8119, 200 Cowichan Way, situated on a five-hectare (13-acre), tree-lined stretch of the Cowichan River. At the Longhouse Story Centre, a film explains the history and legends of the Cowichan people. At the carving house, visitors can see

ABOVE: The fearsome image of the thunderbird sits atop a totem pole in Victoria's Thunderbird Park. OPPOSITE: The handsome caboose of a vintage Canadian Pacific Railroad train.

artisans at work, and at noon there's a salmon barbecue and dance presentation. The village is open daily from 9 AM to 5 PM; an admission is charged for the village and for the barbecue/show.

Highway 18 takes you 31 km (19 miles) westwards to **Lake Cowichan**, the largest freshwater lake on the island. It is known mainly for its good fishing but it is also good for swimming, camping, or canoeing, and the surrounding forest is laced with hiking trails. The valley is a lumbering area and one of the better logging roads will take you westwards from the lake to Port Renfrew on the island's west coast, the beginning of the Pacific Rim National Park's famous West Coast Trail.

About three kilometers (one and a half miles) north of Duncan the **British Columbia Forest Museum** ✆ (250) 715-1113 offers a fascinating look at the history of the forestry industry in the province through both indoor and outdoor exhibits. Here you can take a ride on a narrow-gauge steam railway, visit a reconstructed logging camp, see old equipment, and walk through the surrounding forest. It's open daily May to September and an admission fee is charged.

Twenty kilometers (12 miles) north along the highway from Duncan lies the curious town of **Chemainus**. To avert the disaster that threatened when the town's sawmill closed down in 1983, the community set out to find itself a new source of revenue by commissioning murals to grace the town's buildings. The idea worked: visitors came to look, shops and restaurants opened, and murals depicting the town's history have spread like wildfire, covering not only walls but also litter bins and anything else that stands still long enough. BC Ferries operates from here to nearby **Thetis** and **Kuper islands**, part of the Southern Gulf Islands.

A little further north the attractive waterfront town of **Ladysmith** sits right on the 49th parallel which divides the mainland between Canada and the United States (aside from Victoria Island). The old buildings here have been nicely renovated and it makes a pleasant stopping place.

For lodging in Duncan there is the **Best Western Cowichan Valley Inn** ✆ (250) 748-2722 TOLL-FREE (800) 528-1234 FAX (250) 748-2207, 6474 Trans-Canada Highway, Rural Route 4, Duncan V9L 3W8, located opposite the British Columbia Forest Museum. It offers 42 comfortable rooms and suites, a dining room, and a coffee shop. Prices are solidly mid-range.

At Ladysmith the **Yellowpoint Lodge** ✆ (250) 245-7422 FAX (250) 245-7411, 3700 Yellow Point Road, Rural Route 3, Ladysmith V0R 2E0, is set in delightful parkland overlooking the sea, and inexpensive accommodation — with three full meals included in the rate — is available either in the main lodge or in rustic cottages. There is a saltwater pool, a hot tub, a sauna, sports facilities, and a restaurant.

NANAIMO

Nanaimo, 110 km (68 miles) north of Victoria, is the second largest city on Vancouver Island and a major deep-sea fishing port. Several First Nations tribes lived in peaceful coexistence here until the Hudson's Bay Company discovered coal in the 1850s. Nanaimo remained a thriving coal mining area until demand dwindled with the coming of the oil-burning ships, at which point it turned to logging and fishing. Now an important BC Ferries terminus with a direct link to the mainland, the town has adapted itself to the tourist industry. Increased facilities, renovated buildings, smart boutiques, jolly festivals, and inhabitants renowned for their friendliness draw many visitors.

In 1853 the Hudson's Bay Company built the fortified **Bastion** as defense against possible native attack. Now the symbol of Nanaimo, this stout fort serves as a museum, and during the summer months its three cannons are ceremonially fired each day at noon. To find out a little more about Nanaimo's history, visit the **Nanaimo Centennial Museum** ✆ (250) 753-1821 at 100 Cameron Street, which is open daily during the summer and from Tuesday to Saturday in the winter.

The wealth of parks and lakes in and around Nanaimo gives anglers, boaters, canoeists, windsurfers, and hikers plentiful opportunities to pursue their sports. Departure Bay at the north end of town is a popular windsurfing spot and whatever equipment you need can be rented from an outlet actually on the beach. If island-hopping appeals to you, there's a regular BC Ferry service to nearby **Newcastle** and **Gabriola islands**. Newcastle Island is a provincial park inhabited only by wildlife, park keepers, and campers, while Gabriola Island, although home to a small artistic community, is also unspoiled, peaceful, and has some lovely beaches.

Just south of Nanaimo look for **Petroglyph Provincial Park** ✆ (250) 387-5002 where you can see prehistoric carvings on the sandstone rock that were made by native people some 10,000 years ago.

The best place to stay around Nanaimo is the **Coast Bastion Inn** ✆ (250) 753-6601 TOLL-FREE (800) 663-1144 FAX (250) 753-4155, 11 Bastion Street, Nanaimo V9R 2Z9, a large hotel on the waterfront with pleasant views from all of its rooms. The hotel has a café and a pub. The **Best Western Dorchester Hotel** ✆ (250) 754-6835 TOLL-FREE (800) 661-2449 FAX (250) 754-6835, 70 Church Street, Nanaimo V9R 5H4, has rooms and suites with harbor views, a restaurant, a rooftop garden, and a library. Prices at both the Best Western Dorchester and the Coast Bastion fall into the expensive category. Conveniently situated for the Nanaimo Ferry Terminal is the **Colonial Motel** ☎ (250) 754-4415 FAX (250) 753-1611, 950 Terminal Avenue North, Nanaimo V9S 4K4. Rooms have private bathrooms, cable television, telephones, and kitchenettes. Kayaks can be rented on site, and restaurants and shopping are close by. Rates are inexpensive.

PARKSVILLE TO PORT ALBERNI

About 38 km (24 miles) north of Nanaimo, **Parksville** is well situated for a variety of outdoor activities. It lies along a coastal stretch popular for its lovely, sandy beaches and waters said to be the warmest in Canada. To the west of Parksville lie wooded slopes threaded with nature trails, and in the winter months nearby Mount Arrowsmith attracts skiers. This is also where the scenic Highway 4 cuts westwards, crossing the island's central mountain range and leading to its star attraction — the magnificent Pacific Rim National Park, 154 km (96 miles) away.

After a steep five kilometers (three miles) along Highway 4, a deviation of about eight kilometers (five miles) to the left will bring you to **Englishman Falls Provincial Park** where the Englishman River rushes over waterfalls down into lush, ferny forest, and brims with rainbow trout and steelhead. With beautiful clear pools for swimming, it is a delightful spot to pitch a tent. Back along Highway 4, a further 20 km (12 miles) will bring you to **Little Qualicum Falls Provincial Park**. A delightful forest trail leads to this series of waterfalls and ice-cold pools, while nearby tree-fringed **Cameron Lake** teems with trout. About nine kilometers (five and a half miles) along the road in **MacMillan Provincial Park** stands the magnificent **Cathedral Grove**, an awesome sight that is not to be missed. Some of the Douglas firs in this grove are 800 years old and reach heights of 76 m (250 ft).

Halfway across the island, **Port Alberni** sits at the head of the deep-cutting Alberni Inlet that widens into the West Coast's Barkley Sound. It is a large town with a thriving lumber industry; a fact unfortunately borne out by the pungent smell that emanates from the mills. Its other main revenue comes from fishing, as anglers come here for the excellent salmon. From the harbor the stately **MV *Lady Rose*** ☎ (250) 723-8313 takes passengers down the inlet to Bamfield and Ucluelet via the Broken Islands. This cruise is a pleasant way to observe some of the wildlife of the sky and sea, and those intending to canoe or kayak around the Broken Islands are allowed to take their vessel aboard. You can rent whatever equipment you need for canoeing, kayaking, or diving from outlets in Port Alberni. The *Lady Rose* operates from April to September. Departures are daily at 8 AM.

From Port Alberni, Highway 4 continues towards the West Coast by **Sproat Lake**, which attracts many watersports enthusiasts and anglers. It proceeds through some beautiful mountain scenery, marred only by evidence of the extensive logging that has taken place in the area. The road follows the Kennedy River to Kennedy Lake, and

On Vancouver Island's Barkeley Sound eagles are so numerous that locals joke, "They're like crows to us."

then reaches the junction with the Ucluelet road where it bends sharply to the right and continues to Tofino.

There's a wide choice of motels and resorts in Parksville and several motels in Port Alberni. Back on the east coast there's some interesting accommodation at **Qualicum College Inn** ☎ (250) 752-9262 TOLL-FREE (800) 663-7306 FAX (250) 752-5144 E-MAIL qcihotel@nanaimo.ark.com, 427 College Road, PO Box 99, Qualicum Beach V9K 2G4. This historic landmark building, once a boys' school, overlooks the sea and has 70 accommodations, including a few honeymoon suites. Fishing and golfing packages are available, and the prices are mid-range.

PACIFIC RIM NATIONAL PARK

The ruggedly beautiful coastal strip that constitutes Pacific Rim National Park ☎ (250) 762-7721, PO Box 280, Ucluelet V0R 3A0, stretches for a dramatic 72 km (45 miles) between Tofino and Port Renfrew and is made up of three sections, all very different in character and equally rich in wildlife. The most northerly section, known as **Long Beach**, lies between the villages of Tofino and Ucluelet and is a driftwood-strewn stretch of white sand and rock pounded by Pacific breakers. The weather is generally cold and wet here, but undeterred sportsmen and women don wetsuits to enjoy some superb surfing, swimming, canoeing, and kayaking. Hikers wrap up warmly and explore the magnificent trails through the rain forest. Porpoises, sea lions, and seals inhabit the waters. Gray whales can be spotted here, most frequently during the spring when they return from their breeding grounds in the south. **Radar Hill** with its telescope offers a good viewing point, but for closer views there are whale-spotting boat trips that operate from Tofino. Humbler marine life can be seen in the tidal pools along the beach — you can look, but you are not allowed to remove any of the little creatures. Another interesting trip from Tofino runs to **Meares Island** where you can follow trails through unspoiled rain forest that has some ancient trees of majestic proportions.

The middle section of the park consists of the **Broken Islands**, 100 or so islands in Barkley Sound that can be reached by the MV *Lady Rose* passenger ship (see PARKSVILLE TO PORT ALBERNI, above), by charter from Port Alberni, or by boat from Ucluelet. The islands are popular with canoeists and kayakers, and the area also offers some wonderful scuba diving with plenty of shipwrecks to be seen, not to mention the world's largest octopi.

Many of the visitors come to Pacific Rim for the third section of the park, the **West Coast Trail**, a tough hiking trail stretching 75 km (47 miles) between Bamfield and Port Renfrew. The trail follows an historic lifesaving route for shipwrecked mariners and requires stamina and endurance, and hikers must carry all food and supplies for the six- to eight-day hike. This trail has become so popular that a quota system has been instituted limiting the number of hikers to 52 per

ABOVE: A kayaker's view of Barkeley Sound near Pacific Rim National Park — the roots of an ancient tree are claimed by the salt water. OPPOSITE: Sea anemone in a Pacific Rim tidal pool.

day. Trailheads are at Port Renfrew and Pachena Bay. Advance reservations are strongly recommended and can be made by calling TOLL-FREE (800) 663-6000. There is a nonrefundable reservation fee. For more information on the West Coast Trail, call the Bamfield Infocentre ☎ (250) 728-3234 or the Port Renfrew Infocentre ☎ (250) 647-5434.

At the entrance to Barkley Sound sits the little town of **Bamfield**, rather unusual in that its main highway is the inlet that divides it into two. A boardwalk two kilometers (one mile) long links East and West Bamfield.

In the Pacific Rim National Park area most of the accommodation is to be found at Tofino and Ucluelet. Bamfield also has a few lodges, resorts, and bed and breakfast places. In recent years fishing charters, lodges, resorts, and other kinds of accommodation have appeared in Bamfield in response to the growing demands of tourism, but during the high season the town still groans under the influx of tourists, mainly fishermen, so everything fills up quickly. You can explore Pacific Rim and the Broken Islands in high style from **Eagle Nook Ocean Wilderness Resort** ☎ (250) 723-1000 TOLL-FREE (800) 760-2777 FAX (250) 723-9842 E-MAIL eaglenk@cedar.alberni.net, PO Box 575, Port Alberni, British Columbia V9Y 7M9. The resort is accessible by water taxi or ferry from Port Alberni (see PADDLE THE PACIFIC RIM, page 15, in TOP SPOTS).

Qualicum Beach to Campbell River

Ten kilometers (six miles) north of Parksville, **Qualicum Beach** is a popular spot for anglers, sunbathers, and swimmers, with plenty of accommodation and facilities geared to visitors' needs. Alternatively, there are the quiet beaches of **Denman** and **Hornby Islands**, home to small communities and accessible by ferry.

A little further north, the towns of **Comox** and **Courtenay** sit in the lovely **Comox Valley**. Both are commercial centers that also serve as bases for the surrounding recreational areas. Golf courses, fishing lodges, mountain trails, and campsites abound, and during the winter skiers flock to the nearby slopes of **Mount Washington** and Strathcona Park's **Forbidden Plateau**.

Campbell River, the gateway to Strathcona Park, is another town that is dedicated to outdoor sports, with skiing, hiking, mountaineering, and canoeing all catered for. The scuba diving here is very highly rated, but above all it is famous for its salmon fishing, which is probably the best anywhere, while its first-class fishing lodges attract enthusiasts from all around the world. It is hardly surprising, therefore, that the town's central attraction seems to be the **Discovery Pier**, a boardwalk that has shelter and facilities for anglers. From here it is well worth a trip on the ferry to historic **Quadra Island** to see the **Kwagiulth Museum and Cultural Centre** ☎ (250) 285-3733 where there are displays of some fascinating carvings and ceremonial objects, many of which were seized by the authorities during the banning of potlatches — elaborate ceremonies involving ritual and feasting that were deemed heathen by the church. Potlatches were outlawed by the Canadian government in 1922 as part of a forced-assimilation program. The ban was lifted in 1951. The museum is open daily from 10 AM to 4:30 PM; closed Sunday and Monday off-season. An admission fee is charged.

From Campbell River, Highway 28 runs west to **Strathcona Park**, the largest on Vancouver

Island. It is a magnificent preserve of wilderness and wildlife that contains the **Golden Hinde**, the island's highest peak, as well as the magnificent **Della Falls**. Highway 28 cuts westwards across Strathcona Park to the small town of **Gold River**, where the *Uchuck III*, a converted mine sweeper, will take you along Nootka Sound to **Friendly Cove**, the place where Captain Cook first landed and met with the natives in 1778.

Comox and Courtenay both have a large number of inexpensive motels, and at Campbell River there are also a lot of fishing lodges. One of the most distinguished lodges in town is the **Painter's Lodge and Fishing Resort** ☎ (250) 286-1102 TOLL-FREE (800) 663-7090 FAX (250) 598-1361, 1625 MacDonald Road, PO Box 560, Department 2, Campbell River V9W 5C1, open April to October. It overlooks the ocean and guests stay either in the main lodge or in cottages, where the rooms are very well-equipped. There's a heated outdoor pool, a pub, and seaside dining, and the lodge organizes just about any kind of package you could want. Prices here range from mid-range to expensive. At the **Strathcona Park Lodge** ☎ (250) 286-8206, Highway 28, PO Box 2000, Station A, Campbell River V9W 5C9, there are many kinds of accommodation to be had: campsites, hostel accommodation, apartments, cottages, and chalets. The lodge organizes packages for every kind of outdoor sport, including rock climbing, canoeing, and sailing. **Tsa-Kwa-Luten Lodge** ☎ (250) 285-2042 TOLL-FREE (800) 665-7746 FAX (250) 285-2532 E-MAIL gbryson@online.bc.ca, Lighthouse Road, Quadra Island, PO Box 460, Quathiaski Cove V0P 1N0, at Cape Mudge, is owned and operated by the Cape Mudge First Nations band. Here guests can relax in an environment steeped in native history, culture, and architecture, and dine in the Big House where traditional West Coast fare is served. Accommodation is in the comfortable main lodge or waterfront cottages. All the typical island activities can be pursued here, including hiking, mountain biking, paddling, scuba diving, fishing, and beach combing.

NORTH ISLAND

The best reason for a stop at **Port McNeill** is to take the ferry to the island of **Alert Bay**, home of the **U'Mista Cultural Centre** ☎ (250) 974-5403. On display here are more of the confiscated ceremonial objects that were used for the native potlatch ceremonies; excellent films on aspects of Northwest Coast native culture are shown. The island is also a good place for **whale watching**. Seasmoke Tours ☎ (250) 974-5225 TOLL-FREE (800) 668-6722 has been leading killer-whale watching educational tours for 20 years. You can choose a six-hour tour aboard their sailing yacht or the three-hour Zodiac tour.

Further north the highway ends at **Port Hardy**, where BC Ferries ply the scenic Inside Passage to and from Prince Rupert on the mainland, a 441-km (274-mile) journey (see CRUISE THE INSIDE PASSAGE, page 16, in TOP SPOTS). For the intrepid, trails run from Port Hardy to the splendidly isolated **Cape Scott** and **San Josef Provincial Parks**.

The Inside Passage ferry leaves from **Port Hardy** early in the morning, so most passengers spend the night somewhere in the vicinity. Always book ahead on nights before ferry departures. Comfortable rooms with shared bath and a hardy breakfast are the trademark of **This Old House** ☎ (250) 949-8372 FAX (250) 949-8390 E-MAIL oldhouse@trinet.ca, 8735 Hastings Street, PO Box 2301, Port Hardy V0N 2P0. Built in 1925 and originally used as a boarding house, it's the oldest residence in Port Hardy. Jean, a former pilot and now part-time mail carrier, knows everything there is to know about the town. Hostel-type accommodation is also sometimes available here. For additional bed and breakfast listings,

Now you see them, now you don't: trees ABOVE of British Columbia's great forests are reduced to timber OPPOSITE to feed the printing presses of several nations.

BRITISH COLUMBIA
YUKON
NORTHWEST TERRITORIES
ALASKA
BRITISH COLUMBIA
ALBERTA
PACIFIC OCEAN
U.S.A.
CASSIAR MOUNTAINS
SKEENA MOUNTAINS
COAST MOUNTAINS
ROCKY MOUNTAINS
Teslin
Bennett
White Pass
Atlin
Nakina
Tulsequah
Nahlin
Porter Landing
Sheslay
Telegraph Creek
Mount Edziza Park
Dease Lake
Stikine River Park
Spatsizi Park
Boundary
Iskut River
Tatlatui Park
Premier
Stewart
Alice Arm
New Aiyansh
Watson Lake
Lower Post
Coal River
Liard River
Kechika River
Gataga River
Kwadacha Park
Ware
McConnell Creek
Ft. Grahame
Muncho Lake
Nelson Forks
Fort Nelson R.
Summit Lake
Muskwa
Fort Nelson
Trutch
Alaska Highway Halfway
Beatton River
Beatton R.
Fort St. John
Fort Simpson
Petitot River
High Level
Grimshaw
Dawson Creek
Chetwynd
Tumbler Ridge
Grande Cache
Prince Rupert
Skeena Valley
Skeena River
Porchar Island
Port Edward
Terrace
Smithers
Hazelton
Fort Babine
Babine Lake
Trembleur Lake
Stuart Lake
McLeod Lake
Kitimat
Pitt Island
Banks Island
Houston
Morice Lake
Ootsa Lake
Fort St. James
Bear Lake
Summit Lake
Vanderhoof
Prince George
Red Rock
Stoner
Hixon
Rennel Sound
Queen Charlotte Islands
Gwaii Haanas National Park Reserve
Princess Royal Island
Eutsuk Lake
Kimsquit
Tweedsmuir Park
Price Island
Green Falls
Hunter Island
Namu
Charlotte Lake
Quesnel
Kersley
Wells
Bowron Lake Park
Mt. Robson 3954
Mt. Robson
Jasper
Jasper National Park
Maligne Lake
Mt. Edith Cavell 3363
Dawsons Landing
Calvert Island
Rivers Inlet
Goose Bay
Allison Harbour
Tatla Lake
Castle Rock
Soda Creek
Keithley Creek
Quesnel Lake
Williams Lake
Wells Gray Provincial Park
Hanceville
Big Creek
Eagle Lake
Tatlayoko Lake
Alkali Lake
Chilko Lake
Taseko Lake
Cape Scott Park
San Josef Park
Queen Charlotte Strait
Sullivan Bay
Port Hardy
Port Alice
Port McNeill
Kingcome Inlet
Thompson Sound
Minstrel Island
Brooks Peninsula
Kyuquot
Kinbasket Lake
Mica Creek
Schoen Lake Park
Blind Channel
Tahsis
Campbell River
Vancouver Island
Courtenay
Strathcona Park
Comox
Jervis Inlet
Pemberton
Whistler
Garibaldi Park
Squamish
Qualicum Beach
Parksville
Port Alberni
Tofino
Barkley Sound
Nanaimo
Pacific Rim National Park
Port Renfrew
Ladysmith
Duncan
Sidney
Saanich
Sooke
Victoria
Vancouver
Seattle
Kamloops
Adams Lake
Mt. Revelstoke National Park
Glacier National Park
Salmon Arm
Vernon
Okanagan Lake
Okanagan Valley
Kelowna
Monashee Lake Park
Upper Arrow Lake
Penticton
Osoyoos
Grand Forks
Lower Arrow Lake
Kokanee Glacier Park
Nelson
Kootenay Lake
Creston
Duncan Lake
Bugaboo Park
Golden
Field
Yoho National Park
Lake Louise
Banff
Banff National Park
Radium Hot Springs
Fairmont Hot Springs
Top of the World Park
Spar
N
E
S
W
0 25 50 75 100 miles
0 75 150 Km

contact the **Port Hardy Visitor Information Centre** ☎ (250) 949-7622, 7250 Market Street, PO Box 249, Port Hardy V0N 2P0; it's open from June 1 to Labor Day. If a hotel is more your style, the locally owned and operated **Airporter Inn** ☎ (250) 949-9434, 4030 Byng Road, Port Hardy, is a reliable choice.

How to Get There

A few airlines serve Vancouver Island cities and link with Vancouver, while there are also regular float-plane flights between Nanaimo and the mainland.

BC Ferries ☎ (250) 381-1401 TOLL-FREE (888) 223-3779 run between Port Hardy in the northern part of the island and Prince Rupert on the mainland. This scenic trip along the Inside Passage takes 15 hours, with ferries operating every second day in the summer and once a week in winter. Reservations are required. BC Ferries also connects Horseshoe Bay in Vancouver with Nanaimo.

Island Coach Lines ☎ (250) 724-1266 runs between Nanaimo and Port Alberni, and **Orient Stage Lines Ltd.** ☎ (250) 723-6924 covers the run from Port Alberni to Ucluelet, Pacific Rim National Park, and Tofino.

Esquimalt & Nanaimo Rail Liner (VIA Rail) ☎ (250) 383-4324 TOLL-FREE (888) 842-7733, 450 Pandora Avenue, Victoria, runs from Victoria to Courtenay, stopping at Courtenay, Nanaimo, Duncan, Qualicum Beach, and points along the way. You need to make reservations for trips during the summer.

If you're traveling by car, the road that connects Victoria to the North Island is the Trans-Canada Highway. To reach Ucluelet and Tofino on the West Coast you need to take Highway 4 from Parksville.

THE OKANAGAN VALLEY

This beautiful ribbon of valleys, lakes, and beaches lies in south central British Columbia and stretches from Osoyoos near the United States border to Vernon in the north — a distance of roughly 180 km (112 miles). It is centered around the Okanagan River and a long string of lakes, the largest being the magnificent 144-km (90-mile) Lake Okanagan, which according to First Nations legend is the home of the serpent-monster N'ha-A-Itk, or "Lake Demon," called Ogopogo in English after the popular nineteenth-century music hall tune, "The Ogopogo Song." The lakes are surrounded by arid, rolling hills, lakeside provincial parks, beautiful smooth beaches, and, inevitably, vacation resorts. Highway 97 runs the length of the valley and those who travel it can appreciate the fascinating Okanagan landscape that changes from a "pocket desert" around Osoyoos, where cactus thrives and rainfall is lightest, to the green farmlands in the north. Throughout the valley orchards flourish, and many believe the Okanagan is at its most seductive during April and May when blossoms cover the trees and their scent fills the air.

The valley averages some 2,000 hours of sunshine a year, summers are hot, winters are mild, and the rainfall is low. This congenial climate, together with the vast tract of water that makes irrigation possible, has turned the area into a major fruit-producing region with crops of apples, peaches, grapes, apricots, cherries, plums, and pears. From late June to October the roadside is lined with stands selling these fruits. Vineyards cover the hillsides and eleven of the province's thirteen wineries are here, extending warm welcomes to the visitors who come to be shown around, to taste the wines, and to enjoy the hilltop views. The various fruit harvests are celebrated with events and festivals, and in early fall the whole valley joins in the biggest and jolliest one of all — the Okanagan Wine Festival ☎ (250) 861-6654. The valley has the largest concentration of population in the interior; its main towns are Penticton, and Vernon. The valley has become a popular vacation spot and attracts Canadians from colder regions who come to soak up some of the abundant sunshine. In and around the main towns vacation resorts line the lakes and spread over the hillsides. There are noisy waterslide parks and theme parks. In the summer,

A steamer on Lake Okanagan calls at Kelowna.

water sports enthusiasts flock to the lakes, while the winter brings skiers to the nearby mountainsides. If you are in search of quieter beauty spots then by far the best way to visit the valley is by car. In this way you can appreciate the variation in the scenery and have the freedom to stop your car where you please.

GENERAL INFORMATION

Apart from the information available from the provincial tourist information offices, you can get more specific information on the region from the **Okanagan-Similkameen Tourism Association** ☎ (250) 860-5999 FAX (250) 861-7493, 1332 Water Street, Kelowna V1Y 9P4. In addition, there is the **Penticton Wine and Information Centre** ☎ (250) 493-4055, 888 Westminster Avenue West, and a smaller Information Centre along Highway 97, seven kilometers (four miles) south of downtown. At **Kelowna** you can drop in on the Travel Infocentre ☎ (250) 861-1515, at 544 Harvey Avenue. **Vernon** has a year-round Travel Infocentre ☎ (250) 542-1415, at 3700 33rd Street, and a couple of other seasonal centers stationed on the main highway at the northern and southern edges of town.

The Okanagan Valley is a popular resort area and there are masses of motels, resorts, and campgrounds that usually fall within the inexpensive and mid-range price brackets. For lists of **bed and breakfast** accommodation in the area contact the Okanagan Bed and Breakfast ☎ (250) 764-2124, PO Box 5135, Station A, Kelowna V1Y 8T9.

OSOYOOS

At the southern end of the Okanagan Valley, just north of the United States border, the little town of Osoyoos sits on the shore of Osoyoos Lake. The town has cultivated a Spanish look to suit its dry, sunny climate, and as is characteristic of the Okanagan Valley, it is a fruit-growing area that celebrates its harvests with colorful festivals. Sandy lakeside beaches and warm trout-filled waters make this a popular spot for sunbathing, swimming, angling, windsurfing, boating, and the site for a variety of water sports events. Although fruit-laden orchards cluster around the lake, cacti and sagebrush grow on the arid hills that surround the town. This sandy area, which extends northwards to Skaha Lake, is often referred to as Canada's "pocket desert." It is a region that supports horned lizards, rattlesnakes, burrowing owls, and other life forms associated with the desert. Take Highway 3 slightly east of Osoyoos to **Anarchist Mountain** for views that allow you to appreciate fully the varied landscape.

West of the town Highway 3 leads into the neighboring Similkameen Valley. Highway 97 continues northwards following the Okanagan River through its valley past Vaseux and Skaha lakes, a route that is lined with orchards and, in the summertime, with stands selling succulent fruit. Eleven kilometers (seven miles) south of Penticton the **Okanagan Game Farm** ☎ (250) 497-5405, occupies a large area of scrubland above Lake Skaha. A five-kilometer (three-mile) drive through the zoo allows visitors to see over 130 species of animals from all around the world and also has some good views of the lakes.

There are some 20 hotels and motels around the lakeside in Osoyoos, several with their own private beach and shaded lawns. Assistance with other options is available at the local **Visitor Infocentre** ((250) 495-7142 TOLL-FREE (888) 676-9667 FAX (250) 495-6161, at the junction of Highways 3 and 97, PO Box 227, Osoyoos V0H 1V0.

PENTICTON

The town of Penticton lies along Highway 97, 395 km (245 miles) east of Vancouver, between Skaha Lake and the southern shore of the larger Okanagan Lake. Its name is derived from Salish words meaning "place to stay forever," and the combination of a warm, dry climate and the lovely beaches of two lakes make it as appealing today as it obviously was to the natives who named it. The town is very popular with vacationers and has become tourist-oriented with water slide parks, motels, and other facilities lining Highway 97 as it cuts through the center of the town. The waters of the lakes are ideal for all kinds of water sports and during the high season the beaches get very busy.

The first orchards were planted here in 1874 and the town is now famous for peach-growing. In late July and August the **Penticton Peach Festival** celebrates the harvesting of the crop with sports events, music, dancing, and the extensive drinking of peach brandy. Penticton also celebrates the grape harvest in September but you don't have to wait until then to enjoy a taste of the local wine (see SPECIAL INTERESTS, PAGE 38, in YOUR CHOICE).

Along the Okanagan lakefront the pleasant **Art Gallery of the South Okanagan** ((250) 493-2928, at 199 Front Street, exhibits local and Canadian works, and can be visited Tuesday to Friday from 10 AM to 5 PM, Saturday and Sunday from 1 PM to 5 PM; an admission fee is charged, free on Tuesday.

About a 30-minute drive west of Penticton along Green Mountain Road lies the **Apex Resort** ((250) 492-2880, where there is a well-equipped ski center. From here, Highway 97 continues its scenic route along the west side of Lake Okanagan, through orchards, vineyards, provincial parklands, and some smaller towns.

At Penticton there are a few places that stand out above the rest, such as the **Clarion Lakeside Resort and Conference Centre** ((250) 493-8221 TOLL-FREE (800) 663-9400, 21 Lakeshore Drive West, Penticton V2A 7M5. It stands on the shores of Lake Okanagan and offers top-line accommodation with all kinds of recreational facilities and services. The rooms are attractively furnished, all have balconies, and there's a restaurant, cocktail lounge, indoor pool, and a fitness center. Golf courses and tennis courts are nearby, and the beach and lake are at your disposal. Prices here range from expensive to mid-range. The **Best Western Inn** ((250) 493-0311 TOLL-FREE (800) 668-6746

Profiles in the Okanagan Game Farm: a mountain goat OPPOSITE and a bighorn sheep ABOVE.

is at 3180 Skaha Lake Road, Penticton V2A 6G4, and has 67 accommodations, including family and honeymoon suites, plus housekeeping units. There are indoor and outdoor pools, a sun deck and a restaurant, and the beach is nearby. Prices here are mid-range. Just across the road from Okanagan Lake Beach, the **Tiki Shores Condominium Beach Resort** ((250) 492-8769 FAX (250) 492-8160, 914 Lakeshore Drive, Penticton V2A 1C1, has one-, two-, and three-bedroom housekeeping units, some with rooftop patios. There's an outdoor pool, an indoor hot tub, and a (seasonal) restaurant. Prices fall into the mid-range category.

In the inexpensive bracket there's the **Three Gables Hotel** ((250) 492-3933, at 353 Main Street, Penticton V2A 1K9, which is in the city center but only a short walk away from the beach. Rooms have private bathrooms, and there's a restaurant and a pub.

Granny Bogner's ((250) 493-2711, 302 Eckhardt Avenue West, is widely held to be the best restaurant in the Okanagan. The theme is homey; the fare is European. It's open for dinner only, and reservations are essential. You can sample Greek specialties in pleasant surroundings at **Angelinis** on Skaha Lake Road, or some hearty good-value food at the **Elite Restaurant** ((250) 492-3051, 340 Main Street, where they do burgers, soups, and puddings. For Mexican food you should try **Taco Grande** at 452 Main Street.

KELOWNA

About halfway along Lake Okanagan, Highway 97 crosses a floating bridge to Kelowna, the largest city in the Okanagan Valley, with a population in the region of 70,000, and the center of this fruit-growing and wine-producing region. This attractive lakeside city with its many vineyards,

parks, gardens, and orchards is an island of greenery set among rolling semiarid hills. It has pleasant, sandy beaches and the lake provides plenty of scope for just about every water sport. The largest of Kelowna's parks is the lovely **City Park**, which has busy beaches, shady retreats, lawns, and tennis courts. In the summer it is sometimes the site of free outdoor concerts.

For a cruise of the lake and maybe a meal, get aboard the **MV *Fintry Queen*** ☎ (250) 763-2780, a paddle wheel that moors in the City Park at the foot of Bernard Avenue. There are also evening cruises, which offer dining and dancing.

At the **Father Pandosy Settlement** ☎ (250) 860-8369 south of downtown you can see some of the mission buildings that the oblate founded in 1859 and which formed the first white settlement in the valley. The original church and school still stand and some other buildings of similar age have been brought to the site to give the visitor a fuller picture of life in those pioneering days. The site is open daily, and admission is free.

The province's largest and oldest winery is Kelowna's **Calona Wines** ☎ (250) 762-9144 at 1125 Richter Street, where visitors are welcome to look around and taste the wine.

During the winter there's plenty of skiing on the slopes around Kelowna. Near the town on the other side of the lake is **Last Mountain**, which has chair lifts, a school, and something for skiers of all abilities, while about 57 km (35 miles) east of Kelowna is the **Big White Ski Area**, which is a ski resort with full facilities.

Continuing northwards along Highway 97 the scenery gradually becomes greener and cattle farming begins to take over from fruit growing.

Seventeen kilometers (11 miles) outside Kelowna lies the **Lake Okanagan Resort** ☎ (250) 769-3511 TOLL-FREE (800) 663-3273 FAX (250) 769-6665, 2751 Westside Road, Kelowna V1Y 7V8. This is an attractive lakeside resort set in landscaped gardens with luxurious condominiums, chalets, rooms and suites, and two dining rooms. It is an ideal haven for sports enthusiasts as it has tennis courts (some of which are floodlit for night games), a par-3 golf course, horse riding, heated outdoor pools, and a marina where guests go to water-ski, windsurf, and sail. Prices here run from mid-range to expensive.

In Kelowna the **Coast Capri Hotel** ☎ (250) 860-6060 TOLL-FREE IN CANADA (800) 663-1144 FAX (250) 762-3430, 1171 Harvey Avenue, Kelowna V1Y 6E8, offers all the creature comforts you could want, with a heated pool, poolside café, restaurant, pub, and a cold beer and wine store. There are comfortable units and suites, all with television and telephone. Prices here are in the mid-range category.

The **Ponderosa Motel** ☎ (250) 860-3982, at 1864 Harvey Avenue, Kelowna V1Y 6G2, has a warm, friendly atmosphere and low prices. It has 16 one- and two-bedroom housekeeping units, all with television. Tea and coffee is on the house and shops and restaurants are nearby. Not far from the lake and park, the **Willow Inn Hotel** ☎ (250) 762-2122, 235 Queensway Avenue, Kelowna V1Y 6S4, has 40 rooms with telephones and televisions, and has a coffee garden. Prices are inexpensive and include full breakfast.

For dining, Kelowna has the popular **Earl's Hollywood on Top** ☎ (250) 763-2777, 211 Bernard Avenue, a smart modern-looking place with a rooftop garden. It serves just about everything — tapas, pasta, ribs, steak, seafood and salads — and also has a busy cappuccino bar. It is open for lunch and dinner daily. There are all kinds of interesting snack items on the menu at **Jonathan L. Seagulls**

Eventide along the South Thompson River at Kamloop's riverfront park.

((250) 860-8449, 262 Bernard Avenue, where you can enjoy lake views and, on weekends, late opening hours. At the attractive **Carmellie's Crêperie** ((250) 762-6350, 1862 Benvoulin Road, a wide choice of sweet and savory crêpes awaits, and the eclectic **Kitchen Cowboy** ((250) 868-8288, 353 Bernard Avenue, has a western decor and fare from basic hamburgers to sundried-tomato pizza that ropes in a trendy clientele.

VERNON

At the northern end of the Okanagan Valley, Vernon is surrounded by Kalamalka, Okanagan, and Swan Lakes, and has more of those pleasant Okanagan beaches that draw the vacationers. At the point where 25th Avenue crosses Highway 97 at the southern approach to the town stands **Polson Park**, where delightful oriental gardens offer a haven of shade and tranquillity. There's also a floral clock in the park. To acquaint yourself with the history of the town you should visit the **Vernon Museum and Archives** ((250) 542-3142, at 3009 32nd Avenue, where you can see old photographs of the town, costumes, carriages, displays on the pioneering days, and a collection of native artifacts. It is open Monday to Saturday and admission is free.

For a fascinating peek at the past take Highway 97 for 12 km (seven and a half miles) north of Vernon to the **O'Keefe Historic Ranch** ((250) 542-7868, one of the first ranches to appear in the area and one of the biggest in the entire province at the turn of the century. You can see O'Keefe's original log house, a general store, a blacksmith's shop, an early Roman Catholic church, and a fully furnished mansion house. Cornelius O'Keefe was one of the first cattle ranchers to come to the area, after which he seems to have made a valiant effort to populate the region. With his first wife he raised nine children, and after her death he remarried and had several more by his second wife. The O'Keefes lived at the ranch from 1867 until 1977, and many of their furnishings and possessions remain here. The site is open daily from mid-May to mid-October; an admission fee is charged.

Summer and winter, the **Silver Star Mountain Resort** ((250) 542-0224 TOLL-FREE IN THE UNITED STATES (800) 663-4431 FAX (250) 542-1236, PO Box 2, Silver Star Mountain V1B 3M1, 22 km (14 miles) east of town, has much to tempt outdoor lovers. From May to September it has some very pleasant hiking or cycling trails with views of the Coast Mountains. The resort, which has been built to look as though it's straight out of a Western, has accommodation, restaurants, and entertainment. In winter the bikes and boots are replaced by skis and snowmobiles, as the resort is awash with cross-country and downhill skiers. To get there, take 48th Avenue off Highway 97. En route you'll come across a turnoff (Tillicum Road) that leads to **Cedar Hot Springs**, where you can relax in warm mineral spring water in a delightful forest setting.

In Vernon there are plenty of motels to choose from, but for something a little different try the **Vance Creek Hotel** ((250) 549-5191 FAX (250) 549-5177, PO Box 3002, Silver Star Mountain V0E 1G0. Like a set out of a spaghetti Western, the Vance Creek has a choice location in the center of the resort. Rooms on the first floor have kitchenettes, bunk beds, and private entrances. Fireplaces and Willow furniture add a touch of additional comfort to suites in the newer annex. Prices fall within the mid-range category.

The Silver Star Mountain Resort has good eating: The **Craigellachie Dining Room** ((250) 542-2459, at the Putnam Station Hotel, serves hearty meals including soups and sandwiches for lunch and traditional favorites such as barbecued spared ribs, lasagna, steaks, and pastas in the evening. The **Silver Lode Restaurant** ((250) 549-5105, at the Swiss Hotel Silver Lode Inn, serves authentic raclettes and fondues in a cheerful atmosphere.

HOW TO GET THERE

Greyhound TOLL-FREE (800) 661-8747 links Vancouver with Penticton, Kelowna, and Vernon. In Penticton the bus station ((250) 493-4101 is off Main Street between Robinson and Ellis streets. In Kelowna there is a station ((604) 860-3835 at 2366 Leckie Road, from which a regular service runs to Banff and Calgary; another links with Vernon, Kamloops and Prince George. In Vernon the Greyhound station ((604) 542-1415 is at 3700 33rd Street.

If you're driving north from Washington State, you'll probably want to take Highway 97. It runs northwards from the United States border through the Okanagan Valley. At the north end of the valley the Trans-Canada Highway links with Highway 97 and 97A, and motorists coming from Vancouver can take Highway 3 then 3A to Penticton.

GLACIER AND MOUNT REVELSTOKE NATIONAL PARKS

Just before it reaches the Rockies, the Trans-Canada Highway runs through Glacier National Park ((250) 837-7500 E-MAIL revglacier_reception @pch.gc.ca, PO Box 350, Revelstoke V0E 2S0, a rugged area high in the Columbia Mountains containing hundreds of glaciers, waterfalls, and rain forests. This is the birthplace of North American mountaineering and mountain climbing challenges abound. There are over 20 hiking trails — some short, some aimed at the more

The Canadian Rockies — A felled evergreen, reminder of Nature's cycle of growth and death.

adventurous hiker. A number of backpacking trails are easily accessed. The more difficult trails often provide the best scenic rewards. The ski season begins in November and lasts almost to June. The spectacular terrain and heavy snowfalls of the Selkirk Mountains combine to produce some of the best ski touring opportunities in North America. Snow shoeing and winter camping. Avalanches are a danger here. At the center of the park, **Roger's Pass** has some magnificent views and the **Roger's Pass Centre** ☎ (250) 837-6274, has maps of the park and pamphlets on the various trails. It's open daily year-round, and admission is free with your park pass.

Just west of Glacier, the smaller Mount Revelstoke National Park ☎ (250) 837-7500 E-MAIL revglacier_reception@pch.gc.ca, PO Box 350, Revelstoke V0E 2S0 is a favorite destination for mountain bikers and hikers. Ten trails with differing levels of difficulty and great Rocky Mountain scenery make it a popular park. Two of the most accessible hikes consist of boardwalks that lead off into the countryside from Highway 1. The **Skunk Cabbage Trail** runs 1.2 km (three quarters of a mile) through towering skunk cabbage patches, and the **Giant Cedars Trail** is a 500-m (one-third-of-a-mile) jaunt through a majestic cedar forest where some of the trees are more than 1,000 years old. You can also drive the 24 km (14 miles) up the **Meadows in the Sky Parkway** (Summit Road) and from the top hike the one-kilometer (half-mile) trail to beautiful alpine meadows. Nearby, the **Revelstoke Dam** ☎ (250) 837-6515 on Highway 23, has a visitor center and a free tour. It's open daily in summer 8 AM to 8 PM, with reduced hours in spring and fall.

At Roger's Pass, you'll find the moderately priced **Best Western Glacier Park Lodge** ☎ (250) 837-2126, Glacier National Park, Roger's Pass V0E 2S0, with heated outdoor pool and 140 km (87 miles) of groomed hiking trails.

PRINCE RUPERT

Situated near the southern tip of Alaska's southeastern panhandle, Prince Rupert is a popular point of departure for trips into northern British Columbia, the Yukon and Alaska, and a pleasant place to spend a day or two.

Until the last decade, Rupert earned its living from the sea. Now that the fish stocks are depleted, the city is casting about for other ways to sustain its economy. Tourism perhaps. If it weren't for the fact that this is the rainiest city in Canada (more than 236 cm or 93 inches fall each year), Rupert would be awash with visitors. It has an excellent regional museum where you can learn about the area's first residents — the Tsimshian and Haida natives, some good seafood restaurants, and it is the gateway to one of the most beautiful valleys in Canada, the Skeena. As it is, there's a steady flow of international visitors since this port town is a major transportation center. Both the ferries and the railroad begin and end here, and a few kilometers west of Rupert is the start of the scenic Stewart-Cassiar Highway, which runs to Watson Lake in the Yukon Territory.

GENERAL INFORMATION

The **Visitor Infocentre** ☎ (250) 624-5637 TOLL-FREE (800) 667-1994 FAX (250) 627-8009 is located inside the Museum of Northern British Columbia, 101 First Avenue East. For advance information, write them at PO Box 669-SATC, Prince Rupert V8J 3S1. There is **Internet access** at the public library, 101 Sixth Avenue West. The major **rental car agencies** are located in the Rupert Square Shopping Centre on Second Avenue. Free transfers from these outlets to and from the airport and ferry docks can sometimes be arranged.

WHAT TO SEE AND DO

The **Museum of Northern British Columbia** ☎ (250) 624-3207, 101 First Avenue West, is housed in an impressive building constructed to resemble a native longhouse. Inside is a small but excellent collection of Tsimshian and Haida artifacts including carved masks in wood and argillite (a rare black stone found only on the Queen Charlotte Islands which by law can only be carved by the Haida), reed baskets, and ceremonial dress. The gift shop is an excellent place to pick up regional souvenirs. Summer hours are Monday to Saturday from 9 AM to 8 PM and Sunday from 9 AM to 5 PM; winter hours are Monday to Saturday from 9 AM to 5 PM. An admission fee is charged.

The museum has a number of special programs. In June and July the **archeological harbor tour** offers a chance to learn about the Tsimshian culture with visits to archeological digs and historic villages and settlements. The Tsimshian have inhabited the area since before the time of the pyramids in Egypt. Across the street from the museum is the **carving shed** — where First Nations carvers can be seen at work in their studio. Hours vary but admission is free. Consult the museum for additional information on special programs.

A short walk from the museum will take you to the harbor front and, more specifically, to Cow Bay, the most delightful part of the town. The **Cow Bay Historic District** has souvenir and craft shops, good restaurants and a fishing village atmosphere that the rest of Rupert lacks, being cutoff from the waterfront by the railway. The best souvenir **shopping** is here where native artwork can be found for sale in shops and workshops. This part of town is quite pleasant for strolling and browsing. But bring an umbrella.

The **North Pacific Cannery Village Museum** ☎ (250) 628-3538 is British Columbia's oldest surviving salmon cannery and is a national historic site and well worth the short drive along Highway 16 to Port Edward. Tours are give throughout the day, along with a live one-woman performance that relates personal stories from an important chapter in the region's history. Visitors can see how the cannery operated and learn about the hundreds of First Nations people, Japanese, Chinese, and Europeans who worked and lived there. The cannery is situated on the scenic Inverness Passage, about 20 km (12 miles) south of Prince Rupert. It's open daily, May 1 to September 30 from 9 AM to 6 PM. An admission fee is charged.

Where to Stay and Eat

The inexpensively priced **Parry Place Bed & Breakfast** ☎ (250) 624-5887 TOLL-FREE (800) 565-3500 FAX (250) 624-8176 E-MAIL norwood@itytel.net, 133 Parry Place, Prince Rupert V8J 4B1, offers comfortable rooms, some with private bath. Breakfast is a cornucopia of fresh fruits, pastries, and bagels with cheese, smoked salmon. The hosts are longtime residents — very knowledgeable, good conversationalists, and most welcoming. They're full of ideas for itineraries since they've boated and camped all over the area, including the Queen Charlotte Islands and Southeast Alaska. Parry Place is close to the ferry docks, and pickup and drop off can be arranged. French is spoken.

Downtown, the **Crest Motor Hotel** ☎ (250) 624-6771 FAX (250) 627-7666, 222 First Avenue West, Prince Rupert V8J 3P6, offers run-of-the-mill mid-range accommodation, with a lounge, coffee shop, and restaurant at your service.

For an entirely unique experience stay at the **Inverness Bed & Breakfast** ☎ (250) 628-3375 E-MAIL duggle@well.com, 1889 Skeena Drive, Port Edward V0V 1G0. It's located within the North Pacific Cannery Village Museum (see WHAT TO SEE AND DO, above). Rates are inexpensive and breakfast is served at the historic Cannery Café. It's open April 15 to October 30.

For no-frills lodging, the drab but tidy **Pioneer Rooms** ☎ (250) 624-2334, 167 Third Avenue, one block east of MacBridge Avenue, has the cheapest sleeps in town. Laundry facilities are available.

If you ask locals where to find the best seafood, they'll undoubtedly recommend **Smile's Seafood Café** (250) 624-3072, 1 Cow Bay Road, which has been in business since 1934. **Cow Bay Café** ☎ (250) 627-1212, 205 Cow Bay Road, is good too and has a nice view of the harbor. The chef at the **Cannery Café** ☎ (250) 628-3375 in nearby Port Edward lived and worked at the historic North Pacific Cannery before it's closure in the late 1960s. The quaint building is the former mess house for the cannery. Salmon, naturally, is the specialty. Next to the Museum of Northern British Columbia, the moderately price **Pegleg's Seaside Grill** ☎ (250) 624-5667, 3-101 First Avenue East, has a vast menu including everything from seafood to Tex-Mex and daily specials such as a halibut curry. There's a very pleasant deck that looks out over the Pacific Mariner's Memorial Park, with its beslickered sailor pointing wistfully out to sea

How to Get There

The **Alaska Marine Highway** ☎ (907) 627-1744 or (907) 627-1745 TOLL-FREE (800) 642-0066, PO Box 25535, Juneau, Alaska 99802 USA, links Rupert with the Alaska panhandle, including

Skagway where there are bus, train and road connections to the Yukon. **BC Ferries** ☎ (250) 624-9627 serve the Queen Charlotte Islands and Port Hardy on Vancouver Island. The ferry docks are at the west end of town on Fairview Road.

Greyhound ☎ (250) 624-5090 has daily service to Vancouver and Prince George. The station is at 822 Third Avenue West. The **VIA Rail** station ☎ (250) 627-7589 is located toward the waterfront on Bill Murray Way. Trains run to Prince George where BC Rail continues to Vancouver (but an overnight stay is required). The airport is on Digby Island, and the ferry/bus connection to downtown takes about 45 minutes. **Air BC** ☎ (250) 624-4554, 112 Sixth Street, and **Canadian Airlines** (250) 624-9181, ground floor of Rupert Square Mall, Second Avenue, connect Rupert with Vancouver. Ask about standby flights as they can sometimes be the cheaper than the bus or train.

Motorists will have no trouble getting into and out of Rupert since there's only one road: Highway 16, the Yellowhead Highway from Prince George.

ABOVE: "North to Alaska!" The intersection of British Columbia's Skeena and Cassiar highways beckons the adventurer to northern British Columbia and beyond. OVERLEAF: On the Queen Charlotte Islands, sea kayaks bear classic Haida designs representing the fauna of the region.

THE SKEENA VALLEY

From Prince Rupert, the Yellowhead Highway runs through a major cleft in British Columbia's Coast Mountains forming the **Skeena Valley**. It was once a vital trade and travel link for Tsimshian and interior native bands who's name for the valley, K'Shian, means "river of mists." One of the most beautiful drives in Canada, the Skeena's fog-shrouded karst mountain scenery is reminiscent of a Chinese silk painting. The drive is also an excellent opportunity to spot wildlife such as black bears, and bald eagles. Recreational possibilities abound along the valley.

The **'Ksan Historical Village** ☎ (250) 842-5544, PO Box 326, Hazelton V0J 1Y0, is a replica of an ancient village along the Skeena River where for thousands of years the Gitksan people lived. Guided tours take visitors through longhouses where artifacts and multimedia exhibits tell the story of how the clan lived before and after European contact. On display are marvelously complex Chilkat blankets, "button" blankets, wood carvings including painted spirit masks, totem poles, and ceremonial costumes. There are dance performances periodically throughout the summer months. The village is open daily from mid-April through September. Admission is by donation, and guided tours of the three longhouses housing exhibits are offered several times daily.

THE QUEEN CHARLOTTE ISLANDS

Sometimes referred to as "the Canadian Galapagos" for their ecological uniqueness, the Queen Charlotte Islands, 130 km (78 miles) west of Prince Rupert, form an archipelago made up of two principle islands, Graham and Moresby, and 180 surrounding islets. Most of the islands' 5,000 inhabitants live on Graham Island, in six communities, and about a third of the islands' residents are Haida.

The **Visitor Information Centre** ☎ (250) 559-8316 or (250) 559-8594 FAX (250) 559-8952 is in Queen Charlotte City on Wharf Street at the east end of town. They have information on Gwaii Haanas and the islands as a whole as well as natural history presentations. They sell the useful *Guide to the Queen Charlotte Islands* and detailed maps of the towns. For information specifically on Gwaii Haanas, contact the Superintendent, Gwaii Haanas (South Moresby National Park Marine Reserve) ☎ (250) 559-8818 FAX (250) 559-8366, PO Box 37, Queen Charlotte V0T 1S0.

WHAT TO SEE AND DO

Visitors are drawn to the Charlottes for a chance to see the ancient remnants of the Haida culture and for the archipelago's gorgeous wilderness scenery. With its rugged west coast and sandy eastern beaches, the islands are a delight for view-seekers, and kayakers come from all over the world to paddle the waterways and coastline. Scuba divers find a watery paradise on Graham Island's west coast at Rennell Sound, where shore dives are possible from many points along the coastal logging road.

The Charlottes have about 120 km (75 miles) of paved roads, mostly along the shoreline on the east coast of Graham Island. In the northeast corner of Graham Island, **Naikoon Provincial Park** ☎ (250) 557-4390 protects a wilderness of rain forest, sandy beaches, dunes, and bogs. In Old Masset (also called Haida) just to the west of Naikoon, there are many Haida sculptors creating works of art in silver, gold, argillite, and wood, as well as prints and woven baskets. You can see the artisans at work here and purchase crafts. On the southern end of Graham Island, in Skidegate, there is the **Queen Charlotte Islands Museum** ☎ (250) 559-4643 with exhibits of Haida totem poles, masks, and carvings of silver and argillite, as well as a natural history exhibit on the wildlife of the islands.

From Graham Island there is hourly BC Ferry service to Moresby Island, a 20-minute crossing. Canada's newest national park, **Sgan Gwaii** — a UNESCO World Heritage Site — is located here, part of **Gwaii Haanas** (also known as South Moresby National Park Marine Reserve). Permission to enter the area is given by the Haida Gwaii Watchmen ☎ (250) 259-8225, PO Box 609, Skidegate, Haida Gwaii, V0T 1S0. The office is located at Second Beach, which is just north of Skidegate Landing along Highway 16. A journey to these sites begins with registration at the Parks Canada office (at the airport or in Queen Charlotte City) and an orientation session. The park, which covers the southern two thirds of the Queen Charlottes, is only accessible by boat or plane. There are some 500 archeological and historical sites here, maintained by the Haida Nation. The best way to experience the park is to go along with an experienced guide, such as **Moresby Explorers** ☎ (250) 637-2215 TOLL-FREE (800) 806-7633, Beach Road, Sandspit, or **Queen Charlotte Adventures** ☎ (250) 559-8990 FAX (250) 559-8983 TOLL-FREE (800) 668-4288, outside Queen Charlotte City on the road to Skidegate.

WHERE TO STAY

Most visitors stay and eat in Queen Charlotte, the largest town in the islands, but all of the islands' communities have a least some tourist facilities,

Queen Charlotte Islands — ABOVE: Haida in ceremonial dress. The drum at right bears the image of the killer whale. BELOW: An ancient Haida totem pole greets the dawn on Ninstits Island.

including many small bed and breakfast places; contact the **Queen Charlotte Travel Infocentre** ☎ (250) 559-4742 FAX (250) 559-8188, 3922 Highway 33, PO Box 819, Queen Charlotte V0T 1S0, for a list of establishments. Reservations are recommended for Queen Charlotte City lodging.

How to Get There

Year-round air service is available with Canadian Airlines International from Vancouver to Sandspit. For transportation from the airport to Queen Charlotte City, contact **Rikka Travel** ☎ (250) 559-4400, 119 Third Avenue in Queen Charlotte City. **Rental cars** are available at Masset, Queen Charlotte, and Sandspit. From Prince Rupert, **BC Ferries** ☎ (250) 559-4485 makes the six-hour crossing six times a week in summer, docking on Graham Island's south side. (Note that this is an open-sea crossing. Landlubbers may want to bring along their favorite seasickness remedy.) Reservations are strongly recommended. There is also daily floatplane service from Rupert to Sandspit, Queen Charlotte City, and Masset.

NORTHERN BRITISH COLUMBIA

A remote and sparsely inhabited area, Northern British Columbia has much in common with the neighboring Yukon Territory. Despite the logging and mining activities that have dominated the region's economy for 100 years, it remains virtually unspoiled — a land of great beauty and seemingly endless bounty. Intrepid travelers come for fishing, hiking through untouched mountain terrain, soaking in hot spring, and for the incomparable solitude.

Starting off from the Trans-Canada Highway (Highway 1) at Cache Creek, the **Cariboo Highway** (Highway 97) runs north, passing through the Fraser Valley to the interior ranch lands. Williams Lake is a major cattle-country pit stop. Further north along the Cariboo, you run into former mining country, then into the lumber and paper mill hub of Prince George. From Prince George the route divides: the northern section crosses the Rockies then joins the **Alaska Highway** at Dawson Creek; the west fork traverses the Hudson Bay Range, through the Skeena Valley with its First Nations villages to the port of Prince Rupert.

A flock of plovers takes to the air.

The Canadian Rockies

STRADDLING THE BORDER OF ALBERTA AND BRITISH COLUMBIA, the Rocky Mountain parks encompass some of the most breathtakingly beautiful scenery on earth. The area encompassing Kootenay, Banff, Jasper, and Yoho national parks, together with Mount Robson Provincial Park and Mount Assiniboine, is recognized as a UNESCO World Heritage Site, one of the largest protected areas in the world. In this vast nature preserve, white mountain peaks and glaciers tower over aquamarine lakes, rivers and waterfalls rush through forested valleys, and wild animals run free. North American mountaineering had its birthplace in these mountains, and adventurers from all over the world continue to pour in each year.

All of the parks present a wealth of opportunities for outdoor enthusiasts, with trails to be walked, mountains to be climbed, lakes and rivers to be fished and navigated, and in the winter a thick coat of snow turns it all into a skiers' paradise. Here in the mountains the temperature varies quite a lot, and the higher you are, the colder it is, making warm clothing an essential part of vacation luggage, even in July.

Wildlife abounds in this protected area and visitors need not go off the beaten track for glimpses of elk, deer, bighorn sheep, and an abundance of clever squirrels. Moose, black bears and grizzlies, and mountain goats are often spotted by hikers. Throughout your visit you will be constantly reminded not to feed the animals, both for their good and for your own, and to keep your distance. These animals are wild, despite their apparent ease around people. To drive the message home, the park authorities have imposed heavy fines on those caught feeding animals.

Besides being rich in wildlife and spectacular scenery, the Rocky Mountains are an open book on the earth's geological history. The sedimentary rock that makes up the mountain chain was laid down over eons beginning 600 million years ago when a vast sea covered the region. Eventually these sediments built up a 20-km (12-mile) thick layer of rock. One hundred and forty million years ago, continental drift caused the mountains to begin to rise of out of the sea. At the same time that the mountains were lifting up the force of water and weather were wearing them down, reshaping the landscape until it began to take on the grand aspect that we see today.

BANFF NATIONAL PARK

Banff National Park is the most famous of the mountain parks, and the most popular. Situated about 113 km (70 miles) west of Calgary along the Trans-Canada Highway, Banff has two townsites that attract thousands of visitors from around the world: Banff and the smaller Lake Louise, both of which have splendid and superbly located castle-like hotels built by the Canadian Pacific Railway. The town of Banff is the park's main center for entertainment, accommodation, and restaurants, and is also the starting point for tours and trails into the park.

Banff was the first national park to be established in Canada. The region was explored in 1841 by the governor of the Hudson's Bay Company, but it was in the 1880s with the coming of the Canadian Pacific Railway that word of the area's great beauty began to spread. During the laying of the tracks three workers discovered some hot sulfur springs, and as soon as word of them got out, visitors began to arrive. In 1885 the government created the Rocky Mountain Park around the springs to preserve the area, and in 1888 the Canadian Pacific Railway opened the magnificent Banff Springs Hotel, a summer resort that was the last word in luxury. A beautiful golf course was laid, trips and expeditions were organized for its guests, and every whim was catered for. People came from far and wide, the town developed, the boundaries of the park were expanded and its name was changed to Banff National Park. Today it covers an area of 6,640 sq km (2,600 sq miles).

GENERAL INFORMATION

Travel Alberta ☎ (403) 427-4321 TOLL-FREE (800) 661-8888 WEB SITE www.discoveralberta.com/html/Canada/Alberta/, PO Box 2500, Edmonton, Alberta T5J 2Z4, **Tourism British Columbia** ☎ (604) 685-0032 TOLL-FREE (800) 663-6000 WEB SITE www.tbc.gov.bc.ca/tourism/, Parliament Buildings, Victoria, British Columbia V8V 1X4, and **Parks Canada** ☎ (403) 292-4401 TOLL-FREE (800) 651-7959 FAX (403) 292-6004 WEB SITE parkscanada.pch.gc.ca/, 220 Fourth Street SE, Room 552, Calgary T2G 4X3, are all good sources of informa-

Visitors to Banff and Jasper need not get off the beaten track for glimpses of bighorn sheep ABOVE and elk OPPOSITE BOTTOM. A snow-covered Banff church TOP rests below Mount Rundle.

THE CANADIAN ROCKIES
0 20 40 miles
0 33 66 Km
N
E
S
W
BRITISH COLUMBIA
ALBERTA
ROCKY MOUNTAINS
Westlock
Barrhead
Whitecourt
Gibbons
St. Albert
Edmonton
Spruce Grove
Peers
Edson
Leduc
Drayton Valley
Wetaskiwin
Robb
Wilmore Wilderness Park
Miette Hot Springs
Medicine Lake
Jasper National Park
Rocky Mountains Forest Reserve
Red Deer Lake
Jasper
Maligne Lake
Mt. Edith Cavell 3363
Red Deer
Nordegg
Rocky Mountain House
Columbia Icefield
Sunwapta Pass 2035
Athabasca Glacier
Icefields Parkway
Olds
Kinbasket Lake
Mistaya Canyon
Peyto Lake
Didsbury
Banff National Park
Mica Creek
Bow Lake
Airdrie
Hector Lake
Lake Louise
Lake Louise Village
Yoho N.P.
Lake Minnewanka
Cochrane
Mt. Stephen 3149
Donald
Field
Bow River
Calgary
Golden
Banff
Canmore
Glacier National Park
Kootenay National Park
Mt. Assiniboine National Park
Mt. Revelstoke N.P.
Revelstoke
Bugaboo Alpine Recreation Area
Radium Hot Springs
Trout Lake
Salmon Arm
Fairmont Hot Springs
KANANASKIS COUNTRY
Monashee Lake Park
Upper Arrow Lake
Duncan Lake
Nakusp
Vernon
Top of the World Park
Sparwood
Arrow Park
Kokanee Glacier Park
Kootenay Lake
Kimberley
Fernie
Kelowna
Cranbrook
Lower Arrow Lake
Nelson

tion on the parks. The park information centers carry maps, pamphlets, and brochures, which include details of the various trips and trails throughout the area. They also give valuable advice on how to protect yourself against attack from animals, on weather conditions, and on survival skills.

For information specifically on Banff and region, contact or visit the **Park Information Centre** ☎ (403) 762-1550 at 224 Banff Avenue, PO Box 900, Banff T0L 0C0, **Banff-Lake Louise Tourism Bureau** ☎ (403) 762-8421 at the same address, or the **Lake Louise Visitor Centre** ☎ (403) 522-3833, Village Road, beside Samson Mall, PO Box 213, Lake Louise T0L 1E0. If you're planning on an overnight hiking trip, you must sign in at either the Banff or Lake Louise information center. **Internet access** is available in Banff at Internet Services ☎ (403) 762-5149, 210 Bear Street, but rates are steep.

WHAT TO SEE AND DO

Banff

Sixteen kilometers (10 miles) beyond the park gates, the town of Banff lies in the Bow River valley, nestling close to the base of Cascade Mountain and shadowed by snowy peaks on all sides. It is the hub of the Banff National Park and Canada's favorite year-round resort. You'll find everything you need here. It is the starting point for scores of trips, some on horseback, some in the bicycle saddle, some on coaches, and others tailored for a variety of outdoor pursuits. There are all kinds of walking trails to places that cars cannot reach, and the most timorous to the most intrepid of hikers will all find something to suit them. But unless you are prepared to hike long distances you will require transport to take you at least part of the way to many of the top attractions.

The town is small, however, and during the peak season of July and August it gets jam-packed, parking becomes a problem, and it can get quite claustrophobic — especially along Banff Avenue, the town's busy main street lined with shops and restaurants.

A Victorian wooden building houses the **Banff Park Museum** ☎ (403) 762-1558, 93 Banff Avenue, where you can see old-fashioned displays of stuffed animals and birds from the park: the only place where you can study some of them up close. There is also a reference library where you can read up on the area. It's open daily year-round; an admission fee is charged. A little further along the road, the **Natural History Museum** ☎ (403) 762-4747, 112 Banff Avenue, deals with the geological formation of the Rockies and the early life forms that inhabited them. There are audiovisual displays, exhibits on dinosaurs, and a model of Sasquatch, the Rockies' version of the abominable snowman. It's open daily; admission is free.

At the southern end of the town near the Bow River, a fortified log building houses the **Luxton Museum** ☎ (403) 762-2388, 1 Birch Avenue, where there are displays on the various native tribes of Alberta, featuring photographs, clothing, and crafts. It's open year-round, daily in summer, Wednesday to Sunday afternoon in winter; an admission fee is charged. The **Whyte Museum of the Canadian Rockies** ☎ (403) 762-2291, at 111 Bear Street, has a gallery devoted to paintings and sculptures of the mountains as well as exhibits chronicling the human history of the region. It also houses archival material, and some historical log cabins. Tea is served on weekend afternoons by the fireside. The museum is open daily from mid-May to mid-October, and is closed on Mondays and on Thursday mornings during the rest of the year. An admission fee is charged.

West of downtown along Cave Avenue you can see the original hot sulfur spring that first brought tourism to the area. Railway workers discovered the Cave and Basin Hot Springs in 1883 and the spa building that surrounds them has been rebuilt in the original 1914 style. Here at the **Cave and Basin Centennial Centre** ☎ (403) 762-1566 you can visit the interpretive display that details the history of the area. It is open daily throughout the year; an admission fee is charged. At the **Upper Hot Springs Pool** ☎ (403) 762-1515, south of town at the top of Mountain Avenue, you can enjoy a dip in the outdoor hot-spring pool (average

Banff Avenue — a corridor of commercialism, but the mountains are never out of view for long.

temperature: 40°C or 108°F), and soak up the glorious mountain views. It's open daily year-round; an admission fee is charged.

About three kilometers (two miles) south of town and next to the Upper Hot Springs is the **Sulphur Mountain Gondola Lift** ☎ (403) 762-2523. Completely remodeled in 1998, the gondola is a gleaming, Swiss-made state-of-the-art aerial tramway to the top of Sulphur Mountain (2,285 m or 7,500 ft). Once at the top you can feast your eyes on the wonderful views from an observation deck with its 360-degree view of the Bow Valley, or follow one of several hiking trails and see bighorn sheep grazing. You can also enjoy a repast at the moderately priced Panorama Room with set dinners featuring salmon and prime rib; or have a light meal or a snack at the Summit Restaurant. The gondola is open daily year-round; a fare is charged.

Following the discovery of the springs, the Canadian Pacific Railway built the **Banff Springs Hotel** (see WHERE TO STAY, below), a magnificently located tourist resort close to the springs. So great was its success that in 1910 the hotel was rebuilt to accommodate the growing number of visitors, and a majestic Scottish baronial-style structure emerged from the pine-covered slopes. If you're not staying at Banff Springs during your visit, you should at least make sure to have a meal there, or take the historical tour, so you can take a look around it and admire the beautiful setting.

The other mountains around the town also have hiking trails, and one of the more gentle climbs close to downtown is up **Tunnel Mountain** along Tunnel Mountain Drive, where you can see the strange column-like rock formations known as **hoodoos**.

For a different angle on the landscape take a trip to **Lake Minnewanka** 11 km (seven miles) west of the town where Lake Minnewanka Tours ☎ (403) 762-3473 will take you on a 90-minute cruise across the waters. Boats sail daily at 10:30 AM, 12:30 PM, 3 PM, and 5 PM, with an evening cruise in July and August at 7 PM; a fare is charged. You can contact the same outfit for guided fishing trips. Nearby, **Two-Jack Lake** is a popular spot for rowing and canoeing.

Northwest of Banff, 28 km (17 miles) along Highway 1A, there's a lovely one-and-a-half-hour hiking trail leading from **Johnston Canyon** that takes you by waterfalls and pools. You can extend the hike by a couple of miles into a lovely meadow where there are some deep-colored underground springs known as the **Ink Pots**.

Lake Louise

In 1882, the explorer Tom Wilson became the first European to lay eyes on Lake Louise, proclaiming: "As God is my judge, I never, in all my explorations of these five chains of mountains throughout western Canada, saw such a matchless scene." The lapis-blue Lake Louise, mirroring the 3,464-m (1,154-ft) tall Victoria Glacier, has been enchanting visitors ever since.

The first question most people ask on arriving at Lake Louise is: "Where's the lake?" That's because the *village* of Lake Louise is located some distance below the actual *lake* of Lake Louise. Most of the amenities are located in the village along with restaurants and lodging. Up at the lake, the Canadian Pacific hotel, Château Lake Louise is piled high along the shore and a few other hotels are strung out along the road to the lake.

The **Samson Mall** is the center of village commercial life with several retail shops and restaurants. Right next door is the **Lake Louise Information Centre** ((403) 522-3833, Village Road and Lake Louise Drive, just off the Trans-Canada Highway. Parks Canada staffs the center year-round and the Banff/Lake Louise Tourism Bureau operates there during summer months. There is an excellent and entertaining interpretive display on mountain formation — a good overview of the fascinating geological history of the Rockies.

Of course, you can't miss seeing Château Lake Louise. Though its exterior is an eyesore, the interior is tastefully lavish. The lobby has a lovely lounge with an arched window looking out on the Victoria Glacier, a wonderful place to stop for refreshment.

Back in the village there are a couple of side trips worth considering. On the other side of the Trans-Canada Highway, four and a half kilometers (almost three miles) from the village, the **Lake Louise Summer Sightseeing Lift** ((403) 522-2095 takes you up Mount Whitehorn (2,040 m or 6,700 ft). There's a teahouse, picnic areas and all sorts of hiking trails to explore at the top. The lift runs daily from June 1 to September 15. And 15 km

(eight miles) south of Lake Louise lies **Moraine Lake**, another beautiful and improbably colored lake that is surrounded by the Wenkchemna Peaks, named for the Stoney native word for the number "ten." Until 1989, these mountains were featured on the Canadian twenty-dollar bill. You will find picnicking and boating facilities here in season.

There are several options for laid-back **hikes** around the village, the most obvious being a the valley-bottom stroll along the Riverside Loop (seven kilometers or four and a half miles) which takes you along the Bow River and past the old train station. If you want to stretch your lungs a bit, take the four-and-a-half-kilometer (three-mile)-long footpath to Lake Louise from the village.

Up at the lake the favorite pastime is gazing at the scenery. As you stroll around the shore on the paved footpaths, look for golden-mantled ground squirrels amongst the rocky banks and Clark's nutcrackers, large gray and black birds with a long black beak. The lake is the starting point for some challenging hikes that lead to the base of the glacier or to a number of other, smaller but equally beautiful glacier-fed lakes. The visitor center has complete and current information on all of the hikes and activities in the area.

SPORTS AND OUTDOOR ACTIVITIES

Both Banff and Lake Louise have a wealth of **hiking** trails of all lengths. Some are little more than short walks, while others are wilderness expeditions that take several days to complete. Parks

All quiet at the boat house — OPPOSITE: Inside Maligne Lake Boathouse, guidesman Barry Wood organizes his gear. ABOVE: Lake Louise canoes wait patiently for the spring melt.

Canada ☎ (403) 292-4401 TOLL-FREE (800) 651-7959 FAX (403) 292-6004 WEB SITE parkscanada.pch.gc.ca/ produces brochures detailing the trails, and copies of these can be picked up from the information centers. If you're planning an overnight hike into the backcountry you will need to buy a permit from either an information center or a park warden. There are also numerous **cycling** trails, which must be strictly adhered to. A few companies operate cycling tours, and renting bikes is easy in both towns. Several companies offer **heli-hiking**, which involves a helicopter trip out to remote spots high on the mountaintops or onto glaciers for some extra-special hiking. If you intend to do a spot of **fishing**, and there certainly are some ideal opportunities in both parks, you must get a national parks fishing license, which can be bought either from an information center or an outfitter. Several places run fishing trips and rent out tackle.

Rivers throughout both parks offer opportunities for **whitewater rafting**, and information centers can supply you with lists of the companies who operate guided trips. If you're interested in **boating** or **canoeing**, there are many beautiful lakes to choose from, most of which have places that rent out a variety of vessels. **Motorboats** are permitted only on Minnewanka Lake.

Horseback riders have a choice of many treks of varying lengths and designed for all abilities. There are several stables in both parks, including one at the Banff Springs Hotel. The information centers have details of where the stables are and what they have to offer.

During the winter there's excellent **skiing** throughout the parks. Banff's nearest slopes are at Mount Norquay ☎ (403) 762-4421 SNOW PHONE (403) 762-4421 extension 6, only five kilometers (three miles) away from town, and the well-equipped Sunshine Village Resort ☎ (403) 762-6500 SNOW PHONE (403) 760-6543, about 16 km (10 miles) west of the town, where there are ski lifts and more than 60 runs. Sunshine Village comprises a 1960s-era hotel and several restaurants. In summer there are hiking trails that lead through alpine meadows. At Lake Louise there's the Lake Louise Ski Area ☎ (403) 522-3555 SNOW PHONE (403) 762-4766 offering runs of up to eight kilometers (five miles), some of the longest runs in the Rockies.

NIGHTLIFE AND THE ARTS

Banff's cultural life revolves around the **Banff Centre** ☎ (403) 762-6300 TOLL-FREE (800) 413-8368, which is near downtown at St. Julien Road. You'll almost always find there's a concert, a play, or a film presented here, and between June and August it is the venue for the world-famous **Banff Arts Festival**, when a program of theater, music, and dance is presented. For information on current and upcoming events, phone or visit the box office in the lobby of the Eric Harvie Theatre ☎ (403) 762-6301 TOLL-FREE (800) 413-8368, St. Julien Road.

There are several busy bars in Banff, mostly around Banff Avenue, and some in the hotels. Several have live musical entertainment. **Barbary Coast** ☎ (403) 762-4616, 119 Banff Avenue, has blues, funk, and jazz bands in its upstairs lounge. Celtic and maritime bands are featured at the **St. James's Gate Olde Irish Pub** ☎ (403) 762-9355, 205 Wolf Street. For country and western as well as live rock bands, there's **Wild Bill's** ☎ (403) 762-0333, upstairs at 201 Banff Avenue, which also has line-dancing lessons every Wednesday night.

WHERE TO STAY

Reservations are strongly advised for the summer season in both Banff and Lake Louise. **Banff/ Lake Louise Central Reservations** ☎ (403) 762-5561 TOLL-FREE (800) 661-1676 can help you sort out the dizzying options.

Banff

EXPENSIVE

The most renowned accommodation in the Rockies is at the **Banff Springs Hotel** ☎ (403) 762-2211 TOLL-FREE (800) 441-1414 FAX (403) 762-5755, on Spray Avenue, PO Box 960, Banff, Alberta T0L 0C0, a splendid château overlooking the Spray Valley and surrounded by towering peaks. It was here in 1882 that the Canadian Pacific Railway built its first resort hotel, to encourage tourism in the area. It was so popular that it soon had to be replaced by this larger structure, which was completed in 1928 — with no expense spared. It remains a resort with riding stables, skiing and fishing packages available, almost every kind of sports facility, including one of the most spectacular golf courses anywhere. There are 841 beautiful rooms and suites, 14 restaurants, a library, shops, and services. At the new European-style spa **Solace** you can bask in the myriad mineral pools or simply lounge by the fireside. A frighteningly thorough list of "therapies" is available here, from "fresh cell RNA/DNA" to "alphahydroxy AHA peels" — all designed to make you beautifully relaxed. Despite its many offerings, this massive hotel may not be to everyone's tastes. Its very fame works against it: Tour groups may receive preferential treatment, and overbooking can be a problem in peak seasons. Rates start in the expensive category and mount skyward.

Though the Banff Springs is more famous, many say the **Rimrock Resort** ☎ (403) 762-3356 FAX (403) 762-4132 TOLL-FREE (800) 661-1587, 100 Mountain Avenue, Banff, Alberta T0L 0C0, on the road to the Sulphur Mountain Gondola, is the place to go if you want to do Banff in style. This 345-room hotel is magnificently situated, and amenities are superlative. Equally luxurious, but with a rustic Rocky-mountain atmosphere, the **Buffalo Mountain Lodge** ☎ (403) 762-2400 FAX (403) 762-4495 TOLL-FREE (800) 661-1367, on Tunnel Mountain Road, PO Box 1326, Banff, Alberta T0L 0C0, has 100 rooms and suites with fireplace, whirlpool, and kitchenette. Recent renovations have made this old standby quite popular.

A number of Banff hotels offer good value at the low end of the expensive price range: The **Banff Park Lodge** ☎ (403) 762-4433 TOLL-FREE (800) 661-9266 FAX (403) 762-3553, 222 Lynx Street,

OPPOSITE: The view from Château Lake Louise. ABOVE: The elegant Banff Springs Hotel.

PO Box 2200, Banff, Alberta T0L 0C0, is just a couple of blocks away from the town's main street, and elegantly decorated throughout, with 210 rooms with balconies. There is an indoor swimming pool, restaurants, and a lounge. **Inns of Banff** ☎ (403) 762-4581 TOLL-FREE (800) 661-1272 FAX (403) 762-2434, 600 Banff Avenue, PO Box 1077, Banff, Alberta T0L 0C0, is an attractive resort, where the rooms have balconies and lots of luxurious touches. It has an indoor and a large outdoor swimming pool, a squash court, a good dining room and lounge, and a Japanese restaurant. The hotel offers special winter ski packages with a ski rental and repair shop on site. The newly renovated **Douglas Fir Resort and Chalets** ☎ (403) 762-5591 FAX (403) 762-8774, PO Box 1228, Banff, Alberta T0L 0C0, is a particularly good choice for families with its tangle of indoor water slides. Accommodation is in rustic chalets with kitchenette, fireplace and patio looking out onto wooded grounds where elk graze. There's a small grocery store on the premises.

MID-RANGE TO INEXPENSIVE

At the high end of the mid-range price category, there are two hotels at which share the excellent facilities at the Inns of Banff resort: **Rundle Manor Apartments/Hotel** ☎ (403) 762-5544 TOLL-FREE (800) 661-1272 FAX (403) 762-0703, 348 Marten Street, PO Box 1077, Banff, Alberta T0L 0C0, is an attractive stone building which has 24 large units with kitchenettes, including some one- and two-bedroom suites. The **Swiss Village** ☎ (403) 762-4581 TOLL-FREE (800) 661-1272 FAX (403) 762-2434, 600 Banff Avenue, Banff, Alberta T0L 0C0, has 50 units and offers ski packages.

Whatever the season, our favorite place to stay in Banff is **Eleanor's House** (403) 760-2457 FAX (403) 762-3852 E-MAIL info@bbeleanor.com, 125 Kootenay Avenue, PO Box 1553, Banff, Alberta T0L 0C0. Here guests have the best of both worlds: a friendly host with boundless energy (that's Eleanor) and the comfort and privacy of an inn (rooms are located in an addition to a private home). You can enjoy the company of other guests at breakfast or at evening cocktails in front of the cozy fireplace. Rooms are tastefully and comfortably furnished with en-suite bath, and the house is conveniently located in a quiet residential area within a few paces of downtown. Rates are in the high end of the mid-range. Winter ski-week packages are inexpensive — an excellent deal.

In all there are some 25 bed and breakfast places in Banff. For a list, contact the **Bed and Breakfast Bureau** ☎ (403) 762-2110, 121 Cave Avenue, Banff, Alberta T0L 0C0.

The **Banff International Hostel** ☎ 403) 762-4122, PO Box 1358, Tunnel Mountain Road, Banff, Alberta T0L 0C0, three kilometers (two miles) outside downtown on Tunnel Mountain Road, is an attractive building with good facilities and accommodation for 154 people.

Lake Louise

In Lake Louise Village, the **Post Hotel** ☎ (403) 522-3989 TOLL-FREE (800) 661-1586 FAX (403) 522-3966, PO Box 69, Lake Louise, Alberta T0L 1E0, is a lovely alpine-style building with 100 rooms and suites, some of which have lofts and large riverstone fireplaces, while others have self-catering facilities. Suites have generous bathrooms with Jacuzzi and plush bathrobes to snuggle into afterwards. Balconies look out over neatly trimmed lawns with stands of spruce and the sparkling Pipestone River. The hotel has an indoor swimming pool, the best dining room in the region, and a cozy tavern. In winter, the Post is the perfect ski lodge; in summer, it's just plain paradise. Rates are solidly in the expensive category.

Above the village, overlooking the beautiful ultramarine-blue waters of the lake, **Château Lake Louise** ☎ (403) 522-3511 TOLL-FREE (800) 441-1414 FAX (403) 522-3834, Lake Louise, Alberta T0L 1E0, is another historic Canadian Pacific hotel. This pile of a hotel adds nothing to the scenic beauty of the lake, but inside there are 510 attractive rooms and suites with spectacular views. The hotel boasts a good restaurant, evening entertainment, riding stables, indoor pools — and there's canoeing on the lake. Room rates are in the expensive range. Canadian Pacific recently announced an expansion of the hotel with 80 new guestrooms to be added. This will be the last expansion of this already immense property as the government of Alberta has (thankfully) banned further construction around Lake Louise. Renovations are slated to be completed in 2002.

The **Lake Louise Inn** ☎ (403) 522-3791 TOLL-FREE (800) 661-9237 FAX (403) 522-2018, 210 Village Road, PO Box 209, Lake Louise, Alberta T0L 1E0, has 220 rooms and suites, including some with fireplaces and kitchenettes, all with beautiful views of the surrounding woods. It has tennis courts, and an indoor swimming pool. The inn runs a free shuttle to Ski Lake Louise. Prices here vary between mid-range and expensive.

Despite its reputation as an exclusive destination, Lake Louise does have a good budget option. Conveniently located in the village center, the **Canadian Alpine Centre & International Hostel** (HI) ☎ (403) 522-2200, PO Box 115, Village Road, Lake Louise, Alberta T0L 1E0, is jointly run by Hostelling International and the Alpine Club of Canada. There are two-, four-, and six-person rooms, private showers and bathrooms, laundry facilities, a central kitchen for self-catering, and a café.

Skiers at Lake Louise.

WHERE TO EAT

Banff

Many of Banff's best tables are found in its hotels. You could eat your way through the restaurants at Banff Springs Hotel for two weeks without exhausting the options. The top table here is the elegant **Rob Roy Dining Room** ☎ (403) 762-6860, specializing in tableside flambées. But you'd miss something special indeed if you limited yourself to Banff Springs' 11 restaurants, because the best restaurant in Banff is the **Dining Room at the Buffalo Mountain Lodge** ☎ (403) 762-2400 FAX (403) 762-4495 TOLL-FREE (800) 661-1367 on Tunnel Mountain Road. Here, under a high ceiling built of rough-hewn timbers, diners enjoy unique Canadian cuisine featuring game and fresh flavors. Also at the lodge is the less formal **Cilantro Café** ☎ (403) 760-3008, where California and Southwestern cuisine is served in a quaint log cabin setting or on a pleasant patio.

At least two other hotel restaurants merit mentioning. **The Pines** (Rundlestone Lodge) ☎ (403) 760-6690 serves inventive Canadian cuisine, and like Buffalo Mountain, wild game is a specialty. Under the same ownership is **Ticino's** (High Country Inn) ☎ (403) 762-3848, 415 Banff Avenue, where Swiss-Italian cooking is featured. The antipasto of air-dried beef, coppa ham, and mountain cheeses is a great way to begin your repast. Raclette (melted cheese with boiled potatoes, cured meats and pickles) and pasta dumplings are specialties of the house. You must save room for a *gelato* made from Ticino's specially brewed coffee.

Grizzly House ☎ (403) 762-4055, 207 Banff Avenue, is known for its exotic fondues, some of which feature alligator and rattlesnake. For a more classical approach, there is excellent French cuisine at **Le Beaujolais** ☎ (403) 762-2712, at the corner of Buffalo Street and Banff Avenue. Choose from à la carte dining, the three-course *table d'hôte* dinner, or the six-course "chef's surprise." The sophisticated menu is complemented by an award-winning wine list.

Banff has a multitude of informal dining spots. Steak features on the menu along with burgers at **Melissa's** ☎ (403) 762-5511, at 218 Lynx Street. For good Italian fare try **Giorgio's Trattoria** ☎ (403) 762-5114, at 219 Banff Avenue, where there's a warm, intimate atmosphere, or if pizzas and subs will do, you could go to **Aardvark's** ☎ (403) 762-5500, 304a Caribou Street. For English-style food try the **Rose and Crown** ☎ (403) 762-2121, 202 Banff Avenue (upstairs), and for pan-European dining try the **Paris' Restaurant** ☎ (403) 762-3554, 108 Banff Avenue, with its reputation for generous servings of steak and seafood. Whole Atlantic lobster and schnitzel are house specialties. **Bruno's Café & Grill** ☎ (403) 762-8115, 304 Caribou Street, is a great spot for a casual lunch or dinner; "wraps" (burritos) and paninis are popular choices — but not as popular as the cookies. There's a takeout counter for those in a rush.

The best place for coffee and morning pastries is **Evelyn's Coffee Bar** ☎ (403) 762-0352. Located on Banff Avenue near corner of Caribou Street. This cozy hole-in-the-wall is renowned for its delicious homemade baked goods, which you can enjoy along with French roast coffee or iced cappuccino.

ABOVE: The wintery landscape LEFT at Lake Louise, and the Weeping Wall RIGHT along the Icefields Parkway. OPPOSITE: Moraine Lake, a few kilometers east of Lake Louise.

Lake Louise

Canada's highest village has some very high-caliber dining establishments. Most notable, and not to be missed, is the **Post Hotel** ☎ (403) 522-3989, in Lake Louise Village. Many people consider this the best table in the Rockies. Built in 1942 for alpine enthusiasts, the Post offers European cuisine with a California influence. The dining room is cozy with its low exposed-beam ceiling and wood-burning fireplace. Reserve early to get a window table and a view of the Victoria Glacier. Among the four restaurants at Château Lake Louise is the elegant **Edelweiss Dining Room** ☎ (403) 522-3511 where diners can also revel in glacier views and enjoy Canadian and continental cuisine.

The Samson Mall has a number of inexpensive places to eat, including **Bee Line** ☎ (403) 522-2077, with chicken and takeout pizza by the slice; the small eat-in or takeout café/bakery **Laggans Deli** ☎ (403) 522-2017; and the **Village Grill and Bar** ☎ (403) 522-3879, for a family sit-down dinner. At the end of Sentinel Street is the **Lake Louise Station Restaurant** ☎ (403) 522-2600, situated in a hundred-year-old log station surrounded by vintage rail cars and gardens. The food is good, if not too imaginative, with Alberta beef and pasta dishes dominating.

How to Get There

The nearest major airport to Banff is **Calgary International**. At the airport you can rent a car from one of several car rental companies if you wish to drive the 120 km (75 miles) to Banff. There is scheduled Airporter motor coach service between Calgary International, Banff, and Lake Louise with **Brewster** ☎ (403) 762-6767 or **Laidlaw Canadian Rockies** ☎ (403) 762-9102 TOLL-FREE (800) 661-4946.

You can join the private train tour to Vancouver, the **Rocky Mountaineer Railtours** ☎ (604) 606-7245 TOLL-FREE (800) 665-7245, at Banff. The depot is at the end of Lynx Street.

In Banff, **Greyhound** ☎ (403) 762-6767 TOLL-FREE (800) 661-8747 operates frequent service to Calgary, Edmonton, and Vancouver. The bus station is on Gopher Street near the train depot. The Trans-Canada Highway (Highway 1) runs through Banff National Park, linking it with Calgary in the east and with Vancouver in the west.

THE ICEFIELDS PARKWAY

Linking Banff with Jasper, the Icefields Parkway is one of the most beautiful drives anywhere, offering those who travel it a spectacular overview of the two national parks. It follows the continental divide along a route lined with glaciers, lakes, valleys, and mountains, where wildlife roams — sometimes into the middle of the road, so you must beware. You should set aside at least a day for traveling the Parkway to allow time for stopping and enjoying the views.

Start at the Lake Louise Visitor Centre (see GENERAL INFORMATION, page 122, under BANFF NATIONAL PARK) where you can get a map and up-to-the-minute information on road conditions (also available by calling ☎ (403) 762-2266). The Parkway runs north from the Trans-Canada Highway. Some 16 km (10 miles) along the Parkway north of Lake Louise you'll see the bright waters of **Hector Lake** fringed by dark green forest. Eighteen kilometers (11 miles) further along the road, the glacial waters of **Bow Lake** reflect the surrounding peaks, and a few miles beyond a trail leads to **Peyto Lake** where the waters change from green to blue as the year advances — a phenomenon caused by the presence of glacial silt. Other sights along the way include the **Mistaya Canyon** and the **Weeping Wall**, where melting snow streams down the cliff face at the bottom of Cirrus

Mountain. It is most spectacular in June when the snow melt is at its highest; in winter climbers come from all over to scale the ice.

At the **Sunwapta Pass**, 122 km (76 miles) north of Lake Louise and 108 km (67 miles) south of Jasper town, you enter Jasper National Park. This is the edge of the huge **Columbia Icefield**, an area of glaciers and snow that covers 325 sq km (129 sq miles) of the Canadian Rockies. The **Icefield Interpretive Centre** ☎ (403) 762-6735 has a museum detailing the geological and human history of the area, with a scale model of the **Athabasca Glacier**, the toe of which stops just short of the Parkway — so close in fact that you can wander up to its edge. Between May and late September, **Brewster Snocoaches** will take you right out onto the glacier for a closer look. The six-wheel-drive Snocoaches are built especially for traveling on the Athabasca Glacier and surrounding gravel fields. Up on the ice you can walk around and even take a sip of pure glacial water. Tours operate from the interpretive center; a fee is charged. Guided ice walk tours of the glacier will safely shepherd you over the surface, away from the deep and treacherous crevasses that thread through the ice. There is a **Parks Canada Information Desk** ☎ (403) 852-6288 within the Icefields Centre.

Continuing towards Jasper, there are two spectacular waterfalls to be seen. The first is the **Sunwapta Falls**, 175 km (108 miles) north of Lake Louise and 55 km (34 miles) south of Jasper, which is reached via a short access road off the Parkway, and further along the Parkway there's access to the **Athabasca Falls**, where the river rushes over a ledge and down into a narrow gorge.

The spectacular Icefields Parkway links Banff with Jasper following the Continental Divide along a route lined with glaciers, lakes, and mountains. OVERLEAF: The Pipestone River tumbles down the mountainside to Lake Louise Village.

Where to Stay and Eat

Forty kilometers (25 miles) north of Lake Louise, **Num-Ti-Jah Lodge** ☎ (403) 522-2167 FAX (403) 522-2425 E-MAIL reserve@num-ti-jah.com, PO Box 39, Lake Louise, Alberta T0L 1E0, nestles in a lovely spot on the banks of Bow Lake below the Crowfoot Glacier. An old hunting lodge (circa 1898), its common areas are decked with animal pelts and unusual furnishings — check out the moose-antler chairs in the library. There are 25 comfortable guestrooms and a large restaurant and lounge. It's a wonderfully isolated spot with marvelous cross-country skiing and snowshoeing in winter and horseback riding, fishing, and hiking in summer. The lodge is closed in November; rates are in the expensive to mid-range category.

JASPER NATIONAL PARK

Jasper sits in a broad valley at the point where the Icefields Parkway crosses the Yellowhead Highway. It is smaller than Banff, less spectacular in its setting, but quieter and considerably less congested during the summer season. The main street is Connaught Drive, and along it stands the Canadian National Railway station which links the town with Edmonton to the east and Vancouver to the west. The town is the starting point for many excellent hiking trails, riding treks, rafting tours, and various other excursions into the beautiful wilderness beyond that teems with wildlife.

Jasper National Park, the largest of the mountain parks, was developed later than Banff. In the early nineteenth century the Athabasca River and Pass were part of the overland fur trading route, and at one time a trading post existed not far away from the present town of Jasper. Apart from these traders and some gold prospectors on their way to the Cariboo (the Canadian Wild West in British Columbia), the area was not visited until the national park was created in preparation for the transcontinental railway that was to cross the Rockies at Yellowhead Pass. The railway brought with it visitors, and the opening of the Icefields Parkway in 1940 made Jasper Park even more accessible. Although Jasper is today a major tourist attraction, it remains quieter and wilder than its older neighbor.

GENERAL INFORMATION

The **Visitor Information Centre** ☎ (403) 852-6176 is at 500 Connaught Drive; information is also available from the **Superintendent**, **Jasper National Park**, PO Box 10, Jasper, Alberta T0E 1E0, or **Jasper Tourism and Commerce** ☎ (403) 852-3858 at the same address. As in Banff, it is necessary to sign in at the information center if you're planning an overnight hike in the park. There is **Internet access** at the Soft Rock Jasper Internet Café ☎ (403) 852-5850, in the Connaught Mall, 622 Connaught Drive.

WHAT TO SEE AND DO

Before you head out of town to enjoy the scenery, you might want to drop by the **Jasper-Yellowhead Museum and Archives** ☎ (403) 852-3013 on Pyramid Lake Road. Historical exhibits show what life in the area was like when the first European explorers and settlers arrived a century ago. It's open daily from mid-May to early September; donations are accepted.

Once you have an historical overview, you can take in a visual overview by taking a ride on the **Jasper Tramway** ((403) 852-3093, seven kilometers (four miles) south of Jasper. The tramway whizzes you up Whistlers Mountain for panoramic views of the ice field and of Mount Robson — the highest mountain in the Canadian Rockies. At the top terminal you'll find a restaurant, a café, an interpretive center, and hiking trails that lead up to the top of the mountain. Once at the top you may discover for yourself the reason for the name of the mountain when you hear the whistling noises made by the little animals there, known as hoary marmots. The tramway operates from March 28 to October 31; a fare is charged.

There are several lakes within easy reach of the town that make lovely spots for outdoor sports and general relaxation. Just seven kilometers (four miles) northwest of town at Pyramid Lake Road, **Patricia** and **Pyramid lakes** are set amidst cottonwood forest and make fine places to picnic, boat, ride horses, hike, or canoe. The former was the sight of the bizarre *Project Habbakuk*, a wartime scheme to create the ultimate weapon: an unsinkable boat made of ice. (Needless to say, the project failed.) Three kilometers (two miles) east of town at Lodge Road, **Lake Edith** and **Lake Annette** both have picnic areas, beaches and hiking trails, and Lake Annette has a bike trail. Closer to town still is **Lac Beauvert**, where the famous **Jasper Park Lodge** (see WHERE TO STAY, below) spreads out along the shore, offering some of the area's best accommodation and catering for all kinds of activities.

To the east of the town lies **Maligne Canyon**, which is reached by the Yellowhead Highway and then Maligne Road, about 10 km (six miles) outside Jasper. The water has worn away the limestone to create this deep, and in parts very narrow, slash across the landscape, which can be explored by means of paths and bridges. Begin your hike along the canyon at the trailhead to the right of the tea house for maximum drama. Six bridges span the canyon at heights of up to 50 m

(150 ft). In winter there are guided ice walks through the canyon (see SPORTS AND OUTDOOR ACTIVITIES, below) when you can explore fantastically shaped and colored ice formations.

Fourteen kilometers (nine miles) further along Maligne Road lies the mysterious **Medicine Lake**, where the water level changes throughout the year, causing it virtually to disappear during the autumn, although water is seen to enter continually. The reason behind this phenomenon is that the water constantly seeps away through holes in the bedrock, but during summer the water level is maintained because melting snow increases the amount of water entering the lake.

The crowning glory of this trip — some might say of the entire tour of the parks — is **Maligne**

Along the Icefields Parkway in Jasper National Park — OPPOSITE: The Athabasca Glacier and Num-ti-Jah Lodge ABOVE.

Lake, which lies a further 21 km (13 miles) along Maligne Road. This delightful lake stretches a length of 22 km (14 miles) and the amount of still and motion film that has been shot here would probably cover that distance several times over. Snowcapped mountains rise up from the deep blue glacial waters, and at its center lies the magical **Spirit Island**; a tiny spit of land — not really an island at all — crowned with trees. A Maligne Tours boat trip will take you along the lake and to Spirit Island between mid-May and mid-October; a hefty fare is charged.

At the Maligne Lake Boat House you can rent rowboats, canoes or kayaks, as well as rod and tackle. Professionally guided fishing trips and fly-fishing lessons can also be arranged. You can make reservations for all of your Maligne Lake activities in Jasper at **Maligne Tours** (403) 852-3370, 626 Connaught Drive.

For a relaxing treat after a hard day's hiking or skiing, visit the **Miette Hot Springs** ☎ (403) 866-3939 which lie 60 km (37 miles) northeast of the town off Highway 16 on Miette Road. The springs are the hottest in these mountains, and their soothing properties can be enjoyed in outdoor pools against a stunning alpine backdrop. The pools are open to the public from mid-May until mid-October; an admission fee is charged. The road to the springs runs through big horn sheep country.

To the south of the town **Mount Edith Cavell** looms magnificently. For a closer look, take a 30-km (18-mile) trip south of Jasper along Highway 93 and turn onto Highway 93A, a winding access road (open only from June to October) that will bring you to the foot of the mountain. It was named in honor of the heroic British nurse shot by the Germans in 1915 for helping Allied soldiers, and such a majestic sight makes a fitting memorial. A trail will take you to **Angel Glacier**, a wing-shaped tongue of ice that clings to the northeastern slopes of the mountain. There's another path that will take you into the alpine Cavell Meadows, and further back along the access road a trail leads to **Cavell Lake**.

If you'd like to see the area with a knowledgeable guide by your side, contact **Thompson Tours** ☎ (403) 852-7269 MOBILE (403) 852-0146 E-MAIL tomtour@telusplanet.net, which offers personalized tours for individuals and small groups at reasonable rates. The owner–guides have years of experience in the Rockies with some of the best historical-cultural commentary and wilderness-sports guiding in the Jasper area. Tours are offered in English, German, and French.

Excursions from Jasper

Contiguous with the Jasper Park boundary, **Mount Robson Provincial Park** makes a nice hour-long trip from Jasper townsite. Following Highway 16, the terrain and scenery are similar to Jasper's; though more lush, as this area receives more rainfall.

The highest mountain in the Canadian Rockies, Mount Robson towers 4,324 m (12,972 ft) high. After five unsuccessful attempts, Robson was finally scaled in 1913. Certain routes on this forbidding mountain are still considered to be among the worlds' most difficult. Viewing conditions are rarely perfect, as Mount Robson is notorious for bad weather and clouds often obscure the top.

There are good views of the mountain (weather permitting) from the parking lot of the **Mount Robson Visitor Information Centre** ☎ (250) 566-9174, which is open mid-May to early October;

there is also a small restaurant here. The park has five hiking trails, ranging from eight-kilometer (five-mile) day hikes to 70-km (44-mile) tramps; a permit is required.

SPORTS AND OUTDOOR ACTIVITIES

You can get a complete list of **day hikes**, the *Day Hiker's Guide to Jasper National Park*, from the Visitor Centre. **Horseback riding** and a dozen other outdoor activities are available at Jasper Park Lodge ☎ (403) 852-3301 which also has an excellent 18-hole **golf** course.

With so many lakes, Jasper is a boater's paradise. There are several outfitters offering **river rafting**, while **canoeing** is mostly reserved for

OPPOSITE: The blue ice of Maligne Falls remains locked in winter's embrace. ABOVE: Fog shrouds Spirit Island on Maligne Lake.

experienced paddlers, as the mountain waterways are swift and dangerous. Route information is available at the park information center. **Motorboating** is allowed only on Pyramid Lake.

There's excellent **skiing** at Marmot Basin ☎ (403) 852-3816 SNOW PHONE (403) 488-5909, 19 km (12 miles) south of Jasper on Highway 93-93A. Here there are slopes to suit beginners and experts, and cross-country trails sweep through the stunning scenery surrounding Maligne Lake. For information on **ski packages** in the area you can call Ski Jasper ☎ (403) 852-5247 TOLL-FREE (800) 473-8135. Also in winter, the popular **Canyon Crawl** offered by Maligne Tours ☎ (403) 852-3370, 626 Connaught Drive, takes the hardy adventurers on ice-climbing and walking trips along the multicolored ice falls at Maligne Canyon. Ice-gripping "super soles" and boots are provided on this three-hour tour.

NIGHTLIFE

Jasper is a much quieter place than Banff, and most people like it that way. What drinking and dancing goes on there tends to take place in the hotel lounges, sometimes to the accompaniment of live music. The **De'd Dog Bar & Grill** ☎ (403) 852-3341, 404 Connaught Drive, in the Astoria Hotel, has a good selection of local ales and rare scotch, and there's a big-screen television and pool and darts. **The Whistlestop Pub** ☎ (403) 852-3361, at the Whistlers Inn, Connaught Drive and Miette Avenue, is a similar setup. There's a nightclub at the **Athabasca Hotel** ☎ (403) 852-3386, 510 Patricia Street, hosting top-40 bands and dancing until 2 AM. For a quiet drink in an elegant setting, there's the Jasper Park Lodge's **Emerald Lounge** (with fireplace) and **Palisade Lounge**, overlooking beautiful Lac Beauvert.

WHERE TO STAY

In splendid solitude, the **Jasper Park Lodge** ☎ (403) 852-3301 FAX (403) 852-5107, PO Box 40, Jasper, Alberta T0E 1E0, unrolls along the milky green Athabasca River to the east of the townsite. This Canadian Pacific hotel on Lac Beauvert has riding stables, luxurious log cabin lodges, and a famous golf course. A famous resort hotel, it has entertained many celebrities since it opened in 1922, and between the main lodge, cabins, and outbuildings it has 440 accommodations — some with fireplaces, all with beautiful views, lots of character, sitting rooms, and creature comforts. It also offers fishing, boating, and skiing packages. Prices vary according to the type of accommodation and the setting, but generally fall high in the expensive bracket. Many of the activities offered here can be enjoyed by nonguests as well.

Charlton's Château Jasper ☎ (403) 852-5644 TOLL-FREE IN CANADA (800) 661-9323 FAX (403) 852-4860, 96 Geikie Street, PO Box 1418, Jasper, Alberta T0E 1E0, tries hard to live up to its expensive bracket prices, but is frankly overpriced. Rooms and suites are very large, but the hotel suffers from ambient noise, and some of the highest-priced rooms look out over a dreary jumble of air-conditioning vents. The dining room has a good reputation, however, and there is an attractive indoor pool.

Lobstick Lodge ☎ (403) 852-4431 TOLL-FREE IN WESTERN CANADA (800) 661-9317 FAX (403) 852-4142, close to the center on the corner of Geikie and Juniper Street, PO Box 1200, Jasper, Alberta T0E 1E0, has 140 comfortable motel units and lots of home-away-from-home comforts, making it an ideal choice for families. There is an indoor pool, outdoor hot tub, a restaurant and lounge. Prices straddle the mid-range and expensive brackets.

Located just opposite the VIA Rail station, **Whistlers Inn** ☎ (403) 852-3361 TOLL-FREE (800) 282-9919 FAX (403) 852-4993, 105 Miette Avenue, PO Box 250, Jasper, Alberta T0E 1E0, is a busy hotel with 40 nicely furnished rooms and suites, all with bathrooms, televisions, and telephones. It has an outdoor rooftop hot tub, a cocktail lounge, and two restaurants, and prices vary from the low to the high end of the mid-range category.

Also mid-range in price, the **Athabasca Hotel** ☎ (403) 852-3386 TOLL-FREE (800) 563-9859 FAX (403)

ABOVE: Rocky Mountain flora — a tiny conifer welcomes spring. RIGHT: Eons of erosion by the rushing water of Maligne Falls dug this deep canyon.

852-4955, 510 Patricia Street, PO Box 1420, Jasper, Alberta T0E 1E0, has simply furnished rooms, about two-thirds of which have private bathrooms. There's a popular pub, an attractive dining room, and a cocktail lounge.

Mid-range to inexpensive accommodation is available on the outskirts of the townsite: A kilometer (about half a mile) south of the town, nestled along the Athabasca and Miette rivers, **Tekarra Lodge** ☎ (403) 852-3058 TOLL-FREE (800) 661-6562 FAX (403) 852-4636, off Highway 93A, PO Box 669, Jasper, Alberta T0E 1E0, offers cozy and peaceful self-catering cabins with fireplaces at inexpensive to mid-range prices. It's open May to October. At **Patricia Lake Bungalows** ☎ (403) 852-3560, PO Box 657, Jasper, Alberta T0E 1E0, 35 tidy, rustic cottages and clumps of aspen and fir dot the banks of an ultramarine lake. There's a new playground, and cabins come equipped with kitchenettes, making this a good place for families. **Pyramid Lake Resort** ☎ (403) 852-4900, PO Box 388, Jasper, Alberta T0E 1E0, has a restaurant that serves seafood and barbecue. Some accommodations have fireplaces. Rates here are in the mid-range, but more expensive than at Patricia Lake.

The mainstay of the Jasper lodging scene is **home accommodation**, a tradition since the park's early days. You'll see signs posted throughout the residential area of Jasper. These accommodations range from basic to very comfortable, from full apartments with kitchen to rooms with private or shared bath. Many are self-contained; some provide breakfast. Rates range from very inexpensive to the low end of the mid-range category, depending on facilities. The association prints an annual brochure that provides contact information for the individual homes. Write to Jasper Home Accommodation Association, PO Box 758, Jasper, Alberta T0E 1E0.

The hostels nearest to the townsite, both open year-round, are the **Maligne Canyon Hostel-HI** ☎ (403) 852-3584 FAX (403) 852-5560, PO Box 387, Jasper, Alberta T0E 1E0, on Maligne Lake Road, 11 km (six and a half miles) east of town; and the **Jasper International Hostel-HI** ☎ (403) 852-3215 FAX (403) 852-5560 E-MAIL jihostel@telusplanet.net, PO Box 387, Jasper, Alberta T0E 1E0, on Whistler's Mountain Road, seven kilometers (four miles) southwest of the townsite. The Jasper International offers downhill skiing packages.

Where to Eat

Fiddle River ☎ (403) 852-3032, 620 Connaught Drive, is one of the newest entry in the Jasper dining arena and is quickly gaining an excellent reputation for its delightful Pacific Rim cuisine featuring innovative dishes such as their pan-seared, peanut-crusted shrimp in strawberry purée. **Something Else Greek Taverna** ☎ (403) 852-3850, 621 Patricia Street, is well-loved and well-patronized for its mouth-watering traditional dishes and suitably Greek decor.

For sushi and other Japanese dishes go to **Tokyo Tom's** ☎ (403) 852-3780, 410 Connaught Drive. The **Soft Rock Jasper Internet Café** ☎ (403) 852-5850, Connaught Mall, 622 Connaught Drive, spins the town's best selection of CDs — from Bob Marley to native chants. Breakfast is served all day with bagels, omelets, waffles, pancakes, and more for a very reasonable price. You'd never know the modern **Mountain Foods & Café** ☎/FAX (403) 852-4050, 606 Connaught Drive, is housed in a former dance hall. "Jaspers best bartender" and a pack of friendly locals are two among many reasons to

pay a call. Quesadillas, bagel sandwiches, and creatively conceived omelets are all made from fresh ingredients. It's directly across from the train station.

Outside the townsite, the **Jasper Park Lodge** ☎ (403) 852-3301 on Lac Beauvert has nine restaurants. The flagship is the Four-Diamond-Award-winning Edith Cavell Dining Room, featuring freshly baked breads and herbs grown in the lodge greenhouse. The cafeteria-style **Maligne Canyon Teahouse** ☎ (403) 852-5565, at Maligne Canyon, has a generous salad bar and hot meals which can be enjoyed on chilly days by the hearth or in summer on the terrace; avoid peak hours as this is a favorite pit stop for coach tour groups. The **Maligne Lake Restaurant**, at Maligne Lake, is another good spot run along similar lines. There's a pleasant terrace and the cafeteria serves hot meals, big sandwiches, and homemade breads and pastries.

HOW TO GET THERE

Jasper is 292 km (184 miles) north of Banff along the Icefields Parkway, making Calgary International Airport 412 km (259 miles) away from Jasper. Edmonton International Airport is 350 km (215 miles) away from Jasper along the Yellowhead Highway. If you're aiming for Jasper during the winter you may want to drive via Calgary and Edmonton rather than taking the Icefields Parkway from Banff — winter conditions on this mountain road are sometimes hazardous.

The **VIA Rail** station TOLL-FREE (888) 842-7733 is in the town center along Connaught Drive, and

trains run west to Kamloops and Vancouver, eastwards to Edmonton, Winnipeg and beyond, and northward to Prince George and Prince Rupert. The **Greyhound** station ☎ (403) 852-3332 shares the train station in the town center, and regular services operate to Vancouver via Kamloops, to Edmonton, and to Banff.

The Yellowhead Highway runs through Jasper from Edmonton in the east and to Prince George in the west, also linking with Vancouver via Kamloops.

YOHO NATIONAL PARK

Making up British Columbia's share of the Rocky Mountain national parks, Yoho and Kootenay lie alongside Banff, accessible off the Trans-Canada Highway for day trips. Both have much to offer outdoor enthusiasts and easily merit extended stays.

Yoho National Park is a land of towering rock walls and thundering waterfalls, and has 28 peaks over 3,000 m (9,000 ft) high. Once you visit, you'll understand why the Cree natives called this place "Yoho," an expression of wonder and astonishment. In addition to its scenic attractions, the park is noted for its fossil beds where the remains of more than 120 species of marine animals from 515 million years ago is the subject of ongoing investigation.

Field, British Columbia, is the administrative and supply center for the park, a compact little village with a history as a railway and mining town. Here you'll find the Field Visitor Centre ☎ (250) 343-6783, which has all the information

you'll need for your visit, including up-to-date news on trail and weather conditions.

There are some 400 **hiking trails** in Yoho that lead to glaciated peaks, rolling alpine meadows, deep forests and thundering waterfalls. If you're making a drive-through tour, look for roadside signs pointing the way to the **Spiral Tunnels** viewpoint where you can watch passing trains corkscrew down a 2.2% grade. **Takakkaw Falls** ("magnificent" in Cree) are the highest in Canada at 254 m (84 ft). There is a parking lot, and several popular hiking trails begin here.

With so much natural history and beauty packed into such a small space (1,310 sq km or

Water, water everywhere — OPPOSITE: The Pipestone River at Lake Louise Village. ABOVE LEFT: The glacially-fed Lake Annette in Jasper National Park. RIGHT: Ice clings to the surface of the Pipestone.

507 sq miles), Yoho is sometimes overburdened with admirers. Park authorities have thus established limited access to certain areas: There is a quota on the number of people who may use the bus service up to **Lake O'Hara**. In addition, no bicycles are permitted; however, there is no limit on the number of people who may hike in. Reservations for the bus service to the lake must be made up to 90 days in advance by calling ☎ (250) 343-6433.

Walcott's Quarry and its **Trilobite Beds** can be visited by guided hikes only. Yoho-Burgess Shale Foundation ☎ (250) 343-6006 TOLL-FREE (800) 343-3006 E-MAIL burgshal@rockies.net, PO Box 148, Field, British Columbia V0A 1G0, offers earth science hikes to both sites. The Walcott's Quarry hike departs from the Yoho Brothers' Trading Post each Friday, Saturday, Sunday, and Monday morning at 8 AM. Guided hikes to the **Mount Stephen Fossil Beds** depart every Saturday and Sunday at 10 AM, also from the Trading Post. This hike is shorter than the Walcott's Quarry hike is, but more difficult. The local mountaineering club cut the trail; it climbs up at a very steep grade and trilobites are everywhere — you have to be careful to avoid stepping on them and crushing them. You must be in good physical condition to undertake either hike. Reservations are required.

For accommodation in Yoho, there is the **Cathedral Mountain Lodge & Chalets** ☎ (250) 343-6442 FAX (403) 762-0514, Yoho Valley Road, Yoho National Park, PO Box 40, Field, British Columbia V0A 1G0. Located four kilometers (two and a half miles) east of Field, along the road to Takakkaw Falls, the lodge offers log cabins with fireplaces situated in quiet wooded grounds along the Kicking Horse River. There is a licensed restaurant and a grocery store. The lodge is open mid-May to mid-October and can be contacted during the off season period at the above fax number. Rates range from moderate to expensive.

From Takakkaw Falls, you can hike up to the **Twin Falls Chalet** ☎/FAX (403) 228-7079, PO Box 23009, Connaught Post Office, Calgary, Alberta T2S 3B1, where there is more cabin accommodation. Day hikers are welcome here for lunch, which is served between noon and 4 PM. It's open from July to Labor Day, and reservations are required. Rates, which include all meals, are in the mid-range category. A number of other **backcountry lodgings** are dotted throughout Yoho. For information, write to the Superintendent, Yoho National park, PO Box 99, Field, British Columbia V0A 1G0. Anyone who is planning an overnight trip into the backcountry must buy a wilderness pass. They're available from any Parks Canada center.

The **Whiskey Jack Hostel (HI)** ☎ (403) 762-4122 FAX (403) 762-3441, at Yoho National Park, PO Box 1358, Banff, Alberta T0L 0C0, has an ideal setting about a kilometer from Takakkaw Falls; it's open mid-June to mid-September.

When you're in Field, be sure to stop in at the **Yoho Brothers Trading Post** ☎ (250) 343-6030, where you can pick up souvenirs and have a sandwich of barbecued wild game or salmon.

Continuing west from Field brings you to the town of Golden in Glacier National Park (see GLACIER AND MOUNT REVELSTOKE NATIONAL PARKS, page 110, in BRITISH COLUMBIA), 78 km (48 miles) from Lake Louise.

KOOTENAY NATIONAL PARK

Lying southwest of Banff and Yoho national parks, Kootenay is accessible via Highway 93 off the Trans-Canada Highway south of Castle Junction. Highway 93, the Banff-Windermere Highway was the first major road to cross the Rockies and runs right through the park to its southern edge; it's a magnificent drive. As you travel through Kootenay look out for such marvels as **Marble Canyon** (take the 20 minute interpretive walk) and the ochre-tinted **Paint Pots**.

At the southern edge of the park, **Radium Hot Springs** ☎ (250) 347-9485 features a hot pool (40°C or 104°F) and swimming pool (27°C or 80.6°F); towel and suit rentals are available. The **Visitor Information Centre** ☎ (250) 247-9595 is located at the hot springs and has the usual raft of maps, brochures, and backcountry permits.

Kootenay and Yoho excursion specialists, **Kootenay Country Expeditions** ☎ (403) 762-5627 TOLL-FREE (888) 899-7999, are located at the corner of Wolf and Bear streets in Banff townsite. They offer all sorts of ways to enjoy the British Columbia Rockies including glacier air tours, whitewater rafting, golf packages, horseback riding, four-wheel-drive tours, nature tours, jet-boating, and parasailing. They will also arrange accommodation in all price ranges from luxury resorts to backcountry cabins. Tours depart from Banff and Canmore.

The town of Radium Hot Springs is 129 km (80 miles) from Banff, and **Panorama Resort** ☎ (250) 342-6941 TOLL-FREE (800) 663-2929 FAX (250) 342-3395, Toby Creek Road, Panorama V0A 1T0, is a further 20-minute drive. **The Springs at Radium Golf Resort** ☎ (250) 347-9311 TOLL-FREE (800) 667-6444 FAX (250) 347-6299, 8100 Golf Course Road, Highway 93/95, PO Box 310, Radium Hot Springs V0A 1M0, is a year-round destination packed with activities. Its 119 rooms are mid-range in price and there is a restaurant and lounge as well as an indoor swimming pool.

Pebbles sparkle like flakes of gold in Banff's Bow River.

Alberta

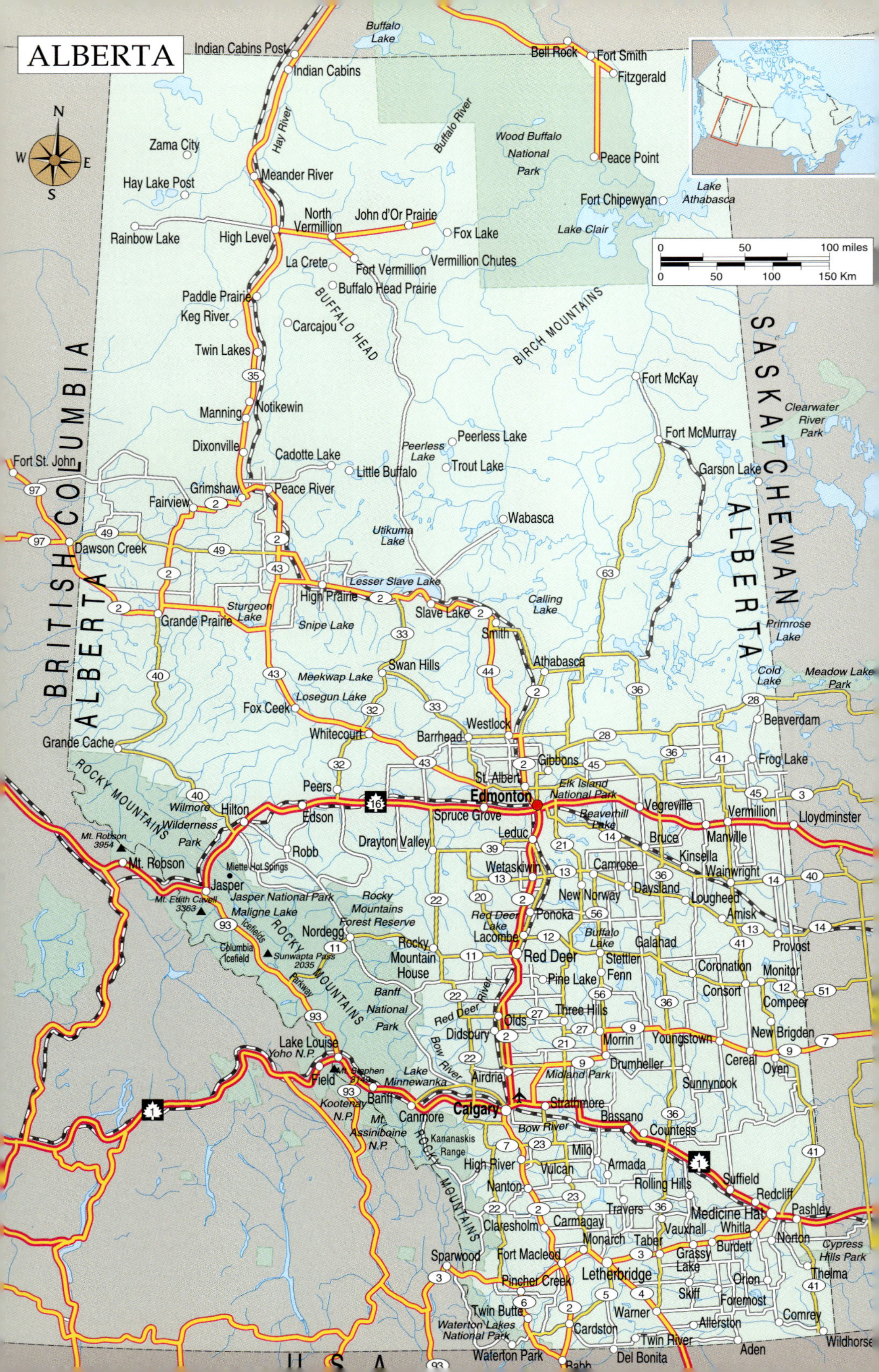
ALBERTA
N
S
E
W
Indian Cabins Post
Indian Cabins
Buffalo Lake
Bell Rock
Fort Smith
Fitzgerald
Hay River
Buffalo River
Wood Buffalo National Park
Peace Point
Zama City
Hay Lake Post
Meander River
North Vermillion
John d'Or Prairie
Rainbow Lake
High Level
Fox Lake
Fort Chipewyan
Lake Athabasca
Lake Clair
La Crete
Fort Vermillion
Vermillion Chutes
Buffalo Head Prairie
Paddle Prairie
Keg River
Carcajou
BUFFALO HEAD
BIRCH MOUNTAINS
0 50 100 miles
0 50 100 150 Km
Twin Lakes
35
Manning
Notikewin
Fort McKay
SASKATCHEWAN
ALBERTA
BRITISH COLUMBIA
Clearwater River Park
Fort McMurray
Peerless Lake
Dixonville
Cadotte Lake
Trout Lake
Fort St. John
Little Buffalo
Garson Lake
97
Grimshaw
Peace River
Fairview
2
Wabasca
49
Utikuma Lake
Dawson Creek
Lesser Slave Lake
43
63
High Prairie
Slave Lake
Calling Lake
Sturgeon Lake
Grande Prairie
Snipe Lake
Smith
Primrose Lake
33
Athabasca
Swan Hills
44
40
Meekwap Lake
Losegun Lake
36
Cold Lake
Meadow Lake Park
28
Fox Ceek
32
Beaverdam
Westlock
Whitecourt
Barrhead
Grande Cache
Gibbons
45
Frog Lake
41
ROCKY MOUNTAINS
St. Albert
Peers
Elk Island National Park
Edmonton
16
Wilmore Wilderness Park
Hilton
Edson
Vegreville
Vermillion
3
Lloydminster
Spruce Grove
Beaverhill Lake
Mt. Robson 3954
Drayton Valley
Leduc
14
Bruce
Manville
Robb
Mt. Robson
39
Kinsella
Miette Hot Springs
Wetaskiwin
Camrose
Wainwright
13
Jasper
Rocky Mountains Forest Reserve
Daysland
Mt. Edith Cavell 3363
Jasper National Park
22
20
New Norway
Lougheed
Maligne Lake
Red Deer Lake
Ponoka
Amisk
Icefields
Lacombe
56
Buffalo Lake
Provost
Columbia Icefield
Nordegg
12
Galahad
Sunwapta Pass 2035
11
Rocky Mountain House
Red Deer
Stettler
Coronation
Parkway
Monitor
Pine Lake
Fenn
Consort
51
Banff National Park
Red Deer River
Compeer
Olds
Three Hills
Didsbury
27
9
Morrin
Youngstown
New Brigden
7
93
Lake Louise
Yoho N.P.
Bow River
21
Drumheller
Cereal
Oyen
Mt. Stephen 3199
Lake Minnewanka
Airdrie
Midland Park
Field
Sunnynook
Banff
Strathmore
Kootenay N.P.
Calgary
Canmore
Bassano
Mt. Assiniboine N.P.
Bow River
Countess
Kananaskis Range
23
Milo
High River
Vulcan
Armada
Suffield
Nanton
Rolling Hills
Redcliff
Travers
Medicine Hat
Pashley
Claresholm
Carmagay
Vauxhall
Whitla
Monarch
Taber
Burdett
Norton
Cypress Hills Park
Sparwood
Fort Macleod
Grassy Lake
Letherbridge
Thelma
Orion
Pincher Creek
Skiff
Foremost
6
5
4
Twin Butte
Warner
Comrey
Waterton Lakes National Park
Cardston
Allerston
Twin River
Waterton Park
Aden
Wildhorse
Del Bonita
Babb
U.S.A.

REACHING FROM THE NORTHWEST TERRITORIES to Montana, Alberta is bordered by the Canadian Rockies to the west and Saskatchewan to the east. It shares Canada's vast prairie land with Saskatchewan and Manitoba, and, covering 650,000 sq km (250,000 sq miles), it is the largest of the three Prairie Provinces. It has a population of 2.8 million, half of whom live in Calgary and Edmonton, leaving vast areas of the province uninhabited by humans.

Alberta has the cowboys, cattle, and wide-open spaces that epitomize prairie land, but it is also famous for the magnificent Rocky Mountain landscape of snowy peaks, sweeping slopes, and brilliant lakes that characterize the Banff, Jasper, and Waterton Lakes national parks to the southwest. The prairie lands of the southeast offer three different landscapes: in the southeastern corner there is an area of arid cattle-raising grassland and badlands surrounded by a larger wheat-growing belt that in turn gives way to an even larger area of parklands, trees, and mixed farming. It is in this last region that the province's major cities, Calgary and Edmonton, are located. The north of the province is a sparsely inhabited region of forests and lakes.

The exploitation of the province's oil and natural gas resources sparked a period of rapid growth and prosperity in the 1970s that brought the cities of Edmonton and Calgary to the fore. Fluctuations in oil and grain prices brought hard times in the 1980s, but these days Alberta is booming again with the fastest-growing economy in Canada. The province remains a producer of beef and grain as well as a major producer of oil and gas, with forestry. The endless outdoor opportunities that the province offers and the stunning scenery of the national parks contribute to a flourishing tourist industry.

The first European to explore the area was Anthony Henday, who acted on behalf of the Hudson's Bay Company. Among those who eased the way for the settlement of the area was Father Albert Lacombe, who founded a mission, schools, and churches, and established good relations with the Prairie natives. In 1869 the Hudson's Bay Company sold the land to the government and so Alberta became part of Canada's Northwest Territories. Whisky peddlers and fur traders descended on the area, and there followed a period of lawlessness and bloodshed, which continued until the arrival in 1874 of the North West Mounted Police.

The traders introduced guns to the native tribes, and the ease with which the buffalo could be slaughtered spelled the end of the massive herds that once roamed the prairie and had been the mainstay of the native way of life. With the herds gone, the natives were willing to negotiate treaties, and cultivation of the prairie by the whites began in the 1880s along with immigration from Europe, Russia, and the United States. The province of Alberta was created in 1905 and the subsequent world wars and various political upheavals brought more immigrants to the province in search of a new life.

Although the discovery of oil brought Alberta prosperity and wealthy, modern cities, the province has steadfastly retained the spirit of its early ranching days. The picture-book image of the cowboy riding among herds on the plains is not an uncommon sight in the south of the province, while the days of the Wild West are celebrated each year with great gusto in the famous Calgary Stampede and Edmonton's Klondike Days festival.

EDMONTON

Alberta's capital city stands on the outer rim of the prairie, right at the center of the province, and is set around the deep valley of the North Saskatchewan River. Shiny modern high-rises testify to the prosperity of this oil town, a wealth that Edmonton seems to have handled wisely. The town is well planned: Streets conform to a grid system, underground and sheltered walkways protect citizens from the winter cold, and the river banks have been turned into parklands that provide winter and summer recreation.

With a population of 890,000, Edmonton is the largest city in Alberta and the northernmost major city in North America. It is Canada's oil capital, with some 2,000 wells within 40 km (25 miles) of

The West Edmonton Mall is not just for shopping.

the city, producing approximately 10% of Canada's oil. It deals with all the technological and scientific aspects of the oil industry, having refineries and petrochemical plants, but it leaves the administrative side of the industry to Calgary.

BACKGROUND

In the late eighteenth century two fur trading posts were established in the area, one belonging to the Hudson's Bay Company and the other to its rival the North West Trading Company. When the two companies merged in 1821 the fort that had been established in 1795 by the Hudson's Bay Company, known as Edmonton House, became the trading and administrative center of the northwest and the jewel in the company's crown. The fort traded with the Blackfoot confederacy of warrior tribes who together with the Cree then inhabited the land.

In 1870 the Hudson's Bay Company sold the land to the Canadian government and the area opened to settlers. Here as elsewhere in Alberta there followed a wild and lawless period during which the town of 600 inhabitants was incorporated. Law and order finally arrived with the North West Mounted Police in 1875. In 1891 the railroad reached Edmonton, increasing its importance as a transportation center and triggering an influx of settlers. The discovery of gold in the Klondike in 1898 brought Edmonton its first boom period as prospectors flooded to the town to prepare for the long trek, increasing the population to around 4,000 and bringing prosperity to the merchants. This period of Edmonton's history is affectionately remembered every year in the town's annual Klondike Days celebrations.

When the province of Alberta was created in 1905, Edmonton, then with a population of 8,000, was elected its capital, much to the disappointment of the rival town of Calgary. It continued to grow rapidly, with a further surge of immigration during the construction of the Alaska Highway. The biggest boom of all started with the discovery of oil in 1947 at Leduc, to the south of Edmonton. The discovery of further oil fields followed and by 1965 the population had quadrupled. The 1960s and 1970s brought a period of great prosperity and frantic urban development, which in the 1980s declined with the drop in oil prices. The economic mood of the 1990s, however, has been decidedly upbeat. Edmonton remains Canada's oil center, but is not wholly dependent on this one commodity. It is also the handling and supply center for the rich agricultural area that surrounds it. Its situation also makes it the main distribution center for the mineral-rich northern Alberta, and for northern Canada as a whole.

GENERAL INFORMATION

There are visitor centers at all of the major points of entry into the province. For information on Edmonton visit one of the **Edmonton Tourism Information Centre**'s three locations: Gateway Park ☎ (403) 496-8400 TOLL-FREE (800) 463-4667 E-MAIL edeinfo@ede.org WEB SITE www.info edmonton.com/, 2404 Calgary Trail Northbound

SW; downtown at the Shaw Conference Centre, 9797 Jasper Avenue NW; and in the Spruce Grove & District Chamber of Commerce Building, Highway 16A West, one kilometer (half a mile) west of Spruce Grove. In advance of your trip you can write to **Edmonton Tourism**, Department VG98, 9797 Jasper Avenue NW, Edmonton T5J 1N9.

Getting Around

Like most Canadian cities, Edmonton's **street plan** is laid out on a numbered grid, making it easy to find your way around. Numbered avenues run east to west. Numbered streets run north to south. Odd numbered buildings are on the east side of the street and on the south side of the avenue. Edmonton's **Light Rail Transit (LRT) System** ☎ (403) 496-4611 runs north from the city center to Commonwealth Stadium, the Coliseum and Northlands Park, across downtown from Churchill Station to Grandin Station at 111th Street and then south to the university.

WHAT TO SEE AND DO

Should you find yourself with time on your hands, there are a handful of sites in downtown where you can while away a few hours. In the heart of the downtown area is the **Edmonton Art Gallery** ☎ (403) 422-6223, 2 Sir Winston Churchill Square. The gallery holds temporary exhibitions of works from its own collection of contemporary and historical art, or visiting exhibitions, usually of quite a high standard. It's open daily; an admission fee is charged, free Thursday from 4 PM to 8 PM.

Southwest of the downtown core, the **Alberta Legislature**, home of the provincial government, is a dignified building of yellow sandstone, fronted with a columned portico and capped with a stately dome. Built between 1907 and 1912, it occupies the site of the original Fort Edmonton, overlooking the river and surrounded by landscaped grounds with fountains, pools, formal gardens, and lawns. Below ground, the Government Centre Pedway links the Legislature building to other government buildings and has an exhibition area where there are displays on various aspects of Alberta. The Legislature Building is at 109th Street and 97th Avenue, and there are free **tours** ☎ (403) 427-7362 daily throughout the year.

Over on the south side of the river close to Macdonald Bridge is the unmistakable **Muttart Conservatory** ☎ (403) 496-8755, 9626 96A Street, a group of four striking glass pyramids. Three of the structures simulate different climatic zones — tropical, arid, and temperate — and contain plants indigenous to each climate. The fourth pyramid houses changing displays. The conservatory is open daily, and an admission fee is charged.

West of downtown the **Provincial Museum of Alberta** ☎ (403) 453-9100, 12845 102nd Avenue, is pleasantly situated in parkland that overlooks the riverbank. This modern building contains four galleries, each devoted to a different aspect of Alberta's natural and cultural heritage. The Habitat gallery has displays that recreate the various aspects of Alberta countryside such as the mountains, the forests of the north, and the grasslands, complete with animal and plant life. The Natural History gallery deals with the geology of the area, its fossils, and the days of the dinosaurs, while the History gallery looks at the white settlement of the province. The Aboriginal Peoples Gallery has a fine collection of native artifacts. It's open daily from May 16 to September 1, Tuesday to Sunday the rest of the year. An admission fee is charged.

For a particularly enjoyable history lesson visit one of Edmonton's top attractions, the **Fort Edmonton Park** ☎ (403) 496-8787 on the south bank of the river just west of Whitemud Freeway and close to Quesnel Bridge. This is an ambitious project that aims to recount the history of the white settlement of Edmonton in the most vivid terms. It has a detailed reconstruction of the palisaded Fort Edmonton, the 1846 Hudson's Bay Company trading post complete with "inhabitants" who are happy to chat to you about their life in the employ of the company. Outside the fort there is a recreation of village life in Edmonton during 1885 before the coming of the railroad, an Edmonton street in 1905 when the town was an expanding capital city, and a 1920 street scene showing Edmonton as a prosperous business city. Meticulous attention is given to detail, and there are shops that carry stock appropriate for the period, as well as schools, churches, and offices. To complete the experience you can ride in a restored streetcar, a steam train, a stagecoach, or a horse wagon. Special events are held here throughout the year. It's open daily, and an admission fee is charged.

OPPOSITE: The little steam train chugs its way across Fort Edmonton Park. ABOVE: Edmonton's skyline at night.

Local history will tell you that to the south of the river lies an area that was once the town of Strathcona, which joined with Edmonton in 1912. In the **Old Strathcona Historic Area** ☎ (403) 433-5866, between 101st and 106th streets and Saskatchewan Drive and 80th Avenue, many of the buildings predate the union and have been restored. Pick up a walking tour brochure from a Tourism Information Centre and enjoy a stroll along these Victorian streets.

Coming back to modern times with a jolt, the **West Edmonton Mall** ☎ (403) 444-5300, at 170th Street and 87th Avenue, is to date the world's largest mall, which covers a staggering 500,000 square meters (five and a half million square feet). Despite recent reports of shady dealings and mismanagement by its owners the mall is still thrivingly devoted to shopping and recreation. It holds about 800 stores, including six major department stores, over 100 places to eat, 20 cinemas, a vast water park, a large amusement park with roller coaster, a mini-golf course, and a casino. There are caged animals and performing dolphins for your entertainment, and much more besides. Like it or hate it, it's there and worth a visit for the experience alone. The mall is open weekdays from 10 AM to 9 PM, Saturday from 10 AM to 6 PM and Sunday from noon to 5 PM. An admission fee is charged.

The **Space and Science Centre** ☎ (403) 452-9100, 11211 142nd Street, northwest of the city center in Coronation Park, is a suitably spaceship-like building containing Canada's largest planetarium, displays on astronomy and science. It's open daily from mid-June to early September from 10 AM to 10 PM; and early September to mid-June from Tuesday to Sunday from 10 AM to 10 PM. An admission fee is charged.

Each year, Edmonton really lets its hair down around mid-July when it celebrates **Klondike Days** ☎ (403) 479-3500. Not to be outdone by Calgary's Stampede celebration, Edmonton introduced this 10-day knees-up in honor of the 1898 gold rush that brought prospectors here on their way to Dawson City. There are parades, silly competitions, music, dancing, parties, and breakfasting in the open air. Northlands Park becomes Klondike Village, and everyone from the bank manager to the shopkeeper joins in by dressing up in period costume.

Excursions from Edmonton

If you hear the call of the wild it could be coming from **Elk Island National Park** ☎ (403) 922-3293, Site 4, Rural Route 1, Fort Saskatchewan T8L 2N7, an unspoiled wilderness of forests and lakes which is a wildlife reserve, only 48 km (29 miles) east of Edmonton on Route 16 (the Yellowhead Highway). Elk, wood bison, moose, and deer roam here, and hundreds of species of birds can be seen. The park has hiking trails varying in length from 2.5 to 18 km (1.5 to 11 miles), cross-country skiing trails over rolling terrain, and a lake for canoeing and swimming. Camping is permitted throughout the year. The Astontin Interpretive Centre tells you all about the park, which is open year-round. An admission fee is charged.

Further east along Highway 16 and about 50 km (31 miles) east of Edmonton lies the **Ukrainian Cultural Heritage Village** ☎ (403) 662-3640, a reconstruction of an early settlement of these immigrants who arrived in Alberta in droves during the 1890s and contributed greatly to the cultural development of the province. A reception area has exhibitions on the lives of these pioneers and on the story behind their immigration. It's open daily between May 15 and October 14; an admission fee is charged.

SPORTS AND OUTDOOR ACTIVITIES

The North Saskatchewan River snakes its way east-west through the city with a long green belt of parkland running along both banks. This is Canada's largest stretch of city parkland, one long recreation area strewn with cycling paths and trails. The River Valley Parks and Outdoor Centre ☎ (403) 496-7275 that stretches for nearly 30 kilometers (19 miles) along both banks of the North Saskatchewan River has all kinds of facilities, including networks of **jogging**, **running**, and **cycling** trails. In the winter there are **cross-country skiing** trails here and also at Elk Island Park. In the summer Elk Island is also a pleasant spot for **swimming**.

NIGHTLIFE AND THE ARTS

You'll find Edmonton to be particularly well-endowed with theaters and theatrical companies. To check what's on in Edmonton, pick up a copy of one of the free monthlies, *The Edmonton Bullet* or *Something Entertaining*.

The **Citadel Theatre** ☎ (403) 425-1820, 99th Street and 101A Avenue, is a major Canadian performing arts center. This impressive glass-and-brick complex houses five theaters where a variety of first-rate stage and musical productions are performed, and there is also a pleasant indoor garden where you can while away some time. The **Northern Alberta Jubilee Auditorium** ☎ (403) 427-9622, 87th Avenue and 114th Street, is another venue for theater, ballet, and concerts, and is home to the **Edmonton Symphony Orchestra** ☎ (403) 428-1414, the **Edmonton Opera** ☎ (403) 424-4040, and the **Alberta Ballet Company** ☎ (403) 428-6839. There are also many other theater venues scattered throughout Edmonton, including a couple of dinner theaters. Edmonton holds the **Fringe Theatre Festival** ☎ (403) 448-9000 for 10 days in late August when alternative theater productions crop up all over the city, both indoors and outdoors.

For jazz, there's the **Yardbird Suite** ☎ (403) 432-0428, 10203 86th Avenue, and there are occasional jazz concerts at the **Northern Alberta Jubilee Auditorium** (above). The city has dozens of bars and eateries that double as nightclubs and feature a wide range of music. You can hear rhythm and blues at the **Sidetrack Café** ☎ (403) 421-1326, 10333 112th Street, where you can also enjoy some excellent food.

Café Select ☎ (403) 423-0419, 10018 106th Street, is the after-theatre spot for a quiet drink. The city's biggest patio at **Earl's** ☎ (403) 448-5822, 11830 Jasper Avenue, is jammed every Friday night before the club scene gets underway. Don't forget, though, that this is cowboy country: Down a cold one at **Cowboys Country Saloon** ☎ (403) 481-8739, 10102 180th Street, then move along to the dance floor at **Cook County Saloon** ☎ (403) 432-2665, 8010 103rd Street, voted Canada's nightclub of the year for five years running.

Edmonton's casino is the **Baccarat** ☎ (403) 413-3178, downtown at 10128 104th Avenue. It's open every day from 10 AM to 3 AM for the slot machines and from noon to 2 AM for live action gambling.

WHERE TO STAY

Mid-range

The superb **Sheraton Grande Edmonton** ☎ (403) 428-7111 TOLL-FREE (800) 263-9030 FAX (403) 441-3098, 10235 101st Street, Edmonton T5J 3E9, has some of the best accommodation in town and is conveniently connected to a major shopping mall. The hotel has two good restaurants, a beautiful lounge set amid an indoor garden, a pub, and an indoor swimming pool. The rooms are elegantly

A ride in one of Fort Edmonton Park's horse-drawn wagons.

furnished and have well-equipped bathrooms. The **Westin Hotel** ☎ (403) 426-3636 TOLL-FREE (800) 228-3000 FAX (403) 428-1454, at 10135 100th Street, Edmonton T5J 0N7, is another first-rate hotel. Its rooms and suites are beautifully decorated and luxuriously furnished. It houses the excellent Carvery Restaurant, and has an indoor pool.

If you feel like being really frivolous, take one of the themed rooms at the **Galaxyland Hotel & Resort** ☎ (403) 444-3000 TOLL-FREE (800) 661-6454, 17700 87th Avenue, Edmonton T5T 4V4, over in northwest Edmonton in the larger-than-life West Edmonton Mall (formerly called Fantasyland). There is a Polynesian room, a Roman room, a Hollywood room, an Arabian room, and the intriguingly named Truck room, to name but a few, all with whirlpools, and some with steam baths. Prices vary between mid-range and expensive.

Mid-range to Inexpensive

Downtown, the **Edmonton House Suite Hotel** ☎ (403) 420-4000 TOLL-FREE (800) 661-6562 FAX (403) 420-4008, at 10205 100th Avenue, Edmonton T5J 4B5, has 300 attractive suites with balconies and kitchens, and a very good range of facilities and services that include an indoor pool, an exercise room, and a bar. They also offer a free shuttle to the Edmonton Mall. The neighboring **Econo Lodge** ☎ (403) 428-6442 TOLL-FREE IN CANADA (800) 613-7043 FAX (403) 428-6467, at 10209 100th Avenue, Edmonton, T5J 0A1, is very good value with 73 nicely furnished rooms. There's a pub as well as a restaurant. Also downtown, the **Alberta Place Suite Hotel** ☎ (403) 423-1565 TOLL-FREE (800) 661-3982 FAX (403) 426-6260, 10049 103rd Street, Edmonton T5J 2W7, has 86 apartments comfortably furnished with compact but well equipped kitchens. The hotel has an exercise room, a sun deck, and most things you need for self-catering. For an added touch there's complimentary coffee, fruit juice, and morning paper. Weekly and monthly rates are available.

For accommodation in one of Edmonton's few older establishments, try **La Bohème** ☎ (403) 474-5693, 6427 112th Avenue, Edmonton, T5W 0N9. Known primarily as a very good French restaurant, it now offers a few charming suites, which, like the service, are continental in style and quite charming. Breakfast is included in the price.

Assistance with **bed and breakfast** accommodation is available through Alberta's Gem B&B Reservation Agency ☎/FAX (403) 434-6098, 11216 48th Avenue, Edmonton T6H 0C7.

The **Edmonton International Hostel (HI)** ☎ (403) 429-0140 FAX (403) 421-0131 E-MAIL eihostel @HostellingIntl.ca, is located at 10422 91st Street, Edmonton T5H 1S6, and has 50 beds and offers mountain bike rentals.

WHERE TO EAT

Edmonton's cultural mix makes for a healthy restaurant scene with a wide choice of cuisines, but as a prairie town it has its own specialty: some of the best beef in Canada. You will find concentrations of restaurants in the Old Strathcona district between 101st and 106th streets, the downtown area, and the Boardwalk Market at 103rd Street.

La Bohème ℂ (403) 474-5693, at 6427 112th Avenue, is housed within an older building close to downtown and is decidedly French in both cuisine and ambiance. You'll find some of the best French fare in town here, and there is a wine cellar to match. It is open throughout the week; reservations are recommended. The menu is also French at **La Ronde** ℂ (403) 428-6611, the revolving restaurant at the top of the Crown Plaza Château Lacombe, 10111 Bellamy Hill. Unlike many of its counterparts, it is not only a feast for the eyes: the food and the service are also of a high standard.

One of the best steak houses in town, **Hy's Steak Loft** ℂ (403) 424-4444, 10013 101st Street, is a good place to sample some of the province's first-rate

beef. The **Unheardof** ℂ (403) 432-0480, at 9602 82nd Avenue, offers *prix-fixe* menus featuring excellent international cuisine prepared with fresh ingredients; desserts are to die for. **The King and I** ℂ (403) 433-2222, 8208 107th Street, in Old Strathcona, serves the best Thai cuisine in town.

The family-run **Smokey Joe's Hickory Smokehouse** ℂ (403) 413-3379, at 156th Street and 87th Avenue, serves hickory-smoked ribs, poultry, and sausages in large helpings and in a warm, friendly atmosphere. There are light meals at the much-loved **Vi's** ℂ (403) 454-4300, 13408 Stony Plain Road, where desserts, including homemade pies, are a specialty. The cozy and affordable **Crêperie** ℂ (403) 420-6656, at 10220 103rd Street, is Edmonton's most romantic restaurant, where the French cuisine is country style.

Doan's has authentic Vietnamese cuisine at two locations: downtown ℂ (403) 424-3034, at 10023 107th Avenue, and on the south side ℂ (403) 434-4448, at 7909 104th Street.

The stylish **Russian Tea Room** ℂ (403) 426-0000, 10312 Jasper Avenue, does indeed serve Russian tea along with wonderful cakes and pastries; it also has a restaurant menu where you'll find traditional Russian dishes.

HOW TO GET THERE

Edmonton International Airport is located 28 km (17 miles) south of the city along Highway 2, and the drive into downtown takes about 30 minutes. The **Sky Shuttle** ℂ (403) 465-8515 runs between some of the big downtown hotels and the airport.

Edmonton lies at the center of the what remains of Canada's trans-national rail network, with three weekly **VIA Rail** ℂ (403) 422-6032 TOLL-FREE (888) 842-7733 trains scheduled, which also connect with Jasper. The new station is at 12360 121st Street.

The **Greyhound** bus terminal ℂ (403) 413-8747 is at 10324 103rd Street, and operates services that extend north to Hay River in the Northwest Territories and to Whitehorse in the Yukon Territory, west to Prince Rupert, and south to Drumheller and Calgary. **Red Arrow** ℂ (403) 424-3339 TOLL-FREE IN ALBERTA (800) 232-1958, 10014 104th Street, serves Calgary, Red Deer, Rocky Mountain House and Fort McMurray. **Motorists** will find the Trans-

Children splash OPPOSITE while adults ABOVE shop at the West Edmonton Mall, the world's largest shopping complex. OVERLEAF: Telephone poles stand single-file across the prairies of eastern Alberta.

Canada Yellowhead Highway (Highway 16) — which runs from Winnipeg through Edmonton to British Columbia — easy to join. Highway 2 runs the 514 km (320 miles) from the United States Montana border via Calgary to Edmonton, and continues northwards.

CALGARY

Calgary sprawls over prairie land that seems to stretch ever eastwards, but it lies in the foothills of the Canadian Rockies and so to the west of the city you can see the magnificent snow-tipped mountains some 80 km (50 miles) away. Originally a small settlement at the confluence of the Bow and Elbow rivers, Calgary now spreads over the largest land area of any Canadian city, and has become a high-powered city of mirrored high-rises, malls, and other modernities. The climate here is generally dry and sunny with hot summers, and winters that can get bitterly cold but are tempered by the warming Chinook winds from the mountains. These winds can raise temperatures quite dramatically within hours and also have the delightful effect of creating some of the most dramatic sunsets that you'll see anywhere on the prairie.

The character of the city also has its contrasts: On the one hand it is undeniably an oil boom town, with glittering skyscrapers and busy traffic, but it also retains the identity of the cow town it once was, and this is the image that the residents are eager to nurture. The people behave in a way you don't quite expect from the inhabitants of an oil-rich city of glass and steel: they are almost aggressively friendly, and they love to lay on the welcome for visitors. And of course it's almost impossible to think of Calgary without the word "Stampede" springing to mind. This annual festival — held in early July — seems to get the whole of Canada reaching for cowboy hats and boots. Visitors and cowboys pour in from all over the world to join in the yeehawing and the explosion of rodeos, chuck-wagon races, dancing, parades, and general merrymaking.

BACKGROUND

In 1875 the newly formed North West Mounted Police were sent here to restore peace to an area where whisky traders and fur trappers had been cooking up trouble and fanning wars between the natives. They set up a fort at the point where the Bow and Elbow rivers meet; the commander of police named it after Calgary Bay in his native Scotland. Settlers clustered around the post almost immediately, and in 1877 a treaty was signed, without bloodshed, in which the native tribes who roamed the area relinquished the land to the government in return for certain provisions and rights.

The Canadian Pacific Railway came to Calgary in 1883, and this together with the offer of free land to settlers brought about rapid population growth. The excellent grazing lands of the prairie brought the ranchers and their huge herds from the United States, so the town continued to expand, becoming an important meat-packing center and the hub of the farming and ranching region. By 1891 the population was around 4,000; in 1893 the city was granted a charter.

In 1914 the discovery of oil in the Turner Valley just southwest of Calgary brought prosperity to the area, but it was the big strike in Leduc in 1947 and subsequent discoveries in the Edmonton area that triggered the meteoric rise in Calgary's fortunes. The city has become the administrative center for Canada's petroleum industry and now over 500 oil and gas companies have their headquarters here. In the late 1960s there began a 20-year period of frantic development with sky-

scrapers breaking out like a rash, dramatically changing the face of the city and turning it into a perpetual building site while the population exploded to around 640,000. Though things quieted down in the 1980s, the city's hosting of the Olympic Games in 1988 brought the area to the world's attention. The 1990s have brought yet another surge of development and Calgary is now second only to Toronto as a Canadian financial center. The city is growing at an astonishing rate, and the visitor information center is as much a welcome wagon as it is a tourist service.

GENERAL INFORMATION

For information on Calgary and the surrounding area, call or drop by the **Calgary Convention and Visitors Bureau** ((403) 263-8510 TOLL-FREE (800) 661-1678 E-MAIL tourismcalgary.com WEB SITE www.visitor.calgary.ab.ca/, whose main office is at 237 Eighth Avenue SE, Suite 200, Calgary T2G 0K8. There is also a year-round visitor center at the Tower Centre, junction of Ninth Avenue and Centre Street and two others at the Calgary International Airport on the arrivals and departures levels, open 10 AM to 10 PM daily.

Getting Around

Calgary is divided into northwest, southwest, southeast, and northeast sections, and this is important to note as you'll find NE, SE, SW, or NW forming part of the addresses here. The east and west dividing line is Centre Street, and the Bow River separates north from south. Streets follow a grid system, and virtually all of them in the downtown section are one-way. Getting around the city is easy if you use the network of enclosed walkways called "Plus 15s" (because they are a

A polar bear in Calgary Zoo.

minimum of 15 ft or 4.5 m above the ground). Although this all makes for a somewhat characterless shopping scene, it provides welcome protection from the bitter cold of the winters. Just about everything in Calgary — excluding the Stampede grounds — is accessible on foot, but should you want to save some shoe leather, there is a public transportation system consisting of the **C-Train** — which runs along Seventh Avenue SW — and a bus network.

WHAT TO SEE AND DO

Begin your tour of the downtown section with a trip up **Calgary Tower** ☎ (403) 266-7171 at Ninth Avenue and Centre Street South. A high-speed lift will whisk you to the observation deck close to the top of this 190-m (625-ft) landmark, from where you can see seemingly endless prairie land stretching to the east and the magnificent Canadian Rockies to the west. The tower contains the almost statutory revolving restaurant, and there's a café for light lunches. The Olympic flame atop the tower is lit on occasion. The observation deck is open daily year-round 7:30 AM to midnight, with slightly shorter hours between September and May; an admission fee is charged.

Over the road from the tower is the excellent **Glenbow Museum** ☎ (403) 777-5506, 130 Ninth Avenue SE, which has an art gallery on one floor with permanent and temporary exhibitions, a floor devoted to the history of western Canada, and another to an extensive military and weaponry collection that spans medieval to modern times. One of the most noteworthy sections here is the excellent collection of native art, including Inuit crafts. The Alberta Children's Museum is a recent addition to the complex. The museum is open daily Saturday to Thursday from 9 AM to 5 PM, Friday from 9:30 AM to 9 PM, closed Monday in winter. An admission fee is charged.

If you feel like a respite from the concrete jungle, take yourself up to the fourth level of the nearby Toronto Dominion Square at 317 7th Avenue SW, where you'll find the **Devonian Gardens** ☎ (403) 268-3888, a one-hectare (2.5-acre) indoor oasis with fountains, pools, waterfalls, a stage for lunchtime entertainment, and, we were told, some 20,000 local and Californian tropical plants. This entirely organic indoor botanical garden gives visitors a clue about how Calgarians make it through those long days of 30-below winter weather. In addition to the foliage, there are fish ponds where muscular carp-koi-goi and turtles swim, as well as waterfalls and garden sculptures. There are a few snack bars here and it makes a very agreeable meeting place. It is accessible daily from 9 AM to 9 PM, except for times when it is rented out for a private function.

To understand a little more about what made Calgary rich, visit the **Energeum** ☎ (403) 297-4293 at the main floor of the Energy Resources Building, 640 Fifth Avenue SW. The formation, exploitation, and uses of Alberta's energy resources are described through fascinating displays that involve models, computer games, hands-on presentations, and even hands-in (you can feel the oil with gloved hands). It's open Monday to

Friday all year from 10:30 AM to 4:30 PM and on Sundays between June and August. Admission is free.

Turning from the ground to the heavens, slightly to the west is the **Alberta Science Centre and Centennial Planetarium** ☎ (403) 221-3700 at 701 11th Street SW, where there are star shows and hands-on displays that help you understand the laws of physics. There's also a small observatory where you can stargaze through telescopes. It's open Tuesday to Sunday, 10 AM to 5 PM, and an admission fee is charged. Walking distance away and to the north of downtown, **Prince's Island Park** in the Bow River offers a very pleasant and shady retreat. It makes a good picnic spot, with cycling and jogging trails, and is accessible by footbridge from both banks of the river.

Fort Calgary Historic Park ☎ (403) 269-7747, 750 Ninth Avenue SE, lies at the east end of the city center at the confluence of the rivers. This was once the site of Fort Calgary, established by the North West Mounted Police in 1875. It was the birthplace of the city. Set in 16 hectares (40 acres) are the 1875 fort reconstruction, and a number of historical buildings. The Interpretive Centre offers a vivid picture of life in the days of the early settlers and traces the history of the city. It's open every day from 9 AM to 5 PM, May 1 to October 13; an admission fee is charged.

From Fort Calgary, cross the bridge to St. George's Island to see the excellent **Calgary Zoo** ☎ (403) 232-9300. Here some 300 species of creatures great and small are represented by over 1,200 animals — in environments that simulate their natural habitats. Glass panels allow visitors to observe the seals, polar bears, penguins, and others in the water. A large **Botanical Gardens** filled with thousands of tropical plants also provides an ideal setting for exotic birds and butterflies. Attached to the zoo is the **Prehistoric Park**, where a group of life-size replica dinosaurs are set in a prehistoric landscape. The zoo is open daily throughout the year, and an admission fee is charged. There's yet more wildlife to be seen at the **Inglewood Bird Sanctuary** ☎ (403) 269-6688, about two and a half kilometers (one and a half miles) from the zoo and southeast of the city center at Ninth Avenue and Sanctuary Road SE. In this forested reserve on the west bank of the Bow River there have been sightings of over 250 species of birds. A new Visitor Centre here offers information and natural history courses. It's open year-round; admission is free.

Stampede Park ☎ (403) 261-0101, southeast of downtown at 14th Avenue and Olympic Way SE, is where the big events take place during the Calgary Stampede (see THE CALGARY STAMPEDE, below). It's worth a trip even when the Stampede isn't in progress just to see the stunning **Canadian Airlines Saddledome** ☎ (403) 777-2177, a sports arena with a roof in the shape of a gigantic saddle. The Saddledome ☎ (403) 777-2177 is the home of the Calgary Flames, the city's National Hockey League

Costumed interpreters talk shop OPPOSITE at Heritage Park's turn-of-the-century village. ABOVE: Calgary's Old City Hall, an architectural survivor amongst the modern skyscrapers.

team. While you're in the park you might like to visit the **Grain Academy** ☎ (403) 263-4594 on the upper floor of the Round-Up Centre, a museum where models and a miniature railway show how grain is transported from the prairies to the Vancouver docks. It's open Monday to Saturday; admission is free.

For a full reconstruction of life in pioneer times and other periods of Calgary's history, you must go to **Heritage Park** ☎ (403) 259-1900, 16 km (10 miles) southwest of town at the Glenmore Reservoir. This is the largest "living-history" village in Canada. Many original buildings have been brought here from various parts of Alberta, and an early-1900s village has been reconstructed with

a working bakery, a mill, a newspaper office, stocked-up stores, and housing. You can enjoy the antique midway rides, take a trip on a restored steam train or go out onto the reservoir aboard the old sternwheeler the **SS *Moyie***. There are also plenty of places to snack or dine here. It's open daily year-round; an admission fee is charged. An old-fashioned pancake breakfast (9 AM to 10 am) is included in the price of admission.

Continuing south along the Macleod Trail, then left along Bow Bottom Trail SE, you'll come to **Fish Creek Provincial Park** ☎ (403) 297-5293 which spreads out along eight kilometers (five miles) at the edge of the city boundary. This parkland, through which Fish Creek runs, is a wildlife sanctuary but is also where people come simply to escape from city life. There is a magnificent colony of great blue heron here as well as archeological sites, a lake for swimming — and in winter there's cross-country skiing and ice skating. The park is open daily and admission is free.

The impressive facilities which Calgary built for the 1988 Winter Olympics are still in use, and the **Olympic Park** ☎ (403) 286-2632, which was the main site for free-style skiing, ski jump, luge and bobsleigh events, stands to the west of town, a 10-minute drive along Highway 1 (the Trans-Canada Highway) from the center. You can explore the site for yourself or join a guided tour (highly recommended). A ski lift takes you to the top of the course from where you can gaze down the 90-m (295-ft) ski jump tower and see the courses from the perspective of the Olympic athletes who tackled them. The **Olympic Hall of Fame and Museum** has three floors stacked with Olympic memorabilia, photographs, and films and a virtual trip down all 14 twists and turns of the bobsleigh track. You can also take the Bobsleigh Bullet — a summer luge ride on the ice. Olympic park is open year-round. Admission fees are charged for the tour, museum, and Bobsleigh Bullet.

The Calgary Stampede

Billed as "The Greatest Outdoor Show on Earth," the Calgary Stampede is a 10-day celebration of Calgary's Wild West days. It takes place every July and has been going since 1912. Everyone gets into the spirit of it, donning Stetsons, jeans, and boots. There is a big parade with dancing in the streets, while hearty breakfasts are served up around town. Calgary's nightlife percolates, too, with all sorts of special events. The **Radisson** and **Westin** feature nonstop dancing in the hotel ballrooms. Southeast of the town at Stampede Park there are bands, more dancing, food, livestock shows, and the real business of the Stampede: the rodeo and the chuck-wagon races. For the professional cowboys who take part in the rodeo and make their living from the sport, this is serious business with big prize money awaiting only the first-prize winner in each of seven main events. Visitors need to reserve their tickets and accommodation well in advance. For details of the event contact the Calgary Exhibition and Stampede ☎ (403) 261-0101 TOLL-FREE (800) 661-1260, PO Box 1060, Station M, Calgary T2P 2K8.

Excursions from Calgary

The foothill region of **Kananaskis Country** lies between Calgary and the Rocky Mountains. This area is protected by several provincial parks, created to take some of the pressure off Banff. Along the Trans-Canada Highway 106 km (66 miles) west of Calgary and 20 minutes east of Banff townsite, the community of **Canmore** is nestled at the base of the Three Sisters Mountain Range. The town center has plenty of shops, and eateries and is a good base for outdoor activities in the Kananaskis region which encompasses three provincial parks, including the **Peter Lougheed Provincial Park** ☎ (403) 591-6344, Alberta's largest. With 500 sq km (190 sq miles) of valleys and lakes and hiking trails. Canmore was the sight of the 1988 Olympic cross-country skiing and biathlon events, and the **Canmore Nordic Centre** ☎ (403) 678-2400 still draws skiers in winter and mountain bikers in summer.

The resort of Kananaskis Village and the adjacent **Nakiska Ski Area** ☎ (403) 591-7777, and **Kananaskis Country Golf Course** ☎ (403) 591-7272 are reached via Highway 40, south of the Trans-Canada Highway. The Canmore Nordic Centre and Nakiska Ski Area were 1988 Winter Olympic sites. Kananaskis Village is the departure point for many hiking and cross-country skiing trails.

The small town of **Fort Macleod** is approximately a two-hour drive south of Calgary, and is one of Alberta's earliest settlements. It is the site of the first North West Mounted Police post, and is named after their first commander, Lieutenant Colonel James Macleod. This force (now the Royal Canadian Mounted Police) was formed in 1873 to enforce law and order in the west, where at that time the whiskey traders were wreaking havoc, and their first action was to set forth on a grueling march from Manitoba through the northwest which brought them here in 1874. The **Fort Macleod Museum** ☎ (403) 553-4703 is built in the fashion of a police post, with log buildings surrounded by a wooden palisade. The log buildings contain displays on the way of life of the Mounties, of the province's pioneers, and of the natives. The **town center** is itself worth a visit as it contains many old buildings and has been declared a Provincial Historical Area. Drop by the visitor booth ☎ (403) 553-2500 for information on self-guided tours.

The luridly named **Head-Smashed-In Buffalo Jump** lies 18 km (11 miles) northwest of Fort Macleod along Highway 2 and Secondary Highway 785. For over 5,000 years natives stampeded herds of buffalo to their deaths over the edge of this steep cliff. These hunts were an important part of the native culture, involving hundreds of men,

OPPOSITE: In the badlands a Richardson's ground squirrel packs in the peanuts. Calgary's Olympic Park LEFT and ABOVE — the main site for the 1988 Winter Olympics — is now enjoyed year-round by skiers, bobsledders, and mountain bikers.

precise planning, and religious rituals. The hunt would provide the natives with food, hides, and bone. Archaeological digs at this UNESCO World Heritage Site have uncovered bones, village sites, and First Nations artifacts. The Head-Smashed-In Buffalo Jump **Interpretive Centre** ☎ (403) 553-2731 is a seven-level complex built into the cliff; it describes the culture of the Plains native people, in particular the Blackfoot, and the business of the hunt itself through films, displays, and guided walks of the site. It's open daily throughout the year; an admission fee is charged.

Approximately 55 km (33 miles) south of Fort Macleod, the lower peaks of **Waterton Lakes National Park** ascend abruptly from grasslands

of the extreme southwestern corner of Alberta — giving rise to the park's sobriquet "the place where the mountains meet the prairie." Waterton Lakes is situated along the Montana-Alberta border where it joins with the United States' Glacier National Park — with which it shares the designation of a "Biosphere Reserve" that is a UNESCO World Heritage Site because of the region's unique geological history.

Accommodation and visitor services are located in the townsite of **Waterton Park**, and the Parks Canada Visitor Centre ☎ (403) 859-2445 or (403) 859-2224 is just north of the townsite, on Highway 5.

Though only 525 sq km (189 sq miles) in area, Waterton Lakes contains scenery as wondrous as any of the bigger Canadian Rockies parks, as well as abundant recreational activities. Backpackers and hikers can enjoy the park's 225 km (135 miles) of trails. There are motorboating and boat tours on Upper Waterton Lake, as well as canoeing at the townsite marina and at Cameron Lake. Upper Waterton Lake has an almost constant wind, averaging 32.5 kph (19.5 mph) making windsurfing a top draw. Scuba divers can explore the wreck of a sunken paddle steamer in Emerald Bay. Picnicking, tennis, bicycling, and swimming round out the summer activities. Winter access is restricted by road closures, but skiing, snowshoeing, and waterfall ice climbing take place.

A one-and-a-half-hour drive northeast of Calgary will bring you to the strange, lunar-like landscape of the **badlands**, characterized by gullies and deeply carved canyons. This area was once a subtropical marshland where dinosaurs roamed, and there have been many discoveries of fossils and skeletons in the area.

Located in this strange landscape is the small city of **Drumheller**, the starting point of the **Dinosaur Trail**, a 48-km (30-mile) circular driving route taking you to various places of interest in the area and offering some good views of the badlands. The Infocentre ☎ (403) 823-6300 is at 703 Second Avenue West, where you can pick up a copy of the *Visitors Guide to the Drumheller Valley* which lists 30 separate stop-offs.

Though mostly commercial and an attempt to capitalize on the dinosaur theme that is well-enough spun out by the Royal Tyrrell Museum and the provincial parks (see below), the Dinosaur Trail is a fun jaunt through the badlands history and geography. You can take an all-terrain vehicle ride through **Horsethief Canyon**, cross the Red Deer River on the 1913-vintage **Bleriot Ferry** that works on a pulley system, cross the **Rosedale Swinging Suspension Bridge**, visit the tumbleweed town of Rosedeer, and drop in to the **Last Chance Saloon** where wagon wheels and elk horns decorate the façade and bullet holes riddle the interior.

On Highway 10, shortly after the hamlet of Cambria (don't blink), turn left into the **Hoodoos Provincial Recreation Area**. These bizarre rock formations were created by 10,000 years of wind and rain erosion; protective caps of hard sandstone prevent the pillars from eroding as quickly as the surrounding rock. Cross-sections of the regions geological history, the hoodoo's shale base was once the floor of an ancient sea, now some 73 million years old; the sandstone above this was deposit by swamps and streams in the dinosaur era 70 million years ago.

About six kilometers (four miles) northwest of Drumheller, the **Royal Tyrrell Museum** TOLL-FREE (888) 440-4240 FAX (403) 823-7131 E-MAIL rtmp@dns.magtech.ab.ca WEB SITE www.tyrrellmuseum.com, PO Box 7500, Drumheller, Alberta T0J 0Y0, contains the largest exhibition of dinosaurs in the world. This excellent paleontological museum presents theories about evolution up until the appearance of man with over 35 complete dinosaur skeletons, hands-on displays, and a variety of special programs. You can watch museum technicians at work behind a glass window, chipping away a millimeter at a time at huge stone-encrusted skeletons. The curators are clearly aware of the esthetic as well as the scientific interest of the fossils, and offer displays emphasizing the myriad patterns and colors of petrified organisms, such as delicate million-year-old seed ferns, swirling ammonites, and rainbow-hued ammolite, a gemstone that is unique to Alberta. The star exhibit at the Tyrrell is the Burgess Shale blacklight presentation where you can see the oldest known multicellular marine animals — "weird wonders" — at 12 to 20 times their actual size.

There are multilingual audio-guides available for taking a self-guided tour of the museum. It's open in summer daily from 9 AM to 9 PM, and in winter Tuesday to Sunday from 10 AM to 5 PM. An admission fee is charged.

The museum is situated in **Midland Provincial Park** and a trail system gives you the chance to walk through the grounds where exposed fossils are often found. But remember that Alberta has strict laws to preserve the province's heritage. All fossils are the property of the people of Alberta; collecting is permitted only outside of the provincial parks.

The museum's Day Digs program gives you the chance to go out and **dig for dinosaurs** with trained technicians, and do the actual work of excavating.

Those who have caught the dinosaur bug may want to extend their journey to the **Dinosaur Provincial Park**, environs and excursions Dinosaur Provincial Park ☎ (403) 378-4342 FAX (403) 378-4247 WEB SITE discoveryweb.com/aep/parks/dinosaur, PO Box 60, Patricia T0J 2K0, 140 km (87 miles) southeast of Drumheller, an area of the Red Deer Valley badlands that is also a UNESCO World Heritage Site. It is one of the most extensive dinosaur graveyards in the world, and throughout the park skeletons are on view exactly in the position that they were discovered. So extensive are the remains that they say you're never more than two feet from a fossil here. In the park you can visit the **Royal Tyrrell Museum Field Station** ☎ (403) 378-4342 where you can see the paleontologists working on finds. It's open daily from mid-May to mid-October, weekends only in winter. An admission fee is charged.

There's an interpretive display here, and it is also the starting point for a bus tour of the park and guided walks. Interpretive programs run daily mid-May to early September. Admission is free; there is a fee for the bus tour To reach the park from Drumheller, take Route 56 to Brooks then Highway 873 and follow the signs.

Those who wish to continue to walk with the dinosaurs can journey even further back into prehistory with trips to the Burgess Shale fossil beds in Yoho National Park (see YOHO NATIONAL PARK, page 145, in THE CANADIAN ROCKIES).

Cochrane, 25 km (16 miles) west of Calgary, is a favorite spot for trail rides and canoe trips on the Bow River. It's western style buildings house some interesting local arts and crafts. The **Western Heritage Centre** ☎ (403) 932-3514, near the junction of Highways 22 and 1A, is a new hands-on interpretive center with exhibits that tell the story of ranching, farming, and rodeos in the province. You can learn about the first Alberta ranchers and the families who still perform those same chores today. It's open daily year-round and an admission fee is charged.

SPORTS AND OUTDOOR ACTIVITIES

There are **cycling**, **hiking**, and **jogging** trails in the pleasant Prince's Island Park, which is accessible by footbridge from downtown, and also at

Fish Creek Provincial Park at Calgary's southern border. The Olympic Park has a brand new **mountain bike** course with lots of challenging trails; bikers and their steeds ride the ski lift to the top of the mountain and zigzag their way down. For **horseback riding**, the Happy Trails Riding Stable ☎ (403) 251-3344 in Fish Creek Park, gives lessons and also operates guided or unguided trail rides.

The Bow and Elbow rivers are popular for **canoeing**, particularly at Bowness Park ☎ (403) 288-5133 at 48th and 90th Street NW. There's world-class fly **fishing** and trout fishing in the section of the Bow River between Carseland and east Calgary, and lists of the many places that offer fishing trips are available from information centers.

In winter there's **skating** on the lagoon at Bowness Park, 48th Avenue and 90th Street NW, also at Fish Creek Provincial Park, and year round in the covered speed-skating track at the Olympic Speed Skating Oval ☎ (403) 220-7954 at the University of Calgary, which is open for public use. In all, there are 17 skating rinks in Calgary; contact Calgary Parks and Recreation ☎ (403) 268-3888

OPPOSITE: One of the Royal Tyrrell Museum's Jurassic monsters. This scale model shows a T-Rex, one of the dinosaurs that once walked the badlands. ABOVE: Home on the range — a latter-day monster haunts the streets of Calgary.

for information. The **downhill ski slopes** at the Olympic Park are open to the public, and there's **cross-country skiing** at Fish Creek Provincial Park.

NIGHTLIFE AND THE ARTS

For **entertainment listings** you should check the local daily and weekly newspapers, especially the Friday *Herald*, and the *Sun*. Several large hotels have nightclubs, and offer quite a variety of entertainment.

Calgary's cultural life centers around the **Centre for the Performing Arts** ☎ (403) 294-7455 at 205 Eighth Avenue SE. This excellent arts complex comprises the Jack Singer Concert Hall, which is

home to the Calgary Philharmonic Orchestra. The Alberta Ballet Company performs at the **Jubilee Auditorium** ☎ (403) 297-8000, 14th Avenue and 14th Street NW. The **Pumphouse Theatre** ☎ (403) 263-0079, 2140 Ninth Avenue SW, features a variety of theatrical performances during its September to June season. Concerts and dramatic works both classical and contemporary are presented at the **University of Calgary Theatre** ☎ (403) 220-4900, 2500 University Drive NW.

Calgary has hundreds of bars and clubs, many of which have live music. Jazz and blues can be enjoyed at **Kaos Jazz and Blues Bistro** ☎ (403) 228-9997, 718 17th Avenue SW, or at **McQueen's** ☎ (403) 269-8889, 317 10th Avenue SW. Local and touring alternative bands can be seen at **Republik** ☎ (403) 244-1844, at 219 17th Avenue SW, or at **The Night Gallery** ☎ (403) 266-5116, 1209B First Street SW, which is primarily known for its theme nights, often with live bands. For country & western there's the **Ranchman's Restaurant** ☎ (403) 253-1100, 9615 Macleod Trail South, where there's also beer swilling and dancing; or **Dusty's Saloon** ☎ (403) 263-5343, 1088 Olympic Way SE, where there are free two-step lessons on Tuesday and Wednesday nights. There's a stretch of 11th Avenue known as **Electric Avenue** that consists of a stretch of bars, clubs and pubs, or there's the less noisy and older neighborhood of **Kensington** centered around Kensington Road and 10th Street NW — a good area for restaurants, pubs, bars, and nightlife.

Calgary has several casinos, including Alberta's largest, the **Stampede Casino** ☎ (403) 261-0422, at Stampede Park. It's open Monday to Saturday from noon to 1 AM.

WHERE TO STAY

Expensive

Downtown, the **Palliser Hotel** ☎ (403) 262-1234 TOLL-FREE (800) 441-1414 FAX (403) 260-1260, at 133 Ninth Avenue SW, Calgary T2P 2M3, was built by the Canadian Pacific Railway in 1914. With its pillars, stately staircases, and crystal chandeliers, it remains an oasis of old-fashioned splendor in this city of steel high-rises. It has just about every comfort provided for. There are exercise facilities, a splendid dining room, a café, and a lovely bar. For a more modern kind of elegance there's the centrally located **Calgary Marriott** ☎ (403) 266-7331 TOLL-FREE (800) 333-3333 FAX (403) 262-8442, at 110 Ninth Avenue SE, Calgary T2G 5A6, which is within the Convention Centre complex. It is luxurious without being brash, and the service echoes this quality with its understated excellence. Rooms and suites have all kinds of special features, and there's an indoor pool and garden, two dining rooms, and a bar with live entertainment.

Also downtown, the **Westin Hotel** ☎ (403) 266-1611 TOLL-FREE (800) 228-3000 FAX (403) 233-7471, 320 Fourth Avenue SW, Calgary T2P 2S6, offers modern luxury with 525 attractive bedrooms and suites, and lots of complimentary touches. The lobby is large and sumptuously decorated, there is a beautiful indoor swimming pool, and the hotel has several dining spots including the city's famous Owl's Nest restaurant. The **Delta Bow Valley Inn** ☎ (403) 266-1980 TOLL-FREE (800) 665-8571 FAX (403) 266-0007, 209 Fourth Avenue SE, Calgary T2G 0C6, is another large, top-rated, downtown hotel that has exercise facilities, a children's center, indoor swimming pool, and a restaurant. The **International Hotel of Calgary** ☎ (403) 265-9600 TOLL-FREE IN WESTERN CANADA (800) 661-8627 TOLL-FREE IN EASTERN CANADA AND THE UNITED STATES (800) 223-0888 FAX (403) 265-6949, 220 Fourth Avenue SW, Calgary T2P 0H5, is a modern highrise that exudes luxury. It has 250 attractive suites. All have balconies and are extremely comfortable. It also has a health spa, a gym, a restaurant, and a piano bar.

Located in a leafy residential area, northwest of the city center, **A Good Knight Bed & Breakfast** ☎ (403) 270-7628 TOLL-FREE (800) 261-4954, 1728 Seventh Avenue NW, Calgary T2N 0Z4, is one of the new breed of luxury bed and breakfast accommodations. A happy combination of homespun style and soothing comforts make this a good choice for anyone looking for a relaxing, friendly stay. Throughout the house, decor is quaint in the extreme — all part of your eager hosts' efforts to make you feel at home. Their teddy bear collection is astounding. While two of the three individually decorated rooms are smallish, a third is quite spacious; a cathedral ceiling, a king-size bed and a jet bath complete the picture. An ample breakfast is served downstairs in the dining room each morning, and special dietary needs are gladly catered for. Rates range from moderate to expensive.

Mid-range

The **Sandman Hotel** ☎ (403) 237-8626 TOLL-FREE (800) 726-3626 FAX (403) 290-1238, 888 Seventh Avenue SW, Calgary T2P 3J3, is centrally situated and offers an excellent range of facilities. It has 300 attractively furnished rooms, some with good views, with all kinds of comforts and conveniences. There is a fitness center, a glass-roofed swimming pool, and a Denny's Restaurant, which is open 24-hours. The **Prince Royal Inn All Suite Hotel** ☎ (403) 263-0520 TOLL-FREE (800) 661-1592 FAX (403) 298-4888, downtown at 618 Fifth Avenue SW, Calgary T2P 0M7, has 300 one- or two-bedroom suites with kitchens, making it good value for families. The hotel has laundry facilities, a health club, and a dining room.

In northwest Calgary there is a motel strip along Banff Trail, near the point where Crowchild Trail crosses the Trans-Canada Highway. Along this strip, the **Quality Inn-Motel Village** ☎ (403) 289-1973 TOLL-FREE (800) 661-4667 FAX (403) 282-1241, 2359 Banff Trail NW, Calgary T2M 4L2, has one of the best ranges of facilities. The 100 suites and rooms have telephones and televisions, and there is a poolside dining room as well as a cocktail lounge.

Inexpensive

Downtown is the **Lord Nelson Inn** ☎ (403) 269-8262 TOLL-FREE (800) 661-6017 FAX (403) 269-4868, 1020 Eighth Avenue SW, Calgary T2P 1J2, with 55 rooms and suites that have private bathrooms, refrigerators, televisions, and telephones. There are also some bridal and executive suites. The hotel has a warm and attractive lobby, a dining room, and a pub.

There is a cluster of motels along Macleod Trail near Stampede Park. Among them is the **Elbow River Inn & Casino** ☎ (403) 269-6771 TOLL-FREE (800) 661-1463 FAX (403) 237-5181, 1919 Macleod Trail SE, Calgary T2G 4S1. It sits on the banks of the Elbow River and is connected by an underpass walkway to Stampede Park. All of its 75 rooms have bathrooms, some have kitchenettes. There is a dining room with pleasant riverfront views, and a full breakfast is included in the rates, which vary from mid-range to inexpensive. The **Flamingo Motor Hotel** ☎ (403) 252-4401 FAX (403) 252-2780, 7505 Macleod Trail South, Calgary T2H 0L8, is set in pleasant grounds and has 50 good-sized rooms and suites with bathrooms, some with kitchenettes. Rates here range between inexpensive and mid-range. The **Stampeder Inn** ☎ (403) 243-5531 TOLL-FREE (800) 361-3422 FAX (403) 243-6962, at 3828 Macleod Trail SW, Calgary T2G 2R2, has nicely appointed rooms and suites, meeting facilities, an indoor pool, shops, a pub, a cocktail bar, and a dining room that lays on an generous buffet.

For **bed and breakfast**, **farm** and **ranch** or **back-country lodge accommodation**, contact the Bed

& Breakfast Agency of Alberta ☎ (403) 277-8486 TOLL-FREE (800) 425-8160, 410 19th Avenue Northeast, Calgary T2E 1P3. In Drumheller, there's the Drumheller Valley Bed and Breakfast Association ☎ (403) 823-5379 FAX (403) 823-9712 E-MAIL gkashuba@telusplanet.net, 71 McDougall Lane, Drumheller T0J 0Y1. Specifically for guest ranch accommodation in the area there's the **Homeplace Guest Ranch & Trail Rides** ☎/FAX (403) 931-3245, Rural Route 1, Priddis T0L 1W0. Rooms come with private bathrooms, family meals are provided, riding lessons and trips are organized, and horse pack trips up into the Rockies with teepee accommodation are also available. The ranch is just outside the city's south perimeter.

OPPOSITE: Calgary's nighttime skyline rides the Saddledome, home of the city's National Hockey League team, the Flames. ABOVE: Public art in downtown Calgary.

The **University of Calgary** has some good accommodation during the summer months, and also a few rooms available during term-time. For details contact the university at ☎ (403) 220-3210, 2500 University Drive NW, Calgary T2N 1N4.

The **Calgary International Hostel (HI)** ☎ (403) 269-8239 FAX (403) 266-6227 E-MAIL chostel@HostellingIntl.ca, has six- to eight-bed dormitory rooms and is located at 520 Seventh Avenue SE, Calgary T2G 0J6.

WHERE TO EAT

La Chaumière ☎ (403) 228-5690, at 139 17th Avenue SW, offers traditional French cuisine prepared

to gourmet standards and excellent service in a charming, intimate setting. The **Owl's Nest** ☎ (403) 266-1611 in the Westin Hotel, 320 Fourth Avenue SW, is one of Calgary's best-known and finest dining spots. It is a splendidly decorated place serving continental cuisine, with the region's excellent beef featuring largely on the menu.

The **Green Street Restaurant** ☎ (403) 266-1551, 815 Seventh Avenue SW, is a popular downtown spot, with a glass wall affording good views of the nearby park. The surrounding greenery, a restful color scheme, and the spaciousness make for a relaxing atmosphere. There are Cajun, French, and Italian dishes, steaks and seafood — in short, a bit of everything — on offer. Prices here range between moderate and inexpensive.

Informal and inexpensive places abound. **4th Street Rose** ☎ (403) 228-5377, at 2116 Fourth Street SW, is a trendy place where you can get very good pizzas, salads, and pasta. There are several other eateries around this section of Fourth Street. Along 17th Avenue SW you'll find another such cluster of restaurants. The **Unicorn Restaurant and Pub** ☎ (403) 233-2666, at 304 Eighth Avenue SW, is a busy, snug place that serves traditional pub grub and lots of beer on tap. Over in the Kensington neighborhood the **Take Ten Café** ☎ (403) 270-7010, 304 10th Street, has German food and lots of home baking on the menu.

Calgary's **Chinatown**, the second largest in Canada, begins at the downtown end of the Centre Street Bridge and extends across the river. There are plenty of Asian restaurants to choose from, some of which serve dim sum. In the back of the Hang Fung supermarket, 119 Third Avenue SE, is the **Hang Fung Foods** ☎ (403) 269-4646, one of the best places in the city to get salt and pepper squid. It's a bit difficult to find (go through the supermarket) but worth the effort for some truly authentic Chinese food.

HOW TO GET THERE

The **Calgary International Airport** is about eight kilometers (five miles) northeast of downtown, a 30-minute drive. Canadian Airlines International runs a frequent Airbus service between Calgary and Edmonton. To get you to the town, there's the **Airporter Bus** ☎ (403) 531-3909 which runs every 30 minutes from Level 1.

With the closure of its more scenic southern rail route through Calgary, VIA Rail no longer serves Calgary. **Rocky Mountain Railtours** TOLL-FREE (800) 665-7245 operates a scenic two-day rail tour from Calgary to Vancouver, with a one-night hotel stay in Kamloops included in the price of the fare (see RIDE THE LEGENDARY RAILS, page 11, in TOP SPOTS).

Greyhound ☎ (403) 265-9111 operates bus services to Calgary from all directions. **Red Arrow** ☎ (403) 531-0350 TOLL-FREE IN ALBERTA (800) 232-1958, serves Edmonton, Red Deer, and Rocky Mountain House. The station is at Eighth Avenue SW and 16th Street. It's a 30-minute walk from the city center, but during the day there's a free shuttle that will connect you with the C-Train.

The Trans-Canada Highway (Highway 1) runs through Calgary, linking it with British Columbia to the west and Saskatchewan to the east. West of Calgary the Trans-Canada Highway runs through Banff National Park and through Glacier National Park in British Columbia. Highway 2 runs north from the United States–Montana border to Calgary, continuing on to Edmonton and beyond.

ABOVE: Calgary's Chinatown is the second-largest in Canada. OPPOSITE: A Plains Indian in full regalia.

Saskatchewan

SASKATCHEWAN
NORTHWEST TERRITORIES
ALBERTA
SASKATCHEWAN
MANITOBA
N
S
E
W
0 50 100 miles
0 50 100 150 Km
Camsell Portage
Waterloo Lake
Uranium City
Lake Athabasca
Beaver Lake
Fond-du-Lac
Athabasca Sand Dunes
Richard Lake
Black Lake
Milton Lake
Lac Brochet
Cluff Lake Mine
Pasfield Lake
Points North Landing
Wollaston Lake
Wollaston Lake
Close Lake
Wollaston Lake Landing
Weitzel Lake
Cree Lake
Cree Lake
Reindeer Lake
Kinoosao
Descharme Lake
Key Lake Mine
Clearwater River Park
La Loche
Turnor Lake
Turnor Lake
Garson Lake
Black Point
Peter Pond Lake
Churchill Lake
Southend
Brabant Lake
Michel
Dillon
Buffalo Narrows
Dipper Lake
Elak Dase
McLennan Lake
Grandmother's Bay
Île-à-la-Crosse
Pinehouse Lake
Lac La Ronge Park
Sandy Bay
Canoe Narrows
La Ronge
Lac La Ronge
Stanley Mission
Pelican Narrows
Primrose Lake
Cole Bay
Beauval
Air Ronge
Deschambault Lake
Jan Lake
Flin Flon
Cold Lake
Meadow Lake Park
Waterhaven Lake
Dore Lake
Dore Lake
Creighton
Sled Lake
Weyakwin
Molanosa
Denare Beach
Green Lake
Montreal Lake
Whelan
Loon Lake
Meadow Lake
Montréal Lake
Cumberland Lake
Prince Albert National Park
Nipawin Park
St. Walburg
Chitek Lake
Waskesiu Lake
Pemmican Portage
Cumberland House
The Pas
Paradise Hill
Spruce Lake
Birch Lake
Big River
Candle Lake
Red Earth
Lloydminster
Debden
Waskesiu Lake
Choiceland
Tobin Lake
Shoal Lake
Spiritwood
Smeaton
Tobin Lake
Lashburn
Glaslyn
Wildcat Hill Park
Prince Albert
Nipawin
Maidstone
Shell Lake
Meota
Birch Hills
Pontrilas
Carrot River
Baldwinton
Delmas
North Battleford
Macdowell
Melfort
Erwood
Tisdale
Wilbur
Battleford
Blaine Lake
Duck Lake
Prairie River
Hudson Bay
Unity
Wilkie
Rosthern
Wakaw
McKague
Porcupine Plain
Porcupine Forest
Archerwill
Greenwater Lake Park
Radisson
Warman
Endeavour
Cando
Martensville
Rose Valley
Biggar
Englefeld
Swan River
Saskatoon
Humbolt
Watson
Kerrobert
Springwater
Vanscoy
Preeceville
Wadena
Tessier
Dundurn
Viscount
Dafoe
Big Quill Lake
Canora
Elfros
Duck Mountain Park
Kindersley
McGee
Rosetown
Hanley
Watrous
Wynard
Foam Lake
Gorlitz
Outlook
Kenaston
Eatonia
Brock
Dinsmore
Hawarden
Imperial
Raymore
Ebenezer
Glidden
Elrose
Bladworth
Kelliher
Yorkton
Leader
Tyner
Birsay
Elbow
Dunleath
Davidson
Craik
Melville
Rokeby
Saltcoats
Kyle
Beechy
Holdfast
Portreeve
Abbey
Fort Qu' Appelle
Waldron
Stewart Vally
Lumsden
Balcarres
Richmound
Fox Valley
Success
Chaplain
Moose Jaw
Qu' Appelle
Herbert
Regina
Indian Head
Qu'Appelle River
Beverly
Erbfold
Hatton
Tompkins
Antelope
Swift Current
Parkbeg
Bushell Park
White City
Grenfell
Whitewood
Pashley
Gull Lake
Wymark
Corderre
Old Wives Lake
Francis
Moosamin
Maple Creek
Kennedy
Cypress Hills Park
Fillmore
Shaunavan
Glenbain
Vantage
Lang
Moose Mountain Park
Thelma
Eastend
Cadillac
Weyburn
Carlyle
Antler
Kincaid
Assiniboia
Rosbart
Dollard
Trossachs
Stoughton
Forget
Govenlock
Mankota
Wood Mountain
Benough
Canuck
Midale
Benson
Divide
Climax
Val Marie
Oungre
Estevan
Almeda
Wildhorse
Willow Creek
Masefield
Canopus
Big Beaver
Minton
Torquay
West Poplar
Fortuna
1
16
155
2
106
55
4
3
40
11
41
6
5
35
9
14
7
21
49
15
44
19
32
39
33
13
18

SITUATED BETWEEN MANITOBA IN THE EAST AND ALBERTA IN THE WEST, Saskatchewan contains the largest area of Canada's three Prairie Provinces. It is the country's most important wheat producer, and has become a byword for the endless, treeless plain that in the minds of many typifies the word "prairie." This is unfortunate and somewhat unfair, as Saskatchewan does have quite a varied landscape, both within the prairie and beyond it. Besides that vast, flat, and treeless wheat-growing belt, there are some 100,000 jewel-blue lakes for fishing and recreation, 200,000 hectares (five million acres) of parkland, the lunar-like landscape of the badlands, as well as green valleys and acres of boreal forest.

In the south of the province the badlands, a mixture of semiarid grasslands and desert-like areas, occupy a large semicircular portion of the prairie. This section is surrounded by a wheat-growing belt in which the provincial capital of Regina lies, and beyond that strip is the outer section of the prairie, known as the parkland, an area of gently rolling hills and trees, through which the North and South Saskatchewan rivers flow. Beyond the prairie, Prince Albert National Park stands at the edge of the remote North Country, a wilderness of forests and marshlands, crisscrossed with a latticework of lakes and rivers, much of which is Canadian Shield country. Here the roads peter out, and it is very sparsely populated. These wide-open spaces, ideal for fishing and canoeing, attract adventurers and urban refugees.

When in 1858 John Palliser led an expedition through the southwest of the province, he deemed the land unsuitable for agriculture, but subsequent irrigation proved his assessment wrong, turning Saskatchewan into North America's largest wheat-growing region. More than 50% of Canada's crop is produced here, while the grasslands of the south have made good cattle-raising country. The mineral wealth of the province has also proved profitable; oil is now an important part of the economy. The favorable summer weather and hundreds of parks attract outdoors lovers, making the tourist industry a newer strand in an economy that is rapidly growing.

Saskatchewan has a population of about a million in an area of 651,900 sq km (251,700 sq miles), leaving a lot of empty space, and the citizens of its two major cities revel in the opportunities that their parklands provide. The relaxed character of the people masks a fighting spirit and a willingness to work together for the common good that has brought them through some very difficult times. They are also unafraid of change: In 1944 Saskatchewan elected the first Socialist government in North America and embarked upon a series of innovative social programs. The people are proud of their pioneering past, which they commemorate in many museums — Saskatchewan has the most museums per capita of all the provinces. There are frequent reminders of the remarkable contribution made by the North West Mounted Police in the development of the area, and also of the bitter Northwest Rebellion that once shook the province and still seems to send out shock waves.

Saskatchewan has quite a colorful history. The first white man to explore the territory was Henry Kelsey in 1690, acting on behalf of the Hudson's Bay Company. Trading posts were then established in the region, and throughout the nineteenth century the fur trade flourished here. As a result the Métis people came into being, children of French fathers and native mothers who lived the native way of life but followed Roman Catholicism.

A vehicle decorated for Regina's Buffalo Days.

In 1870 the Canadian government, seeing the agricultural potential, bought the land from the Hudson's Bay Company and began to negotiate treaties in preparation for the settlement of the area. The government advertised free land to settlers, and ranchers began to move their herds into the southwest. In 1873 the North West Mounted Police was formed to enforce law and order in the Northwest Territories. But it was the coming of the Canadian Pacific Railway in 1882 that began to reel in settlers from the United States, Britain, and Europe.

The arrival of the settlers and the surveying of the land in preparation for further immigration caused great consternation among the Métis, who stood to lose rights to the lands they already inhabited. As their pleas to the government went unheeded, they turned to the leadership of a young man named Louis Riel. They set up their own provincial government in an attempt to establish their rights, but the English Métis did not lend their support to this faction, and conflict arose between Riel's people and some of the settlers. This resulted in Riel having one of them killed following an attempt on his life. The Métis were eventually granted some land for settlement and Riel was forced into exile, but when the Métis and the natives again found themselves about to be dispossessed, Riel returned to lead them in the Northwest Rebellion of 1885, dubbing himself "Prophet, Infallible Pontiff and Priest King."

This was a bitter conflict that ended with a hopeless but noble stand by the rebels at Batoche, against government troops using Gatling guns. Riel surrendered, was brought to trial in Regina, and was hanged for treason there.

Subsequently the Métis received the land rights they had sought, but the death of Riel had other political repercussions. For many it came to represent the French-English conflict, and to this day it remains an emotive subject. Saskatchewan does much to keep the memory alive, and each year in Regina the trial of Riel is reenacted.

In 1905 Saskatchewan was incorporated, with Regina as its capital, and immigration to the province steadily continued along with prosperity and growth. The Depression of the 1930s hit Saskatchewan particularly hard, and to add to the misery 10 years of drought brought crop failure, creating a depressing brown landscape dotted with starving cattle. Now, half a century later, the region thrives; like the other Prairie Provinces, the 1990s have ushered in a period of great economic growth in Saskatchewan.

REGINA

Saskatchewan's capital is one of Canada's sunniest cities, and as befits its name Regina rises regally from the center of the flat prairie wheat fields. With the Canadian Pacific Railway and the Trans-Canada Highway running through the city, it is the financial, industrial, and agricultural center of Saskatchewan, with a population of around 200,000. It has a healthy cultural life with a good number of theatre and dance companies, as well as Canada's oldest symphony orchestra and one of her top concert halls. Regina is home to Canada's only training academy for the Royal Canadian Mounted Police, which adds a splash of red color and some ceremonial pomp to the city. The museum that traces the development of the force and other museums throughout the city afford visitors a fascinating window on the province's past.

Once a miserable, muddy, and unpromising site along the banks of the Wascana, Regina has been transformed into a dignified and serene city of parklands and well-considered public facilities, offering travelers welcome respite from the vast plains that surround it. The core of the city and the buildings that house some of its major attractions lie in Wascana Centre, a pleasant parkland of trees and gardens surrounding a man-made lake.

BACKGROUND

When the Canadian Pacific Railway was planning its route across the plains, the government, realizing that the erstwhile capital of the Northwest Territories would be nowhere near the railway, entered into discussions with the Canadian Pacific Railway to decide on a site for a new settlement that would lie along the line. The place they settled upon was far from being an obvious choice. It lay along the banks of an almost dried-up creek, with only a few stagnant pools remaining — an area that varied from being too muddy to too dusty. The banks had been used by the Cree for slaughtering buffalo and drying the skins, and because of the large numbers of buffalo skeletons there they had given it the inauspicious name Oskana — meaning "Pile of Bones." However, settlement was soon under way, and in 1882 the first train chuffed into the station. Princess Louise, wife of Canada's governor-general, bestowed upon it the more dignified name of Regina, in honor of her mother, Queen Victoria.

The North West Mounted Police set up headquarters here, and in 1885 Regina became the focus of attention when, following the Northwest Rebellion, it was the scene of the trial of the Métis leader, Louis Riel. Opinion was divided over Riel, as many believed his cause to be a just one that highlighted the French-British conflict in Canada, but Riel was found guilty of treason and hanged in November of that year.

When the province of Saskatchewan was incorporated in 1905, Regina was its capital city and immigrants began to flood in. Gradually the problems of the location were solved: the creek was dammed to create an artificial lake, the surrounding parkland was landscaped, the dignified Legislative Building was planned, and present-day Regina began to take shape.

GENERAL INFORMATION

For information on Regina and vicinity contact **Tourism Regina** ☎ (306) 789-5099 TOLL-FREE (800) 661-5099 extension 277 FAX (306) 789-3171, which is located on the Trans-Canada Highway at the eastern edge of the city at Highway 1 East, PO Box 3355, Regina S4P 3H1. It's open year-round, seven days a week in summer and weekdays only in winter.

WHAT TO SEE AND DO

Along the banks of Wascana Creek lie several parks, but Regina's pride is the **Wascana Centre**, a 930-hectare (2,300-acre) park that forms the heart of the city. Once a muddy area with an uncertain water supply, settlers dammed the creek here to create Wascana Lake and a water reserve. It is now one of the largest urban parks in North America — a beautiful green space where trees have been planted and flowerbeds cultivated. Around the lake a pleasant marina has been built where you can take a ferry over to Willow Island, a lovely spot for a picnic. With canoeing, sailing, boating, windsurfing, and many picnic areas, it is a place of recreation, but the art gallery and science center located here also make it a place of culture and education.

On the western side of the park stands the stately domed **Legislative Building** ☎ (306) 787-5357, built between 1908 and 1912 in the style of the English Renaissance Revival, lavishly decorated within, and set in pleasant gardens. It is open to the public and tours can be arranged that take visitors around the huge library, the Legislative Chamber, and the art galleries on the lower levels. Admission is free.

Over on the north bank of Wascana Lake at the corner of College Avenue and Albert Street stands the **Royal Saskatchewan Museum** ☎ (306) 787-2815, a low building built in Tyndall stone and decorated with a frieze. If you intend visiting the Saskatchewan that lies beyond the cities, this is an excellent introduction to the flora and fauna you will encounter. There are dioramas of various regions, complete with wildlife and sound effects that add to the realism, and with displays

OPPOSITE: Regina's skyline as seen from the Wascana Centre. ABOVE: The iron-and-wood stitchery that since 1885 has sewn Canada together.

on wildlife biology. The Earth Sciences Gallery traces the province's geological history and features some hands-on displays, while another gallery deals with Native American history.

Close by stands the **Mackenzie Art Gallery** ✆ (306) 522-4242, at Albert Street and 23rd Avenue. This began as a private collection bequeathed to the University of Regina, and it now includes both contemporary and older works from a variety of countries, but with an emphasis on Canadian art. It is open daily, with evening hours on Wednesday and Thursday, and admission is free. In August a theatre company reenacts the trial of Louis Riel here from court transcripts, which never fails to stir up controversy.

many other species. There's a naturalist on hand to answer questions and to arrange guided tours. As well as the information center, there's a gift shop and a small art gallery. It's open daily, year-round.

Close to the Legislative Building stands **Government House** ✆ (306) 787-5717, Dewdney Avenue at Connaught Street. This served as the residence of the Lieutenant-Governors between 1891 and 1945. The rooms have been beautifully restored and contain period furnishings. Hours are Tuesday to Sunday from 1 PM to 4 PM. Admission is free.

North of the Wascana Centre, the famous Royal Canadian Mounted Police, or Mounties, have their

Also on the north shore of the lake the old city power station has been converted to house the **Saskatchewan Science Centre** ✆ (306) 522-4629 TOLL-FREE (800) 667-6300, on the corner of Winnipeg Street and Wascana Drive, where hands-on exhibits help to explain some of the laws of physics. It is open daily year-round. An admission fee is charged.

Also within the Wascana Centre on Lakeshore Drive you'll find the **Saskatchewan Centre of the Arts** ✆ (306) 565-4500, which contains two theaters, the larger of which serves as an excellent concert hall where you can hear the Regina Symphony Orchestra play, Canada's oldest continuously operating symphony orchestra. The Centre presents operas, theatrical productions, dance, and other musical presentations. Nearby on the lake shore is the **Waterfowl Park** (306) 522-3661, where you can see Canada geese, swans, pelicans, and

training academy and also the **RCMP Centennial Museum** ✆ (306) 780-5838, off of Dewdney Avenue West. The museum traces the colorful history of the Mounties and the vital role they played in Canada's development — a role that far exceeds that normally fulfilled by a police force. Archival material, uniforms, weaponry, artifacts, and a wealth of memorabilia recall the famous and grueling march that the newly formed force made through the west to establish law and order. Various other events in the force's history are also recalled. There are some curiosities on display here, such as Chief Sitting Bull's tobacco pouch, while some exhibits add a lighter touch, such as the Hollywood representations of those who "always get their man." It's open daily; admission is free.

For lovers of military drills, the **Sergeant Major's Parade** takes place weekdays at 1 PM, and from July to mid-August the colorful **Sunset**

Retreat Ceremony draws the crowds on Tuesday evenings when the flag is lowered.

Excursions from Regina

Seventy-one kilometers (44 miles) west of Regina along the Trans-Canada Highway lies **Moose Jaw**, Saskatchewan's third largest city. A prosperous railroad and industrial center, Moose Jaw was renowned in the Roaring Twenties as a haven for American bootleggers. Various schemes to attract tourists based on the city's gangster-ridden past have proved unpopular with residents, especially those who experienced this unhappy period.

The city's principal attraction is the huge **Western Development Museum** ☎ (306) 693-5989, 50 Diefenbaker Drive at the junction of the Trans-Canada Highway and Highway 2. There are four Western Development museums in Saskatchewan, each dealing with a different area of provincial history. This branch covers the history of transportation, with displays on aviation, the railway, plus land and water transportation. Exhibits include vintage cars and aircraft, an old Canadian Pacific Railway train, a reconstructed railway station, wagons, and old snowmobiles. It's open daily during summer, closed on Mondays during winter; an admission fee is charged.

If you're keen on visiting another of the four of the Western Development museums, then you need to travel to Yorkton, which 187 km (116 miles) northeast of Regina along Highway 10 (for the two others, see WHAT TO SEE AND DO, pages 184 and 185, under SASKATOON). Yorkton is a major distribution center with a population of around 16,000, and some decent accommodations. If you visit in late May or early June, you can catch the **Yorkton Short Film and Video Festival**. The **Western Development Museum** ☎ (306) 783-8361, is on the west side of town along Highway 16. The museum depicts "The Story of People," daily life in Saskatchewan during the eighteenth and nineteenth centuries, with displays of tools and machinery both old and new. The interiors of early homes are recreated, reflecting the style of the various ethnic groups, such as the Plains natives, the English, French, and Ukrainians. It's open daily May to mid-September; an admission fee is charged.

The **Qu'Appelle Valley** cuts through the prairie from Lake Diefenbaker to the northwest of Regina up to the Manitoba border to the east, a route that stretches across roughly two-thirds of the province. This long, green valley of trees and lakes was a favorite place for fur traders and natives as it offered welcome respite from the prairie and was a valuable source of wood. Today it is as green as ever and is lined with parks, villages, and resorts. Route 10 from Regina will bring you to **Fort Qu'Appelle**, some 70 km (43 miles) away, which is a good place to buy local crafts. In this stretch of the valley there are a series of lakes that are excellent for fishing and swimming. The string of lakes here is popular with boaters and water-skiers. These are also ideal fishing lakes, but make sure to get a license first and familiarize yourself with the regulations.

OPPOSITE: Pinning down enthusiasm for Buffalo Days. ABOVE: The Legislative Building in Regina.

WHERE TO STAY

Expensive to Mid-range

The **Regina Inn** ☎ (306) 525-6767 TOLL-FREE (800) 667-8162 FAX (306) 525-3630, 1975 Broad Street, Regina S4P 1Y2, is a top-rank modern hotel and convention center in the heart of downtown. It has 235 rooms and suites, most of which have balconies, and good facilities. There is a fitness center with a massage therapist on call, two attractive dining spots, and a dinner theater. There are similarly high standards at the **Sands Hotel and Resort** ☎ (306) 569-1666 TOLL-FREE (800) 667-6500 FAX (306) 525-3550, 1818 Victoria Avenue, Regina S4P 0R1. It has particularly attractive public areas and 250 rooms and suites, all very well-equipped. There's a lovely indoor swimming pool, a restaurant and a pub. Prices at both hotels vary between expensive (for a suite with a Jacuzzi) and inexpensive (for a standard room on the weekend).

For first-class accommodation in older surroundings, book into the **Hotel Saskatchewan Radisson Plaza** ☎ (306) 522-7691 TOLL-FREE (800) 333-3333, 2125 Victoria Avenue, Regina S4P 0S3, a grand building that dates from 1927. The public areas have an old-fashioned grandeur, and the generously proportioned rooms are furnished in modern style and with many creature comforts. There are 215 rooms and suites, including the "Royal Suite," which has indeed housed royalty. There is a cocktail lounge, and a restaurant. Prices here are in the expensive category.

Situated downtown, the **Chelton Suites Hotel** ☎ (306) 569-4600 TOLL-FREE (800) 667-9922 FAX (306) 569-3531, at 1907 11th Avenue, Regina S4P 0J2, has 56 large rooms and suites, attractively decorated and equipped with refrigerator, microwave, and wet bar. A restaurant, a friendly atmosphere, and prices that vary from inexpensive to mid-range make this good value.

Inexpensive

The **Plains Motor Hotel** ☎ (306) 757-8661 TOLL-FREE (800) 665-1000 FAX (306) 525-8522, downtown at 1965 Albert Street, Regina S4P 2T5, has 60 rooms with bathrooms and television. There's a pub and a dining room. Slightly to the north of the center, the **Inntowner Motor Inn** ☎ (306) 525-3737 TOLL-FREE (800) 667-7785 FAX (306) 525-5548, 1009 Albert Street, Regina S4R 2P9, has 43 good size rooms with television, some with queen-size beds, and the hotel has a dining room and a coffee shop.

South of downtown the **Landmark Inn** ☎ (306) 586-5363 TOLL-FREE (800) 667-9811 FAX (306) 585-2303, 4150 Albert Street South, Regina S4S 3R8, is virtually a resort hotel incorporating a large recreational complex including an indoor swimming pool with a water slide. There are 186 rooms, all well-equipped, a restaurant, and a pub.

Close to Wascana Park, the **Turgeon International Hostel (HI, IYHF)** ☎ (306) 791-8165 TOLL-FREE (800) 467-8357 FAX (306) 721-2667, 2310 McIntyre Street, Regina S4P 2S2, is a restored heritage house with lots of character, offering dormitory-style rooms, good self-catering facilities, a laundromat, and a lovely old sitting room. It operates February 1 to December 23, and doors are open from 7 AM to 10 AM and from 5 PM to midnight.

WHERE TO EAT

The **Diplomat** ☎ (306) 359-3366, 2032 Broad Street, is one of Regina's most elegant restaurants. Seafood and steaks, prepared expertly, are complemented by an excellent wine list.

A multitude of choices is available for moderately priced to inexpensive dining. Good Cajun cuisine is served at **Orleans Café and Oyster**

Bar ☎ (306) 352-2000, in the Chelton Inn, 1907 11th Avenue, which is a favorite with locals who appreciate the fine service and the room's casual elegance. **Bartleby's** ☎ (306) 565-0040, at 1920 Broad Street, is a popular dining spot and bar, with a menu that has a United Nations feel, but it's the decor that they really come here for. Heaps of Victorian curiosities adorn the place and just about every corner has some piece of memorabilia or hardware poking out of it. For English-style pub grub go to the **Elephant & Castle** ☎ (306) 757-4405, in the Cornwall Centre at 11th Avenue and Scarth Street.

There's spicy Caribbean fare at **Brown Sugar** ☎ (306) 359-7355, including jerk, curry dishes, and salads featuring tropical fruits and vegetables. It's located downtown at 1941 Scarth Street. **Heliotrope** ☎ (306) 569-3373, at 2204 McIntyre Street (14th Avenue), serves vegetarian food with global influences. And, **Orleans** ☎ (306) 525-3636, downtown at 1822 Broad Street, serves authentic Cajun cuisine in a lively Mardi-Gras style atmosphere.

HOW TO GET THERE

The **Regina Airport** is seven kilometers (just over four miles) southwest of the city center. It's about a 10- to 20-minute ride to downtown.

Greyhound TOLL-FREE (800) 661-8747 buses run from Regina to Saskatoon where connections can be made with **VIA Rail** TOLL-FREE (888) 842-7733. Buses also run to Calgary and Vancouver, Winnipeg, Toronto, and Montréal. The bus station is close to downtown at 2041 Hamilton Street ☎ (306) 787-3340.

The two main highways into Regina are the Trans-Canada Highway (Highway 1) that runs

Royal Canadian Mounted Police at their training academy in Regina.

east and west of the city, and Highway 6 that runs from the United States Montana border to the south through the town, continuing northwards beyond Melfort. Just north of the city, Highway 11 from Saskatoon links with Highway 6, just north of Regina, which runs into the city center.

SOUTHERN SASKATCHEWAN

In the southwest corner of Saskatchewan, and stretching into southern Alberta, **Cypress Hills Interprovincial Park** ☎ (306) 662-4411 comes as something of a surprise. It is an area of forests, hills, valleys, lakes, and streams that rise out of the prairie plains to heights of almost 1,500 m (5,000 ft). There are pine forests (which were mistaken by the French explorers for cypresses, hence the name), rare flowers, birds, and other wildlife. An area of the park is set aside for a resort with campsites, cabins, hiking trails, riding stables, tennis courts, golf courses, and a beach. Located on Route 21, it is open daily and a per-vehicle admission fee is charged.

This is also an area of historical significance. In 1873 it was the scene of a massacre when some Montana wolf hunters who mistakenly believed the Assiniboines were responsible for stealing their horses killed Assiniboine. The illegal trading of whisky in the area had played its part in the affair, and the massacre spurred the creation of the North West Mounted Police. In 1878 they set up headquarters at Fort Walsh, now the center of the **Fort Walsh National Historic Site** ☎ (306) 662-3590. It is located 55 km (34 miles) southwest of Maple Creek along Highway 271. The fort has been restored both inside and out, so that visitors can see for themselves the tough living conditions that the men endured. The interpretive center here shows films and has displays on the fort and the history of the police force. Among the more difficult tasks assigned to them was that of trying to persuade Chief Sitting Bull and his 5,000 braves to return to the United States after they had fled here following their defeat of Custer at Little Big Horn.

A bus from the fort will take visitors to **Farwell's Trading Post**, where costumed guides take you through the buildings and help recreate the lawless days of the whisky traders. It's open daily mid-May to mid-October; admission is free.

SASKATOON

Saskatoon sits in the center of the prairie parkland, an area of trees and farmland that lies to the north of the wheat-growing belt and south of the forested northern wilderness. It is a small, pleasant city of around 220,000 people that lies along both banks of the South Saskatchewan River, which runs northeast to southwest through the city. Several bridges cross the river, and its banks are lined with parks offering peaceful retreats and recreation. There is a mixture of old and new buildings, generally low-rise, and there are wide downtown streets that die out around the edges of the town.

Saskatoon was founded as a temperance colony in 1882 by a group of Methodists from Ontario. They christened it after the purple berries that grew plentifully in the area. Temperance seems to have been unpopular, for at the turn of the century there were only 113 inhabitants, and even the coming of the railroad in 1890 didn't tempt new settlers here. However, in the early 1900s the agricultural potential of the area began to attract settlers from Europe and the Ukraine, and in 1906 the city was incorporated. A year later Saskatoon University was founded.

The city can offer its visitors some decent accommodation, several interesting eateries, and a warm, friendly welcome, making it a good stopover if you are on your way to the wild North Country. The Saskatoon University campus, the city's largest employer, dominates the east bank of the river. Although the university has been at the forefront of medical technology development, the city has still not shaken off the aura of a frontier town.

GENERAL INFORMATION

The local branch of **Tourism Saskatchewan** ℂ (306) 242-1206 TOLL-FREE (800) 567-2444 FAX (306) 242-1955 offers information on the province and is situated in the Old Canadian Pacific Railway station, at 305 Idylwyld Drive North S7L 0Z1.

WHAT TO SEE AND DO

The downtown core lies along the west bank of the South Saskatchewan River and is a fairly small area, so most of the main attractions, with a few exceptions, are within walking distance of one another. The streets conform to a grid system, and 22nd Street cuts across the city dividing it into north and south, while Idylwyld Drive forms the east-west dividing line. Several galleries and shops downtown sell **arts**, **crafts**, and **antiques**, and some other outlets can be found on the east side of the river, particularly along Victoria and Broadway Avenues.

The river banks are lined with pleasant parks, trees, and recreation areas. One of the most distinguished landmarks on the west bank is the **Delta Bessborough Hotel**, a 1930s railway hotel built in the grand château style favored by the railway companies of that time. Near the Bessborough Hotel lies **Kiwanis Park**, a picnicking spot, where you can rent a canoe if you fancy some paddling.

A little further north along the river bank, the **Ukrainian Museum of Canada** ℂ (306) 244-3800, 910 Spadina Crescent East, preserves examples of the culture of these peasant immigrants who settled in the region during the late nineteenth and early twentieth centuries. There are displays of costumes, arts and crafts, artifacts, textiles, and photographs documenting the history of their immigration. The gift shop here sells Ukrainian cookery books, arts, and crafts. The museum is open daily from mid-May to September and closed on Mondays during the rest of the year. An admission fee is charged.

Continuing northwards along the riverbank, the **Mendel Art Gallery and Civic Conservatory** ℂ (306) 975-7610 is housed in a modern building at

OPPOSITE: The campus of Saskatoon University.
ABOVE: Bison roam at the Forestry Farm Park and Zoo in Saskatoon.

950 Spadina Crescent East. The gallery has a permanent collection of contemporary and older works from Europe and Canada, and also hosts visiting exhibitions. The building contains a small but pleasant conservatory and an interesting gift shop. It's open daily, and admission is free.

Looking across the river from the gallery you'll see the attractive gray-stone buildings of the **University of Saskatchewan** ☎ (306) 244-4343. Tours of the campus start from Place Riel Campus Centre; places of interest here include the Biology Museum ☎ (306) 966-4399 (open weekdays), and the Museum of Antiquities ☎ (306) 966-7818 (open weekdays). The university's Diefenbaker Canada Centre ☎ (306) 966-8384 (open daily) is a museum, art gallery, and research center in Canadian studies commemorating Canada's 13th prime minister. Also on the campus stands the Little Stone School House ☎ (306) 966-8384 (open daily in summer, weekdays the rest of the year), Saskatoon's first schoolhouse and oldest public building, dating from 1887. Admission is free for all of these museums.

One of Saskatoon's two major tourist attractions is the **Western Development Museum** ☎ (306) 931-1910 at 2610 Lorne Avenue South. It is one of four such museums in Saskatchewan (the others are in Yorkton, Moose Jaw — see WHAT TO SEE AND DO, page 179, under REGINA; and North Battleford — see below), each of which is devoted to a different aspect of the province's history. The subject dealt with by this museum is "Boomtown 1910," and the museum brings that period of Saskatchewan's history very much to life in an impressive indoor reconstruction of an entire street of that year, complete in every detail. Care has been taken to represent the period not only in visual terms but also in smells and sounds, creating a vivid impression of life at that time. As you stroll along the wooden sidewalks, past the horse-drawn buggies and automobiles, you can peruse the remedies on display at the pharmacy, look in the windows of the stores, and even see a silent movie at the picture house. The street also has a fully equipped Chinese laundry, a bank, a railway station, and a school. Other areas of the museum have collections of old cars, aircraft, and farming equipment. There's also a display on the mail order services that were an important part of life for many families until quite recently. The No. 1 bus will take you from Second Avenue downtown to the museum. The museum is open daily, year-round; an admission fee is charged.

Saskatoon's other big attraction is **Wanuskewin Heritage Park** ☎ (306) 931-6767, RR 4, located five km (three miles) north of Saskatoon on Highway 1. This museum complex is built around the ongoing archeological excavation of 19 ancient Indian sites. You can walk the trails and observe archeological digs in progress, including living areas, teepee rings, bison jumps, and other remnants of the Northern Plains peoples who once inhabited the area. At the amphitheater, there are performances presented by native dancers and storytellers, while at the outdoor activity area visitors can learn how to build a teepee, bake bannock, or tan a moose hide. The main exhibition halls feature artifacts, interactive computer displays, multimedia shows exploring the archeology and culture of the Plains peoples, and contemporary art. The park complex is open from Victoria Day to Labor Day daily from 9 AM to 9 PM; fall and winter Wednesday to Sunday from 9 AM to 5 PM. An admission fee is charged.

Eight kilometers (five miles) northeast of downtown along Attridge Drive lies the **Saskatoon Zoo** ☎ (306) 975-3382. This pleasant verdant area houses around 300 animals and birds, mainly those indigenous to North America. There are recreation areas as well (including cross-country skiing in winter) along with picnic and barbecue facilities, making it a nice spot for a family outing. It is open daily throughout the year, and an admission fee is charged, with a additional vehicle fee in the summer months.

Excursions from Saskatoon

The **Batoche National Historic Site** ☎ (306) 423-6227, lies 88 km (55 miles) northeast of Saskatoon along the banks of the South Saskatchewan River, and is a must for anyone interested in the history of the Northwest Rebellion. Batoche was the site of a major Métis settlement in the nineteenth century and was the headquarters for Louis Riel's Provisional Government, which was set up to fight for the lands of the Métis people. At the park you can tour four battlefield areas and view a film at the visitor center. The Interpretive Centre has displays on the Métis culture and the rebellion, and altogether the park pays a moving tribute to Métis people and their plight. The park is open from mid-May until mid-October; an admission fee is charged. To get there, take Highway 11 from Saskatoon, turn onto Highway 312 at Rosthern, then north onto Highway 225, which brings you to the park.

There are more history lessons in store, quite fun ones too, at the **Battlefords**, the two communities of Battleford and North Battleford, divided from one another by the North Saskatchewan River and lying 140 km (87 miles) northwest of Saskatoon. Battleford sits on the south side of the river and was once the capital of the Northwest Territories, but it lost this status when the Canadian Pacific Railway laid their line further south. It was the site of a North West Mounted Police fort built in 1876, and at **Fort Battleford National Historic Site** ☎ (306) 937-2621, Central Avenue, you can see the restored fort which has been fitted with authentic artifacts and furnishings. Within the palisades there are five buildings, including the Officers' Quarters, the Commanding Officer's Residence, and the Barracks. The Interpretive Centre provides some good displays on the 1885 rebellion. It's open daily, and an admission fee is charged.

Across the bridge, North Battleford was created because the Canadian National Railway ran its line along the north shore of the river, and it contains another **Western Development Museum** ☎ (306) 445-8033 located at the junction of Highways 16 and 40. This one takes the "Heritage Farm and Village" as its theme, and there are extensive displays on agricultural equipment and techniques, as well as a reconstruction of a small village of 1925 vintage. The village includes pioneer homes, a Ukrainian Orthodox church, and a railway station. It is open from the beginning of May until mid-September. To get to the Battlefords from Saskatoon, the most direct route is along the Yellowhead Highway (Highway 16) to North Battleford. An admission fee is charged.

Protecting a slice of northern coniferous forest and wildlife at the center of Saskatchewan, **Prince Albert National Park** ☎ (306) 663-4522 TOLL-FREE RESERVATIONS (888) 333-7267 FAX 306-663-5424, PO Box 100, Waskesiu Lake, SK S0J 2Y0, lies 200 km (124 miles) north of Saskatoon and 90 km (54 miles) north of Prince Albert, is a preserve of lakes, streams, hills, and forest — where coyotes, black bears, elk, moose, beavers, and many others roam free. As well as canoeing it offers its visitors hiking trails ranging from easy walks to backpacking hikes that last for days, and cross-country skiing in winter.

Just inside the eastern entrance of the park lies **Waskesiu Lake**, and along its shores the Waskesiu townsite. With accommodation of all descriptions, cafés, and shops, it makes an excellent base from which to explore the park. Waskesiu has a beach, a golf course, tennis courts, stables, and boat rentals, and you can take a leisurely cruise along the lake aboard a paddle-wheel. The **Nature Centre** ☎ (306) 663-4509, gives interesting and entertaining presentations on the park, telling the story of Grey Owl, the self-styled naturalist who lived in the park during the 1930s and spoke out for the cause of conservation. There's an interactive exhibit on the boreal forest and its inhabitants, and the center offers guided walks. It's open daily from June to September.

WHERE TO STAY

Expensive to Mid-range

The **Sheraton Cavalier** ☎ (306) 652-6770 TOLL-FREE (800) 325-3535 FAX (306) 244-1739, 612 Spadina Crescent East, Saskatoon S7K 3G9, is a modern downtown hotel that has just about all the facilities you could wish for, including special executive facilities. There are 250 rooms, with lots of comforts and enough recreational features to keep all the family happy. There are two indoor water slides, a sun deck, an attractive dining room, a café, and a nightclub.

Close to the airport, the **Saskatoon Inn** ☎ (306) 242-1440 TOLL-FREE (800) 667-8789 FAX (306) 244-2779, 2002 Airport Drive, Saskatoon S7L 6M4, has 250 sumptuously decorated rooms with sitting areas. The hotel has a lovely courtyard filled with tropical plants, a pleasant indoor pool and whirlpool, a smart restaurant, and a more casual dining spot. There's nightly entertainment and dancing in the hotel lounge.

The **Delta Bessborough** ☎ (306) 244-5521 TOLL-FREE (800) 268-1133 FAX (306) 653-2458, 601 Spadina

Crescent East, Saskatoon S7K 3G8, is Saskatoon's most distinguished hotel, built in the grand château style of railway hostelries and set in attractive gardens overlooking the river. The hotel retains its 1930s splendor while incorporating modern conveniences. There are 225 rooms, all slightly different but quite spacious with old-style furnishings. There is an indoor swimming pool, a Japanese steak house, a bistro, a pleasant lounge, and a coffee shop. The hotel also has special business facilities. Also on the riverbank is the **Radisson Hotel Saskatoon** ☎ (306) 665-3322 TOLL-FREE (800) 333-3333 FAX (306) 665-5531, 405 20th Street East, Saskatoon S7K 6X6, a newish 18-story building with an ornate lobby and 290 well-decorated rooms. There are luxury suites available, and

There is superb fishing to be found in the many lakes of central Saskatchewan.

the hotel offers guests an excellent range of recreational facilities, including two indoor water slides. There are also several dining spots to choose from.

At Prince Albert National Park there is lodge and convention center in Waskesiu townsite at the **All Season Waskesiu Lake Lodge** ☎ (306) 663-6161 FAX (306) 663-6144, 175 Lakeshore Crescent, Saskatoon S7J 3T4. Despite the name, it's open May to mid-October.

Inexpensive

The **King George Hotel** ☎ (306) 244-6133 TOLL-FREE (800) 667-1234 FAX (306) 652-4672, 157 Second Avenue North, Saskatoon S7K 2A9, is conveniently located downtown opposite The Bay department store. The building dates from 1905, but all rooms are equipped with modern facilities. There's a restaurant and a bistro. The **Senator Hotel** ☎ (306) 244-6141 FAX (306) 244-1559 is of a similar vintage and is also in the downtown area at 243 21st Street East, Saskatoon S7K 0B7. The hotel retains a rather grand style throughout, and its 45 rooms are all slightly different but with the same modern amenities. The dining room has lots of character and there is an English-style pub. Also centrally located, the **Park Town Hotel** ☎ (306) 244-5564 TOLL-FREE (800) 667-3999 FAX (306) 665-8697, 924 Spadina Crescent East, Saskatoon S7K 3H5, has newly renovated and attractive rooms all with televisions and telephones, and offers guests the use of an indoor pool.

There's no hostel in Saskatoon, but the **Patricia Hotel** ☎ (306) 242-8861, 345 Second Avenue North, Saskatoon S7K 2B8, is just as inexpensive as one. It's located a couple of blocks from the bus depot, on the corner of 25th Avenue.

For details of **farm vacations** and **bed and breakfast** accommodations, contact the Saskatchewan Country Vacation Association ☎ (306) 664-3278 FAX (306) 664-6822, 1308 Fifth Avenue North, Saskatoon S7K 2S2.

WHERE TO EAT

This is prairie land and consequently there are some excellent steak houses in town. **Cousin Nik's** ☎ (306) 374-2020, 1110 Grosvenor Avenue, specializes in moderately priced surf and turf, but adds a Greek touch, both in the food and the decor. The attractive outdoor courtyard makes a particularly appealing dining spot. The splendid Delta Bessborough Hotel, 601 Spadina Crescent East, houses the two reliable restaurants: the **Samurai Japanese Steak House** ☎ (306) 244-5521, and the **Garden Bistro**. You'll find elegant continental dining at the Ramada Inn's **R.J. Wiloughby** ☎ (306) 665-7576, 90 22nd Street East.

St. Tropez Bistro ☎ (306) 652-1250, 238 Second Avenue South, is a pretty and popular spot for inexpensive snacking. **Fuddruckers** ☎ (306) 955-7777, 2910 Eighth Street East, also inexpensive, serves good homemade hamburgers.

HOW TO GET THERE

Saskatoon International Airport is about a 10- to 20-minute drive west of downtown.

The **VIA Rail** TOLL-FREE (888) 842-7733 terminal, is at the western edge of the city on Chappell Drive. It's a five-minute walk to the bus that takes you downtown.

The **Greyhound** bus station ☎ (306) 933-8000 is downtown at 50 23rd Street East, and it handles services between Saskatoon and Regina, Winnipeg, Calgary, Edmonton, and Jasper.

If you're **driving** to Saskatoon from Regina, you'll arrive on Highway 11, and if you're coming from Manitoba in the east or Alberta in the west, you'll probably need to take the Yellowhead Highway (Highway 16) which becomes Idylwyld Drive within the city limits. If you're driving from Prince Albert National Park or Lac La Ronge Provincial Park further to the north, you need to take Highway 2 and then pick up Highway 11 south of Prince Albert, which will bring you to the northern edge of Saskatoon.

NORTHERN SASKATCHEWAN

About 150 km (95 miles) north of Prince Albert National Park lies **Lac La Ronge Provincial Park** ☎ (306) 425-4245 TOLL-FREE (800) 772-4064, with 340,500 hectares (841,035 acres) of lakes and forests. Over 100 lakes, including the huge Lake la Ronge, plus waterfalls and rapids, make this an ideal place for canoeing and fishing. It is open year-round. Accommodation can be found in the town of La Ronge on the southwestern edge of the lake, as well as agencies offer canoeing and camping package trips.

Northeast of Prince Albert National Park lies **Meadow Lake Provincial Park** ☎ (306) 236-7680, a horizontal strip of parkland that surrounds a string of lakes. Like Prince Albert, it is an area of forests, lakes, and rivers that marks the transition between the northern Saskatchewan wilderness and the prairie parkland area. Visitors come here to enjoy its beautiful lakeside beaches and its wildlife, and to canoe, fish, and hike. There are tennis courts, stables, and in the winter cross-country skiing trails. The park is open year-round, and there are campsites in the park and cabins for rent.

OPPOSITE: Images of life on the prairies.

TEA

Manitoba

MANITOBA
NUNAVUT
SASKATCHEWAN
MANITOBA
ONTARIO
U.S.A.
Hudson Bay
Seal River
North Knife River
Churchill River
Tadoule Lake
Big Sand Lake
Northern Indian Lake
Southern Indian Lake
Amisk Natural Park
Wapusk National Park
Churchill
Herchmer
Thibaudeau
Weir River
York Factory
Gillam
Kinoosao
Lynn Lake
South Indian Lake
York Landing
Kelsay
Heaman
Highrock
Nelson House
Thompson
Pukatawagan
Takipy
Sipiwesk
Oddhill
Knee Lake
Oxford House
Gods Lake
Gods Lake Narrow
Flin Flon
Snow Lake
Grass River Park
Ponton
Atik
Cormorant Lake Park
Wekusko
Clearwater Lake Park
Cormorant
The Pas
Moose Lake
Norway House
Warren's Landing
Waasagomach
St Theresa Point
Overflowing River
Cedar Lake
Dawson Bay
Grand Rapids
Lake Winnipeg
Big Black River
Denbeigh Point
Porcupine Forest
Lake Winnipegosis
Swan Pelican Forest
Birch Island
Reindeer Island
Berens River
Swan River
Duck Bay
Cowan
Camperville
Dauphin River
Princess Harbour
Duck Mountain Park
Atikaki Wilderness Park
Meadow Portage
Hecla Heritage Park
Pine Dock
Roblin
Dauphin
Dauphin Lake
Fisher River
Ashern
Dallas
Grandview
Riding Mountain National Park
Mulvihill
Arborg
Hecla
Russell
Silver Ridge
Victoria Beach
Wasagaming
Lake Manitoba
Gimli
Pine Falls
Foxwarren
St. Georges
Nopiming Park
Minnedosa
Neepawa
Gladstone
St. Laurent
Lac du Bonnet
Grosse Isle
Selkirk
Whiteshell Park
Rivers
Winnipeg
Portage la Prairie
Oak Lake
Brandon
Elm Creek
Richer
Falcon Lake
Reston
Souris
Wawanesa
Holland
Steinbach
North Angle Forest
Lake of the Woods
Melita
Boissevain
Rosenfeild
Morris
Killarney
Delraine
Winkler
St Jean Baptiste
0 25 50 75 100 miles
0 75 150 Km
N
E
S
W
10
6
39
60
77
49
83
5
68
16
50
7
8
59
11
44
1
21
34
2
13
12
71
29

OFTEN REFERRED TO AS CANADA'S "KEYSTONE PROVINCE" because of its central position, Manitoba is bordered by the states of North Dakota and Minnesota to the south, by the province of Saskatchewan to the west, Ontario to the east, and Nunavut and Hudson Bay to the north. It stretches over a vast 650,088 sq km (251,000 sq miles), approximately one-sixth of which is covered with rivers and lakes. It has a population of just over one million, more than half of whom live in the capital city of Winnipeg, the province's only major city.

Of all three Prairie Provinces, Manitoba has the smallest portion of prairie land, with the wheat-growing belt intruding only into its southwest corner. Beyond the prairies lie the Great Lakes of Winnipeg, Manitoba, and Winnipegosis; beyond them a vast, rugged, rocky wilderness of forests, bogs, and more lakes stretch northwards to the sub-Arctic coastline of Hudson Bay. With the Northern Lights and polar bears of Hudson Bay, around 100,000 lakes, the desert-like landscape of Spruce Woods Provincial Park, and numerous parks offering escape routes into the wilderness, there is a lot more to Manitoba than wheat fields.

Agriculture, however, has always played an important role in the province's growth and economy. Wheat is the major crop, with other grains and cattle-raising also important sources of revenue. Food processing and manufacturing are the province's main industries, and the rich mineral deposits of the Canadian Shield form the basis of several others. The tourist industry is developing and outdoor enthusiasts are attracted to the province by the wonderful opportunities that the lakes and forested wilderness have to offer. The climate, however, is a limiting factor for adventurers: it varies between hot summers, when the temperature often soars above 30°C (90°F), particularly in the southwest, and bitterly cold winters, when it's often well below freezing.

In 1612 an Englishman named Thomas Button sailed into Hudson Bay and spent the winter at the mouth of the Nelson River. He came in search of the fabled Northwest Passage to the Orient, but the disappointment at coming up against the mass of mid-Canada was diminished by the discovery that it was a hunter's paradise, teeming with furry animals and cut by rivers that brimmed with fish. In 1668 the ketch *Nonsuch* sailed from England to Hudson Bay and returned laden with furs. As a result, the Hudson's Bay Company was formed and was granted the vast territory, then known as Rupertsland, by Charles II, and trading posts were established around the province.

French trappers were the first white settlers in the prairie and they were the fathers of the Métis race, a half-French, half-Cree people who held with the Catholic faith but led the native way of life. The fur trade continued to flourish and eventually the French posts were surrendered to the British.

Because of the success of trade and transportation in the area, the province began to open up, but this success brought with it a threat to the Métis way of life.

In 1870 the Hudson's Bay Company sold its lands to the Dominion of Canada, which immediately commissioned surveys of the area in preparation for land allotment to new settlers. This prompted the Métis people to rise up in defense of their land rights, and, under the leadership of the young Louis Riel, they set up their own provisional government. As a result of their action and negotiations, a small area around the Red River Valley was declared the province of Manitoba with land allocated to the Métis, and in 1870 Manitoba was incorporated into the Dominion of Canada.

The coming of the Canadian Pacific Railway in the 1880s heralded a period of great change, bringing with it immigrants from Ontario, Iceland, Eastern and Western Europe, and the Ukraine. By 1912 the ever-growing province had been extended to its present-day boundaries, farming was flourishing, and good communications increased the province's supply lines, thus strengthening the economy.

WINNIPEG

Halfway across Manitoba, at the very center of Canada, the city of Winnipeg rises out of the vast flat prairie land rather like a mirage, so far away is it from any other city. It lies at the junction of the Assiniboine and Red rivers, 2,093 km (1,300 miles) west of Toronto, and 572 km (355 miles) east of Regina, connected by rail and the Trans-Canada Highway. It is Manitoba's only major city. Around 675,000 people live in it, over half the entire population of the province. It is also Western Canada's oldest city, and its nucleus is, and always has been, the junction of Main Street and Portage Avenue, streets that stretch out for miles across the prairie, following the direction of the city's two rivers.

Winnipeg is a very likable city, quite cosmopolitan in character and very cultured. It has pleasant parks, lovely riverside walks, wealthy suburbs with old mansion houses, and at the north-eastern end of the city an old area of warehouses and depots reminds visitors of its early importance as a distribution center. The buildings along the wide, flat downtown streets testify to a policy of urban development that has respect for the city's stately older buildings, while remaining unafraid of change and innovation.

The famous corner of Portage Avenue and Main Street has benefited from such innovation, with an underground mall and walkways now offering shelter from what is billed as the windiest and coldest spot in Canada. The summer temperatures in the city can hit upwards of 30°C (the high 80s Fahrenheit), but the winter sees temperatures of minus 20°C (minus 4°F) with snow and blizzards that chill to the bone. Winnipeggers seem to take pride in their ability to withstand the bitterness of these long winters, and they will boldly go forth in search of an evening's entertainment. The combination of this harsh weather and Winnipeg's isolation from other urban centers may be the reason why it has created such a gloriously rich cultural scene for itself. It boasts the world-famous Royal Winnipeg Ballet, a widely acclaimed symphony orchestra, the Manitoba Opera, the excellent Manitoba Theatre Centre, and one of the country's finest museums, the Manitoba Museum of Man & Nature.

Another enriching factor in Winnipeg's cultural life is the diverse ethnic mix of its population. It started out with a mixture of natives, British, French, and Métis, but the coming of the Canadian Pacific Railway added more to the melting pot. Chinese came as laborers working on the construction of the railway, then came other Western and Eastern Europeans, Ukrainians, Mennonites, and Icelanders. The various nationalities tended to settle in ethnic-based communities around the city, and though this arrangement has to a large extent broken down, certain districts still retain a strong cultural identity. The downtown area has a sizable Chinatown, while the St. Boniface district to the south of the river has a large French-speaking community, and the southern part of town generally tends to be British in origin. Each August the city celebrates its ethnicity with the Folklorama festival that takes place in 40 pavilions throughout the town, each representing a different culture. You buy a "passport" which gains you admission to the various pavilions and also allows you to travel on the special buses that shuttle you between pavilions.

Maybe it is again the city's isolation and self-sufficiency that underlies its strong character. Even the cityscape, with its cast-iron buildings, huge stockyards, warehouses, and mansion-like houses, has solidity and a sense of security about it. Winnipeggers are themselves a resilient bunch, proud of their city, whose feelings of intense loyalty bind them to it wherever they wander.

BACKGROUND

This was once a region where the Cree and Assiniboine roamed, but change began when the first white man set foot in the area in 1738. He was the French explorer and fur trapper Pierre Gaultier de la Verendrye, and he established a fort near the confluence of the Red and Assiniboine rivers. The fur trade flourished in the area, albeit with a good deal of friction between rival factions, and in 1812 the Hudson's Bay Company gave land in the Red River valley to Lord Selkirk, allowing him to establish a Scottish settlement, thus creating a supply center for the traders.

These Scottish Highlanders came here in search of a more prosperous life, and they began to farm the area, slowly at first, as regular flooding and pestilence made for a difficult start. To the Métis people who lived by hunting buffalo, the settlement and farming of the area was a threat to their survival, and in 1816 they attacked the settlement, killing 20 of the Scots in what has become known as the Seven Oaks Massacre. The colony faltered, but continued to grow slowly. A commercial center developed around the junction of the two rivers that served as trading trails, with river and road transportation linking it to the United States.

In 1870 the province of Manitoba was created, and by 1873 the city of Winnipeg was incorporated. The Canadian Pacific Railway arrived in 1886, sparking the rapid expansion of the city and bringing large numbers of immigrants to the city. The agricultural industry flourished, and Winnipeg's position as a distribution center and financial capital was strengthened. Today it has a thriving manufacturing industry, and it remains a major financial and distribution center with a large Commodity Exchange. The junction of Portage Avenue and Main Street, shadowing the two old trade routes, remains at the center of the city's financial district, a reminder of its past.

GENERAL INFORMATION

At The Forks waterfront complex (next to the Johnston Terminal), you can visit the huge **Manitoba Travel Idea Centre** ☎ (204) 945-3777, extension SJ9, where exhibits and travel counselors will help you sort through your options; another walk-in visitor center is located at the Legislative Building at Broadway and Osborne Street. Information on camping in Manitoba can be obtained from **Manitoba Natural Resources** ☎ (204) 945-6784 TOLL-FREE (800) 214-6497. For information specifically on Winnipeg, there is **Tourism Winnipeg** ☎ (204) 943-1970 TOLL-FREE (800) 665-0204, 279 Portage Avenue, Winnipeg R3B 2B4, with a second location at the Winnipeg International Airport ☎ (204) 774-0031, main Level, North End, and a third at the Legislative Building, at Broadway and Osborne Street.

WHAT TO SEE AND DO

The **Exchange District** lies at the very heart of Winnipeg, a 20-block area stretching from Portage Avenue and Main Street to the Centennial Centre, and incorporating the famous Canadian cold spot at the corner of Portage Avenue and Main Street. Today the large buildings that stand here

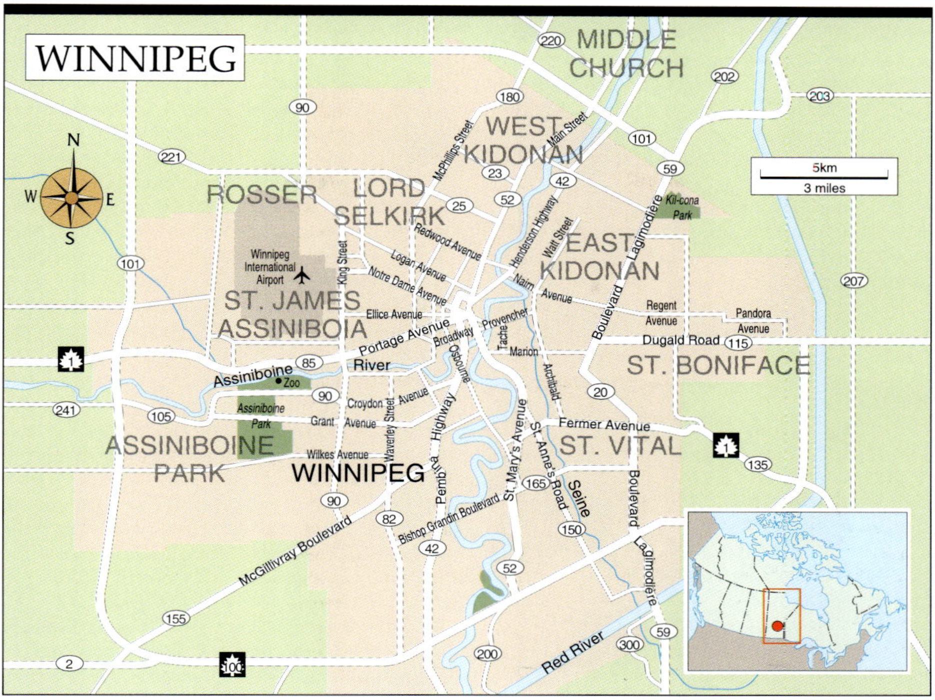

are all linked together by an underground shopping mall. This area has always been the commercial hub of the province and many of its beautiful old buildings still stand. The **Winnipeg Commodity Exchange** ☎ (204) 925-5015, after which the district is named, is still located here. Originally the world's largest grain exchange, it has expanded into other commodities and now occupies the fifth floor of a tower block at 360 Main Street. Visitors can watch the action on the trading floor from a gallery and join a guided tour. Trading takes place between 9:30 AM and 1:20 PM. One particularly attractive building in the area is the ornate **Electric Railways Chambers Building**, which is a reminder of the importance of the railway in Winnipeg's development.

This is not purely a business district, however, as many of the restored buildings now house restaurants and boutiques. The **Market Square** at King Street and Bannatyne Avenue is a popular gathering place where there are shops, market stalls selling arts and crafts, trendy restaurants, and street entertainment during the summer months. The Exchange District is also a lively nighttime spot when the theaters, clubs, and restaurants open up.

On the edge of the Exchange District at Main Street stands the **Centennial Centre**, a complex comprising several buildings, including the **Centennial Concert Hall** ☎ (204) 956-2171 (information) or (204) 986-6069 (tours), the **Planetarium** ☎ (204) 943-3142, and the **Manitoba Museum of Man and Nature** ☎ (204) 956-2830 or (204) 943-3139 (24-hour recorded information), 190 Rupert Avenue. As its name suggests, this splendid museum is devoted to the development of the province in geological, natural, historical, and cultural terms. There are realistic dioramas of Manitoba's various natural regions — combining sight, sound, and smell — and there's a gallery devoted to the prairie lands with reconstructions of pioneer dwellings and displays describing the native way of life. The highlight of a visit here is the *Nonsuch*, a full-scale replica of the ketch that left London in 1668 for Hudson Bay and returned laden with furs. It was this success that brought the famous Hudson's Bay Company into existence. The museum is open daily year-round, and an admission fee is charged.

Close by stands the **Ukrainian Cultural and Educational Centre** ☎ (204) 942-0218 FAX (204) 943-2857, 184 Alexander Avenue East. Housed within this old building is an art gallery and a museum that contains archival material and presents changing exhibitions on the history and rich culture of the Ukrainian people, the second largest group of immigrants to settle in the province. Exhibits include samples of embroidery, ceramics, carving, costumes, and the delicately painted Easter eggs called *pysankys*. It's open Tuesday to Saturday and Sunday afternoons; an admission fee is charged.

Moving south along Main Street and opposite the railway station there's a tiny park in which you can see **Upper Fort Garry Gate**, all that remains of the early nineteenth-century Hudson's Bay Fort. To the east along Broadway, another Winnipeg landmark carries on the name — the **Fort Garry**, a château-like hotel built by the Grand Trunk Railway in 1913.

Behind the station, on four hectares (10 acres) of land is the **Forks National Historic Site** ☾ (204) 943-6757, where you can learn about the region's history through interpretive displays, or wander along riverside pathways. Next to the historic site and sharing the riverside promenade with it is **The Forks** ☾ (204) 943-7752, a sprawling complex

of renovated railway buildings and parkland. There's a lively public market in a former stable, a playground, Johnston terminal with shops and restaurants, and the **Manitoba Children's Museum** ☾ (204) 956-5437, a state-of-the-art hands-on space that appeals equally to adults. Five different sections cover aspects of history, science, nature and technology. Kids can climb aboard a vintage steam-engine, try out a fully functioning television studio, and more. It's open daily; an admission fee is charged.

The magnificent **Legislative Building** ☾ (204) 945-5813 stands at the junction of Broadway and Osborne Street, an excellent example of neoclassical architecture, built in 1919 and designed by English architect Frank Worthington Simon. It is an H-shaped structure made of Tyndall limestone, a substance rich in fossil deposits that gives it a special texture. Atop its dome stands the gold-plated figure of the **Golden Boy**. This figure of a boy holds the torch of progress in one hand and carries a sheaf of wheat in the other to symbolize its importance in the development of Winnipeg. It is the work of French sculptor Charles Gardet, and has become itself a symbol of the city. The building is set in lovely grounds dotted with statuary honoring the city's various ethnic groups with depictions of some of their distinguished countrymen. One statue of particular note is that of Louis Riel. The interior of the building is also quite spectacular and free guided tours that allow visitors a look at the Legislative Chamber are conducted between July and Labor Day, weekdays from 9 AM to 6 PM; Labor Day to June by appointment.

South of Broadway, you can take a look at what high-tech meant to the late Victorians at the **Dalnavert Museum** ☾ (204) 943-2835, 61 Carlton Street, a house that was built for the son of John A. Macdonald, Canada's first prime minister. It is a red-brick building that was built with indoor plumbing, electric lighting, and was fitted with all kinds of household gadgetry. It is closed on Fridays and Mondays. Call for opening hours; the admission fee includes a guided tour.

Winnipeg has a superb **Winnipeg Art Gallery** ☾ (204) 786-6641 housed in an unmissable wedge-shaped building at 300 Memorial Boulevard. It has a varied collection of international art, but is most famous for its wonderful collection of Inuit works, which are exhibited in continually changing displays. The gallery hosts some major temporary exhibitions, and is a center for other cultural events. It is open Tuesday and Thursday to Sunday from 11 AM to 5 PM, Wednesday from 11 AM to 9 PM (though times may vary with seasons). An admission fee is charged, free on Wednesday.

Across the Red River lies the **St. Boniface** district, the oldest French-speaking community in Canada and the largest in the west. French traders lived in the area from 1738 when Pierre Gaultier de la Verendrye arrived here. In 1819, following the building of a church here, a French community began to develop that included French Canadians and Métis. The **St. Boniface Basilica** ☾ (204) 233-7304, 190 avenue de la Cathédrale, that stands today is a modern structure built among the ruins of an earlier cathedral that burned down in 1968. In the old cemetery lies the body of Louis Riel, who was executed following the defeat of the Northwest Rebellion.

Next to the basilica stands an oak structure that was built in 1846 as a convent for the Grey Nuns who arrived here from Montréal. It now contains the **St. Boniface Museum** ☾ (204) 237-4500, 494 avenue Taché, which has a large collection of artifacts belonging to the Métis and to other early settlers in the district and includes some memorabilia of Louis Riel. The museum is open daily. Also in the area is the **Church of the Precious**

Blood, an interesting modern structure that is shaped like a teepee.

At the southern edge of the city you can visit **Riel House** ☎ (204) 257-1783, which stands close to the river at 330 River Road in St. Vital. It was the home of the Riel family although Louis Riel never lived there. It has been restored to the year 1885, when Riel was executed, and tours and exhibits offer glimpses into Métis life of the period. It's open daily, mid-May to Labor Day, and an admission fee is charged. Moving eastwards, a striking glass pyramid houses the **Royal Canadian Mint** ☎ (204) 257-3359, at 520 Boulevard Lagimodière. The mint produces coins for Canada and various foreign nations. Guided tours — offered in English and

French — show you the processes and high-tech equipment involved in making money. It's open year-round, and an admission fee is charged. Tours run weekdays from May to August, and by appointment from September to April

Assiniboine Park ☎ (204) 986-3130, at 2355 Corydon Avenue, over in the west end of the city is a large, pleasant park with recreation areas, a miniature railway, flowerbeds, an English garden where a statue of Queen Victoria stands, and an attractive old pavilion where you can sometimes catch a game of cricket. It also contains a **zoo** ☎ (204) 986-6921 with a population of around 1,300 — including many native species — and a conservatory where there are tropical plants, birds, and monkeys. The park is on the southern bank of the Assiniboine River about 11 km (seven miles) from downtown. There is an admission fee for the zoo, which is open daily, year-round.

The **Fort Whyte Centre for Environmental Education** ☎ (204) 989-8355, 1961 McCreary Road, stands on 80 hectares (200 acres) of land in Winnipeg's southwest corner. Here the natural habitat of the province's lakes and rivers has been recreated in and around several former cement quarries. Self-guided nature trails and an interpretive center tell all about it. It's open weekdays from 9 AM to 5 PM, weekends from 10 AM to 5 PM; an admission fee is charged.

Excursions from Winnipeg

Lower Fort Garry ☎ (204) 785-6050, about 32 km (20 miles) north of Winnipeg along Highway 9, was built by the Hudson's Bay Company in the

1830s and is the only remaining stone fort of that era in North America. It has been carefully restored and visitors can see the various living quarters, the fur loft, and the governor's residence as they were when the fort functioned as an important trading post. Before you begin your tour of the buildings, it's a good idea to watch the film shown in the reception area, which fills you in on the background. Inside the compound, costumed "workers" will demonstrate crafts in the various workshops. In the grounds you'll see a restored York boat, a vessel that was designed for transporting furs. Buses run to the fort from the downtown bus station. The fort is

OPPOSITE: Walking out the past in Lower Fort Garry. ABOVE: Part of the façade of the Legislative Building LEFT and the towers of the Ukrainian church at the Ukrainian Cultural and Educational Centre RIGHT.

open daily from mid-May to Labor Day; an admission fee is charged.

The **Mennonite Heritage Village** ☎ (204) 326-9661 lies 61 km (38 miles) southeast of Winnipeg, about two and a half kilometers (one and a half miles) outside the village of Steinbach, a living museum where you can see a working mill and watch the Mennonites demonstrate their crafts, just as they would have in the nineteenth century. The Mennonite sect is one that is totally committed to pacifism and has been frequently persecuted because of its beliefs. The Mennonites who settled in Manitoba came from Russia in the 1870s and 1880s, and this heritage village presents a colorful picture of their way of life. There is a restaurant here that serves traditional Mennonite food. The village is open daily from May to September. To get there from Winnipeg, take Highway 1 to Highway 12 North, and watch for signs just north of Steinbach. It's open daily from May to September, weekdays only from October to April. An admission fee is charged.

If you like scenic train rides you should find out if the *Prairie Dog Central* is back in operation. At the time of research the train was not operating, but it may resume service in 1999; check with Tourism Winnipeg (see GENERAL INFORMATION, above). A trip aboard this early twentieth-century steam train takes you on a two-hour trip to **Grosse Isle**, 58 km (36 miles) northwest of Winnipeg. It's worth the trip not only to see the countryside rolling by, but also for the delightful experience of traveling in grand old-fashioned style.

SPORTS AND OUTDOOR ACTIVITIES

There are **hiking** trails and **cycling** paths in the city parks, details of which are available from information centers. There are several **skating** rinks throughout Winnipeg, and when the snow comes there's **snowmobiling** at Birds Hill Provincial Park, about 32 km (20 miles) northeast of the city.

There's excellent **fishing** in the province, as you would expect with so many lakes, but you need to venture outside Winnipeg. The tourist information centers can help you with information on where to go and how to get there. Likewise they can help you with details of the excellent **canoe** routes that the province is famous for.

NIGHTLIFE AND THE ARTS

Winnipeg has a lively nightlife. To find out what's going on check the entertainment listings that appear in the daily *Winnipeg Free Press* and the *Winnipeg Sun*. The **Centennial Centre** ☎ (204) 956-1360, 555 Main Street, is the hub of Winnipeg's cultural scene. The area comprises the Centennial Concert Hall, the Manitoba Theatre Centre, the

Warehouse Theatre, and the excellent Manitoba Museum of Man and Nature.

The theatre season in Winnipeg is really under way between September and early May, and during those months the **Manitoba Theatre Centre** ☎ BOX OFFICE (204) 942-6537, 174 Market Avenue, stages a variety of comedy and serious drama, while nearby the smaller **Warehouse Theatre** ☎ (204) 956-1340, stages experimental productions. There are several other companies scattered around town, including the innovative **Gas Station Theatre** ☎ (204) 284-9477 FAX (204) 284-9478, 445 River Avenue, in Osborne Village.

The most cherished and famous of Winnipeg's cultural institutions is the **Royal Winnipeg Ballet**, which performs a program of classical and modern works at the **Centennial Concert Hall** ☎ (204) 956-2792, Room 101-555 Main Street, and also gives a free open-air performance in Assiniboine Park in the summer. The acclaimed

Winnipeg Symphony Orchestra and the **Manitoba Opera** also perform at the Centennial Concert Hall.

A mixture of jazz, folk, and classical music can often be heard at the **Winnipeg Art Gallery** ☎ (204) 786-6641, 300 Memorial Boulevard. You'll find rock and other live music playing at various bars and clubs in the town, often in hotel lounges. The **Palamino Club** ☎ (204) 772-0454, 1133 Portage Avenue, is a country-and-western hangout. Winnipeg has quite a lively nightclub scene and one that is rapidly changing, like the city itself. The Exchange District is a nighttime hot spot where many of these clubs can be found.

Winnipeg has two **casinos**, both of which were under renovation at the time of research: Club Regent TOLL-FREE (800) 493-4652, at 1425 Regent Avenue, is installing a gigantic walk-through saltwater aquarium; and McPhillips Station TOLL-FREE (888) 493-4652, 484 McPhillips Street, will have the Manitoba Millenium Theatre where multimedia and "multisensory" presentations will explore the province's history and culture. In addition to their new, John Waters-esque attractions and the usual mass of gaming tables, both casinos feature Vegas-style entertainment, restaurants and lounges.

WHERE TO STAY

Expensive

The **Crown Plaza Winnipeg Downtown** ☎ (204) 942-0551 TOLL-FREE (800) 2CROWNE FAX (204) 943-8702, 350 St. Mary Avenue, Winnipeg R3C 3J2, is part of a complex that connects with the Convention Centre. There are 390 pleasant rooms including several suites, indoor and outdoor pools, and a good range of services. There's a choice of

Feathers for sale in the Old Market Square.

restaurants within the hotel, and several more inside the complex. Also top notch, the **Radisson Winnipeg Downtown** ✆ (204) 956-0410 TOLL-FREE (800) 333-3333 FAX (204) 947-1129, 288 Portage Avenue, Winnipeg R3C 0B8, is a downtown highrise hotel with 270 rooms above its multistory parking facility. The rooms are smart and have good views; the service is first-rate. There are two attractive restaurants, one formal and one casual, and a comprehensive range of amenities that include an indoor swimming pool, a cinema, and a supervised children's activity center. Under renovation at the time of writing, the Radisson will sport a new lobby and entrance by the spring of 1999.

Mid-range

The Lombard ✆ (204) 957-1350 TOLL-FREE (800) 441-1414 FAX (204) 956-1791, at 2 Lombard Place, Winnipeg R3B 0Y3, is in the very center of town and is one of the city's top-rated hotels. There are 340 luxurious rooms, excellent service, and guests have the use of an indoor swimming pool. There is a choice of restaurants, a café, and in-house entertainment. The hotel is conveniently linked to a large shopping complex. The **Sheraton Winnipeg** ✆ (204) 942-5300 TOLL-FREE (800) 463-6400 FAX (204) 943-7975 is another top downtown hotel located close to the Convention Centre at 161 Donald Street, Winnipeg R3C 1M3. Rooms here are large, well-equipped, and have balconies with some excellent views from the top floors. The hotel has an indoor pool, a sun deck, and a pleasant restaurant, with nightly entertainment in the lounge. Both hotels have prices that vary between mid-range and expensive.

For some old-style grandeur, you must go to **Hotel Fort Garry** ✆ (204) 942-8251 TOLL-FREE (800) 665-8088 FAX (204) 956-2351, 222 Broadway, Winnipeg R3C 0R3. This castle-like hotel was built by the Grand Trunk Railway in 1913 and subsequently underwent extensive renovation. The refurbishment has been done with great care, so the original splendor has been preserved throughout the hotel. There are 240 elegant rooms and suites, and two beautiful dining rooms. Breakfast is included in the price of accommodation.

For accommodation with lots of character and excellent service, book in at the **Ramada Marlborough Hotel** ✆ (204) 942-6411 TOLL-FREE (800) 667-7666 FAX (204) 942-2017, 331 Smith Street, Winnipeg R3B 2G9, which is in the town's financial district. It is a Victorian Gothic building with a grand interior of vaulted ceilings, stained glass, and polished wood. The rooms and suites are stylish with modern conveniences, and the hotel has a delightful restaurant as well as a coffee shop.

Inexpensive

The **Gordon Downtowner Motor Hotel** ✆ (204) 943-5581 FAX (204) 947-3041, 330 Kennedy Street, Winnipeg R3B 2M6, has comfortable, convenient accommodation, bars, and a restaurant, and is excellent value. The **Charter House Hotel** ✆ (204) 942-0101 TOLL-FREE (800) 782-0175 FAX (204) 956-0665, 330 York Avenue, Winnipeg R3C 0N9, is a good downtown choice. It has 90 rooms, some of which have balconies, a dining room, and an outdoor swimming pool. The **St. Regis** ✆ (204) 942-0171 TOLL-FREE (800) 663-7344 FAX (204) 943-3077, 285 Smith Street, Winnipeg R3C 1K9, has basic but pleasant rooms, and a nice atmosphere.

The **Ivey House International Hostel** ✆ (204) 772-3022, 210 Maryland Street, Winnipeg R3G 1L6, is located in a turn-of-the century residence within walking distance of the city's cultural attractions. It's open year-round. During the summer break the **University of Manitoba** has accommodation for visitors. For details contact the Conference Coordinator ✆ (204) 474-9942, 26 MacLean Crescent, Pembina Hall R3T 2N1.

For a list of bed and breakfast accommodation in the area contact an Information Centre or Bed and Breakfast of Manitoba ✆ (204) 661-0300, 434 Roberta Avenue, Winnipeg R2K 0K6. If a rural retreat appeals, get in touch with the **Manitoba Country Vacations Association** ✆ (204) 776-2176, c/o Ernest Fraser, Fairfax R0K 0V0. The Information Centres also have information on campgrounds in the region.

WHERE TO EAT

Winnipeg's diverse ethnic mix makes for some exciting dining, and there are a surprisingly large number of restaurants for a city of its size. Many of the restaurants, like the shops, are closed on Sundays.

Moderate to Expensive

Restaurant Dubrovnik ✆ (204) 944-0594 FAX (204) 957-7750, 390 Assiniboine Avenue, is one

Winnipeg's skyline.

of the city's best restaurants. It is in a large Victorian house on the riverbank, with a charming interior that has retained many of the original features. Some beautiful examples of Yugoslavian crafts adorn the walls. The food is continental but with Yugoslavian specialties on the menu, and it is quite delicious. Proof of its excellence lies in its popularity, so be sure to make a reservation. Prices vary between expensive and moderate.

Another popular dining spot is the **Royal Crown Revolving Restaurant** ℂ (204) 947-1990, at Fort Garry Place, 83 Garry Street. The menu here is continental on the whole, and the interior is quite plush. There are two restaurants that revolve in different directions, the Tiara Dining Room being the more exclusive of the two. Although the food is quite good, people come here mainly for the panoramic views of the city. In addition to daily à la carte dining, there's a Sunday brunch and a Sunday evening buffet. The **Velvet Glove** ℂ (204) 985-6255 in The Lombard, 2 Lombard Place, is a top-rated restaurant that specializes in continental food prepared to gourmet standards. The setting is one of formal elegance amid warm tones of wood and brass, and the dining booths add an element of intimacy. Prices vary widely, but unless you choose some particularly expensive dishes your bill is likely to land in the moderate range.

Victor's ℂ (204) 947-2751, in the Ramada Marlborough, 331 Smith Street, bears out the Gothic exterior of this lovely hotel with arches, stained glass, and Victorian furnishings creating a delightful atmosphere. The menu concentrates on steaks, seafood, and continental dishes. Over in the French district of St. Boniface, **Le Beaujolais** ℂ (204) 237-6306, 131 Provencher Boulevard, serves traditional French and nouvelle dishes, all expertly prepared, and elegantly served in attractive surroundings.

For good northern Italian cooking in a cultivated setting, go to **Amici** ℂ (204) 943-4997, 326 Broadway. There's delicious Swiss fare at the **Old Swiss Inn** ℂ (204) 942-7725, 207 Edmonton Street, where you'll find more than fondue on the menu, and warm, friendly surroundings. **Hy's Steak Loft** ℂ (204) 942-1000, 216 Kennedy Street, serves good quality steaks and seafood in old-fashioned surroundings, and **Rae and Jerry's** ℂ (204) 783-6155, in the west end of the city, at 1405 Portage Avenue, is another popular steak house that includes chicken and fish dishes on its menu. Prices here vary between inexpensive and moderate. For steaks served in a rather different way, go to the **Ichiban Japanese Steak House and Sushi Bar** ℂ (204) 925-7400, 189 Carlton Street, where meats and vegetables are stir-fried with tremendous flair in front of diners. There's also a wide choice of other traditional dishes. The decor here is easy on the eye, and an artificial brook adds the soothing sound of running water. The Ichiban is a good choice for a Sunday when your options are limited in Winnipeg.

Inexpensive

One of Winnipeg's ever-popular restaurants is the **Bistro Dansk** ℂ (204) 775-5662, 63 Sherbrooke Street. It is a cheerful, friendly place with good Danish food and pleasant, helpful staff.

The north end of town has a plethora of delis and cafés that make for some interesting and enjoyable dining. **Alycia's** ℂ (204) 582-8789, 559 Cathedral Avenue, serves homemade Ukrainian food in cozy surroundings decorated with traditional arts and crafts. Both **Oscar's** ℂ (204) 947-0314, 175 Hargrave Street, and **Simon's** ℂ (204) 589-8269, 1322 Main Street, are well-established Jewish delicatessens which are open into the small hours. For a taste of Indonesia, try **Betsy's Place** at 1134 Main Street North.

In Osborne Village you can go English at the **Tea Cozy** ℂ (204) 475-1027, 99 Osborne Street. Here you can eat breakfast, or have a spot of lunch, or take tea with crumpets, cakes, or biscuits. For a completely different cultural experience, **Carlos and Murphy's** ℂ (204) 284-3510, 129 Osborne Street, has a bar and a restaurant serving good Mexican food in a congenial atmosphere.

Winnipeg's **Chinatown** lies to the north of the Exchange District, stretching between James and Logan avenues and covering an eight-block area. As is the norm, you'll find good-value Chinese restaurants here and a variety of Chinese cuisines.

HOW TO GET THERE

Winnipeg International Airport is approximately 10 km (six miles) northwest of downtown, about a 20-minute drive away, but allow longer during rush hours. An airport shuttle runs between the airport and some of the big hotels.

The **VIA Rail** ℂ (204) 949 1830 TOLL-FREE (888) 842-7733 station is downtown at 101-123 Main Street. Trains run to Vancouver via Kamloops, Jasper, Edmonton, and Saskatoon. From the east the line runs into Winnipeg from Toronto. VIA Rail runs the *Hudson Bay* train to Churchill via Dauphin, The Pas, and Thompson.

The bus station is downtown at 487 Portage Place. **Greyhound** ℂ (204) 982-8747 buses operate to and from this terminal. **Grey Goose Lines** ℂ (204) 784-4512, 301 Burnell Street, links Winnipeg with other towns in Manitoba.

Winnipeg is quite isolated, so if you're driving the chances are that wherever you're coming from (unless it's the airport), you'll have quite a long drive ahead. The Trans-Canada Highway (Highway 1) runs through the city, linking it with Toronto, 2,093 km (1,300 miles) east, and Calgary, 1,359 km (844 miles) to the west. Minneapolis in Minnesota is 734 km (456 miles) from

Winnipeg via Interstate-94 and Interstate-29 in the United States, becoming Highway 75 in Manitoba.

ELSEWHERE IN MANITOBA

WHITESHELL PROVINCIAL PARK

There are wonderful opportunities for all kinds of outdoor pursuits in this large wilderness park that lies close to the Ontario border, 144 km (89 miles) east of Winnipeg. It is Canadian Shield country, an area rich in lakes, rivers, forest, and wildlife — ideal for hiking, canoeing, horseback riding, fishing, and all kinds of water sports. Areas of the park have been developed for tourism, and at **Falcon Lake** a recreational development offers a golf course, tennis courts, a ski resort, shops, and accommodations. If you prefer to get away from all that, there are quieter areas in the northern reaches of the park.

LAKE WINNIPEG

This vast lake lies to the north of Winnipeg and is lined with sandy beaches, making it an excellent place for relaxation and water sports. The fishing town of **Gimli** stands at the southwestern shores of the lake, 90 km (56 miles) north of Winnipeg. Back in the 1870s Icelanders came to the area in search of a new home free of the tyranny of the volcanoes that so disrupted their lives in their native land. They found that this area could offer them a good living through fishing and farming, and for a time the region was an independent country known as New Iceland. The community of Gimli retains a strong Icelandic identity and culture, and in August it celebrates the **Icelandic Festival**, a celebration of sports, music, parades, art, and traditional food. There is a museum on the waterfront that has displays on the history of the settlement.

Hecla Provincial Park ☎ (204) 378-2945, PO Box 70, Riverton ROC 2R0, encompasses a collection of islands in Lake Winnipeg. These islands are wildlife preserves and a bird-watcher's delight, while hikers, fishermen, canoeists, and winter sports enthusiasts also find much to enjoy here. Hecla Island is accessible by car, and at its northern end the **Gull Harbour Resort** (204) 475-2354 TOLL-FREE (800) 475-5992 manages to offer recreation facilities, attractive accommodation, and good Icelandic hospitality without marring the natural beauty of the island. The hotel is open year-round.

RIDING MOUNTAIN NATIONAL PARK

Riding Mountain National Park is an outdoor playground that lies 248 km (154 miles) northwest of Winnipeg, on the highlands of a prairie escarpment. It has been partially developed in **Wasagaming** on the shores of Clear Lake, where there's a variety of accommodation and extensive recreational facilities, but the area remains largely unspoiled, with bison, elk, deer, and beaver inhabiting the parkland. In the winter there are cross-country skiing trails through the park and downhill skiing at Mount Agassiz. The **Visitor Centre** ☎ (204) 848-PARK TOLL-FREE (800) 707-8480, in Wasagaming, will provide guides and maps. Close to Wasagaming the **Elkhorn Resort & Conference Centre** ☎ (204) 848-2802 FAX (204) 848-2109, PO Box 40, Onanole R0J 1N0, has chalets and suites, a nine-hole golf course, and organized horseback riding treks. Prices vary from mid-range to expensive.

CHURCHILL

The small town of Churchill lies on the southwestern shore of Hudson Bay at the estuary of the Churchill River, and is one of the few places in the north accessible from the south — though not by road. It is one of the world's largest grain-handling ports, with huge grain elevators looming overhead, but it is increasingly becoming a popular tourist destination because of its substantial natural attractions. Although weather conditions are very difficult here, with snow during most of the year creating a sparse, subarctic vegetation, the wildlife draws the visitors. It is a great place for **polar bear watching**, especially during October and early November when migration is at its height and the bears are regularly seen wandering around the town. **Tundra Buggy Tours** ☎ (204) 675-2121 TOLL-FREE (800) 544-5049 operates specially built buggies that take visitors out on bear-spotting safaris. Half-day tours are offered July to September, full-day tours in October and early November.

Getting there, as you might expect, is half the fun. **Canadian Airlines International** runs flights between Winnipeg and Churchill; there's also the option of a two-night **VIA Rail** ☎ (204) 949-1830 journey from Winnipeg. VIA's Winnipeg address is 103-123 Main Street, Winnipeg R3C 2P8.

OPPOSITE: Waterfowl and moose share the unspoiled beauty of Riding Mountain National Park.

The North

ONE COULD ARGUE THAT ALL OF CANADA IS THE NORTH. But for Canadians, "true north" is that vast stretch of country that extends from the 60th parallel beyond the magnetic North Pole. This North occupies a special place in the national mythology, forming a significant part of the identity of all Canadians — despite the fact that most of them have never been there. Northerners, for their part, call the rest of Canada "the outside." The Yukoners' history is as closely linked to that of Alaskans as to their fellow Canadians, and the Inuit majority of the northeast shares a common culture with the native peoples of Greenland.

Two-thirds of this surprisingly varied landscape constitute the Northwest Territories and Nunavut — a land of giant lakes, treeless tundra, and the hardy Dene, Inuit and other native groups who have thrived in this rugged environment for thousands of years. This is the least densely populated area in the world, with Canada's highest concentration of Aboriginal peoples (60%). Following decades of land-rights negotiations, on April 1, 1999, the former Northwest Territories was divided. The new border extends north from the Manitoba-Saskatchewan frontier for 500 km (310 miles), veers northwest for 1050 km (650 miles), hooks back east 500 km (310 miles) to 110' latitude, then cuts dead north to the Arctic Ocean. The territory east of this border has been named Nunavut (which means "our land" in Inuktitut), and includes the islands in Hudson Bay, James Bay, and Ungava Bay that are not within Manitoba, Ontario, or Quebec. The lands west of the new border will remain the Northwest Territories until a new name is chosen.

To the west of the Northwest Territories is the Yukon, distinguished from the rest of the North by its indigenous populations, its climate, its geography, and its history. Aside from its cultural and geographical differences, the Yukon is also more accessible than Nunavut and the western Northwest Territories primarily because of its transportation infrastructure. On the whole, the Yukon tends to attract more hikers and paddlers, while Nunavut and the Northwest Territories attract hunters and fishermen, though all three territories offer excellent opportunities for hiking, boating, fishing and hunting.

For the traveler who wishes to explore the North, several aspects of northern travel should be borne in mind. The first is that this is a vast, vast land. "The Canadian north," writes Pierre Berton, "is so big that you could drop the state of Texas or the British Isles in here and never notice either of them." Thus, you will want to choose a specific area to explore, depending on your interests, rather than trying to "do" the North. Second, a trip to Canada's North will probably require more

The Northwest Territories — A hiker surveys the Mackenzie Mountains.

than the usual amount of advance preparation and will certainly demand a significantly greater outlay of money.

Be aware that mosquitoes and changeable weather are major issues in the northern summer. A bug jacket over your T-shirt during the day will be as important a sweater in the evening.

If you intend to do any wilderness hiking or paddling, you should obtain accurate and timely information about conditions to be expected and advise a friend or relative, and the nearest Royal Canadian Mounted Police detachment, where you are going and when you will be back.

Many of the Yukon's roads are now widened, straightened and paved, but major gravel roads

still exist. In the Northwest Territories highways are mainly all-weather gravel roads. Keep your headlights on at all times.

With the exception of Whitehorse in the Yukon, northern communities are not under the 911 emergency system. See under HEALTH AND SAFETY, page 239, in TRAVELERS' TIPS, for police (RCMP) and medical emergency numbers for the North.

THE YUKON TERRITORY

In the far northwest corner of Canada, a rough triangular boundary defines the Yukon Territory's 483,450 sq km (174,000 sq miles). Bordered by British Columbia to the south and the Northwest Territories to the east, the northern tip of the triangle is cut through by the Arctic Circle and ends at the Beaufort Sea, home to musk oxen, polar bears, and beluga whales. Frozen wilderness defines the Yukon's southern boundary as well, where the largest nonpolar ice caps in the world are suspended over the saw-toothed mountains of Kluane National Park. In between all of this frozen water is a semiarid land that, were it not so far north, would be a desert.

The climate of the Yukon comes as a surprise to many visitors. Dawson City's temperature may drop below -50°C (-58°F) in January, but easily rise to 35°C (100°F) in July. The dry climate and long hours of sunshine contribute to this phenomenon.

The Yukon's aridity gives rise to another characteristic of the region: forest fires. Each year thousands of hectares burn. Fires are closely monitored, but generally allowed to take their own course. The prevailing notion is that burning and regrowth is a natural cycle of the habitat.

Some 1,300 species of flowering plants have adapted to ice, wind, and fire to thrive in the territory. Fireweed — so named because it is the first plant to revegetate land cleared by fire — is the Yukon's official flower, seen all summer long blazing along the roadways. The territory is home to 214 bird and 61 mammal species, as well as 28 species of fish. Only a few hardy tree varieties, such as spruce and lodgepole pine, poplar, birch, and willow, are able to tolerate the growing conditions in the Yukon. These trees tend to be smaller and spindlier than their southern relatives.

The Yukon's 33,000 human inhabitants are a ruggedly adaptable bunch as well. Situated 2,720 km (1,700 miles) from Vancouver, 1,440 km (900 miles) from Edmonton, hemmed in by lofty mountains to the south, they are extraordinarily isolated from the rest of Canada. In fact, Yukoners feel stronger ties with their Alaskan neighbors — with whom the Yukon shares its western border and many geographical and cultural characteristics — than they do with Canadians. Yukoners live in one of the earth's last frontier lands — and like all frontiers, it is full of hardship and opportunity. Yukoners, as you might expect, love and revere the outdoors: Though two thirds of them live in the capital city of Whitehorse, much of the residential area of this city rolls out into the countryside, with immediate access to mountain trails and river routes.

The Yukon has much to offer visitors: the ancient cultures of the regions' First Nations peoples, still alive in communities from Whitehorse to Old Crow; historic sites linked to the era of one of the world's greatest gold rushes; wilderness areas where barely a trace of human existence can be found; and some of the most splendid mountainscapes in Canada.

Skookum Jim ("skookum" means handsome), one of the discovers of Bonanza Creek, where the gold was "thick between the flaky slabs, like cheese sandwiches." The discovery touched off the 1896 gold rush.

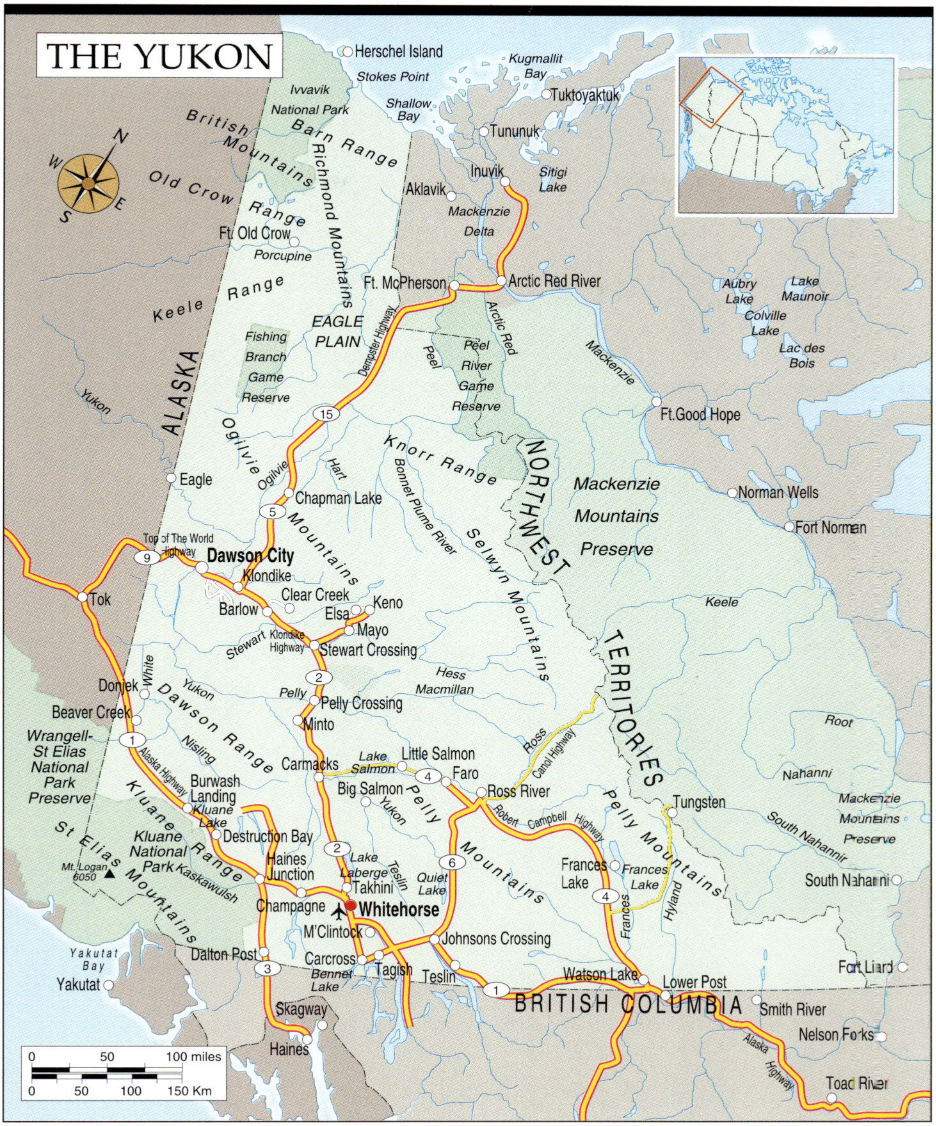

BACKGROUND

Up until around 1800s the region now known as the Yukon was occupied exclusively by bands of Gwitch'in, Kaska, Tagish, Tutchone, and Teslin Hän natives — hunters and nomads who gathered in springtime into larger groups for fishing.

Beginning in the eighteenth century, Russian explorers began trading with the area's natives. Then in 1825 the explorer Sir John Franklin anchored off the Yukon's Arctic coastline. The Hudson's Bay Company moved into the interior in the 1840s, and United States traders arrived after Russia sold Alaska to the America in 1867.

Prospectors began to trickle into the Yukon in the 1870s, following a trail of gold strikes along the Rockies that had begun in California in 1849 and had continued into the interior of British Columbia. By 1882 there were 50 miners in the Yukon Valley searching for and finding small but promising amounts of gold. By the early 1890s the number had grown to nearly 1,000, centered mostly around the community of Forty Mile, near present-day Dawson City.

In 1896 a white prospector, George Washington Carmack, and his native brothers-in-law, Skookum Jim and "Dawson" Charlie, found gold, lots of it, in Rabbit Creek. Carmack brought word back that the rocks of Rabbit Creek had gold "thick between the flaky slabs, like cheese sandwiches." The three men staked their claims and Carmack renamed the creek, Bonanza. The gold rush was on.

Thousands of people poured into this remote corner of Canada, most arriving by way of Skagway, Alaska, and the upper Yukon River. These stampeders had to haul enough provisions to last out the year over the White or Chilkoot pass, then build a boat at the foot of Lake Bennett to carry them the remaining stretch to the Klondike gold fields near Dawson City. In the spring of 1898, Mounties counted 28,000 men and women leaving the shores of Lake Bennett in 7,000 makeshift boats bound for the Klondike. Amidst this hullabaloo, the town of Dawson was born.

Within a few years Dawson was left in the sawdust as gold seekers moved on to Nome, Alaska, where yet another big strike had been found. Gold mining in the Yukon continued (and continues today), but beginning in 1913 the Yukon's economy shifted from gold to other minerals, such as silver and lead at Keno Hill in the central Yukon. The construction of the Alaska Highway and the Canol pipeline and road brought new mineral exploration activity as well as bringing people, services, industries, and tourists to the Yukon. With the highway came permanent non-native settlers, who finally outnumbered Yukon's native peoples.

Though the Yukon contains some 30% of Canada's natural resources, current low prices for precious metals, along with the cost of extraction, have put most mining operations in mothballs. In recent years, mining has been supplanted by tourism as the Yukon's leading industry.

WHITEHORSE

A hundred years ago, Whitehorse was not Whitehorse at all, but a stop on the Southern Tutchone and Tagish peoples' seasonal round of hunting and fishing. When the Klondike gold rush peaked from 1898 to 1900, Whitehorse became yet another stopping point, this time for the stampeders clawing their way to Dawson City, far to the north. Here on the banks of the Yukon, prospectors stopped to wring out their socks after traversing the treacherous rapids upstream. Then in 1900 the White Pass & Yukon Railway was completed with its terminus in Whitehorse, and the settlement began to take shape. The building of the Alaska Highway through its backyard gave the town a further boost: In 1941, the population jumped from 300 to over 3,000. Today, Whitehorse, the territorial capital since 1953, has a population of around 22,000.

If someday there are cities built on planet Mars, they'll certainly look like parched and pragmatic Whitehorse. It's about as homely as cities come, but it grows on you — and quickly. Many are the stories of people who "came for a few days and stayed 20 years." But no matter the length of your stay, you'll discover that Whitehorse is a friendly town with fine, hot, and dry summers with daylight lasting long into the evenings. Everything you need for moving on into the remoter stretches of the territory is available here. There are quite a few historic buildings in the downtown area, and there are some worthwhile museums to explore.

General Information

Once in Whitehorse, your first stop should be the **Visitor Information Centre** ☎ (867) 667-2915 FAX (867) 667-3546 E-MAIL yktour@yknet.ca, at the corner of Hanson Street and Second Avenue. They have stacks of information about the city and the territory, as well as interactive kiosks, video presentations, and helpful staff. Next door, the Whitehorse Public Library ☎ (867) 667-5239, 2701 Second Avenue, has **Internet access** and is open daily. While there are **automated teller machines** on the Interac and Plus systems in Whitehorse, Dawson City, and Watson Lake, Whitehorse has the territory's only ATM operating on the Cirrus system, located at the **Bank of Montréal** ☎ (867) 668-4200, 111 Main Street.

What to See and Do

Though Whitehorse extends over an area of 259 sq km (162 sq miles), the downtown is small and a convenient place to get around. The center, laid out around Main Street, has four blocks of stores and an almost-bustling pace. Several interesting sights, however, are located outside of the downtown area. **Whitehorse Transit** ☎ (867) 668-2831 makes the rounds. We recommend renting a car.

You may want to begin your downtown explorations with the Yukon Historical & Museums Association's 45-minute **historical walking tour** ☎ (867) 667-4704, departing Monday to Saturday from the Donneworth House, at 3126 Third Avenue; a fee is charged.

Even if you're spending a very short time in Whitehorse, make a point to visit the **SS *Klondike* National Historic Site** ☎ (867) 667-3970, near the downtown core at the Robert Campbell Bridge. In the territory's heyday, over 200 sternwheelers steamed up and down the Yukon River and its tributaries. Now only a few of these majestic ships are left, and the SS *Klondike* is the only one to have been restored to its earlier splendor. The park service interpretive tour and video are excellent. It's open daily 9 AM to 5:30 PM, with tours on the half hour. An admission fee is charged which includes a guided tour.

"Oh, for some of that gold," writes a wistful British Columbian in the **MacBride Museum** ☎ (867) 667-2709 guest register. This log structure with a sod roof houses several fascinating exhibits, including an array of gold nuggets — each with its distinctive form — taken from a spectrum of Klondike creeks. Hands on exhibits allow visitors to get a sense of the weight of gold (it's 19 times more dense than water) and see a prospector's sluicebox in action. Archeology, culture, history, natural history, and transportation are other themes. Located on First Avenue between Steele and Wood streets, the museum is open June to August daily from 10 AM to 6 PM. An admission fee is charged.

Below the White Horse Rapids Dam you can see Chinook salmon completing the word's longest salmon migration at the **Whitehorse Fishway** ☎ (867) 667-4263 or (867) 633-5965 (summers). This man-made fish ladder, located at the end of Nisultin Drive in suburban Riverdale, was built to allow the spawning salmon to fight their way upstream during their annual migration, bypassing the dam. There are interpretive displays and tanks that give you a fish's-eye view of the proceedings. The migration takes place in late July and August; the facility is open daily during the summer from 8 AM to 10 PM. Admission is free.

Whitehorse has its share of boutiques and corner pocket malls to browse in. The **Indian Craft Shop** ☎ (867) 667-7216, 504 Main Street, across from the Gold Rush Inn, is a family-run operation selling First Nations arts and crafts. Parkas are available in stock or made to order, and beaded mukluks and moccasins, hides, furs, and souvenirs large and small are on offer. Nancy Huston, owner of **Midnight Sun** ☎ (867) 668-4350, 205C Main Street, has made it her mission to find and market Yukon art and crafts. You'll find Yukon herbal teas, local jams and jelly, pottery, and prints as well as seventeenth-century First Nations trading beads

The Kluane Range, west of Whitehorse — You don't have to go far outside of town to find wide open spaces.

made into works of art and jewelry. The Jetsons-style sign of **Murdoch's Gem Shop** (867) 667-7716, 207 Main Street, is a downtown landmark. On display are "Klondike Kate's diamond belt" and the Yukon's largest selection of gold nugget jewelry.

Outside of the downtown area, there are several worthwhile sights. The **Yukon Art Centre** ☎ (867) 667-8485, Yukon Place at Yukon College, off of Range Road N, is the best place in the territory to see art. Exhibits in this beautiful gallery showcase Yukon artists, both native and non-native, as well as internationally recognized visual artists. While you're on campus, you can find out if there is a prospector in your past at the **Yukon Archives** ☎ (867) 667-5321 TOLL-FREE (800) 661-0408 E-MAIL yukon.archives@gov.yk.ca. Besides genealogical research, staff at the archives are prepared to help you find out more about any aspect of Yukon history. The archive has a file of ready-made historical photos, which get our vote for the best-value souvenir in the territory. Choose from portraits of handsome Skookum Jim or that Yukon iconic image — toilers on the Chilkoot Trail — and many others. Hours are Tuesday and Wednesday from 9 AM to 5 PM, Thursday and Friday 1 PM to 9 PM and 10 AM to 1 PM and 2 PM to 6 PM on Saturday. On the drive up Two Mile Road, on the corner of Fourth Avenue, look for the **spirit houses**, a cluster of small, brightly colored shelters. This is a First Nations burial ground (and thus not to be disturbed).

Continuing onto the Alaska Highway from the Yukon College area, head for the airport where there are two more very good museums. The **Beringia Interpretive Centre** ☎ (867) 667-8855, Alaska Highway Milepost 915, weaves First Nations creation myth and hard scientific evidence to tell the story of Beringia, the land bridge, created during the last Ice Age along which the first inhabitants of North America migrated from Asia. On this continent-sized land bridge, woolly mammoths and giant beavers as big as black bears roamed during the Pleistocene Age. The exhibits present the paleontological and archeological evidence of the age alongside Tlingit native stories about a great flood and how the clever Crow created the world. Fossilized remains include the tooth of a woolly mammoth weighing around five kilograms (11 lb), dioramas showing the flora and fauna of the age and skeleton models of giant beavers and sloths. Interestingly, it was the gold rush that led to the discovery of this mother lode of ice age fossils and remains. As prospectors dug down into the permafrost to release the gold from the gravel, they also discovered (and continue to discover) these remains.

Next to the Beringia Centre is the **Yukon Transportation Museum** ☎ (867) 668-4792, Alaska Highway Milepost 917. In a remote area like the Yukon, the history of European settlement is in many ways the history of transportation. The museum takes you on a fascinating historical journey from snowshoes to moose-skin boats to dogsleds, stage coaches, pioneer aircraft, railroad, riverboat and finally to the military vehicles that helped build the Alaska Highway. There's a very good film about the building of the White Pass & Yukon

Railway. It's open May 19 to September 14 daily from 9 AM to 6 PM; an admission fee is charged.

A hot soak at **Takhini Hot Springs** ☎ (867) 633-2706, 17 miles north of Whitehorse, off the Klondike Loop Road, is surprisingly refreshing on a scorching Yukon summer's day. The hot pool has a grassy area surrounding it; bring a book and you can alternately soak and sun your afternoon away. It's open weekends starting in mid-May, daily from June 1 to mid-October; an admission fee is charged. Suit rental and lockers are available. There is horseback riding here as well.

During the gold rush hundreds of stampeders smashed their crude boats attempting to run the Whitehorse Rapids that once raced through **Miles Canyon**, five kilometers (three miles) south of the city. The canyon's frothing water reminded the prospectors of horses' manes, which is where the capital city's name is believed to have originated. Now that the Whitehorse Dam has tamed the water, the canyon offers a pleasant float. You can take a two-hour Yukon River cruise on the **MV *Schwatka*** ☎ (867) 668-4716, Miles Canyon Road off the Alaska Highway South, accompanied by narration that tells the story of those wilder times. Trips run daily from June 1 to September 7 at 2 PM; additional 7 PM cruises run every day from June 15 to August 15 inclusive. Advance reservations are recommended. The **Scenic Gold Rush Raft Float Tour** ☎ (867) 633-4836, takes passengers through Miles Canyon on a two-and-a-half-hour narrated trip on a quaint (but seaworthy) craft that is a replica of the stampeders rafts. The boat makes a stop at Canyon City, where recent excavations have turned up remnants of stampeder encampments, as well as remains of early native use. Trips depart daily at 10 AM and 2 PM from the office of **Go Wild Tours!** ☎ (867) 668-2411 E-MAIL arctic@yknet.yk.ca, on First Avenue (look for the moose head).

Excursions from Whitehorse

Not far from Whitehorse there are a couple of First Nations camps where visitors can see how Yukon native people lived prior to the arrival of European influences (for other camps see LISTEN TO ANCIENT VOICES, page 18, in TOP SPOTS). First Nations tourism is a rapidly changing and growing scene, so you may want to call or drop by the **Yukon First Nations Tourism Association** ☎ (867) 667-7698 or (867) 667-7699 FAX (867) 667-7527, 1109 First Avenue, to find out about the latest offerings.

Atsua Ku (Grandma's Camp) Riverboat Adventures ☎ (867) 668-6854 E-MAIL dsam@atsuaku.yk.ca, PO Box 5494, Whitehorse Y1A 5H4, takes travelers eight kilometers (five miles) down the Yukon River to visit historic First Nations cabins and an old steamboat wood camp. The trips can be done as lunch, supper or overnight trips with barbecue dinner. Included is wildlife watching, exhibitions of First Nations crafts, storytelling, and nature walks. About a 45-minute drive from Whitehorse is **Kwaday Dan Kenji (Long-**

OPPOSITE: Indigenous mountain goats graze at a Whitehorse wildlife preserve. ABOVE: At Silver City near Kluane National Park you can ramble among the decaying shanties and mining equipment of this boom-and-bust silver mining encampment.

Ago Peoples) ✆ (867) 667-6375, located on the Alaska Highway two kilometers (just over a mile) south of Champagne (contact: Indian Way Ventures, PO Box 33031, Whitehorse Y1A 5Y5). Here you can come and enjoy hot tea and fresh *bannock*, fried biscuits. The family that runs this enterprise is researching and building a traditional First Nations camp showing how their ancestors lived before the introduction of European influences. It is open May to October 9 AM to 7:30 PM.

To see some of the countryside surrounding Whitehorse, drive the **Carcross Loop**, where unique and lovely scenery as well as gold rush and native history are found. Head out of Whitehorse south along the Alaska Highway, then take the Klondike Highway south. You'll shortly reach one of the most photographed scenes in the territory, **Emerald Lake**. Its turquoise hue is caused by the decomposed shells that are suspended in the water. Further along, the **Carcross Desert** is not a true desert at all but a former sandy lakebed, where winds have formed dozens of dunes. At Carcross, you'll want to stop and poke around. Tourism Yukon's **Visitor Reception Centre** ✆ (867) 821-4431 is at the Old Train Depot. The friendly staff will help orient you to the tiny native town where log cabins line the unpaved streets.

Before the gold rush, Carcross (originally Caribou Crossing) at the foot of Lake Bennett was a seasonal hunting and fishing camp for the Tagish natives. During the stampede, Tlingit natives displaced them. The Tlingit who now live here are descendants of the tribe that once traveled and traded across the Chilkoot Trail and became renowned as porters when the gold rush was on. Sites in the tiny town include the **New Caribou Hotel**, built in 1900, the oldest in the Yukon, and the historic **Old North West Mounted Police Barracks**, which is now a curio shop.

You can retrace your route from Carcross back to Whitehorse or head east along Tagish Road through the village of Tagish and reconnect with the Alaska Highway to complete the loop. The distance from Whitehorse to Carcross is 74 km (47 miles).

Sports and Outdoor Activities

Many people come to the Yukon for it's world-class **river running**. Resources are legion, but you might start your research by contacting the Yukon Canoe and Kayak Club ✆ (867) 633-5625 FAX (867) 633-5630 E-MAIL bear@yknet.yk.ca, PO Box 5546, Whitehorse Y1A 5H4. In Whitehorse, canoes and kayaks can be rented from Kanoe People ✆ (867) 668-4899 FAX (867) 668-4891 E-MAIL kanoe@yknet.yk.ca, PO Box 5152, Whitehorse Y1A 4S3. They also offers guided or unguided tours, fishing trips, and rent mountain bikes and camping gear. Also renting canoes is Up North ✆ (867) 667-7905 FAX (867) 667-6334 E-MAIL upnorth@yknet.yk.ca, PO Box 5418, Whitehorse Y1A 5H4, located across the Yukon River from the MacBride Museum.

Nahanni River Adventures (guided trips) ✆ (867) 668-3180 TOLL-FREE (800) 297-6927 FAX (867) 668-3056 E-MAIL nahanni@yknet.yk.ca, PO Box 4869, Whitehorse Y1A 4N6, has guided trips for beginners and experts on the Tatshenshini, Yukon, Nahanni and other northern wilderness rivers. Tatshenshini Expediting ✆ (867) 633-2742 FAX (867) 633-6184 E-MAIL tatexp@polar.com, 1602 Alder Street, Whitehorse Y1A 3W8, has guided **whitewater rafting** trips on the Tatshenshini, from day trips to 11-day excursions, and four- to six-day trips on the Alsek. They also rent rafts and canoes.

The area around Whitehorse affords great opportunities for **fishing**. A sport-fishing license is required, even to catch to the odd grayling by the side of the road. Licenses are available at sporting-goods stores. There are strict regulations governing seasons, sizes, and weights. Guided fly-fishing trips for two or three people are offered by Fly-Fishing Adventures ✆ (867) 667-2359, PO Box 5971, Whitehorse Y1A 5L7, which also rents boats and equipment.

If you are in the Yukon in the spring or winter, take a **dog sledding trip** with Walden Guiding and Outfitting ✆ (867) 667-7040; Blue Kennels ✆ (867) 667-1342, PO Box 5484, Whitehorse, Y1A 5H4, or Sunshine Valley Guest Ranch ✆ (867) 667-RIDE, PO Box 4211, Whitehorse, Y1A 3T3. Sunshine Valley also runs **packhorse trips** in the Yukon wilderness and offers French-speaking guides.

Several operations offer a full menu of activities from guided outdoor adventures to cultural trips: Arctic Vision ✆ (867) 668-2411 FAX (867) 668-2642 E-MAIL arctic@yknet.yk.ca, PO Box 31210(v), Whitehorse Y1A 5P7, offers nature, birding, and cultural tours in the Yukon and Western Arctic. Big Bear ✆ (867) 633-5642 FAX (867) 633-5630 E-MAIL bear@yknet.yk.ca, PO Box 5210, Whitehorse Y1A 4Z1, has canoeing, kayaking, hiking, rafting, and bicycle tours and rentals. Dutch and German are spoken.

Nightlife

Nightlife in Whitehorse centers around cold glasses of excellent Chilkoot Brewery ale, sipped late into the sunlit night on "The Deck" at the Yukon Mining Co., High Country Inn (see WHERE TO EAT, below). Another favorite gathering spot is the small terrace at Sam 'n' Andy's (see WHERE TO EAT, below). But before you've earned the right to kick back with the rest of Whitehorse's night creatures, you must see ***Frantic Follies*** ✆ (867) 668-3225, at the Westmark Whitehorse Hotel. From Dawson City to Beaver Creek, every town in the Yukon will implore, if not order, you to see its "variety" show. Most of them are to be avoided, but the Whitehorse show is a happy exception. The follies pack in plenty of physical comedy, pulled off, in general, with flair, and the Robert Service recitations are truly funny. Even locals go at least once a year to see the new talent and get their fix of high-kicking showgirls. There are nightly performances. Reserve in advance as seats are often filled with coach tour groups.

Where to Stay

Easily the most luxurious accommodation north of 60th parallel, **Hawkins House** ☎ (867) 668-7638 FAX (867) 668-7632 E-MAIL umbrich@internorth .com, 303 Hawkins Street, Whitehorse Y1A 1X5, is an unmissable painted-lady-style Victorian mansion in downtown Whitehorse. Fortunately, the interior is much more soothingly decorated. Rooms are small but beautifully and lovingly decked out in warm wood tones and packed with all the comforts you could ask for, including queen-sized beds, en-suite baths, sinks and refrigerators, and balconies. Two of the rooms have Jacuzzi tubs. A gourmet breakfast is served in the dining room each morning for an additional fee. Prices are at the high end of the mid-range category.

In the heart of downtown, there is the **Westmark Inn** ☎ (867) 668-4700 FAX (867) 668-2789, at Second and Wood streets, Whitehorse Y1A 3T3, part of a northern chain. With 180 rooms this is the largest hotel in the Yukon. Rooms are spacious, nicely furnished, and well-decorated. There are lots of amenities close at hand, including a restaurant and bar, a travel agency, a gift shop, and a barber and a hair salon. Rates are at the top of the mid-range category.

At the end of Main Street, overlooking the Yukon River, the **Edgewater Hotel** ☎ (867) 667-2572 FAX (867) 668-3014, 101 Main Street, Whitehorse Y1A 2A7, is a small, vintage hotel with 20 rooms and the excellent Cellar Dining Room (see WHERE TO EAT, below). Rooms are cozy and come equipped with extra-long beds and air conditioning. There is room service and some rooms are equipped with kitchenettes.

The slightly lower-priced **Best Western Gold Rush Inn** ☎ (867) 668-4500 FAX (867) 668-7432, 411 Main Street, Whitehorse Y1A 2B6, is owned by one of Whitehorse's local characters who refers to himself as Gold Nuggie Dougie. Rooms are clean and comfortable, if lacking in the character one expects from the hunting-lodge-style lobby. There is a predictable restaurant and lounge.

A casual atmosphere, spacious rooms, full breakfast, evening snacks, and a host who will always go out of her way to make her guests' stay as carefree as possible are all trademarks of the **Four Seasons Bed & Breakfast** ☎ (867) 667-2161 FAX (867) 667-2171 E-MAIL jeano@polarcom.com, 18 Tagish Road, Whitehorse Y1A 3P5. The house is located in a quiet residential area, a 15-minute walk from downtown and hillside hikes. Your host can arrange guided tours, access to laundry facilities, and transportation. Prices are at the low end of the mid-range.

Haeckel Hill Bed & Breakfast ☎ (867) 633-5625 FAX (867) 633-5630 E--MAIL bear@yknet.ca, 1501 Birch Street Whitehorse, Yukon, Canada Y1A 3X1, is located at the foot of Haeckel Hill in the rural suburb of Porter Creek, a five-minute drive from downtown. It makes an excellent base for day hiking and exploring the hilly countryside and forest trails; the proprietors are also tour operators who can arrange hiking, bicycling, and river trips. Rooms are sunny and comfortably furnished in white pine with a clean, uncluttered northern European touch. There's a sitting room with views of the mountains and a fireplace. A breakfast of homemade breads and muffins is served each morning. Rates fall in the low end of the mid-range. German and Dutch are spoken.

There is no hostel in Whitehorse, nor is there a YMCA residence or university dormitory housing. In addition, camping is at a premium as hundreds of Canadian college students come north to supply labor for the Yukon summer tourist season. Bargain hunters traveling in groups of three or four can sometimes make arrangements with bed-and-breakfast establishments. For example, Four Seasons Bed & Breakfast (see above) regularly books their spacious double rooms, supplied with an extra cot, to three people for a very reasonable price.

A roadside marker denotes the international boundary between the United States and Canada.

For long-term stays, including winter vacations, **Wild Treats Vacation Property Rentals** ☎/FAX (867) 633-3322 E-MAIL jwebster@yknet.yk.ca, 29 Wann Road, PO Box 9150, Whitehorse Y1A 4A2, rents cozy wilderness cabins.

Where to Eat

Hearty fare is served in Yukon restaurants; steak and seafood are featured on many menus. Arctic char, Alaska king crab, and Yukon or Taku River salmon are some of the local delicacies. You'll also find a variety of ethnic eateries with good, if not authentic, cuisine.

Locals and savvy tourists alike all seem to agree that the **Cellar Dining Room** (Edgewater Hotel) ☎ (867) 667-2572, 101 Main Street, is the best restaurant in Whitehorse. You'll pay top dollar for the excellent prime rib, Alaska king crab, or lobster and prawns served in the plush lower-level dining room The same great food is served in a more casual atmosphere — and for less money — in the Gallery upstairs from the Cellar.

Considering how far "north of the border" they are, **Sam 'n' Andy's** ☎ (867) 668-6994, 506 Main Street, serves fairly good Mexican food. The admittedly overpriced pitchers of margaritas draw the locals to the small, friendly terrace each evening. The post-modern **No Pop Sandwich Shop** ☎ (867) 668-3227, 312 Steele Street, is a trendy bistro-style place serving sandwiches and a number of daily specials, usually featuring fresh fish. On Sunday there is a popular brunch. Reservations are recommended. Also very popular locally, the **Talisman Restaurant** ☎ (867) 667-2736, 2112 Second Avenue at Main Street, has the best tabouli in town. It's open daily for breakfast lunch and dinner.

We love the **Pasta Palace** ☎ (867) 667-6888, 209 Main Street, for its inexpensive and delicious fare. The proprietors don't bother with atmosphere, but concentrate on serving some of the tastiest and best-value meals in the city. In addition to pastas there is an extensive selection of tapas and appetizers. Service is prompt and friendly.

Known locally as "The Deck," the **Yukon Mining Co.** (High Country Inn) ☎ (867) 667-4471, 4051 Fourth Avenue, is the place to go for an excellent cold one from the local Chilkoot Brewery and one of Heinz's juicy barbecued burgers. The best deal is the Deck burger. Also on the menu is a range of seafood, pastas, and salads. There is surprisingly good sushi at the Yukon Mining Co. on certain nights; call to inquire about availability. To find The Deck, just look for the adjoining hotel, an aluminum tower in the neighborhood of the Robert Campbell Bridge.

There are several roasters in Whitehorse where a good cup coffee can be enjoyed. Our favorite is **Midnight Sun Coffee Roaster** ☎ (867) 633-4JOE, 4168C Fourth Avenue, where the organic brew is especially aromatic and the atmosphere is homey. They have great muffins and cookies, too. Another "must" on the Whitehorse scene is the **Alpine Bakery** ☎ (867) 668-6871, 411 Alexander Street, where you can purchase long-lasting expedition bread for your hiking or boating trip. All of the baked goods are terrific, all organic. They also offer homemade yogurt, European cheeses, and organic preserves made with Yukon berries. The Alpine has a reputation for being not only the best bakery in the Yukon, but one of the best in the country. It's open Tuesday to Saturday from 10 AM to 5:30 PM.

How to Get There

The **Whitehorse International Airport** is seven kilometers (five miles) from the downtown core, on a hill above the city. Until recently, there were no international direct flights to the Yukon. That changed with the introduction of a weekly Lufthansa flight from Frankfurt; additional international connections may be added as the Yukon becomes a more popular destination for Europeans.

Most people still fly into Whitehorse via a Canadian city. Daily service is available through Vancouver and Edmonton via **Canadian Airlines International** ☎ (867) 668-7378, or from Juneau and Fairbanks, Alaska via **Air North** ☎ (867) 668-2228. Flying to the Yukon is appallingly expensive. At certain seasons it is possible to arrange one-way charter flights to Vancouver or other Canadian cities for much less than the regular airline fare. The best place to make onward travel arrangements from Whitehorse is **Atlas Travel** ☎ (867) 667-7823, in the Westmark Whitehorse Hotel.

Coming from British Columbia, motorists enter the Yukon via the Alaska Highway (Highway 1) or the **Stewart-Cassiar Highway**, which connects with Highway 1 near the Yukon-British Columbia border. From Alaska, Highway 1 leads from Fairbanks into the southwest corner of the territory. Those heading to Dawson City from Alaska can pick up the **Taylor Highway** (Highway 5) at Tok, Alaska, and from there connect with the Top of the World Highway (Highway 9) which leads to Dawson City.

Greyhound ☎ (867) 667-2223 TOLL-FREE (800) 661-8747 offers daily service from Edmonton. The trip takes 36 hours. The best place to break the journey is Liard Hot Springs. **Alaskon Express** TOLL-FREE (800) 544-2206 has regularly scheduled service from Alaska to the Yukon communities of Carcross, Whitehorse, Haines Junction, and Beaver Creek. Tickets may be booked at any Gray Line Office. In Whitehorse **Gray Line Yukon** ☎ (867) 668-3130 is at 2288 Second Avenue. Cheaper fares are to be had on the **Alaska Direct Bus Lines** ☎ (867) 668-4833 or (907) 277-6652, 125 Oklahoma Street, Anchorage, Alaska 99504-1210 USA, also runs through the Yukon, serving Whitehorse, Haines Junction, Burwash Landing, and Beaver Creek.

The most scenic way to get to the Yukon is via the Alaska State Ferries along the Inside Passage (see CRUISE THE INSIDE PASSAGE, page 16, in TOP SPOTS). Passengers can debark at Haines, Alaska, and follow Haines Road (Highway 3) up to Haines Junction where it connects with the Alaska Highway; or they can get off at Skagway, Alaska, where they can journey over the White Pass by railway (see RIDE THE LEGENDARY RAILS, page 11, in TOP SPOTS). From Skagway, travelers can also follow in the footsteps of the gold-rush stampeders by trekking the Chilkoot Trail (see SKAGWAY, ALASKA, below); or they can reach the Yukon by car via the Klondike Highway (Highway 2).

SKAGWAY, ALASKA

Described in 1898 as nothing more than "a spot of wet, mossy earth at the foot of a high mountain on the seashore," Skagway, Alaska, is one of the primary routes to the Yukon. A popular destination in itself, Skagway is swamped throughout the summer with short-term visitors: some 450,000 cruiseship passengers pass through each season. Most of the 2,500 people who work in Skagway are not residents, but come up early for the summer tourist season. Only around 800 live here year-round. A day is certainly enough time to rest up from your ferry trip, get a feel for the place and make your onward connections to the Yukon. The name, incidentally means, "place of the north wind."

General Information

The overburdened **Convention and Visitor Bureau** ☎ (907) 983-2854 FAX (907) 983-1898, has town

The 1898 Klondike gold rush— "Tenderfeet" labor over the Chilkoot Pass from Dyea, Alaska, to Lake Bennett, British Columbia. ABOVE: A seasoned prospector, or "sourdough."

and trail maps and offers information and advice on all your travel and accommodation needs. **Internet access** is available at Soapy Station ☎ (907) 983-2085, 745 Broadway, where there are also phone and fax facilities and laptop ports.

What to See and Do

The United States park service has done an admirable job of preserving the historical district of this boom-and-bust town, but behind the boardwalks and authentic false-fronted buildings, attractions, eateries, and hostelries of quality number only a few. Skagway's historical district is essentially a show for the passengers of the giant luxury cruise ships that dock by the threes and fours in its small harbor. Much of downtown Skagway constitutes the **Klondike Gold Rush National Historic Park** which also encompasses the White Pass and Chilkoot Trail (as well as Pioneer Square in Seattle, Washington). The park Visitor Centre, Second Avenue and Broadway, is open daily 8 AM to 6 PM from May to September, 8 AM to 8 PM from June to August. The center offers films, ranger talks, and a worthwhile **walking tour of the historic district**; all activities are free of charge.

ABOVE and OPPOSITE BOTTOM: Alaska State Ferries' MV *Matanuska* plies the Inside Passage. TOP: A Dawson cabin sports the traditional moose antler and knotty pine admorments.

Dozens of operators — with mottoes such as "Why pay more?" — offer **sightseeing tours** around and about town. Take your pick. The one stand-out in the crowd is the Skagway Street Car Company ☎ (907) 983-2908, whose costumed interpreters take you around in a shiny yellow 1920s-vintage limousine.

For those who did not arrive in Skagway via boat, a taste of the Inside Passage can be had by booking on the **boat tours** to Haines or Juneau. Chilkat Cruises ☎ (907) 766-2100 TOLL-FREE (888) 766-2103 operates a daily scheduled ferry shuttle service; Auk Nu Tours ☎ (907) 586-8687 TOLL-FREE (800) 820-BOAT, runs the catamaran *Alaskan Dream* on day-long round-trip cruises to Juneau; and the Water Taxi ☎ (907) 983-2083 offers a similar service to Haines.

And, don't worry — Skagway is not under attack; it's only helicopters and planes giving **flightseeing tours** to Mendenhall Glacier. You can hardly miss Temsco Helicopters ☎ (907) 983-2900, near the harbor or Skagway Air Service ☎ (907) 983-2218 E-MAIL skagair@ptialaska.net. They also have flightseeing tours of the spectacular Glacier Bay.

Skagway has two locally owned art and craft shops: **Inside Passage Arts** (907) 983-2585, and **Inhofe's Carvers Gallery** ☎ (907) 983-2434, both located on Broadway. Inhofe's sells his own work and the works of his protégés, chiefly mastodon ivory carvings. At Inside Passage Arts the work ranges wider with Southeast Alaska native arts alongside the hand-carved silver jewelry of the owners. The rest of Skagway's shops are not noteworthy, running the gamut from expensive jewelry stores to trinket shops brimming with big-eyed seal T-shirts.

Excursions from Skagway

For many travelers, the sole reason for passing through Skagway is to access the famed 53-km (33-mile)-long **Chilkoot Trail**. A difficult hike that takes three to five days, it follows the route of the stampeders. The trail begins near the Dyea townsite northwest of Skagway. You must obtain a backcountry permit from the National Park Service before you begin your hike. Only 50 hikers per day are allowed to cross into Canada via the trail. Because of this quota, it may be necessary to obtain your permit as early as six months in advance if you wish to hike the trail at the peak season of mid-July to mid-August. Contact the **Klondike Gold Rush National Historic Park** ☎ (907) 983-2921, PO Box 517, Skagway, Alaska 99840.

Where to Stay and Eat

If you decide to overnight in Skagway, we recommend **Whitehouse Bed and Breakfast** ☎ (907) 983-9000 FAX (907) 983-3210 E-MAIL whitehse@ptialaska.net, Eighth and Main, PO Box 41, Skagway, Alaska 99840. This historic house is located in a quiet street far enough away from Broadway to escape the constant hubbub but close enough for convenience. The spacious rooms have high ceilings and en-suite bathrooms. Full breakfast is served each morning in the dining

YUKON RIVER CRUISES
TICKET OFFICE

room. Prices are in the mid-range category. The **Skagway Inn** ✆ (907) 983-2289 FAX (907) 983-2713 E-MAIL sgyinn@ptialaska.net, Seventh and Broadway, PO Box 500, Skagway, Alaska 99840, is a good choice, if you want to be in the center of the historic district. It's a European-style inn with cozy rooms decorated to commemorate "the girls" of Skagway's gold-rush days. Bathrooms are shared. Rates run from inexpensive to mid-range. For budget travelers, the **Skagway Home Hostel** ✆ (907) 983-2131 FAX (907) 983-2713, Third Street and Main, Skagway, Alaska 99840, has dormitory accommodation as well as inexpensive private double rooms.

It's difficult to make recommendations for restaurants in Skagway, whose dining establishments have begun to suffer from their success. On the ground floor of the Skagway Inn is **Olivia's** ✆ (907) 983-2289, where Caesar salad is prepared at your table. Its reputation as the best restaurant in town is probably deserved, but standards are lamentably low here; nevertheless, reservations are recommended. The **Golden North Hotel** ✆ (907) 983-2451, on Third Street and Broadway, has a restaurant with a delightful terrace, but service is slow. Also on Broadway, the very popular **Sweet Tooth Gertie's** ✆ (907) 983-2450, 315 Broadway, is your best bet for a hearty breakfast. You can count on good solid food here, but be sure to arrive before the morning ferry passengers alight. They'll be hungry.

How to Get There

Skagway can be reached year-round via the **Alaska Marine Highway** ✆ (907) 627-1744 or (907) 627-1745 TOLL-FREE (800) 642-0066, PO Box 25535, Juneau, Alaska 99802-5535, from Bellingham (Washington), Prince Rupert (British Columbia); and Wrangell, Petersburg, Sitka, Juneau and Haines (Alaska); and by air from Juneau, Haines and Whitehorse, Yukon. Road routes to Skagway are the Alaska and Klondike highways from the Yukon.

Once in Skagway, your options are the three Rs: road, rail, or ramble. The Klondike Highway takes you over the White Pass to the Yukon's capital city of Whitehorse. For bus service, there is **Rival Highway Tours** ✆ (867) 667-7896, connecting Whitehorse to Skagway via Carcross and Fraser, British Columbia. Before the highway there was the **White Pass & Yukon Railway** ✆ (907) 983-2217 TOLL-FREE (800) 343-7373 FAX (907) 983-2734, PO Box 435, Skagway, Alaska 99840. Ramblers backpack the steep Chilkoot Trail out of Dyea (see EXCURSIONS FROM SKAGWAY, page 216).

KLUANE NATIONAL PARK

Tucked in the southwest corner of the territory, a two-hour drive from Whitehorse, Kluane (pronounced kloo-*ahn*-ee) National Park is the jewel of the Yukon, a designated UNESCO World Heritage Site. These 22,015 sq km (8,500 sq miles) of glaciers, marshes, lakes, and mountains are unsettled and virtually untouched. There are no ski lifts in Kluane waiting to whisk you to the top of a mountain, no teahouses at the end of the trail. "Kluane," said a transplanted Swiss couple we met there, "is the Swiss Alps without all the people." The Matterhorn of this alpine land is **Mount Logan** (6,050 m or 19,849 ft), Canada's highest peak and the second highest mountain in North America. It is part of the St. Elias Mountains, which contains six other peaks over 5,000 m (16,000 ft).

Much of the reserve's wilderness has been the homeland of the Southern Tutchone people for thousands of years. Many of the trails follow traditional paths of these First Nations people who still use them. The Champagne and Aishihik First Nations have a constitutional right to hunt and fish in the park and are co-managers of Kluane.

Because the park is undeveloped, the interior is only accessible to experienced alpinists (or those with the money to take a flightseeing tour, see WHAT TO SEE AND DO, below). Despite this, parts of Kluane are surprisingly accessible. Rafting, fishing in crystal clear waters, and wildlife watching are the chief activities.

General Information

Kluane has two visitor reception centers, staffed throughout the summer, where expert advice is available on what to see and do in the park. The **Kluane Park Visitor Centre** ✆ (867) 634-2251 provides literature, information, and maps. It's open daily 8:30 AM to 9 PM. Within the same facility is the territorial **Visitor Information Centre** ✆ (867) 634-2345. The **Sheep Mountain Visitor Centre** (867) 841-5161, Km 1707 Alaska Highway, is open daily 9 AM to 7 PM. An interpretive program runs

OPPOSITE and ABOVE: Kluane National Park — The St. Elias Lake Trail, "bear country."

through the summer months with guided hikes and presentations. Haines Junction is the place to stock up on provisions. **Madley's** has everything you need for camping, hiking as well as groceries, fresh produce, and smoked wild salmon which they will ship. Next door, the public library has the only public **Internet access** for miles around.

What to See and Do

You don't have to be a mountaineer to enjoy the many kilometers of trails throughout the park's front ranges. The best time of year for **hiking** is between June 15 and September 15, when temperatures range between a high of 28°C (82°F) and a low of 0°C (32°F). All overnight trips into Kluane

require registration at one of the visitor reception centers where you can also find out about how to avoid sneaking up on a bear (to begin with, always make noise as you are walking). The trailhead for the short hike to **St. Elias Lake Trail** (3.8 km or 2.4 miles) is 60 km (38 miles) south of Haines Junction on Haines Road. The trail leads through wood and meadow to backcountry camping along a lake visited by loons. The **Auriol Trail** (15 km or nine miles) is a popular overnight loop. The trailhead is seven kilometers south of Haines Junction on Haines Road.

Kluane is also a wonderful place for **paddling**. You can rent a canoe, kayak or raft and strike out on your own, or you can hook up with an outfitter (see OUTFITTERS, below).

Just east of the Sheep Mountain Visitor Centre, look for the scenic viewpoint marker for the turnoff (to your left) for **Silver City**, a ghost town located five kilometers (three miles) down a gravel road. It's a worthwhile side trip where you can ramble among the decaying shanties and mining equipment.

The only way to get a glimpse at the St. Elias Mountains, short of mounting a major expedition, is to take a **flightseeing** tour with one of the local operators such as Trans North Helicopters ☎ (867) 668-2177, located along the Alaska Highway east of the Sheep Mountain Visitor Centre. The helicopters will take you to the spectacular **Kaskawulsh Glacier**, part of the world's largest nonpolar ice field. Or you can arrange a **heli-hiking** trip. You'll be dropped off in an alpine meadow with panoramic views of Sheep Mountain, Kluane Lake and the St. Elias Mountains; from there you trek back to Trans North's Kluane base.

Haines Road is a gorgeous drive leading into an uninhabited corner of British Columbia before arriving at Haines, Alaska. At its highest point, the road cuts across a grand plateau guarded by glaciated mountains. Numerous creeks pass through the region, and this area has some of the continent's best river trips (see below).

Outfitters

Paddlewheel Adventures ☎ (867) 634-2683, PO Box 2079, Haines Junction Y0B 1L0, across from the Kluane Park Visitor Centre, has canoe and mountain bike rentals, guided tours, and does bookings for a variety of other tours, including whitewater rafting, flightseeing, horseback riding, and llama hikes. The Tatshenshini Wilderness Area provides some of the best river running in the world. **Tatshenshini Expediting** ☎ (867) 633-2742 FAX (867) 633-6184 E-MAIL tatexp@polar.com, 1602 Alder Street, Whitehorse Y1A 3W8, is one of the Yukon's longest established rafting and kayaking companies. They offer a range of adventures from one-day paddling trips along the Tat to the full 11-day Tatshenshini and Alsek river-rafting experience — this is the one that draws people from all over the world not only for its challenging rapids but for its unparalleled scenery. They also rent boats and all necessary equipment.

Where to Stay and Eat

In Haines Junction, the **Raven Motel** ☎ (867) 634-2500 FAX (867) 634-2517, 181 Haines Road, PO Box 5470, Haines Junction Y0B 1L0, has comfortable rooms ranging in price from inexpensive to moderate. Rooms have direct dial telephones, en-suite bathrooms, and television. The restaurant (expensive) is among the best in the Yukon.

Rooms at the **Gateway Motel** ☎ (867) 634-2371 FAX (867) 634-2833, PO Box 5460, Haines Junction

Yukon flora and fauna — ABOVE: Lichens flourish in an alpine meadow. OPPOSITE: A felled tree offers evidence of beavers.

Y0B 1L0, are of surprisingly high quality given the appearance of the building and office. Standing as it does at the junction of the Alaska Highway and Haines Road, few motels can compete with its stunning views of the snowcapped Kluane Mountain Range. Amenities include satellite television, complimentary coffee, and kitchenettes. The Gateway had a "For Sale" sign attached to it at the time of research, but the cigar-chomping owner (after offering to sell it to us) assured us that it was to remain in operation.

The **Cozy Corner** ☎ (867) 634-2511 FAX (867) 634-2119, PO Box 5406, Haines Junction Y0B 1L0, is another good motel choice. The attached restaurant serves a generous breakfast.

One of the best ways to explore the region is to stay at **Dalton Trail Lodge** ☎/FAX (867) 667-1099, PO Box 5331, Haines Junction Y0B 1L0, nestled at the base of the St. Elias Mountains on Dezadeash Lake. Activities run from horseback riding to dog mushing, canoeing, hiking, fishing for king salmon and Arctic grayling, flightseeing, and snowmobiling all from the comfort of the casual lodge, log cabins, or private outposts. Visitors can opt for full-fledged, guided excursions or relaxed day-long forays into Kluane. The lodge has canoes stationed at many of the lakes, so day hikers can combine a canoe trip with a hike. Finally, the lodge has its own gold claim on Kimberly Creek where visitors can pan for nuggets and learn about placer mining. Full breakfast, a picnic lunch, and a hardy Swiss dinner are included in the prices, which are in the moderate category. German and French are spoken.

DAWSON CITY

At a latitude of 64° 4′ north, Dawson City is a place of strange contradictions. Once the largest metropolis north of San Francisco, it now has a year-round population of less than 2,000. One of the most northerly of Canadian towns, it is also one of the hottest. In June, you can watch the sun sink below the horizon at one o'clock in the morning and stick around to see it come back up three hours later. The town's beer halls are loaded with frontier character, but it also lovingly preserves the cabins of two famous literary men, Robert Service and Jack London.

Dawson's gold rush atmosphere is what draws most visitors. Large portions of the town are part of a registered historical area administered by Parks Canada and the Klondike Visitors Association. Many of the buildings are authentic gold-rush era structures and the rest are good reproductions. The streets remain as they were in 1898, unpaved and lined by boardwalks. Museums, tours, panning for gold, gambling, old-time music, riverboat rides, and can-can girls are all part of the fun. Yet there is much more to Dawson City than turn-of-the-century revelry. Visitors who take a moment to look beyond the gold-rush glitter will also find a welcoming native community composed of descendants of the region's original inhabitants. Outdoor enthusiasts will find abundant opportunities for hiking, fishing, paddling and more, while motorists can enjoy some wonderfully scenic drives.

Background

The first wave of stampeders to arrive in Dawson City were totally unprepared for what lay ahead. The winter of 1897 was a season of shortages: There was not enough food to go around and fearful prospectors began to panic and hoard; candle and lamp oil was in short supply, leaving 3,000 of 6,000 inhabitants without with light for the winter in a land where daylight lasts only from 10 AM to 2 PM; 2,000 people were unsheltered or living in tents.

Despite its rough start, Dawson City was born and prospered. At the height of the gold rush, Dawson had a population of around 30,000, making it one of the biggest cities west of Winnipeg. Between 1897 and 1904, it is estimated that over $100 million in gold was recovered from the Klondike and its tributaries which covered an area of around 64 sq km (40 sq miles). It was a small pocket of land that glittered with gold, yet only a handful of prospectors went home millionaires. Tens of thousands were disappointed, for by the time they reached the gold fields, all of the best claims had been staked.

After the stampede, the population of Dawson City began to decline almost immediately. Many prospectors were soon discouraged and were lured by reports of other gold discoveries (e.g., Nome, Alaska in 1899). By 1906 the most easily worked placer mines (containing gold that is found lose in sand and gravel as opposed to "lode" gold that occurs in hard rock) were finished, leaving claims to be mined by large companies using huge and expensive dredges. The employment offered by these dredging companies kept Dawson City alive for the next 50 years. These days the little town of 2,000 year-round residents thrives on tourism.

General Information

Stop by the excellent **Visitor Reception Centre** ☎ (867) 993-5566 on the corner of Front and King streets, for an orientation before you begin your explorations. It's open daily from May 16 to September 21, 8 AM to 8 PM. The building is a replica of the Alaska Trading Company building. **Parks Canada** ☎ (867) 993-7200, maintains a counter here as well, where you can purchase a Parks Pass — worth the price if you're planning to visit more than three of their sites. For trip planning, you can contact the park service by writing: Superintendent, Klondike National Historic Sites, PO Box 390, Dawson Y0B 1G0. The public library, in the Post Office Building, Fifth Avenue, has free **Internet access**; however, there is usually a long waiting list (we're talking days). It's better to shell out a few dollars to check your e-mail at **Harper Street Publishing** ☎ (867) 993-6671. Call to get their current office location. While you are there, pick up a free copy of their *Guide to the Goldfields*, an annual publication with news, opinions, and essays about the North.

What to See and Do

Begin your visit to Dawson City with a **walking tour** through the historic downtown area. Tours are given by costumed interpreters and depart

Dawson City — OPPOSITE: The Palace Grande Theatre LEFT and a sunny seciton of the city's wooden sidewalks RIGHT. ABOVE: The "Pit" at the Windsor Hotel is a popular night spot.

from the Visitor Information Centre three times daily. The interpreters have an interesting rap, and this is also the only opportunity to see the interior of some of the restored historical buildings. You can, alternatively, rent an audio tape in English, French or German, for a self-guided walking tour.

On the riverbank near Queen Street, you can see an old, grounded sternwheeler, the **SS *Keno***. Built in 1922 to ply the Stewart River around the mining hamlets of Mayo and Keno, it was the smallest in the Yukon fleet. Because of its diminutive size, the *Keno* would have been the first to break through the winter ice to Dawson — a welcome sight after long months without fresh vegetables. Tours of the newly restored boat are offered by the SS *Keno* National Historic Site ☎ (867) 993-5462 FAX (867) 993-5683, C.P. 390 390 Dawson City Yukon, YIA 285.

A few blocks away from the river, he **Dawson City Museum** ☎ (867) 993-5291, Fifth Avenue at Minto Park, features exhibits on the history of the gold rush. There are some 25,000 artifacts on display, though most of it will only be of interest to gold-rush buffs. Exhibits on the native Hän who populated the area before the gold rush and who still live here are lackluster. Silent films of the period, unearthed during a 1978 restoration project, are the best part of the museum's offerings. There's a coffee and gift shop. The museum is open from early June to Labor Day daily from 10 AM to 6 PM; an admission fee is charged.

The **Robert Service Cabin** is a two-room log structure in which the poet lived between 1909 and 1912. Actor Tom Byrne performs a daily recitation of the life and works of the "Bard of the Yukon" — who wrote such classics as "The Shooting of Dan McGrew" and "The Call of the Yukon." It's open daily from 9 AM to noon and 1 PM to 5 PM with recitals at 10 AM and 3 PM; an admission fee is charged. Farther south, on Eighth Avenue at the corner of Fifth, is the **Jack London Cabin**, where the writer lived briefly. Though his time in the Yukon was short, he collected the materials here for such classics as *White Fang*, "The Snow Wolf," and *The Call of the Wild*. There's a talk each day at 1 PM about London's adventures in the Klondike. It's open 11 AM to 3 PM and admission is free.

Souvenir shoppers should not miss the **Dawson Trading Post** ☎ (867) 993-5316, on Fifth Avenue, a gold mine for those on the lookout for the unusual. Besides being a sports-and-adventure outfitter, the store sells local antiques, caribou antlers, and raw mastodon ivory. The **Klondike Nugget and Ivory Shop** ☎ (867) 993-5432, has the Yukon's signature souvenir gold-nugget and mastodon ivory jewelry.

Dawson nightlife retains some of the frontier, whoop-it-up flavor of its heyday. The diminutive and beautifully restored **Palace Grande Theatre** ☎ (867) 993-6217, King Street, was built in 1899 from materials that once made up two steamboats. Parks Canada restored the theater 1962, and now offers guided tours. The theater is also home to the much-vaunted *Gaslight Follies*. Best to tour the theater by day, but if you feel you must see the show, tickets are available at the Historic Post Office; shows run May 17 to September 14 nightly except Tuesday at 8 PM. It's safe to say that your evening might more wisely be spent elsewhere, say at **Diamond Tooth Gertie's Gambling Hall** ☎ (867) 993-5575, at Fourth Avenue and Queen Street. At least here you'll have fun wasting your money. It's open from 7 PM to 2 AM with three floor shows each night, complete with can-can line. Minors are not admitted. It's open from mid-May to mid-September; an admission fee is charged.

The gaudy pink **Westminster Hotel** ☎ (867) 993-5463, 975 Third Avenue, is the home of the "Pit" beer parlor and is stocked with local character and characters. Nightly entertainment is provided by same.

Excursions from Dawson City

A hike or drive up to **Midnight Dome** is another requisite of the Dawson City experience. Dawson sits at the foot of this mountain, and the summit affords views of the gold fields, Yukon River valley, Dawson, and the Ogilvie Mountains. Go up for the late-night sunset for the best vistas.

If you'd like to go with a group, **Gold City Tours** ☎ (867) 993-5175, PO Box 960, Dawson Y0B 1G0, on Front Street across from the SS *Keno* riverboat, takes up to Midnight Dome. They also take sightseers out to the Bonanza Creek gold fields, and on a 12-hour trip via coach along the Dempster Highway to the Arctic Circle and back.

The twin-deck ***Yukon Queen*** takes passengers from Dawson City to Eagle, Alaska, a distance of 174 km (108 miles). The day-long cruise includes two meals and a stopover in Eagle. Trips run from mid-May to mid-September and passengers can choose one-way or round-trips. Book well in advance at Gray Line Yukon ☎ (867) 993-5599 on Front Street near the visitor center.

Dawson City has some wonderful river excursions where you can meet and learn about the regional native cultures. **Ancient Voices Wilderness Camp** ☎ (867) 993-5605 FAX (867) 993-6532 E-MAIL avwcamp@yukon.net, PO Box 679, Dawson Y0B 1G0 (see LISTEN TO ANCIENT VOICES, page 18, in TOP SPOTS) has an evening barbecue, drumming, and storytelling program as well as accommodation and adventure packages and programs including wilderness survival, arts and crafts, and

TOP: A motorboat ride up the Yukon River is a chance to spot wildlife such as moose and black bear. BOTTOM: Permafrost plays havoc with house foundations. These days, pilings that can be raised and lowered stablize the city's buildings.

women's workshops. **Fishwheel Charter Service** ✆ (867) 993-6857, PO Box 891, Dawson Y0B 1G0, runs two-hour historical-cultural tours, where you can see a traditional native method of fishing. *Bannock* and tea are included in the trip.

The gold fields lie just south of Dawson City in the hills and creeks along the Klondike Highway. Though the rush is long over, you can pan for gold — success guaranteed — at **Claim 33** ✆ (867) 993-5303, Mile 7 Bonanza Creek Road. But what's the fun in noodling around in a trough laced with gold flakes? Far better to roll up your sleeves and take your chances in a creek. **Goldbottom Mining Tours** ✆ (867) 993-5023 FAX (867) 993-6715, PO Box 912, Dawson Y0B 1G0, runs escorted trips to an authentic placer mining operation where you'll see a gold processing demonstration and get an hour of gold panning in the creek (daily 11 AM to 7 PM) — rubber boots, pan, and shovel provided. They are located at Goldbottom and Hunker creeks, 30 km (19 miles) south of Dawson City and 15 km (just over nine miles) up Hunker Creek Road from the Klondike Highway.

After the first wave of individual prospecting, companies moved into the Yukon and began large-scale mining with dredges. Until it sank in the 1960s, **Dredge No. 4** ripped 22,000 grams of gold out of the ground each day. The largest wooden-hulled dredge ever built, it is now an historical monument. This dredge and others like it are responsible for the eerie, apocalyptic look of the landscape in the Klondike area. Floating in man-made ponds, the dredges scooped, sifted and spewed out creek gravel, creating huge, caterpillar-shaped mounds of tailings. It's open daily 9 AM to 5 PM, and is located 13 km (eight miles) south of Dawson City on Bonanza Creek Road (off the Klondike Highway).

The best way to get an idea of the extent of the gold fields is to take an **aerial tour** with Trans North Helicopters ✆ (867) 993-5494. They also offer **heli-hiking** in the nearby Tombstone and Ogilvie mountains. The helipad is on the Klondike Highway, half a kilometer (about one quarter mile) south of Dawson City.

One hill over from Dredge No. 4, **Bear Creek** was for 60 years the home of the Yukon Consolidated Gold Corporation. This dredge support camp was where the gold ore was milled and melted down into bullion. This Parks Canada site has 65 buildings to tour illustrating the history of large-scale mining. The turnoff for Bear Creek is 16 km (10 miles) south of Dawson City, off the Klondike Highway.

Where to Stay

A welcome new addition to the mid-range to expensive accommodation available in Dawson City is the **Aurora Inn** ✆/FAX (867) 993-6860 E-MAIL rjansen@yknet.yk.ca, PO Box 1748, Dawson Y0B 1G0. Located on Fifth Avenue, the inn has spacious, sunny rooms with a contemporary Scandinavian look and locally made white pine furnishings. All rooms have en-suite baths. A European breakfast is served at an additional moderate cost. Some rooms come equipped with computers and the proprietors are happy to arrange a variety of supplementary services with its higher-priced rooms.

At the corner of Second and Queen streets, the **Downtown Hotel** ✆ (867) 993-5346 TOLL-FREE (800) 661-0514 or (800) 764-GOLD FAX (867) 993-5076, PO Box 780, Dawson Y0B 1G0, is one of Dawson's two year-round accommodations. The rooms are comfortable and modern. The main building features a restaurant and the plush Sourdough Saloon. The annex (across the street) has a whirlpool. Rates are at the top end of the mid-range category.

The **Westmark Inn** ✆ (867) 993-5542 TOLL-FREE (800) 544-0970 or (800) 999-2570, Fifth Avenue and Harper Street, Dawson Y0B 1G0, is part of the northern chain. It focuses most of its energies on the many coach tours that its parent company brings to Dawson City, but rooms for independent travelers are sometimes available. Though small, rooms are modern and richly furnished. There is room service, a dining room, lounge, and gift shop. Rates are solidly mid-range.

Nondescript but reliable, the **Triple J Hotel** ✆ (867) 993-5323 TOLL-FREE (800) 764-3555 or (800) 661-0405, PO Box 359, Dawson Y0B 1G0, on Fifth Avenue, has a hotel, a motel, and small cabins. All units have private bath. The main hotel building includes a restaurant and lounge with a terrace. It's right next to Diamond Tooth Gertie's Casino, and it is open year-round. Rates are mid-range.

The First Nations-owned-and-operated **Bear Creek Bed & Bannock** ✆ (867) 993-5605 FAX (867) 993-6532 E-MAIL kormendy@hypertech.yk.ca, PO Box 679, Dawson Y0B 1G0, offers inexpensive to mid-range bed and breakfast accommodation in Bear Creek, a quiet subdivision 10 minutes from Dawson. Guests stay in a four-room facility separate from the main house, and a continental breakfast including fresh *bannock* is served daily. Traditional First Nations arts and crafts are on display. Guests have use of a kitchen, living room, dining area, laundry facilities, and a large deck.

The **Dawson City Bunkhouse** ✆ (867) 993-6164 FAX (867) 993-6051, on the corner of Front and Princess streets, PO Box 4040, Dawson Y0B 1G0 has clean, rustic accommodation including rooms with shared bath, or suites with private baths. Rates range from inexpensive to moderate.

Dawson has the Yukon's only Hostelling-International-affiliate, the **Dawson City River Hostel** ✆ (867) 993-6823, PO Box 32, Dawson Y0B 1G0, directly opposite Dawson across the Yukon

At Ancient Voices Wilderness Camp, a moosehide is stretched on a rack for tanning.

River. It's open mid-May through September, has a kitchen and bike and canoe rental, and offers free pickup from the bus depot at designated times. To get there take the free 24-hour ferry from Front Street to West Dawson; the hostel is located 100 m (just over 100 yards) from the landing site.

Where to Eat

Good dining can be found in the local hotels, most notably the Downtown Hotel's atmospheric **Jack London Grill and Sourdough Saloon** ☎ (867) 993-5346. The best restaurant in Dawson City, however, is **Marina's** ☎ (867) 993-6800, Fifth Avenue between Princess and Harper streets. The pasta is heavenly. Located across from the Westmark, it can fill up quickly with hungry coach tour groups, so you may want to arrive a bit early for dinner.

Klondike Kate's ☎ (867) 993-6527, corner King Street and Third Avenue, is housed in an authentic gold-rush-era building. The extensive menu features ethnic dishes such as gyros, falafel, "wraps" (like burritos), seafood, sandwiches, and domestic and imported beers. The breakfast special is one of Dawson's best buys. There's a covered patio in the rear. It's open daily 7 AM to 11 PM.

Along the riverfront, **River West Food & Health** ☎ (867) 993-6339, Front and York streets, is a café where you can get sandwiches, salads, and soups at the counter. The coffee is good and you can order food to take out or to eat in.

How to Get There

You can fly from Whitehorse to Dawson City on **Air North** ☎ (867) 668-2228. If you're driving from Alaska, you'll take the **Taylor** and **Top of the World highways** from Chicken to Dawson City. The **Klondike Highway** runs from Skagway, Alaska, through Carcross, Whitehorse, and on to Dawson. The section of the highway from Whitehorse to Dawson City is 537 km (333 miles) and the road is excellent. Bus service between Whitehorse and Dawson is provided by **Norline Coaches** ☎ (867) 993-6010 (in Dawson City) or (867) 668-3355, 2191 Second Avenue (in Whitehorse).

YUKON HIGHWAYS

The Top of the World Highway

The Top of the World Highway (Highway 9) is a scenic drive that begins just across the Yukon River and leads 105 km (64 miles) to the border where it connects with the historic Taylor Highway (Highway 5). The trip begins with the free automobile and passenger ferry ☎ (867) 993-5441, which operates 24 hours a day (apart from Wednesday mornings when it is closed for servicing from 5 AM to 7 AM.) Expect long lines in peak months. Heaviest traffic is from 7 AM to 11 AM and 4 PM to 7 PM.

This road began as a pack trail connecting Dawson City with Sixtymile and other neighboring mining communities. After crossing the Yukon River, the 175-km (110-mile) highway climbs rapidly above the tree line and meanders along mountain ridges with good views of the surrounding countryside. Moving on into Alaska, the Taylor Highway leads north to Eagle or south to Tetlin Junction and the Alaska Highway. The border area is a good place to spot rough-legged hawks, red-tailed hawks, merlins, and kestrels during spring and fall migrations.

The Alaska Highway

Hastily constructed as a military route during World War II, the Alaska Highway (Alcan) is now a tourist route to the northern frontier. As much a pilgrimage route as a road, the it attracts thousands every year, many of them retirees behind the wheel of their brand new recreational vehicles.

The Alaska Highway (Highway 1) starts at Dawson Creek, British Columbia, and travels northwest for 2,452 km (1,520 miles), ending in Fairbanks, Alaska. Along the way it cuts through the southwest corner of the Yukon. Even up until 10 years ago, sections of the road were unpaved. It is now entirely paved, though you will likely find some rough spots, as construction crews only have the precious summer months to upgrade and maintain the road.

First stop along the Canadian portion of the Alaska Highway is the "Gateway to the Yukon," **Watson Lake** (population: 1,795). Tourism Yukon operates the Visitor Reception and the Alaska Highway Interpretive Centre ☎ (867) 536-7469, at the junction of the Robert Campbell and Alaska highways.

The next long stretch of road travels through **Teslin** and then skims past **Whitehorse**, after which the highway skirts **Kluane National Park**. Spreading south from Alcan, the snow-covered **Icefield Ranges** can be seen behind the rugged Kluane Ranges. This is the most scenic part of the route. Plan to take your time.

As the Kluane Ranges taper off, you'll come to **Burwash Landing**, a tiny native village (population less than 100) which overlooks Kluane Lake. Here you'll find the very worthwhile **Kluane Museum of Natural History** ☎ (867) 841-5561, Mile 1093 Alaska Highway. It has the Yukon's best natural history display along with fine exhibits of Southern Tutchone garments, tools, and weapons, as well as fossils. The museum has a stock of videos, which they will play on demand. It's open daily from mid-May to mid-September from 9 AM to 9 PM; an admission fee is charged. Oddity aficionados may be interested

The Dempster Highway runs from just east of Dawson City to Inuvik in the Northwest Territories.

to know that Burwash Landing is also the home of the "biggest gold pan in the world."

The last Canadian stop on the Alcan is **Beaver Creek** (population 140), the westernmost community in Canada. Like many other small Yukon and Alaskan towns, it began as a settlement during the construction of the Alaska Highway. It is situated 30 km (18 miles) south of the Alaskan border. There's a **Visitor Reception Centre** ✆ (867) 862-7321, on the Alaska Highway, and directly across the street you'll find the **Westmark Inn Beaver Creek** ✆ (867) 862-7501 TOLL-FREE (800) 544-0970 FAX (867) 862-7902, Mile 1202 Alaska Highway, Beaver Creek Y0B 1A0. The hotel has 174 rooms, a dining room, dinner theatre, recreation room, mini-golf, a recreational vehicle park, a laundry, a convenience store and a gas station. Unfortunately the only superlatives we can bestow on this Westmark are that it has the tiniest bathtubs we've ever encountered as well as the thinnest walls. Don't hesitate to ask to be moved if you get stuck next to noisy neighbors.

The Klondike Highway

The Klondike Highway (Highway 2) is a scenic, paved road leading from Skagway, Alaska, north through Whitehorse and on to Dawson City. About 180 km (112 miles) north of Whitehorse and 360 km (224 miles) south of Dawson, the village of **Carmacks** is located on a traditional First Nations trading site. In 1892, George Carmacks (later part of the group that precipitated the gold rush) established a small trading post here. The gravel-paved **Robert Campbell Highway** (Highway 4) intersects the hamlet, going on to Faro, Ross River and various mining operations, and provides an alternative to the Alcan between Whitehorse and Watson Lake, through remote spectacular wilderness. If you need to break the drive from Whitehorse to Dawson City, you can bed down at the **Hotel Carmacks** ✆ (867) 863-5221 FAX (867) 863-5605 E-MAIL hotelcar @yknet.yk.ca, PO Box 160, Carmacks Y0B 1C0.

The Dempster Highway

The start of the Dempster Highway (Highway 5) lies 40 km (25 miles) south of Dawson City. From here, this famed trek runs north 735 km (456 miles) to Inuvik, Northwest Territories, near the Arctic Ocean. The most northerly public road in Canada, the Dempster offers beautiful scenery, especially in early fall when the tundra plants take on autumn colors and migrating caribou are more easily seen.

Driving the Dempster Highway is no more difficult than traveling any other gravel road. Some precautions must be taken, however: The **Northwest Territories Visitor Centre** ✆ (867) 993-6167 on Front Street in Dawson, across the street from the visitor center, is the place get information on traveling the Dempster and on visiting the Northwest Territories. For information on road conditions, call TOLL-FREE (800) 661-0750.

The **Klondike River Lodge** ✆ (867) 993-6892, Klondike and Dempster Highways, Dawson Y0B 1G0, is the place from which to launch your trip up the Dempster Highway. Operated by the Gwitch'in Tribal Council, the lodge includes parking for recreational vehicles, a restaurant, a car wash, and a grocery store.

THE NORTHWEST TERRITORIES AND NUNAVUT

A vast frontier covering an area nearly half the size of the United States, the Northwest Territories and Nunavut are the North American continent's last true wilderness. The 67,500 Dene, Athapaskan, Inuit, and Anglo-Europeans who call these territories home are far outnumbered by the approximately 1,367,000 caribou which roam the land — these two territories have the world's lowest population density per square mile.

In the eastern areas the Inuit form a majority of the population. Although their traditional culture has suffered from contact with Anglo-European settlers, they remain a cultural force. In recent decades they have won significant victories in the fight to preserve a way of life that is so intimately tied to the land. These land-rights negotiations finally led to the partitioning, on April 1, 1999, of the old Northwest Territories into today's eastern Nunavut and western Northwest Territories.

For the adventurer, the Northwest Territories and Nunavut offer incomparable scenic wonders, along with abundant wildlife, world-class fishing, and opportunities to visit and learn from the native inhabitants. Recommended (if not indispensable) publications, should you decide to visit Nunavut or the Northwest Territories, include *The Nunavut Handbook* (Marion Soubliere, ed.) and *The Milepost* (see RECOMMENDED READING, page 247).

You should plan your trip to the Northwest Territories in advance, confirming accommodations and guide services prior to your departure. In many parts of the Northwest Territories transportation is limited to airplanes, snowmobiles, and all-terrain vehicles (ATVs) since there are no roads linking most communities. Dog teams are still used in winter and boats travel during warmer months when the ice comes off the water.

GENERAL INFORMATION

If you hear the call of the North, you're first response should be to get in touch with the government tourism agencies. The **Nunavut Tourism Association** ☎ (867) 979-6551 TOLL-FREE IN CANADA (800) 491-7910, PO Box 1450, Iqaluit X0A 0H0, is the place to contact for planning your trip to Nunavut. Write or call **Northwest Territories Tourism** ☎ (867) 873-7200 TOLL-FREE (800) 661-0788 WEB SITE www.nwttravel.nt.ca/, PO Box 610, Yellowknife X1A 2N5, for information on the Northwest Territories , including Yellowknife and the Western Arctic.

Many northern communities have **regional and local visitor centers** offering information and assistance as well as interpretive displays on the local culture and history. In communities that don't have visitor centers, you can usually get assistance at the community center and from hotel staff.

Inuvik, the town that stays up all summer — OPPOSITE: Our Lady of Victory Church is often called the Igloo Church. ABOVE: A downtown street is backlit by the midnight sun.

CNWX 109721
Canada

Travelers' Tips

THE BEST TIP WE CAN OFFER ANY TRAVELER is to get a good travel agent. There is no substitute — not even this sparkling chapter — for the information and helpful advice that a travel agent has at his or her command. In a world where fares, schedules, even routes are changing hourly, only someone with access to the latest information can give you the sort of guidance necessary to ensure a hassle-free vacation.

GETTING THERE

Almost all of the **major international airlines** fly to Canada, but Air Canada has more flights to more Canadian cities than any other airline. Also,

as you would expect, Air Canada has an extensive network of domestic airlines linking cities within Canada (see GETTING AROUND, below). Contact numbers for **Air Canada** are as follows: TOLL-FREE IN CANADA (888) AIR-CANADA; TOLL-FREE IN THE UNITED STATES (800) 776-3000 (for reservations) or (800) 488-1800 (for flight arrival and departure information); in Australia (C) (02) 9232 5222; in France (C) 01 44 50 20 20; in New Zealand (C) (09) 379-3371 and in the United Kingdom (C) (0990) 247 226.

Other major airlines offering flights to Canada include: **American Airlines** TOLL-FREE (800) 433-7300; **Canadian Airlines** TOLL-FREE (800) 426-7000; **Delta** TOLL-FREE (800) 221-1212; **United** TOLL-FREE (800) 241-6522; **Northwest** TOLL-FREE (800) 447-4747; and **US Airways** TOLL-FREE (800) 428-4322.

One general tip regarding air travel to Canada — or anywhere else for that matter — is to get to the airport early. This is a contentious issue among frequent flyers, some of whom like to arrive at the airport just as the pilot is starting up the engines. But for us there are three compelling arguments in favor of heading for the airport ahead of time. One is that it gives you a safety margin in case you encounter a problem — a traffic jam, a flat tire, a detour — on the way. You would be surprised how many people miss planes because they didn't leave themselves time to absorb unexpected delays. Secondly, by getting to the airport early you have a much better seat selection for your flight — and the longer the flight, the more important it is to have the seat you want. (If you are flying on a British Airways jumbo jet, for example, you can often get a seat upstairs, where it is more comfortable and the service is more attentive.) Thirdly, early arrivals at the airport avoid the long lines at the check-in counter, which means that the time that would otherwise be spent standing around shepherding one's luggage slowly forward can be spent reading, shopping, having drinks, having a meal — in a word, relaxing.

Three **car-ferry** services operate between Victoria, British Columbia and Washington state: **Black Ball Transport** (C) (250) 386-2202 (in Victoria) or (360) 457-4491 (in Port Angeles) operates from Port Angeles; **Clipper Navigation** (C) (250) 382-8100 TOLL-FREE (800) 288-2535 from Seattle; and **Victoria San Juan Cruises** (C) (360) 738-8099 TOLL-FREE (800) 443-4552 from Bellingham with a stop in the San Juan Islands.

There are 13 principal border crossing points where the American highway system connects directly with the Canadian. Crossing into Canada by **car** is usually a quick, simple matter, although in peak season you might want to avoid the busier crossing points such as Detroit-Windsor and Niagara Falls. Once in Canada, no matter where you've crossed, you are only a short drive from the Trans-Canada Highway.

Greyhound TOLL-FREE (800) 661-8747 is the only company operating a cross-border service, but it has such a huge route system that you should have no difficulty in getting to most points in Canada from virtually anywhere in the United States. It also has a hugely complicated system of fares, discount fares, seasonal rates, unlimited-travel passes, and so on. Travel agents can usually help with such things. Major routes include Minneapolis–Winnipeg, and Seattle–Vancouver/Edmonton/Calgary.

Amtrak TOLL-FREE (800) 872-7245, the United States passenger railway system, connects Seattle, Washington with Vancouver, British Columbia.

TOURIST INFORMATION

Rather than having a central source of information for all of Canada, each of the provinces maintains a bureau that dispenses information on subjects of interest to tourists. In the GENERAL INFORMATION sections of the preceding chapters we have listed the local agencies; here, then, are the provincial tourism offices:

Travel Alberta (C) (403) 427-4321 TOLL-FREE (800) 661-8888 WEB SITE www.discoveralberta.com/html/Canada/Alberta/, PO Box 2500, Edmonton, Alberta T5J 2Z4.

British Columbia Tourism ☎ (604) 685-0032 TOLL-FREE (800) 663-6000 WEB SITE www.tbc.gov.bc.ca/tourism/, Parliament Buildings, Victoria, British Columbia V8V 1X4.

Travel Manitoba ☎ (204) 945-3777 TOLL-FREE (800) 665-0040 WEB SITE www.gov.mb.ca/itt/travel/explore/index.html, Seventh Floor, 155 Carlton Street, Winnipeg, Manitoba R3C 3H8.

Northwest Territories Tourism ☎ (867) 873-7200 TOLL-FREE (800) 661-0788 WEB SITE www.nwttravel.nt.ca/, PO Box 610, Yellowknife, Northwest Territories X1A 2N5.

Nunavut Tourism ☎ (867) 979-6551 TOLL-FREE IN CANADA (800) 491-7910 WEB SITE www.nunatour.nt.ca/, PO Box 1450, Iqaluit, Nunavut X0A 0H0.

Tourism Saskatchewan ☎ (306) 787-2300 TOLL-FREE (800) 667-7191 WEB SITE www.sasktourism.com/index.html, Suite 500, 1900 Albert Street, Regina, Saskatchewan S4P 4L9.

Tourism Yukon ☎ (867) 667-5340 WEB SITE www.touryukon.com/, PO Box 2703, Whitehorse, Yukon Y1A 2C9.

EMBASSIES AND CONSULATES

United States Embassy ☎ (613) 238-4470 100 Wellington Street, Ottawa, Ontario K1P 5T1.

United States Consulates: Calgary ☎ (403) 266-8962, Room 1050, 615 Macleod Trail SE, Calgary, Alberta T2G 4T8; **Vancouver** ☎ (604) 685-4311, Columbia Centre IV, 1095 West Pender Street, Vancouver, British Columbia V6E 2Y4.

Australian consulate general ☎ (416) 323-1155, 175 Bloor Street E, Toronto, Ontario M5L 1B9.

British consulate general ☎ (416) 593-1267, Suite 1910, 777 Bay Street, Toronto, Ontario M5G 2G2.

French Embassy ☎ (613) 789-1795, 42 Sussex Drive, Ottawa, Ontario.

Netherlands Embassy ☎ (613) 237-6471, 2020-350 Albert Street, Ottawa, Ontario.

Spanish Embassy ☎ (613)747-2252, 74 Stanley Avenue, Ottawa, Ontario.

TRAVEL DOCUMENTS

United States citizens, permanent residents of the United States, as well as British, Australian, New Zealand and Irish nationals, or citizens of most European Commonwealth countries, require only proof of citizenship to enter Canada (passport, birth certificate, voter registration card, or naturalization certificate). If the identification does not have a photograph on it, some form of additional photo identification may be needed. United States residents who are not citizens must show their Alien Registration Receipt Card. Travelers crossing the border with children should carry identification for them (passport or birth certificate), since Canadian and United States Customs and Immigration are taking measures to reduce parental and other kinds of child abduction. Children traveling with one parent or adult should bring a letter of permission from the other parent, parents, or legal guardian. Divorced parents with shared custody rights should carry legal documents establishing their status.

CUSTOMS

Customs regulations are similar to those in most countries, including the usual restrictions on bringing in meats, plants, and animals. Items intended for personal or professional use do not have to be declared, and you are allowed up to 200 cigarettes or 50 cigars, and 1.1 liters (40 oz) of wine or spirits duty-free. You can bring in gifts up to $60 in value. There are no currency restrictions.

Hunting and fishing equipment may be brought in duty-free as well, but all firearms and ammunition must be declared and a written description of each item, including serial numbers of guns, must be provided. Certain non-firearm weapons are also prohibited. Details of Customs regulations are available from Information Services, Revenue Canada, Customs and Excise, Connaught Building, Sussex Drive, Ottawa, Ontario K1A 0L5, or call Customs Canada TOLL-FREE (800) 461-9999.

OPPOSITE: All aboard! A railway station, though it may be small, is never far away. ABOVE: High over the Atlantic, an Air Canada jet engine glows in the first light of dawn.

If you are planning on purchasing furs or other animal products (e.g., antlers) check with your country's customs regulations to find out which animals are considered endangered and cannot be imported. The same consideration applies to Inuit art, which may be made of whalebone or mastodon ivory, neither of which can be brought into the United States.

TAXES

As a visitor to Canada you can claim a **tax refund** for some of the tax you pay on accommodation, as long as you stay less than one month in that accommodation. In addition, you may

claim a tax refund for certain goods you take home. Look for the "Tax Refund for Visitors" brochure at Visitor Information Centres, ask for it at your hotel front desk, or write the Visitor Rebate Program, Revenue Canada, Summerside Tax Centre, Summerside, Prince Edward Island C1N 6C6.

WHEN TO GO

The decision of when to go will depend on what you are going *for*, and by now you should have a pretty good idea of what each region has to offer at what time of the year.

Generally speaking, the seasons in Canada's more temperate climes divide up as follows: winter occupies most of the long stretch from November to the end of March, summer occurs in June, July, and August, while the "shoulder" seasons of spring and autumn are largely confined to April through May and September through October.

The most temperate climate in all of Canada belongs to British Columbia, where mild summers fade gently into mild winters. In Vancouver, for example, the temperature seldom rises above 21°C (71°F) in summer, and seldom dips below freezing in winter. You will, however, need to take an umbrella: In December and January alone, meteorologists count on seeing 42 days of rainfall, an average that drops to about seven days in July and August.

Once you are east of the Rockies, the climate abruptly changes. The Prairie Provinces of Alberta, Saskatchewan, and Manitoba are known for their climatic extremes. In all three provinces you will find summers that are hot and sunny, though punctuated by the occasional thunderstorm, followed almost immediately by winters that are very cold and generally dry. To give you some idea of the extremes of weather to be encountered in the Canadian prairies, in Saskatchewan temperatures of 45°C (113°F) have been recorded in summer and temperatures of -57°C (-70°F) in winter.

Not surprisingly, weather conditions in the Far North are more extreme than those in the southern provinces. Some visitors are surprised to find out that northern summers can be hot. With the sun out as much as 24 hours a day (above the Arctic Circle), the temperature can reach a balmy 88°F/31°C. But even in July, you should be prepared for cool weather and take sweaters and a fall jacket.

Average monthly temperatures for five western Canadian cities are as follows:

Calgary	
January	-10°C/14°F
April	4°C/39°F
July	16°C/62°F
October	6°C/51°F
Inuvik	
January	-29°C/-20°F
April	-14°C/14°F
July	14°C/57°F
October	-8°C/17°F
Vancouver	
January	3°C/37°F
April	9°C/48°F
July	17°C/63°F
October	10°C/50°F
Whitehorse	
January	-18°C/17°F
April	0°C/32°F
July	14°C/57°F
October	1°C/33°F

Yellowknife

January	-28°C/-18°F
April	-7°C/20°F
July	16°C/61°F
October	1°C/30°F

In the North, daylight hours are an important seasonal factor. Average daylight hours for seven northern Canadian cities are as follows:

	DEC	JUNE
Cambridge Bay	0.0	24.0
Dawson City	4.2	21.1
Inuvik	0.0	24.0
Iqaluit	4.5	20.8
Rankin Inlet	4.5	20.8
Whitehorse	5.4	19.1
Yellowknife	6.5	20.0

WHAT TO BRING

The criterion for what to pack should not be the desirability of having a particular article with you at any given time, but the undesirability of *not* having a particular article with you when you really need it. On that principle, here is our list of things you should never leave home without.

At the top of the list, by a wide margin, is a Swiss Army knife (or, to put it another way, two knives, two screwdrivers, a bottle opener, a can opener, a corkscrew, a toothpick, tweezers, nail file, and scissors). We would also throw in a miniature flashlight and a small travel alarm clock. You will need an adapter and/or transformer if you plan to bring electrical appliances that don't run on 110 volts or don't have an American-style plug.

Because even the most minor physical irritations or afflictions can ruin a trip if they strike at the wrong time (which is the only time they strike), we would be sure to include a small first-aid kit with such items as lip balm for chapped lips, aspirin, anti-diarrhea tablets, antiseptic ointment, a few bandages, and a few packets of tissues (which can also serve as toilet paper in an emergency). Resealable ziplock plastic bags come in handy when you have items that you want to keep apart, or you want to segregate items that are damp or dirty or might be inclined to leak. By the way, everything we have mentioned so far will fit easily into a medium-sized plastic freezer bag.

If you are planning to travel by air and you want to take a Swiss Army knife, or anything else that might conceivably be considered a "weapon," be sure to pack it in the luggage you intend to check. You don't want to be mistaken for an armed passenger. On the other hand, if you are taking any battery-powered gadgets — shavers, cassette players, etc. — carry them with you on the airplane or take the batteries out before packing them, airline security personnel get understandably jumpy when unidentified objects with batteries in them show up on their X-ray screen.

Be sure to take with you lists of the numbers of all travel documents, cards, and checks you will be carrying, along with any telephone numbers included on them. This will greatly facilitate their quick replacement if lost. Also, take photocopies of your passport and any travel tickets: duplicates are issued more speedily if people can see a copy of the original — much more speedily in the case of tickets or refunds. It is a good idea to get an international driver's license, obtainable from your automobile club, so that you can keep your home driver's license tucked away in a safe place. Always leave your inessential credit cards behind when you go on a trip, and of those you take with you carry only a couple in your wallet: any others

should be tucked away in the same safe place as your passport, driver's license, extra travelers' checks, etc. It's just another way of ensuring that any loss causes only a temporary inconvenience.

When it comes to clothing, toiletries, jewelry, and gadgetry, it's up to you to decide what and how much you want to take. Canadians are very casual in their dress, so there is no need to take formal or semiformal wear beyond what your taste and your expected engagements require. There is, however, a need to take some warm clothing — a sweater or two perhaps, the odd woolen or corduroy garment, and a windbreaker — because even in summer, even in the hottest spots, it can turn quite cool in the evenings, especially if you happen to be on or near the water.

OPPOSITE: A "trembling aspen" near Athabsca Falls in Alberta. ABOVE: Winter in Canada is a time for bundling.

BASICS

TIME

Western Canada is divided into three time zones, corresponding to, and continuations of, the three western United States time zones: Central Standard Time, Mountain Standard Time, and Pacific Standard Time.

Manitoba and the eastern half of Saskatchewan are on **Central Standard Time;** the rest of Saskatchewan, Alberta and northeast British Columbia are on **Mountain Standard Time**. All of British Columbia west of the Rockies is on **Pacific**

Standard Time, eight hours behind Greenwich Mean Time.

All of western Canada — with the mysterious exception of eastern Saskatchewan — observes Daylight Savings Time from the first Sunday in April, when the clocks are put forward one hour, until the last Sunday in October.

ELECTRICITY

The electric current is 110–120 volts AC, the same as in the United States, and the sockets only take American-type plugs with two flat prongs.

WEIGHTS AND MEASURES

Canadians, like just about everybody else in the world except their American neighbors, rely almost exclusively on the metric system. Thus, while Canadians are spared the old question, "How much is that in dollars?" they now have to face the new question, "How far is that in miles?" or "What is that in pounds and ounces?"

To make life easier for those not yet numerate in metrics, we have devised our own rough-and-ready (and of course approximate) system for making instant conversions on the spot. It is not only simple, but easy to memorize, so long as you remember that the colloquial term "a bit" here represents one-tenth of whatever it is next to. Thus: a meter equals a yard and a bit; a kilometer equals a half-mile and a bit; a kilogram equals two pounds and a bit (500 grams equals 1 lb and a bit); a liter equals an American quart and a bit.

For converting to degrees Fahrenheit, simply double the figure you are given in Celsius and add 30, topping it up by a couple of degrees when you get above 20°C. The temperature you come up with won't be precisely accurate, but it will be close enough. Note that when temperatures descend into the negative numbers the two scales begin to converge, thus: -40°C equals -40°F. (This may seem like an arcane bit of knowledge, but remember, this is Canada.)

SHOPPING HOURS

Shopping hours are generally from 9 AM to 6 PM, Monday through Friday, with late-night shopping in some stores until 9 PM on Thursday and Friday. Most shops and stores are also open Saturday and some local stores, especially during the summer, are open on Sunday from noon until 5 PM. Stores may have longer hours in summer months.

HEALTH AND SAFETY

You really haven't much to worry about in Canada, because health hazards are few and the health care is excellent. It can be expensive, though, so American visitors should check to make sure that their health insurance provides coverage in Canada, and overseas visitors should arrange short-term medical coverage for the period they expect to be there. An excellent medical emergency policy, which also includes personal travel insurance, is available from the **Europ Assistance Group** through its affiliates in a dozen or so countries, including: United Kingdom ☎ (1444) 411999 FAX (1444) 458173, Sussex House, Perrymount Road, Haywards Heath, West Sussex RH1 IDN, England; and France ☎ (01) 41858585 FAX (01) 41858305, 1 promenade de la Bonnette, 92230 Gennevilliers, France. A similar policy, similarly priced, is offered by **Wexas Interna-**

tional ☎ (071) 5893315 E-MAIL mship@wexas.com, 45–49 Brompton Road, Knightsbridge, London SW3 1DE, England.

Another wise precaution is to carry a card in your wallet giving your blood type and listing any allergies or chronic conditions (including the wearing of contact lenses) that might affect treatment in an emergency.

Beyond that, it's always a good idea to have insect repellent with you, because in summer Canada has plenty of insects to repel, especially black flies and mosquitoes. A sunscreen lotion is also advisable, as the Canadian sun has a burning power out of all proportion to its heating power.

Emergency fire, ambulance, and police services are usually reached by dialing 911. For other emergencies or for areas not serviced by 911 (e.g., the Northwest Territories and Nunavut), you should contact the operator by dialing "0." In the Yukon Territory, only Whitehorse operates a 911 emergency call system. For the rest of the territory, dial Royal Canadian Mounted Police ☎ (867) 667-5555; Medical ☎ (867) 667-3333. Yukon communities also have local police and medical emergency numbers, which you can get a list of from a visitor information center when you begin your trip.

CRIME

Crime? What crime? Canada may well be the most law-abiding of the world's industrialized nations. Violent crime isn't exactly unheard of, but it's not heard of very often. The streets of Canada's cities are as safe at night as they are in the daytime.

All this law-and-orderliness notwithstanding, one should still take the same basic precautions here that a sensible person would take anywhere: leaving valuables in the hotel safe, locking your hotel room and car, not leaving valuable items visible in your car when unattended, not carrying all your cash and cards with you when you go out, not going for late-night strolls through questionable areas. In short, exercise your common sense, secure in the knowledge that Canadians can be counted on to exercise their common decency.

CURRENCY

Canadian currency resembles American currency in every important respect except value: The coins are in the same denominations and go by the same names (penny, nickel, dime, etc.), the paper notes are of uniform size (but in different colors according to value). There are no longer $1 and $2 bills. Instead there are $1 "loonie" coins, nicknamed the after the bird that appears on it, and the $2 "toonie."

At press time the **exchange rate** was: US$1 to C$1.50; and for the euro: €1 to C$1.65. Should you wish to be precisely *au courant*, visit the Universal Currency Converter WEB SITE www.xe.net/

OPPOSITE: A steam-powered clock keeps Pacific Standard Time in Vancouver's Gastown district. ABOVE: Sir Wilfred Laurier (1841–1919), first French-Canadian prime minister of Canada, appears on Canada's five dollar bill.

currency/, or check your local newspaper. American dollars are widely accepted, but using them introduces an unnecessary complication into a transaction, as well as an unnecessary discourtesy.

As in all countries with hard currencies, the banks offer the best exchange rates — much better than hotels, for example. Banking hours are Monday to Thursday from 10 AM to 4 PM, 10 AM to 6 PM on Friday. Trust companies and credit unions tend to have longer hours and may also be open on Saturday morning. Most major credit cards are accepted anywhere you are likely to go — including American Express, MasterCard, Visa, Diners Club, Enroute, and Carte Blanche; consequently you are advised to carry a minimum of cash. If you prefer using non-plastic money, take it in the form of travelers' checks. They can be cashed everywhere, with proper identification (e.g. passport, driver's license), although the larger denominations will not always be welcome in places like restaurants that don't like being used as banks.

In general, however, we recommend floating through Canada on a raft of plastic: your bank debit card. All Canadian financial institutions have automatic teller machines (ATMs), and you'll find ATMs located in large and small shopping centers, airports, train stations, and even many gas stations and corner stores. Before you leave home check with your bank to be certain your ATM card is on the Plus or Cirrus network; they can also provide you with a booklet listing networks worldwide on which your card with operate.

GETTING AROUND

BY AIR

The country's two major carriers, **Air Canada** TOLL-FREE (800) 776-3000 and **Canadian Airlines International** TOLL-FREE (800) 426-7000, along with their regional partners, handle the bulk of the middle- and long-distance air traffic. Dozens of local independent carriers connect the remaining dots on the map. Thus there are very few places in Canada, even including remote islands, that are not accessible by air. The principal regional carriers in the west are: **Air BC** ((604) 688-5515, and **Canadian Regional** ((604) 279-6611 serving British Columbia and Alberta; and **NWT Air** ((867) 423-1222 serving the Northwest Territories and the Yukon.

Anyone purchasing a round-trip trans-Atlantic flight from Europe to Canada on Air France, Continental, Air Canada, or United is eligible to purchase Air Canada's **Ameripass**. (Other transatlantic carriers also participate, but pass prices are higher.) The pass is bought in series of three to eight coupons — each coupon allowing one flight within North America to selected cities. At the time of research, three flights cost around $325, and eight flights around $930. There are restrictions, but it is a wonderful deal for those who want to cover a lot of ground in a short period of time. European travel agents should be able to provide information and make the bookings, or you can go directly to Air Canada.

BY RAIL

Canada's passenger rail carrier is the government-owned **VIA Rail** TOLL-FREE (888) 842-7733 WEB SITE www.viarail.ca. The VIA Rail network is rapidly shrinking due to cuts in government funding, but there is still regular service between the major cities, and it is still possible to make the transcontinental journey by train in the comfort of your own rolling bedroom or roomette. This transcontinental service runs between Toronto and Vancouver, operating three times weekly, east and west, transiting Winnipeg, Saskatoon, Edmonton and Jasper, and passing through three spectacular mountain ranges en route: the Canadian Rockies, the Selkirks, and the Coast Mountains. It takes three days.

VIA Rail issues the **Canrailpass**, which makes possible substantial savings by allowing 12 days of coach-class travel over a 30-day period. Prices are $370 (low season) and $570 (high season). Sleeping cars are available, but must be reserved at least a month in advance during the May to October high season. The pass must be purchased prior to arrival in Canada. Your travel agent will have details. Alternatively, contact VIA Rail's web site (see above), which lists their representatives throughout the world. Local and regional contact numbers for VIA Rail are found throughout the text.

BY BUS

Where there's a way, there's a willing bus to take you just about anywhere you want to go in Canada. Greyhound Canada has a nationwide route system, and there are five or six large regional companies that reach into the nooks and crannies that Greyhound misses. Bus service is frequent, quick and inexpensive, whether intercity or cross-country. The 5,000-km (3,000-mile) from Montréal to Vancouver, for example, takes 69 hours.

With Greyhound's **Domestic Canada Coach Pass** you can travel throughout five of the provinces as well as the Northwest Territories, Nunavut and the Yukon for periods of a week to two months. The pass is available for sale in Canada only, and costs between $209 and $495. You can buy it at any Greyhound Canada terminal, or ask a travel agent. There is also the **International Canada Coach Pass**, which is good on routes in all provinces excluding parts of Québec and the Maritimes; to include these areas you'll have to spring for the **Canada Coach Pass Plus**, available in 15-, 30-, and 60-day limits at a cost of $335, $440, and $545 respectively.

For detailed information contact **Greyhound Canada** TOLL-FREE (800) 661-8747 WEB SITE www.greyhound.ca, 877 Greyhound Way SW, Calgary, Alberta T3C 3V8.

By Car and Motor home

Canada, only slightly less than the United States, is a motorist's dream. The highway system may not be as sprawling as in the United States, but it doesn't have to be, since most of the places visited by tourists and natives alike are within easy driving distance of the Trans-Canada Highway. The gasoline may not be as cheap as in the United States, but it's far cheaper than in Europe.

The major car-rental firms are represented across the country, including: **Hertz** TOLL-FREE (800) 654-3001 TOLL-FREE IN CANADA (800) 263-0600 TOLL-FREE IN THE UNITED KINGDOM (0345) 555888; **Alamo** TOLL-FREE IN CANADA (800) 879-2847; **Budget** TOLL-FREE (800) 527-0700 TOLL-FREE IN THE UNITED KINGDOM (0800) 181181; **Dollar/Eurodollar** TOLL-FREE (800) 800-4000 TOLL-FREE IN THE UNITED KINGDOM (0990) 565656; and **Rent-a-Wreck** TOLL-FREE IN THE UNITED STATES (800) 535-1391 TOLL-FREE IN QUÉBEC (514) 521-5771 TOLL-FREE IN THE UNITED KINGDOM 011-44-21-772-8599 TOLL-FREE IN CANADA (800) 327-0116 Also represented is the largest Canadian rental car company, **National Tilden** TOLL-FREE (800) 387-4747, which has over 370 offices all over Canada.

If you are planning to rent a car in the summer, it's a good idea to reserve before you leave home. In order to rent a vehicle in Canada, you must be at least 25 years old and you must have a credit card.

But, perhaps you had in mind something a bit larger: Each year hundreds of travelers hit the back roads of Canada in rented motor homes (recreational vehicles) and truck campers. This is the American equivalent of a "caravan," especially attractive for those who want to explore Canada as a family or group of friends. In order to rent a recreational vehicle, you must have a driver's license (that you've held for more than one year) and be at least 25 years old. It is strongly recommended that you reserve your recreational vehicle several weeks prior to departure. Contact your travel agent for information and reservations.

By Ferry

There are both car and passenger ferry services available on most of Canada's major lakes and rivers, as well as between the mainland and the offshore islands. Ferries between Vancouver and Vancouver Island don't require reservations, but other ferries should be booked in advance — well in advance if you are taking a car with you.

Information on ferry transportation within various regions is listed under HOW TO GET THERE in the relevant chapters. The Pacific Coast's two major lines are:

Alaska Marine Highway System ((907) 627-1744 or (907) 627-1745 TOLL-FREE (800) 642-0066,

ABOVE: Goldie greets guests arriving by float plane at Eagle Nook Ocean Wilderness Lodge bordering the Pacific Rim National Park.

PO Box 25535, Juneau, Alaska 99802-5535 USA, operates between Bellingham, Washington, Prince Rupert, British Columbia, and Skagway, Alaska with stops in Juneau and Haines, and other Southeast Alaska ports.

BC Ferries ☎ (250) 386-3431 TOLL-FREE IN BRITISH COLUMBIA (888) 223-3779 FAX (250) 381-5452, 1112 Fort Street, Victoria, BC V8V 4V2 Canada, links Vancouver with Vancouver Island, Port Hardy, Prince Rupert, the Queen Charlotte Islands, the Gulf Islands and various southern British Columbia ports.

BY LOCAL TRANSPORTATION

Taxis can always be found at airports, railway stations, and major hotels. They can also be hailed in the street fairly easily in the larger cities; elsewhere they can be ordered by telephone. Rates are quite reasonable by American or European standards, and a tip of 15% or so is normal. In some provinces not all the taxis have meters, making it advisable to agree on the fare before beginning a journey.

DRIVING

You will be required to carry a valid driver's license and it is recommended that you get an international driving permit as well (see WHAT TO TAKE, above). Any standard United States car insurance policy is valid in Canada. If you have time, get a Canadian Non-Resident Inter-Provincial Motor Vehicle Liability Insurance Card from your insurance company. If the car you're driving is not registered under the name of one of the drivers or one of the passengers, bring written proof that you have permission from the owner to take the car into Canada.

The driving regulations will be familiar to anyone used to driving in the United States or in continental Europe: You drive on the right and pass on the left, vehicles approaching from the right have the right-of-way at intersections, the use of seat belts is compulsory, and driving under the influence of alcohol will incur stiff penalties. In Newfoundland, Prince Edward Island, Québec, Ontario, Manitoba, and in the Yukon, Northwest Territories and Nunavut radar detectors are illegal even if not in use.

The speed limit on highways is usually 100 kph (60 mph), on smaller roads 80 kph (50 mph), and in towns 80 kph down to 50 kph (30 mph). You must stop if you come upon a school bus with its red lights flashing. You may turn right at a red light (except in Québec) if you stop first and make sure the road is clear. Some provinces require drivers to keep headlights on for periods after dawn and before sunset. In the Yukon, the law requires drivers to keep headlights on at all times when using territory highways.

There are plenty of 24-hour service stations flanking the major highways, while those in town tend to close around 9 PM (7 PM in small towns, and all day on Sundays). Gasoline (or petrol) is sold by the liter (one liter equals about one quart; there are 3.8 liters to the gallon). Gas is a good deal more expensive than it is in the United States, but cheaper than in Europe. Most stations take credit cards, and most are now self-service.

In the event of an accident, you should get to a telephone and dial the operator ("0") who can connect you with the police and emergency services. Members of automobile clubs affiliated with the Canadian Automobile Association (the American Automobile Association and most European automobile clubs are) should bring their membership cards along with them, as they are entitled to membership benefits. For more information contact the **Canadian Automobile Association** ☎ (613) 226-7631, 1775 Courtwood Crescent, Ottawa, Ontario K2C 3J2; the **American Automobile Association** TOLL-FREE (800) 564-6222; the **United Kingdom Automobile Association** ☎ (0990) 500600; or the **Royal Automobile Club** ☎ (0990) 722722 or (0345) 121345.

ACCOMMODATION

When it comes to accommodation in western Canada, one is spoiled for choice. Wherever you go, you will find that there are types of accommodation to appeal to every taste and to suit every budget. If luxury and comfort are your priorities, there are deluxe hotels to rank with any in the world. If convenient locations while motoring are important, you will be pleased to know that there are motels in every price range sprinkled along the nation's main roads and highways. If economy is the paramount consideration, you will be able to get rooms at a YMCA, YWCA, university, or hostel in all but the most remote spots—and sometimes even there (see BACKPACKING, page 26, in YOUR CHOICE). If conversation and "character" count alongside economy, there is bound to be a bed-and-breakfast house to fit the bill.

If you will be staying in one place for a longish period, particularly with children or in a group, you will get both privacy and savings (on food) in an efficiency apartment in one of Canada's many apartment hotels. If rustic charm is what you're looking for, there are delightful country inns spread across the country. If you want to get into serious rusticity, there is no better way than to stay on one of the hundreds of working farms and ranches that offer accommodation as well as hearty meals and healthy activities (see SPECIAL INTERESTS, page 38, in YOUR CHOICE). If you just want to get away from it all and hunt or fish or think about the human condition, there are some wonderful lodges in remote wilderness areas where Nature starts at your front door.

NATIONAL PARKS

National parks are federally administered, but locally supervised by park information centers. These centers are excellent sources of information, and are the place to pickup permits for fishing or backcountry camping. Exhibits on flora and fauna, interpretive talks and nature walks with park naturalists, and reports on weather and road conditions are often also part of the package.

Motorists must purchase permits when entering national parks, usually from a roadside booth at the park boundary. Each park has its own fee structure, and many offer pass programs. For additional information, contact **Parks Canada** ((819) 997-0055 E-MAIL parks_webmaster@pch.gc.ca, 25 Eddy Street, Hull, Québec K1A 0M5. The Parks Canada WEB SITE parkscanada.pch.gc.ca/ has a list of all park fees and pass programs as well as access to an on-line campground reservation system for a limited (but growing) number of parks.

CAMPING

There are thousands of campgrounds throughout western Canada, of every size and description. Many are in the national and provincial parks, some are municipally owned, others are privately run. Most are open from May until late September, with campsites costing from $10 to $15. Facilities usually include toilets, showers, a laundry, picnic tables, campfire sites, and power hookups for recreational vehicles. The fancier ones will also have a shop and a restaurant. Generally speaking, the privately run campgrounds will have more amenities and will be more expensive, while the public ones in the national and provincial parks will be more scenically situated.

As most campgrounds are run on a first-come, first-served basis, during the high season — July and August — it's a good idea to start looking for a site no later than mid-afternoon.

There are three **nocturnal nuisances** that can thoroughly spoil a camping vacation if you come unprepared. The first is that familiar bane, the mosquito. So bring plenty of insect repellent, as well as a tent fitted with a mosquito net. The second nuisance is scavenging animals — often, in Canada, bears. These creatures can be discouraged by never keeping food in or near the tent (unless it's in the car), and by always disposing of uneaten food and washing up the dishes immediately after meals. No leftovers, no problems. Thirdly, even in midsummer, the temperature at night can suddenly drop, leaving you shivering unless you have brought enough warm clothing.

For lists of campgrounds write to the provincial tourism office in the area you plan to visit or contact Parks Canada (see above).

PRICES

With a few exceptions, we have deliberately avoided giving exact restaurant and accommodation prices. This is because we have learned that the only thing you can absolutely depend on in this business is that the prices will have changed before the ink is dry (sometimes, surprisingly, for the better — as special offers and new types of discounts are introduced). We have therefore confined ourselves to price categories where hotels and restaurants are concerned. Hotels in the **expensive** category, for example, will charge over $150 a night for a double room; **mid-range** hotels will charge between $75 and $149; **inexpensive** hotels will charge less, sometimes much less. At restaurants listed as **expensive** you can expect to pay more than $50 per person for a meal, excluding wine; **moderate** restaurants will charge between $25 and $50; **inexpensive** ones will cost you less — sometimes, again, much less. When hotels or restaurants fall at either of the two extremes — very expensive or very inexpensive — we have so indicated.

Another word about prices. All the prices given in this book, and the categories outlined above, are in Canadian dollars. Most travel guides tell you to remember that the Canadian dollar is worth about 20% to 30% less than the American dollar. My advice is precisely the opposite: forget that the Canadian dollar is worth less. Don't translate; think in United States dollars. This is because all the prices quoted in Canada are exclusive of the layers of taxes that are added later — sales taxes, goods and services taxes, even "taxes on taxes," as one hotel owner wanly pointed out to me. So by

Posing for the folks back home at Maligne Canyon, Jasper National Park, Alberta.

the time your bill is added in Canadian dollars, it will come to almost exactly the original, untaxed figure in American dollars. If you keep in mind this one simple trick, you will know a real bargain when you see one.

TIPPING

In general, you should tip more or less 15% — more if the service is outstanding, less if it is not so good. Tip porters $1 a bag, chambermaids $1 a day — rounding off the total upwards in deserving cases, downwards in undeserving ones.

PUBLIC HOLIDAYS

National holidays include: New Year's Day, Good Friday, Easter Monday, Victoria Day (Monday nearest May 24), Canada Day (July 1), Labor Day (first Monday in September), Thanksgiving (second Monday in October), Remembrance Day (November 11), Christmas Day, Boxing Day (December 26).

In addition to the national holidays, each territory and province has its own local holidays.

MAIL

Although main post offices in Canada may open as early as 8 AM and close as late as 6 PM on weekdays, and some are open on Saturday mornings, you can avoid disappointment by going between 9 AM and 5 PM, Monday to Friday. In fact, you can avoid post offices altogether for most purposes, as stamps can be bought at hotels and from vending machines in airports, railway stations, shopping centers, and drugstores. Letters and postcards can be mailed at most hotels' front desks or at any red mailbox. At press time rates were $.46 for a first-class letter or postcard within Canada, $.55 to the United States, and $.95 to other countries.

If sending mail to a Canadian address, be sure to include the postal code. Also, we are told by the postal authorities that every year there are some Americans who think it is just as good to use American stamps as Canadian ones. It's not. Following are **postal abbreviations** for the provinces and territories: Alberta AB, British Columbia BC, Saskatchewan SK, Manitoba MB, New Brunswick NB, Newfoundland and Labrador NF, Northwest Territories and Nunavut NT, Nova Scotia NS, Ontario ON, Prince Edward Island PE, Québec QP, Yukon Territory YT.

If you want to **receive mail** in Canada, you can have mail sent to you ℅ General Delivery at the mail post office in the town or city where you wish to pick it up. But remember that it must be picked up within 15 days or it will be returned to sender. If you have an American Express card, or traveler's checks from American Express or Thomas Cook, you can have mail sent to you at any office of either company. It should be marked "Client Mail," and it will be held for you for as long as a month.

Telegrams are handled by CN/CP Telecommunications, while most good hotels now have telex and/or fax facilities available for guests' use.

TELEPHONES

The Canadian telephone system is completely integrated with that of the United States, which means that it is splendidly efficient and economical, and that no international codes are necessary for calls between the United States and Canada. As in the United States, for information on local telephone numbers dial 411; for information on long-distance numbers dial 1-555-1212. For calls requiring operator assistance — such as long-distance personal or collect calls, or for emergency calls — dial "0."

To place a long-distance call within the same area code, dial 1 + the number you are calling. To place a call outside your area code, dial 1 + area code + telephone number. For direct dialing of overseas calls, dial 011 + country code + city code + telephone number.

Calls placed in the evening or on the weekend are less expensive, although any call from a hotel will incur a (usually steep) surcharge. There are public telephones just about everywhere; they only accept Canadian quarters, and/or prepaid phone cards.

We have made an effort to provide the specific geographic limitations of the toll-free numbers listed in this book when this information was available. Generally speaking, TOLL-FREE refers to numbers available throughout North America, whereas limitations to Canada, the United States, or a specific province are indicated. TOLL-FREE IN WESTERN CANADA means just that: you can use this number in British Columbia, Alberta, Saskatchewan, Yukon and Manitoba, but will not get through if you dial from elsewhere.

THE INTERNET

Canada is wired. Just about everywhere you go, you will find a bookstore, café, or public library offering access to the Internet for a nominal fee (and sometimes for free). If you've signed up for one of the global e-mail accounts before leaving home (Microsoft's HotMail is one of the most popular free e-mail services) then you are wired, too.

Where available, we have listed local Internet access points in the various destination sections under GENERAL INFORMATION. We found that most libraries offered access, but that actual availability varied greatly because of lack of equipment and high demand. In most cities, you can ask around and find the latest cybercafé where you can settle down with a coffee and get warming news from home.

The Internet is also becoming a powerful tool for researching and planning trips. Many, if not most, organizations, hotels, and tour operators listed in this book have home pages on the **World Wide Web**. Finding one of these home pages is usually a simple matter of logging onto your web browser (e.g., Netscape Navigator™ or Microsoft Internet Explorer™), locating the search function and typing in the name of the organization for

which you are looking. You can also do keyword searches if you don't have a specific organization name in mind. Essentially, once on the web, your access to information is limited only by your ability to ask the right question.

Web sites are of varying quality. Some are quite useful, allowing you to retrieve information quickly, make contact via e-mail direct from the site, or even make a reservation at the touch of a button. Others will have you pulling your cyber hair out.

The following sites are ones that we found particularly useful in our research on this book. They offer essential information and pertinent services, as well as "links" to other home pages that will set you well on your way into cyberspace. (It is the nature of the web to be somewhat ephemeral, and you may find that some of these sites are no longer active.)

SITES

Reference

Canadian Yellow Pages www.cdnyellowpages.com. This is a fairly well organized tool for address and telephone searches. It also offers classified ads, pictures of Canada, and links to other sites.

Ghosts of the Gold Rush www.gold-rush.org/. Find out if Great Aunt Lou climbed the Chilkoot Trail.

Lost Moose, the Yukon Publishers www.yukonweb.com/business/lost_moose/. These publishers specialize in northern literature, including the legendary *Lost Whole Moose Catalog*.

National Archives www.archives.ca. In English and French, this site contains written records, artwork, photographs, and maps that document the history of Canada and the workings of its government.

Sympatico www1.sympatico.ca:80/. This is a comprehensive site, operated by Bell Canada, with all things Canadian and more. It's very well organized, easy on the eye, and an excellent place to start research on the country in any category. The travel sections are especially good.

Universal Currency Converter www.xe.net/currency/. A nifty way to find out what your dollar or euro is worth against any other currency, in real time.

Travel

Airline Network www.airnet.co.uk. Cheap flights departing from the United Kingdom. Unique in that it lists free stopovers.

Atevo www.atevo.com/. A comprehensive travel web site with all kinds of nooks and crannies to explore. It offers online reservations, but we found the engine lacking. It's best used as an online magazine and travel-idea generator.

Rec.Travel Library — Canada www.travel-library.com/north_america/canada/index.html. A homespun site that has plenty of information, including personal advice and a list of answers to frequently asked questions about traveling in Canada. Strong on links to many other Canadian sites.

Travelocity www.travelocity.com. The best choice for straightforward air travel fare search and booking. Sign-up for automatic updates on air routes of your choosing. When the rate drops by $50 or more, you'll be notified via e-mail

Where Magazine www.wheremags.com. These are locally edited, ad-oriented destination magazines. The web site is useful and attractive. You can order magazines from the site, or browse the information on line for a number of Canadian cities, including Winnipeg and Vancouver.

A phone booth in Vancouver's Chinatown.

Airlines

Air Canada www.aircanada.ca. Flight and departure information, reservations and the WebSaver program, a free service with last minute travel bargains to selected destinations. Sign up for automatic e-mail updates at this web site.

Canada Airlines International www.cdnair.ca. A slow site, but it has some interesting features. For example, you can ask its destination locator to list ticketing offices and hotels in your city of destination.

In addition, all of the following airline web sites allow you to get on e-mailing lists and book flights on-line:

American Airlines www.americanair.com

Continental www.flycontinental.com

Delta www.delta-air.com

Northwest Airlines www.nwa.com

United www.ual.com

US Airways www.usairways.com

Travel Guides

Alaska Highway www.peace.bc.ca

Mile marker by mile marker along this epic roadway.

Ferries

Alaska Marine Highway Ferry System www.dot.state.ak.us. Not a particularly glamorous or well-organized site, but key information is not difficult to find.

BC Ferries www.bcferries.bc.ca. Slick and useful. Access information about routes, schedules, fares, and online reservations.

Ground Transportation

Greyhound Canada www.greyhound.ca. An excellent site where you can download your choice of Adobe Acrobat .PDF (Portable Document Format) files of schedules.

VIA Rail www.viarail.ca. Attractive and very useful schedules, fares, and on-line reservations.

Visitor Information

Calgary Convention and Visitors Bureau www.visitor.calgary.ab.ca

Discover Banff www.discoverbanff.com/

Nunavut Handbook www.arctic-travel.com/NUNATOUR/nt.html

Tourism Winnipeg www.tourism-winnipeg.mb.ca

Tourism Vancouver www.tourism-vancouver.org

YukonWeb www.yukonweb.com/

Yukon Wild www.yukonwild.com/

RADIO AND TELEVISION

We are tempted to say that if you are in Canada you should not stay indoors, and leave it at that. We are further tempted to say that if you do find yourself indoors in North America, you certainly shouldn't be watching television. You know the reasons; you've probably seen a number of them already, wherever you live. Even so, it's difficult to convey the feeling of dull despair that comes over you when you contemplate a galaxy of up to 40 television channels — not one of which is shining brightly enough to engage your attention for more than a couple minutes.

If it's any consolation, though, you are better off watching television in Canada then in the United States, simply because you have a choice of programs aside from the American ones (which nonetheless predominate even in areas beyond the reach of American stations). Its precarious finances notwithstanding, the CBC (Canadian Broadcasting Corporation) manages to produce some worthy programming of its own, while the French-language channels serve up the occasional treat. But don't be surprised when you switch channels to escape Teenage Mutant Ninja Turtles only to be confronted with Popeye *et ses fils*.

The Canadian radio dial, like the American, features end-to-end music — classical, pop, rock, country, jazz — interspersed with talk shows, phone-ins, and news.

NEWSPAPERS AND MAGAZINES

Canadian journalism, too, closely resembles its American counterpart. With the exception of the *Globe and Mail*, which is published in Toronto, the newspapers are all local papers. Certainly, some big-city papers such as the *Toronto Star* are national, even international, in stature; but their main emphasis remains on coverage of their own communities. This enlightened parochialism benefits the visitor not only by providing a useful introduction to topics of local interest, but also by providing, through its listings and advertisements, a comprehensive guide to local events and entertainment. As a matter of fact, many of the places to go and things to do that we have recommended in this book were originally suggested to us by articles or reviews we came upon in the local press. So don't neglect this valuable resource whenever you arrive in a new place.

All of the larger newsagents in Canada have shelves that are identical to the ones you would expect to find in comparable shops in the United States — except that in addition to all the American newspapers and magazines you get the Canadian ones as well.

Recommended Reading

BACKHOUSE, FRANCES. *Women of the Klondike*. Whitecap Books, 1995.

BERTON, PIERRE. *The Mysterious North*. Toronto: McClelland and Stewart, 1956. *The Klondike Fever*. New York: Carroll and Graf, 1958.

BERTON, LAURA BEATRICE and PIERRE BERTON. *I Married the Klondike*. Toronto: McClelland and Stewart, 1996.

BROOK, STEPHEN. *Maple Leaf Rag*. London: Pan Books, 1989.

DRISCOLL, CYNTHIA BRACKETT. *One Woman's Gold Rush: Snapshots from Mollie Brackett's Lost Photo Album 1898–1899*. Kalamazoo: Oak Woods Media, 1996.

HARDY, ANNE. *Where to Eat in Canada*. Harvard Common Press, 1997.

MACLENNAN, HUGH. *Papers*. Calgary: University of Calgary Press, 1986.

MALCOLM, ANDREW H. *The Canadians*. New York: Times Books, 1985.

MCNAUGHT, KENNETH. *The Penguin History of Canada*. London: Penguin Books, 1988.

MILEPOST (THE), 50TH EDITION. Bellevue, Washington: Vernon Publications, 1998

MORGAN, BERNICE. *Random Passage*. Breakwater Books, Ltd., 1992.

MORTON, DESMOND. *A Peculiar Kind of Politics*. Toronto: University of Toronto Press, 1982.

MORTON, WILLIAM L. *The Canadian Identity*. Madison: University of Wisconsin Press, 1973.

MUISE, D.A., ed. *Reader's Guide to Canadian History, Vol. I*. GRANATSTEIN, A.L and P. STEVENS, eds. *Reader's Guide to Canadian History, Vol. II*. Toronto: University of Toronto Press, 1982.

PATTERSON, FREEMAN. *The Last Wilderness: Images of the Canadian Wild*. Vanier, Ontario: Canadian Geographic Society, 1991.

RICHLER, MORDECAI. *The Apprenticeship of Duddy Kravitz*. London: Penguin Books, 1991. Broadsides. London: Vintage Books, 1991. Papers. Calgary: University of Calgary Press, 1987.

SOUBLIERE, MARION, ed. *The Nunavut Handbook: Traveling in Canada's Arctic*. Iqaluit, NWT: Nortext Press, 1998.

WALLACE, DONALD C. and FREDERICK A. FLETCHER. *Canadian Politics through Press Reports*. Toronto: Oxford University Press, 1985.

WELLS, E. HAZARD. Randall M. Dodd, editor. *Magnificence and Misery: A Firsthand Account of the 1897 Klondike Gold Rush*. Garden City, New York: Doubleday & Company, 1984.

For Children

CRAVEN, MARGARET. *I Heard the Owl Call My Name* and *Again Calls the Owl*. Laureleaf, 1993.

GALE, DONALD. *Shooshewan, Child of the Beothuk*. Breakwater Books, 1988.

SKOGAN, JOAN. *The Princess and the Sea-Bear and Other Tsimshian Stories*. Polestar Press, 1990.

Treading the Athabasca Glacier while a springtime snow falls in Canada's Rockies.

Quick Reference A–Z Guide to Places and Topics of Interest with Listed Accommodation, Restaurants and Useful Telephone Numbers

K

Photography Credits

All photographs taken by Robert Holmes and Nik Wheeler, with the exception of the following:

David Henry: pages 5 *right*, 7 *right*, 11, 12, 13, 14, 20, 21, 22, 24, 25, 26, 27 *top*, 28, 30, 32, 34 *top and bottom*, 35, 39, 40 *top*, 41, 42, 43, 45, 51, 59, 64, 67, 71, 83, 100, 101, 108, 111, 120, 121, 122, 123 *bottom*, 125, 126, 127, 132 *right*, 137, 140, 141, 142, 143, 144, 145 *left and right*, 147, 163, 164 *left*, 165, 167, 170, 233, 235, 236, 241, 243.

Laura Purdom: pages 3, 15, 17 *top and bottom*, 19 *top and bottom*, 31, 38, 40 *bottom*, 60, 113, 148, 203, 208, 210, 211, 213, 216, 217 *top and bottom*, 218, 219, 220, 221, 222 *left and right*, 223, 225 *top and bottom*, 227, 246.

Banff/Lake Louise Tourism Bureau: 123 *top*.

Dewitt Jones: 23, 36, 37, 46 *bottom*, 50, 62, 65, 99, 115, 117 *top and bottom*.

Yukon Archives: Claude Lidd Collection: 53, Skookum Jim Oral History Collection: 206, McBride Museum Collection: 214, Vancouver Public Library Collection: 215.